The Psychophysiology of Self-Awareness

The Norton Series on Interpersonal Neurobiology
Allan N. Schore, PhD, Series Editor
Daniel J. Siegel, MD, Founding Editor

The field of mental health is in a tremendously exciting period of growth and conceptual reorganization. Independent findings from a variety of scientific endeavors are converging in an interdisciplinary view of the mind and mental well-being. An interpersonal neurobiology of human development enables us to understand that the structure and function of the mind and brain are shaped by experiences, especially those involving emotional relationships.

The Norton Series on Interpersonal Neurobiology will provide cutting-edge, multidisciplinary views that further our understanding of the complex neurobiology of the human mind. By drawing on a wide range of traditionally independent fields of research—such as neurobiology, genetics, memory, attachment, complex systems, anthropology, and evolutionary psychology—these texts will offer mental health professionals a review and synthesis of scientific findings often inaccessible to clinicians. These books aim to advance our understanding of human experience by finding the unity of knowledge, or consilience, that emerges with the translation of findings from numerous domains of study into a common language and conceptual framework. The series will integrate the best of modern science with the healing art of psychotherapy.

A Norton Professional Book

The Psychophysiology of Self-Awareness
Rediscovering the Lost Art of Body Sense

Alan Fogel

W. W. Norton

New York • London

Copyright © 2009 by Alan Fogel

All rights reserved
Printed in the United States of America
First Edition

For information about permission to reproduce selections from this book, write to Permissions, W. W. Norton & Company, Inc., 500 Fifth Avenue, New York, NY 10110

Manufacturing by Quebecor World Fairfield Graphics
Production Manager: Leeann Graham

Library of Congress Cataloging-in-Publication Data

Fogel, Alan.
 The psychophysiology of self-awareness : rediscovering the lost art of body sense / Alan Fogel. -- 1st ed.
     p. cm. -- (The Norton series on interpersonal neurobiology)
  "A Norton Professional Book."
  Includes bibliographical references and index.
  ISBN 978-0-393-70544-7 (hardcover)
  1. Somesthesia. 2. Self-consciousness (Awareness) I. Title.
  QP448.F64 2009
  612.8--dc22
                                            2009017377

W. W. Norton & Company, Inc., 500 Fifth Avenue, New York, N.Y. 10110
www.wwnorton.com

W. W. Norton & Company Ltd., Castle House, 75/76 Wells St., London W1T 3QT

1 3 5 7 9 0 8 6 4 2

Table of Contents

	Preface	vii
Chapter 1:	Rediscovering the Lost Art of Sensing the Body	1
Chapter 2:	Feelings from Within: The Emergence of Embodied Self-Awareness	29
Chapter 3:	Links and Boundaries: Locating Ourselves	71
Chapter 4:	Out of Touch with Ourselves: Suppression and Absorption	102
Chapter 5:	Shelter from the Storm: The Effects of Safety and Threat on Embodied Self-Awareness	141
Chapter 6:	In the Flesh: Moving and Touching	186
Chapter 7:	Catching Our Breath, Finding Our Voice	227
Chapter 8:	Coming Home to Ourselves: Restorative Embodied Self-Awareness	269
Glossary		307
References		323
Index		385

Preface

This book covers both the practice and the science of embodied self-awareness, our ability to feel our movements, our sensations, and our emotions. As infants, before we can speak and conceptualize, we learn to move toward what makes us feel good and move away from what makes us feel bad. Our ability to continue to cultivate and enhance awareness of these body feelings is essential for learning how to successfully navigate in the physical and social world and for avoiding injury and stress.

Embodied self-awareness is made possible by neuromotor and neurohormonal pathways between the brain and the rest of the body, pathways that serve the function of using information about body state to maintain optimal health and well-being. When these pathways become compromised, primarily as a result of physical injury or psychological stress and trauma, we lose our ability to monitor and regulate our basic body functions. The many different types of practices that can enhance embodied self-awareness that has been impaired follow some general principles that can be understood in terms of the psychophysiology of self-awareness.

Parts of this book provide concrete examples of acquisition and loss of embodied self-awareness. Other parts give case reports showing transactions between clients and practitioners in practices that enhance embodied self-awareness. In addition, parts of this book contain technical terminology involving anatomical, physiological, and psychological function in both health and illness. All technical terms are set in bold and their definitions can be found again in the Glossary at the end of the book. The more technical parts of the book can either be read in detail or skimmed, depending upon your purpose. If you would just be pleased to know that there is a scientific explanation for why you feel happier after you do yoga, even though you never talk about your emotional problems in yoga class, then forget about the technical details and focus on the examples and practices. If you are trying to convince the hospital in which you work to include more pre- and postoperative meditation classes, the physiological and anatomical details may be useful in convincing the policymakers.

You do not, however, need a scientific background to profit from the technical material in this book. It is accompanied by many everyday examples that ground the concepts in real experience and practice. There will also be boxes that focus on interesting links between body function and self-awareness (such as how yawning wakes us up to ourselves), and boxes that contain brief experiential exercises through which you can have an opportunity to get out of your conceptual thoughts and into embodied self-awareness.

Who Should Read This Book

This book is meant for people who want to learn more about how to expand their embodied self-awareness or to help others to achieve this goal. It may be read by anyone who engages in awareness-based practices and who wants to know how and why he or she is helped in some way through that practice. It can also be read by teachers, therapists, and other practitioners who want to deepen their understanding of the links between practice, awareness, and physiology.

Here is a sample of the fields in which the practitioners may find this book useful. Teachers at any level of schooling from preschool to postgraduate may use this book to justify bringing the body back into the classroom through touch, movement, and guided self-awareness meditations. Touch-based bodyworkers—including those who work with therapeutic massage, Rosen Method Bodywork, Feldenkrais Method, and other modalities including craniosacral, structural integration, biodynamic massage, Shiatsu, Watsu, Trager, and many others—can find explanations for the links between muscle tension, touch, relaxation, and emotional growth. Body psychotherapists—somatic psychotherapists, dance movement psychotherapists, psychodynamic psychotherapists, process psychotherapists, sex and marriage therapists, those who practice some somatically oriented forms of cognitive behavioral therapy, and many others—can discover how embodied self-awareness has a direct impact on mental health and how cultivating their own embodied self-awareness can enhance their work with clients.

Preface

Those who work in medicine and allied fields such as nursing, pharmacology, psychiatry, rehabilitation, physical therapy, naturopathy, osteopathy, acupuncture, and chiropractics can enhance their understanding of how complementary practices to enhance self-awareness can contribute to healing and recovery from allopathic treatments. It may seem obvious that obesity, eating disorders, some forms of cardiovascular disease, and work-related injuries can arise from lack of awareness of the sensations, emotions, and movements of the body. People who overeat may not sense when their stomach is full. The stress of work situations leads to a diminished awareness of muscle tension and pain that can lead to deterioration in the long term

It is less obvious that persistent lack of embodied self-awareness can also play a role in hormonal dysfunction (as in stress disorders, disorders of sexual function, menstrual and menopausal symptoms) and immune function (leading to tumor growth and other autoimmune disorders like fibromyalgia and chronic fatigue). Awareness is medicine. Many studies show that sometimes alone and sometimes alongside allopathic medicines and interventions, physical and mental health can be improved. This is because of the direct physiological link between awareness of the body and the body's ability to regulate its physiological functions, including hormonal and immunological processes.

Finally, athletes and their teachers could benefit from finding ways to reduce injury and enhance performance through better self-awareness skills. Artists, and especially performing artists who use their whole bodies—actors, dancers, singers, and other musicians—can create a better focus in terms of their work with less pain and less unnecessary effort, by learning simple methods of embodied self-awareness. The practitioners of the meditative disciplines—including the different forms of mindfulness and body-focused meditation methods, yoga, tai chi, and the many martial arts—can enhance their understanding of how their practices can affect mental and physical well-being.

Goals of This Book and This Author

This book is about our lifetime journey toward and sometimes away from embodied self-awareness, sometimes with and sometimes without other people, a journey that begins before birth and continues until the moment of death. The book will address some of the following questions.

Psychophysiology of Self-Awareness

- What are the neurophysiological processes that explain the long-term maintenance of dysfunctional patterns of impaired embodied self-awareness leading to restrictive patterns of relating to others and to somatic symptoms such as muscle pain/tension, restricted movement, sensation, and emotion? Dysfunctional patterns of embodied self-awareness include interpersonal and attachment difficulties and self-regulatory problems such as obesity, eating and body image disorders, the functional somatic syndromes such as fibromyalgia and chronic fatigue, drug abuse and other addictions, depression, anxiety, sexual dysfunction, trauma-induced somatization syndromes, dissociation, as well as physical disorders that have a psychogenic component such as cardiovascular disease.
- What are the individual differences in early childhood related to embodied self-awareness and how do these differences relate to differences in parent–infant interpersonal relationships, attachment, and emotion communication?
- What are the long-term developmental consequences of these individualized preconceptual forms of awareness—experience-dependent and preverbal patterns of relating to self and to others—after we acquire language and thought?
- Finally, what are the currently available therapeutic practices to enhance embodied self-awareness that alleviate dysfunctional patterns in infants, older children, and adults? Research in developmental neurophysiology, biology, and psychology (such as research on the link between self-awareness due to meditation and subsequent increases in physiological and psychological well-being; or research on the long-term health consequences of hyper- or hypoactive neurohormonal processes linked to chronic defensive holding patterns in the muscles that result from "embodied" memories of early trauma) will be used to develop a treatment-relevant neurophysiological model of psychosomatic function and dysfunction.

This book does not advocate a particular program of self-improvement or a treatment method. It does not claim that embodied self-awareness makes you a better person. We cannot tell ourselves to be more self-aware and have

Preface

it suddenly happen. This is because expanding embodied self-awareness requires renewed access to neuromotor circuits that lie deep in the brain, outside of voluntary control. It is mostly not easy to change entrenched and lifelong patterns of embodied self-avoidance; it takes effort and support within therapeutically and educationally facilitative interpersonal relationships, and for some people, it may takes years until those core neural circuits are rebuilt. In my experience one can find temporary relief, but a quick fix for these problems does not exist.

This is a "how it works" book, intended to inform and illuminate the links between the science and practice of embodied self-awareness, from the viewpoint of a behavioral scientist and embodied self-awareness practitioner. Readers can expect to take away a better understanding of why they feel and act as they do, or why a particular awareness-based treatment modality feels particularly helpful for them. Practitioners of the arts of awareness-based treatment and training can expect to better understand why their particular modality is likely to be helpful for some people, some of the time, and perhaps not for others. Because each person's senses, feelings, and movements are unique, there is no one-size-fits-all approach.

Perhaps, like many, you've read a self-help book—for exercising, dieting, meditating, health, or whatever—and found that it did not work for you even after what you thought was a diligent application of its principles. Or, it worked for a while and then you lost your way. This outcome may not be entirely your fault. On the one hand, there truly is no quick fix for what may be lifelong issues of pain, depression, or weight control to name a few symptoms. On the other hand, without the coregulatory communion of a trained practitioner, one who senses when to give you control and when to provide support, you are unlikely to meet your goals. The bottom line is that a self that has been set against self-awareness for a long time will likely continue to do the same without guidance.

Many of the current practices for enhancing embodied self-awareness lack the scientific foundation and credibility of medical practice. Clients and insurers, therefore, are less likely to see their value. As a society, we operate under the illusion that if a body part breaks we can fix it quickly and get on with life. We lack a more sophisticated understanding that no part of our bodies, brains included, can fully function in the absence of links to other parts of the body

Psychophysiology of Self-Awareness

and to embodied self-awareness. We can physically heal from the surgery to repair a bullet wound or the injuries caused by an automobile accident, but unless treated, the effects of the trauma of assault or of the surgery itself will linger with more accompanying long term pain and self-doubt than is necessary. "Undiagnosable" pain, fatigue, and dysfunction have their roots in impaired self-awareness.

I endeavor to base all of the scientific language in some kind of real-life experience. It is not only a way of grounding the conceptual in lived experience, it also helps me test my own understanding of the concepts. If I can't translate the science into something concrete, then I probably don't understand it well enough to write about it.

The concrete experience from which I write is, of course, my own embodied self-awareness. In my view, there is no omniscient nonbiased scientific observer. All scientists are human, all are shaped by their experiences, and each scientist can make the choice either to reveal those biases or to put on the emperor's new clothes of expert objectivity. The truth is that all scientists found their way to their particular domain of interest because of some personal experience, most likely a childhood one. So, whether they want to admit it or not, they have a personal stake in the outcome.

In my view, the role of scientists in society is to examine their own limitations in light of evidence that may require them to change their view of the world and even to honor and thank those with whom they may have most vociferously disagreed. Holding too fast to one's own view, or protecting that view with the shield of authority, is a deliberate blunting of the very embodied self-awareness on which the case of this book is founded.

The personal developmental pathway of the scientist is no different from that of any competent professional. We all have to learn to sift evidence from our senses, movements, and emotions while assessing our own role in the process, and moving toward a broader vision of ourselves in the universe and in relation to other people. Scientists are different from others only in the type of evidence they are likely to employ in this process: particular technical terminology with precise meanings, particular ways of doing experiments, particular techniques of measurement, and particular ways of ensuring that results can be replicated by someone else.

Preface

As a Rosen Method Bodywork (see Chapter 2) practitioner and a scientific developmental psychologist, I have come to the domain of embodied self-awareness via these and other personal life pathways. My experience as a writer, teacher, speaker, and clinician suggests that the better able I am to illuminate my own point of view and my inherent biases, the better able others are to understand themselves and their own life pathways and potentials. If you don't become more self-aware after reading this book, I have not succeeded in this project.

Outline of the Book

Chapter 1 introduces the main themes of the book and sets them in the context of the social and cultural practices that pull us away from and bring us back to our bodies. Chapter 2 covers the aspect of embodied self-awareness related to body sensations (**interoception**) like cold, tingling, softness, or dizziness and our emotions. Chapter 3 describes the other part of embodied self-awareness that involves our sense of movement (**proprioception**), and the size, location, and shape of our bodies (**body schema**). Interoception and proprioception are organized by different sets of peripheral receptors, different nerve and spinal pathways, and different areas of the brain. Yet they become integrated into embodied self-awareness by means of the emotional feelings and motivations we have about these different forms of body awareness.

Chapter 4 deals with the themes of expression or **suppression** of embodied self-awareness and also the normal and pathological **absorption** into particular types of body states. Chapter 5 links these forms of opening and closing to the body with our sense of safety or threat from the environment and from our own bodies. Safety and threat are the fundamental organizing principles of the body, leading to our ability to remain emotionally and interoceptively open to other people and to ourselves. In this chapter, we will also see how traumatic life experiences shape our ability to feel our bodies or to avoid those feelings.

Chapter 6 covers movement and touch and includes the workings of our muscles and why they get stiff and painful. Since moving and touching are almost always linked to other things, especially other people, this chapter will

Psychophysiology of Self-Awareness

also cover the ways in which our bodies relate to others and the formation of **secure and insecure avoidant-dissmissive or insecure-resistant attachments**. Chapter 7 reviews the mechanics of respiration and vocalization, both of which are essential to expression and well-being, and both of which can be impaired in function with loss of embodied self-awareness. Finally, Chapter 8 describes some indicators of having regular and easy access to restorative forms of embodied self-awareness. Our body is always inviting us to come home, to feel safe and secure in its bounty of feeling. We can learn to hear that call.

Acknowledgments

I am grateful to the people who contributed to this book. The staff at Norton, especially editor Deborah Malmud and associate managing editor Kristen Holt-Browning were exceptionally supportive and gave effective feedback for improvement. Vito Rontino, an administrative assistant in the Department of Psychology at the University of Utah was invaluable in compiling the long and complex list of references. Neuroscientists with whom I directly consulted—Bud Craig, Ray Kesner, Marc Lewis, Yana Suchy, Don Tucker, and Jason Watson—were helpful in guiding me toward appropriate research as I mapped out the links between the brain and self-awareness. Suzi Tortora, Roger Russell, and Jacqueline Fogel each graciously donated their time to write illustrative case material from their own practices. Finally, Jacqueline Fogel gave me comments on earlier drafts and provided her ongoing generous and supportive presence in my life.

Alan Fogel
Salt Lake City
2008

1

Rediscovering the Lost Art of Sensing the Body

Only human beings have come to a point where they no longer know why they exist. They have forgotten the secret knowledge of their bodies, their senses, their dreams.
(Lame Deer & Erdoes, 1972, p. 157)

Did you ever feel as if you lost touch with your body? Perhaps you discovered one day that you had put on some extra pounds or that you developed a persistent pain in your shoulders and neck. At the same time, you realized that you could not explain why or how this happened. Somewhere along the way you just stopped noticing what you were doing to yourself.

Check in right now. Can you feel your feet touching the floor? Is there tension in your back or neck? Have you noticed the weather outside? Do you have to go to the bathroom? Are you thirsty or hungry?

This book is about how everyday life, as well as serious stress and trauma, can cause us to lose contact with our sensations and emotions and with the way our body moves, feels, and acts. Once our attention gets caught up in thought, judgment, demands, expectations, and other stressors we have no time left over to attend to ourselves. Maybe tomorrow?

It is not a big surprise that we lose touch with ourselves. Unless we are Buddhist monks, or live close to the land and nature, or have a regular practice of body-centered activity, we are likely to live in a complex social world of appointments, responsibilities, and concerns. What may come as a shock is that the loss of attention to ourselves brings with it additional losses. We risk losing our emotional equanimity, our physical health, and our sense of well-being.

Embodied self-awareness is the ability to pay attention to ourselves, to feel our sensations, emotions, and movements online, in the present moment, without the mediating influence of judgmental thoughts (Am I doing this

Psychophysiology of Self-Awareness

right? Why am I so clumsy? I wonder if anyone is watching?). Embodied self-awareness is composed of sensations like warm, tingly, soft, nauseated, dizzy; emotions such as happy, sad, threatened; and body senses like feeling the coordination (or lack of coordination) between the arms and legs while swimming, or sensing our shape and size (fat or thin), and sensing our location relative to objects and other people.

Embodied self-awareness is fundamental to survival. If we can't feel the heat, we will get burned. If we can't feel the boundaries of our bodies, we will bump into things or fall and get injured. If we can't sense the condition of our digestive system, we could be poisoned and not know it.

In this book, we'll see that we sometimes need to go off-line from our bodies in order to respond to threats and challenges from our environment. Our nervous system has a very efficient way of doing this, directing resources away from self-awareness and self-renewal into arousal and rapid response. We get into trouble, however, if we stay on alert for too long and never let our bodies rest and recover. In that case, we will begin to lose precious metabolic resources. Without anyone at "home" to monitor the system, it will start to break down and fall apart. Pain, mental distress, and physical illness are the inevitable consequences.

Paradise Lost

The first permanent human settlements, tiny villages, were only established 10,000 years ago. Prior to that, *Homo sapiens* lived as nomads for 100,000 years. These people were descended from other human species that arose at the beginning of the Pleistocene Era, about 1.6 million years ago. About 35,000 years ago, *homo sapien sapien* hunter-gatherer groups existed in Africa, Europe, Asia, Australia, and in the Americas. For most humans, their entire society was a small band of 25 to 30 souls who dug roots, cut plants, and hunted game. Their territory would be no more than 20 miles (30 kilometers) across and they seldom encountered another human group.

Observations of the few still surviving hunter-gatherers in Africa, Oceana, and the Amazonian basin reveal a great deal of close physical contact between people of all ages. Individuals are embedded in a *"socio-sensual human organization* which began in infancy during a period of almost continuous, unusually rich tactile interaction" (Sorenson, 1979, p. 289; emphasis added). This sensual network begins in infancy and continues throughout life.

> When not in the sling, infants are passed from hand to hand around a fire for similar interaction with one adult or child after another. They are kissed on their faces, bellies, genitals, are sung to, bounced, entertained, encouraged, and addressed at length in conversational tones long before they can understand words.
> (Konner, 1982, p. 302)

Hunter-gatherer life was not Eden. Old age began at 35 and most people did not live that long. Diseases, predators, accidents, and famine were the main causes of death. Yet while alive, people lived physically close to other people, fully engaging in the complex movements and exertions of hunting and gathering, child care, and love. Living hunter-gatherers have a substantial amount of leisure time which they spend in play with children, games, rituals, and relaxation.

By necessity, hunter-gatherers must have had their senses attuned to the earth's climate and cycles. Different body sensations registered changes in humidity, temperature, and light that presaged rain, an early winter, or drought. Earth, air, fire, and water, the basic elements of life, were not conceptualized in scientific terms. The earth under their feet could be warm or dry, fragrant with living organisms or barren. The taste and smell of water, not chemical testing, led to decisions about whether it was safe to drink. We evolved by honing and indulging our embodied sensations: the softness and warmth of touch, the smells of life and death, the colors of the sky, the sounds and tastes of the natural world (Abram, 1996; Shepard, 1998).

We also think people fully accepted and embraced their emotions because funeral rites, a commemoration of grief, are the oldest rituals in the archaeological record, first appearing some 30,000 years ago. The excitement of the hunt, lust and love, and the pleasures and pains of childbirth were also celebrated in cave paintings and figurines that have been dated to the same era.

Change took place 10,000 years ago, when people began to make permanent settlements and create concepts of ownership and property, and when work became specialized and society stratified. At this point we see a shift toward patterns of dominion and warfare, entitlement and oppression, the loss of connection to the earth, and the loss of the freedom to move and play. Agriculture, the dominion and domestication of animals and plants, was part of this shift away from engagement with the natural world (Eisler, 1987; Wenke, 1990).

Psychophysiology of Self-Awareness

Suppose we represent human evolution, beginning 1.6 million years ago, at noon on an imaginary clock. Those first villages would arise at 4 minutes before midnight. Human civilization, with urban centers and technologies, would awaken at 2 minutes before midnight. However you want to conceptualize this vast scale of time, most of human experience—the experience that created our basic genetic and psychophysiological structure—unfolded in the cradle of a sociosensual human organization.

In the urban technological cultures in which we live today, awareness of the body, our vital connection to other bodies and to the earth, is ignored or minimized. Busy people focus on thinking and doing rather than on feeling, being, and being with. In the global marketplace of ideas and products, a higher value is placed on being rational than emotional. Many of us are likely to have learned from our early school years onward to keep movement to a minimum, to sit up straight rather than sway, rock, or fidget, to pay attention to our thoughts rather than to our feelings.

Being *civilized* in technological societies has come to mean to suppress, contain, prioritize, and push down the body's natural functions. Let's assume at a minimum that societies require at least some hygienic proscriptions such as: do not urinate, defecate, menstruate, or pass gas in public places except where otherwise designated, please cover your mouth when you sneeze, wash your hands before touching food, and I'll thank you to stay at home if you have a contagious disease.

How about the other restrictions on our bodies, especially those found in the urban centers of technological societies?

- Schools in the United States have severely curtailed or eliminated physical education and performing arts programming because of the need to score higher on standardized tests in order to receive federal funding. School children spend their free time at home in front of computer screens, watching TV, or with a cell phone or iPod plugged into their relatively stationary ears. Obesity, diabetes, and asthma have reached epidemic proportions in American children and adolescents. Junk food is no doubt a part of this but so is the lack of physical activity, outdoor play, being in nature, and outlets for creative expression through the body.
- White collar workers worldwide are increasingly confined to small offices and cubicles in which they sit staring at a computer monitor, clicking a

mouse, and typing at a keyboard for most of their work day. This apparent efficiency comes at the cost of repetitive motion injuries of the hands and arms, and lower back pain, ailments once confined primarily to factory workers. Office workers also suffer from a host of stress-related disorders that show up in the form of chronic fatigue, high blood pressure, diabetes, and obesity. These too are likely caused by the unnatural confinement of the body and mind, with no way to blow off the steam of stress caused by external control.
- Homemakers with young children may use their bodies more—lifting a baby, mopping a floor, walking around a supersized market with toys at one end and toiletries at the opposite end of a cavernous indoor space. The stress of many commitments—play dates, school drop-offs and pickups, shopping, cleaning, after school activities, preparing meals, balancing being a marital partner and a parent—takes its toll and once again the body is forgotten until pain or illness show up. Some parents rarely have a moment to rest or even go to the bathroom. Some also suffer from hand, arm, and back strain from the physical labor of moving children's bodies without having the time to focus on how those movements can be done without self-injury. Maternal depression is growing increasingly common and has lasting impacts on young children.

For all these inhospitalities, the culprit is sociocultural demands for productivity lacking in an awareness of the role of the body. In the current state of work in the Western world, the body is put aside as a mere tool, as if that tool could be discarded and replaced when it breaks down. Until it actually does break down, the body is perceived like everything else in a consumer-driven economy, something that might be replaced with a newer model. Bringing an awareness of and commitment to the body could make work healthier for both the economy and the worker.

Not only work lacks embodiment. Leisure is also perversely anti-body. There is the DVD-MP3-TV-texting hegemony. Who doesn't succumb to groggy stiffness after hours of such inactivity, an acquiescent victim of brain-numbing? Exercise, if it does take place, is done because it is supposed to be good for you: walking a treadmill or rowing in place while plugged into the iPod or whatever. No one is going to get a runner's high going down this road. The only kind of body awareness that could enter this theater of surround sound is fatigue or pain. By then, it is too late to make midcourse corrections that adjust body physiology to maximum benefit. Does anyone practice the zen of leaf raking and the meditation of gardening anymore? Or, are those just chores to get done as quickly as possible, openly inviting opportunities for muscle and cardiovascular strain?

Another lost opportunity for sensitivity to the body is in Western culture's predominant approach to health. Physicians work with the body, but the body for many of them is a collection of muscles and bones, vessels and cavities, lumps and microorganisms. The medical body is disconnected from the lived body.

Even in endeavors that should emphasize body awareness, like athletics and the performing arts, competition and money lead to a loss of self-awareness. A musician may be perfectly comfortable in the company of "safe" audiences but the stakes of an audition or a stage performance raise new and uncontrollable emotions. Stage fright is exceptionally paralyzing. The muscles and breath freeze. The knees become weak and shake. There may be dizziness and nausea. One wants to run or hide. Then there are the social emotions like pride and shame that haunt the imagined audience of colleagues, friends, parents, and ticket buyers. Even successful and seasoned performers may battle these "demons" before every public appearance.

The problem with fear, and any type of threat to the self, is that awareness of the body becomes lost and replaced by the need to protect the self or to collapse. **Suppression** is the loss of our ability to feel ourselves. Suppression includes defenses of denial (I'm not really scared, just a little nervous!), intellectualizing (I don't want to be a failure. They're all counting on me to get this part), self-soothing in the service of blunting feelings (eating too much), and the like.

In addition to stage fright, dancers and athletes in particular must also work near the edges of endurance and the outer fringes of metabolic stability. Conditioning and diet allow the athlete to engage at the highest levels of human body performance, incredibly close to the breakdown points of the cardiovascular, respiratory, and digestive systems. With the body close to its limits, the pressures, and the years of effort and expense for training all on the line, it is no wonder that some of our heroes suppress these intense feelings by succumbing to performance-enhancing and pain-alleviating drugs. The surprise is that we are disappointed in them when they are found out, not because we are doing any better in holding it all together without prescribed or recreational pharmaceutical support, but because the weakness of the hero exposes our own insufficiencies and guilty sedations.

For the person taking a written examination, or just attending a typical school or going to work in the industrialized world, there is a lesson to be learned from these exceptional human beings whose work is highly visible performances. The body, no less than the mind, is always involved. In learning thought skills as children we are told to sit still, keep quiet, write clearly, obey instructions, and the like. We must endure sitting for long hours, not being able to go to the bathroom when we need to, eating junk food on the run, all the while suffering from a headache. We have to suppress a constant flood of emotions related to our peers and teachers, pride and shame, fear and infatuation. We often do not get time to move, breathe, rest, or play.

We are expected to know how to "behave" and are likely to be censured if we do not. Thought processes—what the test is supposedly assessing—can be constricted in a constricted body. Recent research suggests that these traditional means of corseting the body in schools and at work are not in fact the most conducive postures for fomenting the kind of in-the-head thinking that institutions would like to foster.

School and white collar work occur in these more or less stationary, more or less sedentary situations. Factory work is similar, with the added disadvantage of repetitive motions that do not offer opportunities for creativity and rest. For perhaps the vast majority of the population in industrialized nations, people learn suppression by avoiding unnecessary movement, shutting off sensation, and putting a lid on their emotions. After a while, in our free time when we have an opportunity to move, we are likely to avoid movement: vegging out in front of a video display seems easier and our bodies mistakenly believe that this is the only means of rest and recovery.

Then we wonder why we have gained so much weight. We stop feeling the pain in our sacrum from the hard seats of school desks, the cramp in our wrists from typing, and the tension in our neck from craning toward a screen or book or power tool. We don't understand why we get headaches so frequently, lower back pain, or carpal tunnel syndrome. We suppress our feelings because they make us vulnerable at school or work; neither girls nor boys, women nor men want to be perceived as weak. We puzzle over why we can't get along with our parents or spouses as we assiduously avoid feeling what's authentic and let anger and resentment take the place of our sadness at the loss of our inner self, a grief so profound and buried so deep inside that we cannot acknowledge its existence, even to ourselves.

The price we pay for ignoring our bodies—its movements, senses, and emotions—is the festering of disease and dysfunction. So far as our bodies are concerned, we are for the most part in a sorry state (see Box 1.1). Fortunate are the enlightened few who radiate well-being, eat healthy foods that satisfy their hungers, who can move in ways that maximize the function of body and mind, who can relax in mindful ways, and who have opportunities for creative embodied self-expression. These individuals are either financially secure and have access to a wide range of contemporary health and wellness resources, or they are poor but living in a society that maintains and supports active embodied work such as manual farming and subsistence hunting on the one hand or embodied spiritual practices such as yoga, meditation, pilgrimage, or ritual ecstatic singing and dancing.

BOX 1.1
Body Count

Since this book is about enhancing embodied self-awareness, our attention to sensations and emotions, it might be worthwhile to take a few moments to assess the ways in which you occupy your attention on a daily basis. You can revisit this assessment after you finish reading the book to see if anything may have changed.

- In what ways do you notice your body during school, work, housekeeping, or childcare?
- Are you aware of stress or tension in your hands, arms, back, belly, neck, legs, or anywhere else as you work?
- Are you aware of any restrictions in your breathing?
- Do you grip the steering wheel tighter than necessary, or stretch your neck forward when trying to read a computer screen, or have restless legs, or hold yourself rigidly at attention when other people are around?

continued

BOX 1.1 (continued)

- Do you do anything to change your movement or posture to alleviate the stress on your body, or do you just keep working?
- Have you developed a painful neuromuscular condition, or chronic fatigue, or nonmedical chest, head, or stomachaches, as a result of not paying attention to the stress on your body?
- When you feel tired or achy, do you know what happened to your body to create this state?
- Aside from sleeping at night, do you ever rest during the day?
- Do you ever stop thinking and just feel yourself?
- Do you practice/receive any type of leisure activity that calls for embodied self-awareness such as yoga, massage and other bodywork, meditation, dance, arts and crafts, music, or sports?
- Do you practice this with the intention to expand self-awareness and relaxation, or are you caught up in achievement at the expense of awareness?
- Do you stop to smell the roses, engage in open-ended play with a child or a companion animal, indulge in prayer, walk in nature with all your senses alert, take a hot bath, or go to a spa with no agenda except to relax?
- Do you ask for help when you need it?
- If you ever suffered a serious injury, were a crime or abuse victim, or were in a natural disaster or at war, have you ever dealt with the emotional aftermath?
- Can you talk about your emotions easily or do you push them aside?

Assuming each item is worth 10 points, there are a few different ways of counting up your self-awareness score in this assessment. One way is to ask whether you do these things or not: "Yes, I confess that I grip the steering wheel too tightly," could be one response. This shows that even though you might not be able to coax your body to relax while driving, you are at least aware that you cannot relax. You can give yourself 6

continued

Psychophysiology of Self-Awareness

> **BOX 1.1** (continued)
>
> points for that awareness. If you are aware of your grip while you drive and you have taught yourself to relax your hands and arms when on the road, you can take all 10 points. Bravo!
>
> Or, you might say, "Wow, now that you ask, I realize that I'm not even aware of how I grip the steering wheel. I need to check that out next time I drive." That is also a positive step toward expanding embodied self-awareness: becoming aware that you were not previously aware. You can take 3 points for that. You get 0 points only if you don't know the answer and you don't care to find out. You just don't want to go there. Fine. But I know that I planted a seed and I think you know that too or you would not be reading this book in the first place.

The Growth and Decline of Embodied Self-Awareness

This book is about **embodied self-awareness**:

- perceiving our *movements* in relation to other people and our surroundings,
- registering the textures and depths of the *senses*, and
- exploring the intricacies of our *emotions* in relation to others and the world.

Formal education around the world emphasizes a heightened awareness of our thought processes with the growing ability to regulate our thoughts toward specific goals such as planning and problem solving, developing effective strategies to reach goals, and censoring our actions to fit in with the culture of the workplace and family.

Thinking about the self, called **conceptual self-awareness**, is not the same as feeling the self in embodied self-awareness. Embodied self-awareness involves **interoception**—sensing our breathing, digestion, hunger, arousal,

Sensing the Body

pain, emotion, fatigue and the like—and the **body schema**—an awareness of the movement and coordination between different parts of the body and between our body and the environment. Conceptual self-awareness is engagement in a thought process of categorizing, planning, reasoning, judging, and evaluating. Embodied self-awareness involves being in the **subjective emotional present**, being able to actually feel one's sadness or pain, for example, without judgment and without trying to escape from it.

Virtually all tests of academic achievement and work-related knowledge are written tests in which the effective awareness of and self-regulation of linguistically based thought is the primary skill. There are some examinations that test the body as well as the thought process. New drivers generally need to demonstrate that they are reasonably competent at obeying traffic signs and signals, changing lanes, making a turn across the oncoming traffic, and parallel parking. Doing this involves the coordination of *movements* involved in steering, shifting, braking, and looking out the rear- and side-view mirrors.

The student driver has to learn to heighten certain senses such as looking and listening as well as the feel of the vehicle going too fast around a turn or having to make a sudden stop. In a real on-the-road driving test, the *emotions* of uncertainty, fear, elation, and possible road rage are likely to cycle rapidly and unexpectedly. The actual embodied task of driving is the awareness of all these feelings—of movement, sensation, and emotion—and learning how to regulate them constructively to get safely from point A to point B and with minimal harm to anything or anyone else.

Embodied self-awareness—awareness of moving, sensing, and emotions—begins prior to birth during the last two prenatal months. Fetal self-awareness already involves both **interoception** (monitoring the internal milieu of the body in relation to the environment) and the **body schema** (the "recognition" of one part of the body by another). Dynamic 4-D ultrasound research films reveal that by the 7th month of gestation, the fetal mouth will open in anticipation if the hand comes near (see Figure 1.1), a striking demonstration that one part of the body recognizes its relation to another part (Myowa-Yamakoshi & Takeshita, 2006). Our inner awareness and our awareness of the links between one and another part—the ability to coordinate movements and senses—continue to grow throughout life as we learn more complex ways of acting in the world.

Psychophysiology of Self-Awareness

Figure 1.1
Fetal hand-to-mouth coordination

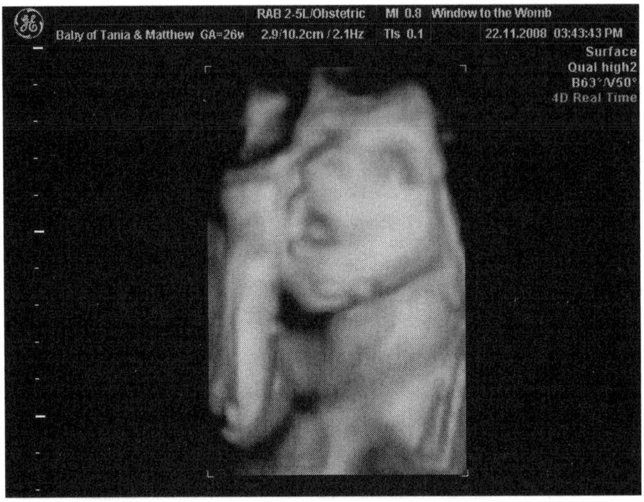

The fetus shows us that expanding self-awareness is our original and primary occupation, so important to well-being that we are equipped to begin our life's work even before birth. It comes as no surprise that the fetus has the ability for basic survival inside, and later outside the uterus. Without the prenatal development of physiological pathways of nerves and muscles for breathing and sucking, for example, we could not get far. The big surprise is that *these neurological circuits for survival are anchored in the brain to pathways for self-awareness* and they can grow or shrink in relation to the presence or absence of opportunities for self-exploration. Yes, the nervous system stimulates respiration and digestion, but it also has simultaneous pathways for feeling ourselves consummate, or fail to consummate, those acts.

There is a primitive sense of self—an **embodied self-awareness** that has the capacity to expand its awareness of itself—at the very core of our psychophysiological being (Stern, 1985). The newborn at the breast is adequately equipped to be self-aware of how to move and sense in a way that facilitates the feelings of pleasure and reduces the feelings of displeasure from the mouth and gut. This is not merely a sucking "reflex" absent of an inner felt sense, not a mere neural discharge. Nursing is one of life's first socially coordinated performances. There is the learning to feel and regulate the self-to-self coordination of sucking, swallowing, and head turning in relation to milk flow. There is an emerging awareness of strong and powerful emotions (unfathomable desires) related specifically to those actions and to the success and failure of those actions (Fogel, 2009).

Freud thought of newborn hunger as emotionally all-consuming, total in its oblivion of anything else, a self-absorption that he thought at once "autistic" and "oceanic" (Freud 1903/1953). He was correct about the oceanic proportions of newborn hunger but entirely wrong about the lack of self- and other-awareness (Stern, 1985). From the perspective of **interoceptive** self-awareness, newborn longing is a longing for connection: a good contact of the lips with the nipple sealed with saliva, the sweetness of the milk that partakes of the sweetness of surrender, and the feelings of warmth exchanged between two vulnerable human beings who cling to each other between hope and despair. In humans, and in most mammals, self-awareness at birth instantly becomes inseparable from other-awareness. Given the stakes, it does not take long for the mother and infant to teach each other how best to signal the need to connect, how best to coordinate their mutual actions, and how best to harness their irrational hungers for each other toward the goal of easily reestablishing, many times each day, this triumph of ordinariness that can only be achieved via socially coordinated embodied self-awareness.

The interpersonal coordination around nursing in all mammals is not simply reflexive and mechanistic, not simply "controlled" by an "innate" neurological pattern generator. It is actually impossible to have smoothly coordinated social action without **body schema** self-awareness, the sense of where "my" body leaves off and "yours" begins. The pathways in the brain for sucking, moving, and touching, therefore, need to loop through neural pathways for self- and other-awareness.

The fetal and infant nervous system, given its limits and immaturity, requires a means to detect the most relevant and important aspects of the myriad of stimulation coming from the body and the world. The brain is put together is such a way that "relevant" means specifically "self-relevant," the part of the manifold of sights, sounds, smells, and visceral feelings which is directly implicated in "my own" sense of stability and well-being. Without this self-referent looping which finds what is most important in the here and now, there could be no learning and no development. The lack of self-reference in the immature brain would in fact engender an autistic state of being overwhelmed by the world without a clear sense of what is important or useful.

Psychophysiology of Self-Awareness

The loss of embodied self-referent awareness at any time in the life course is debilitating. It occurs whenever stimulation from the body or from the world exceeds the ability of the nervous system to track its significance for the self. This state of affairs is typically experienced as trauma. During physical assaults and violent attacks (e.g., automobile accidents, child and sexual abuse, crimes, and warfare) the body's self-referent, self-protective, and self-regulatory circuits are incapacitated. The brain goes on autopilot, invoking some of our basic **biobehavioral responses** to threat—fight, flight, freeze, or faint—that, as we shall see later in this book, fundamentally and perhaps permanently alter the person. Memory, movement, and sensation become impaired and the boundaries of the self shrink to a small sphere of perceived control. So also, the small and persistent insults of our family, work, and school lives can accrue and create over time a similar kind of self-numbing.

As a result, individuals can no longer monitor their internal states. We can no longer tell when we are actually hungry or tired, happy or sad. The reason our body needs us to be self-aware is in order to maintain **homeostasis**, that is, a state of mental and physical health in which our cells are sufficiently nourished to maintain normal metabolism to preserve and grow body function. The neural pathways for embodied self-awareness are directly linked to the pathways for homeostasis.

In these states of traumatic withdrawal, people need supportive personal **resources**, things that promote pleasure and a sense of safety. Only when there is a sense of safety can we access the **biobehavioral responses** related to safety: restoration, engagement, and normal absorption. When an animal is threatened by a predator, once it has escaped it can only recover in the safety of a protected den or burrow. **Restoration**, which involves an awareness and acceptance of the need to recover, occurs in extended periods of licking, rest, sleep, and the comfort of other warm bodies. Following restoration, the individual can then enter states of normal **engagement** with the world and with other people. Later, these states of engagement can expand with more depth into **normal absorption**: the experience of being "lost" in something that one loves (a person or an activity), including creativity, performance and sports "highs," deep states of concentration and meditation, and the "oceanic" feelings described above for the newborn (see Chapter 5).

The startling take-home message in these observations is that:

- *Embodied self-awareness is as fundamental to health and survival as breathing and eating;*
- *The loss of embodied self-awareness at any time in life can be debilitating;*
- *Embodied self-awareness is easily lost while growing up in technological societies, by cumulative deprivation, or by sudden traumas; and*
- *Embodied self-awareness must be actively maintained, cultivated, taught, and renewed to sustain well-being.*

The natural question is, if embodied self-awareness is so important, why is it so easily diluted or impaired? The answer lies in an understanding of the linking pathways in the immature brain of the fetus and infant: the **biobehavioral response** pathways for (1) taking in and responding to the world; (2) for sensing and responding to the organ systems inside the body; and (3) for deciding and bringing to awareness what among these is the most self-relevant.

In an accidental fall, we are not surprised that an ankle is sprained or an arm broken. In a physical assault, we are not surprised at sustained injuries or even by psychological consequences like nightmares and states of paranoia. It is no longer news that a lifetime of anger and impatience (the Type A personality) can lead to cardiovascular disease.

What may come as news to some, and is the purpose of this book to present, is that the reason these insults have their lasting effects on the body and mind is due to an *untreated and unrecognized impairment of embodied self-awareness*, an impairment that, given the architecture of the brain and nervous system, occurs whenever the relationship of the person to the internal and external environment is disturbed or distorted. In humans, restoration of embodied self-awareness occurs in the context of interpersonal relationships.

Self-Awareness Is Fundamentally Linked to Awareness of Others

In a previous book, *Developing through Relationships* (1993), I described a process called **coregulation** in which two individuals dynamically coordinate actions into a smooth joint performance by means of sensing the boundaries

Psychophysiology of Self-Awareness

between self and other (Fogel, 1993). Since many people have told me the example I used in that book was especially helpful in their understanding of this point, I will use it again here.

Imagine an adult taking hold of the hands of a 3-month-old baby, who is lying on her back, in order to assist the baby into a sitting position. As the adult lifts the baby's arms, the adult can feel the baby beginning to contract her own arm muscles, pulling back against the adult's muscle force. If the baby pulls more strongly, the adult needs less force. The baby naturally exerts force in the arm and trunk muscles if she wants to sit up. The baby of this age does not conceptualize the adult as a separate person. She can, however, feel her self being pulled and also feel herself pulling in response.

There is no force at the beginning, when the baby is lying supine, and no force from the arms at the end, when the baby is sitting. As the adult helps to pull the baby up, total force increases, but it may cycle dynamically in relative intensity between adult and infant (see Figure 1.2). The total force exerted is a smooth function over time (Figure 1.3) but it can only be achieved by a mutual sensing of when to pull more or less in relation to the partner, by our brain's ability to sense the self, and the self-in-relation to another.

Figure 1.2
Coregulation in Pull-to-Sit

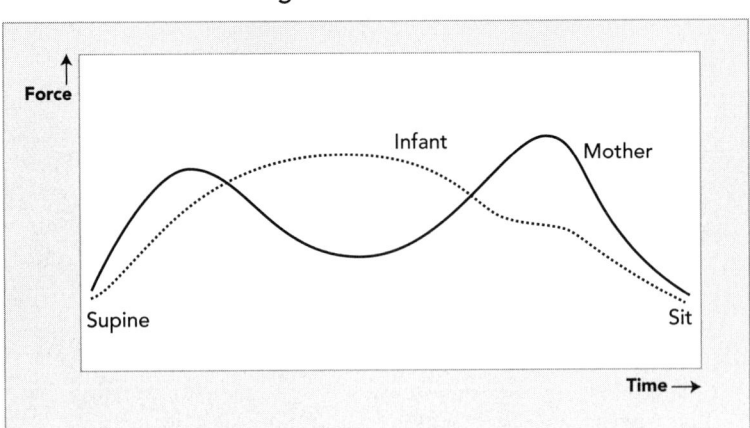

16

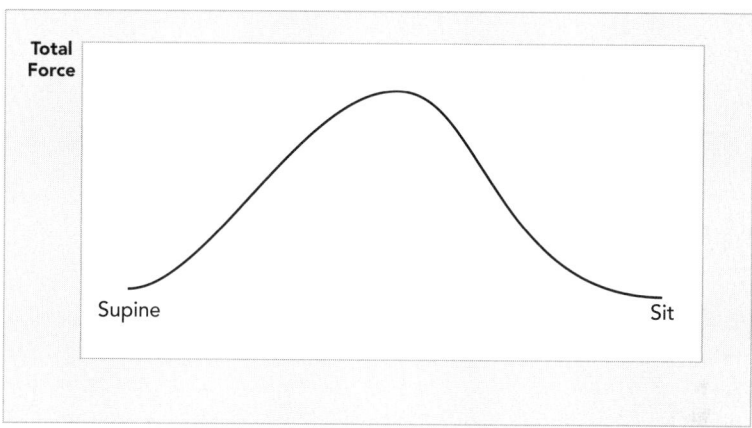

Figure 1.3
Total Force Exerted in Pull-to-Sit

If the adult is too forceful and pulls the baby with a steady and unrelenting power, the baby will either become rigidly tight or limp. In this case, there is no coregulation of mutual forces. And, in this case, the baby either senses the self as helpless against the felt power of the adult, or cannot feel the self at all. Suppose the adult, on the other hand, allows the baby to exert herself to the limit of her ability, and to provide assistance only when the baby's effort lags. In this case, the baby can not only feel what she needs to do to maintain the upward motion, but she can also feel the safety of being held and propelled should her own muscles get tired or her timing is off. The opportunity for self-awareness in the baby that is provided by a coregulating adult leads ultimately to the baby's learning, over repeated occasions, how best to execute a smooth performance on her own and how best to work with another person to do this.

Not only is the immature brain organized around self-awareness, it is also intimately open to others in such a way that the well-being of the self is fundamentally tied to the way in which these early social coordinations of moving, touching, sensing, and feeling play out (see Box 1.2). The brain, and the entire body in humans and other social animals, is at the same time self-aware and other-aware. The newborn's body comes equipped with a mouth of just the right size to engage an adult breast and with a tongue that is able to express milk from a nipple: parent and infant, and lovers, are made to "fit" each other, to couple lips, faces, voices, bodies, and body parts. Our emotions are relational: we are happy to be with someone, angry at someone, sad because of the loss of someone. Of course, an adult may feel sad for "no reason," but upon introspection the reason is always a loss of some relationship quality. Our thoughts are relational: always about something or someone.

Box 1.2
Push Me, Pull You

A unique demonstration of embodied self-awareness in relationships was reported by Daniel Stern, who was one of the first to recognize that the embodied sense of self begins in early infancy and develops through interpersonal relationships (Stern, 1985). Stern describes his observations of conjoined twins who were born connected at their lower abdomens, facing each other. The twins were surgically separated at the age 4 months, but prior to that Stern and his colleagues noticed that the twins sometimes sucked on their own hands and sometimes on their sister's hands.

> When twin A (Alice) was sucking on her own fingers, one of us placed one hand on her head and the other hand on the arm that she was sucking. We gently pulled the sucking arm away from her mouth and registered (in our own hands) whether her arm put up resistance to being moved from her mouth and/or whether her head strained forward to go after the retreating hand. In this situation, Alice's arm registered the interruption of sucking, but she did not give evidence of straining forward with her head. The same procedure was followed when Alice was sucking on her sister Betty's fingers rather than her own. When Betty's hand was gently pulled from Alice's mouth, Alice's arms showed no resistance, but Alice's head did strain forward. Alice seemed, in this case, to have no confusion as to whose fingers belonged to whom and which motor plan would best reestablish sucking. (Stern, 1985, pp. 78–79)

continued

Sensing the Body

> **Box 1.2** (continued)
>
> This shows that the twins were aware of their bodies in two ways: interoception and body schema. Interoceptively, they could sense what it felt like to suck on a hand and that this was something they wanted to repeat. They also clearly had a sense of their own body schema, both in terms of what parts of their bodies needed to move to get the hand to the mouth (the arm) and also what body parts belonged to themselves compared to their sister.
>
> This sense of embodied self-awareness developed as the girls interacted with each other. In the coregulated dialogue of pushing and pulling of their own and their sister's hands and arms and heads, they could begin to sort out which of those movements came under voluntary control and which did not.
>
> Awareness of the body schema arises from the sensorimotor integration across at least two different modalities: in this case, vision, touch, and movement. Interoceptively feeling the muscular effort to move an arm or head, locating that movement to a particular body part through sensation and touch, and seeing that part move in synchrony with the effort is sufficient for the brain to say: this is "my" arm and "my" effort (Stern, 1985).

Our sense organs are directed outward, feelers at the end of neural stalks that are rooted deep in the brain, for the specific and primary purpose of connecting us with the world. Our brain is not fully formed at birth. It awaits engagement, most specifically with other people, to spur cellular growth and inter-neuronal connections. We develop in and through relationships. Each new relationship experience presents another opportunity to move, sense, and feel in deeper, more creative, and more fulfilling ways. Or, the opposite: to limit ourselves so that we do not hurt or get hurt by another person. Our brain is nourished by engagement, knows how to recognize safety and threat, and knows how to metabolize these nutrients and grow differently in response to each. That is also why interpersonal aspects of treatment for trauma and injury are required: the sense of safety and support in the other nourishes the growth of new neuromotor connections.

Infants don't have a full complement of emotions at birth. Enjoyment does not begin until the second month, anger can't be felt before 6 months, fear is absent prior to 10 months, and defiance, pride, and shame don't show up until the end of the second year, guilt not until 3 years, and the depths of love in all its forms take a lifetime to learn. This means that our experiences with other people during the first few years of life can teach us to explore, embrace, accept, live with, and control these feelings and the complexities of feeling and expressing them in the company of other people (Fogel, 2009).

If we are less fortunate, our natural sprouting of anger is met with scorn or with terror. Joy and pride may not be celebrated. The child's greatest asset, creative spontaneity, may be suffocated with demands and expectations. The body goes into a pattern of suppression and defense that is deeply etched into the brain and nervous system, limiting not only our expressive movements and ability to reach out to the world, but also our sense of self as a fully expressive and alive being. To limit emotions is to limit embodied self-awareness. While the person on the outside may seem perfectly compliant and well-behaved, behind the façade there is no room for spontaneity, curiosity, and self-awareness. This person may have no place that feels safe enough to let go of pretension, relax, feel, and recharge the batteries. Connecting with the self and our emotions is like balm for the brain. After a while, the power drain of many years of hiding from self and others leads inevitably to the disease and dysfunction mentioned earlier.

Embodied self-awareness develops initially via interpersonal relationships during the first 3 years of life, to create a foundation of self- and other-approach or self- and other-avoidance upon which patterns of lifecourse mental and physical health or illness are built. Self-awareness in the late-term fetus and in the infant is nonconceptual and nonlinguistic. It is an implicit "knowing" about the self's likes and dislikes, joys and pains, in relation to the world. It is a way of filtering the world into what is self-relevant and what is not. There is a relational component to early self-awareness, however, in the sensing that a "mother's" ever louder footsteps mean that she is coming closer. Self-awareness in early infancy has no concept of "me" and "you" as separate beings. Infant self-awareness is the sense that if I turn my head, I can see "someone," and if I reach out, I can touch "something." It is sensing the difference between touching and being touched.

Over the first 3 years of life, there is a growing awareness that the arms, breasts, and lips that the baby can see and feel and that she can perceive are not initiated by her own muscle contractions, have their own intentions, and do not come and go entirely because of her smiles or cries. By the end of the first year, babies will follow the gaze or point of another person, or themselves point at an object of interest, acts that reveal a sense that there is an "otherness" out there that does not share their own mind. By the end of the second year, toddlers will comfort a distressed adult with their own bottle or blanket: there is an awareness that the "otherness" feels something similar to what the self can feel and can be comforted by the things that comfort the self. Some adults, but not all, can separate their own emotions from those of others, sensing for example that the "other's" pain was the cause of their angry outburst rather than anything that "I" did.

Our growth of the ability to clearly distinguish the self, to feel all of our emotions and to fully empathize with other people and allow them to feel theirs, depends upon our developmental history of self-awareness in relationships. Suppressing feelings at work or school is an adaptive strategy in society. Adults who avoid or suppress their feelings in close relationships, blame those closest to them for perceived transgressions, or fail to recognize a close relation's feelings, have not resolved or recognized a prior threat to their own feelings in past close encounters. They are likely not aware of their avoidance because avoidance is an acquired way of relating that was hidden in the older and deeper parts of the brain at a time when there were no words or concepts to explain what happened.

Coming to Our Senses: Basic Principles of Restorative Interventions for the Loss of Embodied Self-Awareness

Explicating the ailments resulting from lack of embodied self-awareness is enough reason to write a book on this topic, although that alone would fall into the literary domain of tragedy. This book is inspired more by the growing science and clinical practices for the cultivation of embodied self-awareness—the refinement of movement, sensing, and feeling—that can have salutary effects on the well-being of individuals and societies.

Psychophysiological health rests upon the ability to mindfully perceive and monitor bodily states leading to the activation of restorative **neurobiological responses** (including autonomic, immune, and endocrine responses), heightened embodied self-awareness (symptom monitoring, stress minimization), restorative behaviors (rest, self-nurturance) that subsequently facilitate healing processes, and ultimately the ability to be fully alive in the **subjective emotional present**: the ability to enter states of **restoration, engagement** and **normal absorption**. According to health psychologist Donald Bakal (1999), who uses the term *somatic awareness* in the same way that I use *embodied self-awareness*,

> Somatic awareness is at the cutting edge . . . and represents a way to truly empower individuals in their efforts to maintain or restore good health. Somatic awareness constitutes an innate wisdom that people have about their own psychobiological health. . . . Somatic awareness represents the next stage in the evolution of holistic health care. (Bakal, 1999, pp. 4–5)

Some of that evidence for the wide-ranging effects of embodied self-awareness, which are to be reviewed in this book, comes from recent research on contemporary "alternative" health practices such as yoga, meditation, dance, exercise, massage, and other bodywork that fosters self-awareness. There is also a substantial research oeuvre in neuroscience, in human developmental science, in psychology, and in the health sciences, that can be mined for insights about the effects of embodied self-awareness on health and well-being.

Treatments that work best are those that are interpersonal, that focus on the subjective emotional present, and that cultivate the art of regaining health-promoting practices of self-awareness. The basic principles of treatment for lost embodied self-awareness are given in Table 1.1. These principles will be illustrated throughout this book.

Table 1.1
Basic principles for the treatment of lost embodied self-awareness

Principle	Definition
1. *Resources.* Recovering, finding, and maintaining **resources**.	**Resources** are a constant and reliable presence in the body, mental imagery, or surroundings that feels safe, stable, and supportive. People need resources as they reexperience the feelings of threat, anger, or pain that led to the **suppression** of embodied self-awareness.
2. *Slowing down.* Getting off the fast track of thinking and doing in order to learn how to stay longer in the **subjective emotional present**.	Encourage shifting from thinking to feeling by starting with what the person can already feel in their bodies and develop a sense of competence to experience these, to expand their tolerance for more embodied self-awareness, and to come back to resources for safety when needed.
3. *Coregulation.* Therapist as **coregulating** psychobiological regulator to enhance a sense of safety in the relationship and in one's own body.	Monitoring autonomic arousal and relaxation and helping the person to maintain **homeostasis** by shifting intensity, speeding up or slowing down, helping the person to come back to resources when needed; pointing out when the person leaves or comes back to the **subjective emotional present**.
4. *Verbalization.* Verbalizing **interoceptive** body sensations and emotions while remaining in the **subjective emotional present**.	Helping the person find words to describe their experience, encouraging communication about experience without losing contact with embodied self-awareness.
5. *Links* and *boundaries.* Clarifying locations and connections in the **body schema** within the self and between self and others.	Locating sources of sensation in the body, opening defensive or immobilized postures, finding and feeling "lost" body areas (feet and legs, pelvis, the back) coordination of movements, finding links and boundaries between self and others, feeling, moving.

continued

Table 1.1 (continued)

Principle	Definition
6. *Self-regulation.* Taking the initiative on one's own **restoration**.	Becoming one's own resource by being proactive in finding needed resources, asking for and arranging for guidance, healing, and soothing from things and people (warm baths, massages, soft clothing, etc.)
7. *Reengagement.* **Engagement** with active embodied self-awareness.	Ability to remain in the subjective emotional present of embodied self-awareness while experiencing the world with empowerment, triumph, and assertiveness. Using awareness to make choices about well-being such as to leave unwanted situations, to say "yes" and "no," to slow down, or to rest. Growing empathy for others and ability to be in touch with others while staying in one's own subjective emotional present.
8. *Letting go.* Allowing oneself to engage in forms of **restoration**, **engagement** and **normal absorption** in the **subjective emotional present**.	*Only after the previous steps have been achieved* can one "let go" without losing embodied self-awareness. Letting go includes being able to "step off the treadmill" of life to take care of yourself, the acceptance of your limits, a sense of compassion for others, and the ability to let yourself get lost in pleasurable creativity and self-discovery.

Sources: cf., Bakal (1999), Feldenkrais (1981), Levine (1997), Ogden, Minton, and Pain (2006), Rosen (2003), van der Hart, Nijenhuis, and Steele (2006).

For a relatively simple experiential introduction to the principles, try the exercise in Box 1.3. This exercise uses the *Awareness through Movement* method of Moshe Feldenkrais. It can be done while sitting or standing.

Box 1.3
A Pain in the Neck

Moshe Feldenkrais, developed a series of verbally guided classroom exercises, called **Awareness through Movement** lessons, that allow people to slow down and enter a state of embodied self-awareness of their **body schema** and **interoceptive** self-awareness. Many of these lessons play on the theme of how movement of one part of the body is linked to other parts (Feldenkrais, 1981). The goal is to find a less stressful, easier way to move.

As you do this lesson, you may notice changes in your chest and belly, neck and shoulders. You may also notice changes in how you feel emotionally, and your state of tension or relaxation. This lesson is about the stress created when we try to push our bodies beyond our limits.

1. Turn your head to look, look as far as you can, really strain to see. Notice the feeling you have when you reach that extreme limit. Is there any pain? Strain? Holding your breath?
2. Now turn a little less. Now turn still less. And less. Make the turn so small, it feels like floating through air or oil.
3. Now increase the turn slightly, and notice if you feel more resistance, like moving through peanut butter or honey. Maybe there is a wall there. Or maybe something clicks. Do you hold your breath?
4. Increase the turn a little more, and notice if your neck jumps like you are moving over the teeth of a gear, or if there is any sensation of strain or pain.
5. Now go back to that movement that feels like air or oil. This is your TRUE LIMIT. Is it in the same place as it was when you started? Anything that doesn't feel light and smooth is PAST YOUR LIMIT. Is your area of true ease bigger or smaller than you expected?
6. Turn several times staying ONLY within your limit. Keep relaxing any and all effort in yourself. Notice how that light, smooth area grows until you can easily turn your head as far as you wish, with no pain or strain.

(Levenson, 2001–2009)

Psychophysiology of Self-Awareness

If you take the time to do the lesson in Box 1.3 carefully and slowly—probably about 15 minutes—you will find that it may be full of surprise discoveries about yourself. This is because this simple lesson partakes of all of the treatment steps listed in Table 1.1.

- *Resources* are found in the lesson itself, the opportunity it presents for guided practice. A place and time to do the lesson while feeling comfortable and safe is also a resource.
- *Slowing down* is built into the lesson, moving less and paying attention more to the feelings engendered by your movements. We often want to go faster and do more, but slowing down means to deliberately get off this fast track.
- *Coregulation* occurs in the relationship between your awareness and the awareness of person who conceived this lesson. More typically, you would be in a live classroom where that person could continuously alter her responses to what she observed in the students. In some sense, this has already happened because the author of the lesson had learned how best to write it based on live classroom experiences.
- *Verbalization* is being done by the Feldenkrais practitioner in speaking or writing the steps of the lesson but you can link the words to your own experience. In other embodied self-awareness practices, you can have an opportunity to find words for your own experiences.
- *Links* and *boundaries* will be discovered if you are able to use the lesson to feel the relationship between your head movements and other parts of your body, or if you can really slow down and feel yourself move through those stiff or jumpy places. That's when you discover the linkages within yourself and begin to notice where there's pain, stiffness, or ease.
- *Self-regulation* occurs the moment that you decide to stop what you are doing and to invest your attention in this lesson. You can make a deliberate, self-inspired choice to take care of yourself. If you can remember to do this lesson while driving or at work to help ease tension in your neck and shoulders, this is also a way to self-regulate.
- *Reengagement* can happen during the lesson if you have a newfound sense of connection to your interoceptive feelings and body schema. It can also happen if after you finish doing the lesson, you feel more ready

and energized to get back to work without losing your embodied self-awareness.
- *Letting go* may not happen in this single exercise unless you have had lots of practice doing this kind of thing. *Letting go is not the way to start the journey to embodied self-awareness but rather the result of engaging in all the prior steps listed in Table 1.1.* Letting go is earned by practice and requires embodied self-awareness (Bakal, 1999). Examples are falling gratefully and without demands into the caring arms of a loved one when you are tired or sad, or forgiving someone for a past hurt without preconception and precondition. The need to acknowledge one's own feelings and to share them with others is evident in these examples. In this exercise, letting go might be losing touch with everything else around you as you go deeper inside yourself with curiosity and without self-criticism.

If you have ever experienced any of the embodied self-awareness disciplines mentioned in the preface and this chapter, you can use Table 1.1 to see how they measure up in terms of providing some or all of the possible ways to return to yourself, to learn to pay attention and stay present, and to grow in your ability to become more fully alive.

In my experience, one never reaches complete embodied self-awareness or complete letting go. There is always more to feel, more territory to explore within the self and between self and others, more opportunities to open, grow, and change. There are always forms of suppression of which we are not aware, always old baggage that we hold onto even when it is no longer needed. Every time we choose to slow down and come to our senses, and we have to make a deliberate choice to slow down, something new can be discovered. Each person will take a different pathway.

I, personally, love being touched and I find that when I feel out of touch, the interpersonal intimacy of sensitive and caring hands on my body leads me most fully back into states of reengagement and letting go. This may be because at the time I was a young child, in the late 1940s, the men like my father who returned from World War II military service felt that little boys should not be hugged or cuddled, comforted or soothed, even by their mothers. In a human species that thrives on touch, I experienced this as a deprivation. The touch I did receive was less-than-gentle scrubbing in the bath, or punitive and painful

Psychophysiology of Self-Awareness

whipping on the bottom with a belt. My family, however, was loving in the context of these beliefs about how best to cultivate masculinity and impose discipline. For a sensitive boy like me, these experiences were traumatic and I'm still uncovering their traces in my 63-year-old body.

For opening to embodied self-awareness, others find movement to be their preferred pathway, accessing the feelings of joy and the freedom of letting go that can occur when they are doing awareness-based movement practices. Still others seek the stillness of meditation and contemplative forms of yoga or martial arts like Tai Chi. Some find land-based practices to their liking and others become entranced with aquatic practices. Some need to verbalize their self-awareness process and others like silence.

I encourage you to try out some of these practices as an accompaniment to reading this book. If you are already a devotee of one practice, try another new one to see what it has to offer, or to see how it can embody the principles of Table 1.1. There will also be short exercises, like that found in Box 1.3, throughout the book. as well as case reports that may bring some practices more to life even if you cannot experience them personally.

If you "got" Table 1.1, then you already realize that you can't just read and think about the steps of the Feldenkrais lesson in Box 1.3, or in any of the exercises in boxes to come later, and gain new self-awareness. You have to make a choice to stop thinking, to move and feel, a choice to awaken your own embodied self. What resources do you need to support that choice?

2

Feelings from Within: The Emergence of Embodied Self-Awareness

> *There is an obvious and prominent fact about human beings: they have bodies and they are bodies.*
> (Turner, 1996, p. 37)

> *There is one body I know in a rather special way, namely my own... I shall call this "knowing from within."*
> (Harré, 1991, p. 14)

Suppose the human body is just a thing, a flesh and blood thing, but a thing nevertheless, an object, a machine. Like many machines, the body has its fuels and lubricants, its ways of relaying sensory information to and from the central processing unit, and the functions which it performs. Like all machines, it needs maintenance, cleaning, and maybe even some polishing up from time to time. This may be true of your body (from my point of view) but it is not true of mine. My body is a thing only up to a point, after which I start to take it personally. The pleasure and pain that emanate from my body are uniquely mine and no one else's and they establish not just a sense of ownership but a sense of being. I am a person by virtue of the fact that I am located in my body and nowhere else, and that body has a historical and physical location from which I can identify myself within the world. To paraphrase Descartes: "I *feel*, therefore I am."

Embodied and Conceptual Self-Awareness

I could list the facts about my life, such as where I was born and when, the names of my parents, where I lived, my work history, but that is nothing more than a resumé. What I itemize about myself is what I *think* about myself, all in the realm of concepts that obey the rules of grammar, reason, and logic. Let's call this way of understanding and describing myself **conceptual self-awareness**.

Psychophysiology of Self-Awareness

In my world of conceptual self-awareness, I know myself to be at this moment sitting at my desk and facing the computer monitor, observing on that screen what my fingers are typing. It is about 2 o'clock in the afternoon, a Monday in April 2008. I've got books and research articles about the topic of self-awareness arrayed on my desk in neat piles and I'm thinking about how to use these materials in this writing project. I could also be thinking, which I am not at the moment, that I am a scientist, a writer, a grandfather, and an awareness-based bodywork practitioner, and these thoughts would also be counted as part of my conceptual self-awareness. If you happened to be observing me, you could say more or less the same things but you might also notice and think about other "facts" about me that occur to you.

What I *feel*, my **embodied self-awareness**, is fundamentally different. Let me take a second, right now, to shift into an embodied mode of awareness and try to describe my experience in words. OK. Because I am just beginning to write this chapter, I'm feeling rather uncertain about exactly what to say and how the chapter will unfold. I actually like that feeling because I recognize it as creativity, which comes with a kind of edginess, not exactly discomfort but not entirely comfort either. I don't like to map out a whole chapter because it feels too confining (almost disgusting). The closest I can come to this is to organize those readings into rather shabby piles according to my very vague and fuzzy sense about the topics in which they seem to fit as I go through them. I'm not thrilled about this first sort and I have a perverse sense of mischief when I, inevitably, rearrange the piles as the chapter unfolds. This chapter still has not gotten to the point at which it "takes over" and lets me ride playfully on its established momentum but my current uncertainty is less uncomfortable because I trust this moment will come, eventually, although I can't say when.

What makes my experience interesting, to me and to anybody else, is the fact that I live it, I feel it personally, and I take from it those aspects that most touch and move me. I can *define* myself conceptually but I come to *inhabit* myself via the concrete feeling and acting of embodied self-awareness. In order to attend to anything, there must be a movement and therefore an activation of muscles. These may be very tiny movements like the stapes muscle that moves the stirrup in the middle ear to amplify or damp the vibrations that the ear drum creates. It may be the pupillary sphincter muscles that open and close the iris, or the orbital muscles that move the eyeball. They could also be large movements involving many muscles like turning the head or body toward a

Embodied Self-Awareness

sound or sight. We look at or listen to or touch that which arouses some emotional feeling like interest, or delight, or fear. All emotions reflect our immediate concerns, that which is most self-relevant (Frijda, 1986).

Table 2.1 summarizes the distinctions that can be made between embodied self-awareness and conceptual self-awareness. Conceptual self-awareness is primarily expressed and understood with respect to categories that apply to the self, categories that are encoded in language. Language is what runs through our heads when we take the time to notice that we are in fact thinking. Language itself is conceptual: A word has a specific definition; a sentence either is or is not grammatical.

Table 2.1
Comparison between conceptual and embodied forms of self-awareness

Conceptual self-awareness	Embodied self-awareness
Based in linguistic and symbolic forms of expression	Based in sensing, feeling, and acting
Rational, logical, explanatory	Spontaneous, creative, open to change
Abstract, transcends the present moment	Concrete, lived in the present moment

Sources: Abram (1996), Gendlin (1962), James (1912/1976), Varela, Thompson, and Rosch (1991).

Embodied self-awareness exists prior to language and does not require language for its expression (Gendlin, 1962). Language is neither necessary nor sufficient to describe embodied self-awareness. Language is not necessary because I can feel and move in a way that activates my embodied self-awareness without ever bothering to describe my experience in words. Language is also not necessary as a means of communicating my embodied self-awareness to others. Body movements, facial expressions, and gestures are often sufficient, and many of the performing arts play on this fact.

One could say, as the philosopher John Dewey did, that all art (verbal, visual, auditory, gustatory) is the transformation of the artist's embodied self-awareness into a sensory form that leads back to another embodied experience, that of the person appreciating the work of art (Dewey, 1934). But that transformation is never perfect, hence the inherent ambiguity and generativity of art. If I choose to explain in words what I feel, even artistic language is not sufficient to do that job because words, indeed any symbol or gesture, are not the same as the felt experience.

Language, on the other hand, can evoke, sustain, and amplify embodied self-awareness even though it cannot fully describe the experience. This occurs when words are chosen to be expressive about felt experience; this is called **evocative language**. When words describe a category, explanation, or judgment, we remain in the world of conceptual self-awareness.

> If you have trouble getting to work, for example, it is futile to ask yourself, "Am I just lazy?" "Do I have a wish to fail?" . . . Such questions, spoken as it were in mid-air, are ineffective . . . . *Only* by referring directly to his experiencing can the individual even find (and later interpret) in himself that which . . . makes it difficult for him to get to work. Directly, in his experiencing, he can refer to that "draggy feeling" with which he "wrestles" when he tries to work. As he attends directly to it, he may find (differentiate) an apprehension of failure, a conviction that he will fail. . . . It is this "heavy sureness" (so it seems at this moment, now) that he has to "drag" to work, and that makes it so hard. (Gendlin, 1962, p. 35–36)

When referring to the "draggy feeling," words are used to evoke a concrete internal experience, felt directly and in the moment. When used this way, words will "resonate" in the felt experience of that person: they will sound "true" or "deep" or "powerful." Words spoken by other people that similarly address our embodied state can also resonate. Here also lies the power of literature, poetry, and song to "speak to" us, not in the words as concepts that refer to a general state of affairs but rather in the words as vehicles that move us to experience and amplify a feeling.

Asking, "Am I just lazy?" is making a judgment by claiming ownership of a category, laziness, presumed to typify the self. Categories are like traits. If

I'm lazy, there is not much I can do about it. Not only that, I can start to doubt or blame myself. In the process, I've completely lost my embodied self-awareness. I might look to others for a confirmation or a denial of my laziness, I might work more to prove myself or I might throw in the towel and just accept my lazy, good-for-nothing bag of flesh and bones. The category starts to become who I am, at the expense of never finding what might be underneath it, the feelings and sensations in my body that might have (erroneously) created the impression in my conceptual mind that I am in fact lazy.

Virtually all methods used to enhance embodied self-awareness use symbols, gestures, and **evocative language** as tools to reach people's embodied self-awareness. Meditation, Tai Chi, Yoga, music, and dance, for example, are taught with language accompanied by movement and gesture. Psychotherapy is based on talk. Awareness-based therapies like the Feldenkrais Method and Rosen Method Bodywork rely on touch, guided movements, or resonant language to enhance self-awareness.

In a yoga class, there are guided movements and meditations, often with soft lighting and music. In somatic psychotherapy, in which clients are guided to a deeper awareness of their embodied experiences, attention to feeling states may eventually lead back to conceptual self-understanding (It is difficult to get to work because I feel as if I have to drag myself there because I [now can] feel the heaviness of an imagined failure). Further exploration of that felt experience may lead to relating the expectation of failure to feelings of loss and sadness at not meeting the expectations of a demanding parent or some other early life experience that the conceptual self "forgot" but the embodied self "remembered" and transformed into a habitual way of feeling and acting.

People who get lost in judgment and expectation can get worn out with the task of trying to figure out how to behave, how to please, how to be better. It is exhausting because the part of us that trades in concepts has to exert neuromuscular control to suppress the part of us that can open to embodied self-awareness. Opening to the embodied self can bring not only enlightenment but profound relief. Because this opening typically occurs when someone or something resonates with our inner self, our sense of relief is accompanied by an opening of the heart toward that which succeeded in "reaching" us and "touching" us (see Case Report 2.1).

CASE REPORT 2.1
Opening Up to Embodied Self-Awareness

Here I report the first of several cases from my clinical practice of **Rosen Method Bodywork** (Berger, 1997; Rosen, 2003; Wooten, 1994). In order to protect client confidentiality, this case, and all the other cases I report from my practice, is a composite across several similar individuals. Names and other personal details are fictitious. In all other respects, I report my observations of actual case material. Rosen Method Bodywork uses touch and talk to promote a client's emerging embodied self-awareness.

The Rosen Method looks like massage because clients lie unclothed under sheets on a padded table, but the similarity ends there. "**Therapeutic massage** involves the manipulation of the soft tissue structures of the body to prevent and alleviate pain, discomfort, muscle spasm, and stress; and, to promote health and wellness" (http:// www.holisticonline.com/massage/mas_def.htm). Therapeutic massage does not, by itself, focus on self-awareness, although practitioners may promote embodied self-awareness by complementing massage with mindfulness meditation and asking clients to pay attention to how stress and pain may be caused during everyday activities (Plews-Ogan, Owens, Grodman, Wolfe & Schorling, 2005).

Rosen Method Bodywork uses a "listening" form of touch, not meant to manipulate tissues or to alleviate pain directly, but rather designed to allow the client to feel that part of the body being touched and to relate that feeling to other body feelings and emotions. Rosen Method assumes that by paying attention nonjudgmentally—with soft hands and soft eyes— and by helping the client become more aware of herself, her own healing resources can be reactivated. With growing embodied self-awareness facilitated by Rosen touch and a practitioner who is in the subjective emotional present, muscles begin to relax, at which time there may be spontaneous emotions and memories that arise, leading to a expanded self-awareness of how those holding patterns developed.

Getting lost in conceptual judgment and self-evaluation is such a common experience in our culture that even clients who have had many sessions with me, and who have learned to notice their embodied feelings, may begin their session with a description of their conceptual self-awareness about events that occurred since the last time I saw them. What does improve over time, however, is how quickly in the session the client shifts from conceptual to embodied self-awareness. There is also an expansion over time of embodied self-awareness into new domains of experience.

Doug was a successful businessman who had come to see me because of pains in his shoulders and neck. Often, people carry muscle tension and consequent pain in this area because of a perceived need to "shoulder" responsibilities. Although I do not impose this interpretation on clients, I am listening for it, and Doug was a classic example. Since his childhood, his father expected compliance and independence without providing the emotional rewards to honor Doug's achievements. Through his Rosen treatments, Doug came to identify his shoulder pain with the embodied self-awareness of the feeling that he could never be good enough. He felt he always had to prove himself, reflected in the posture of tense readiness in his neck and shoulders with which he approached all of his work and family responsibilities.

In one session, after about 6 months of weekly treatments, Doug began by talking about a business partner, Jack, who was always taking and never giving back (in Doug's view). Doug's need to please had led him, on the other hand, to indiscriminately give himself away—his money, his time, his possessions. Since clients usually start the session lying face down, as Doug talked about Jack, I could feel that his upper back and shoulders were extremely tense. I had the sense that Doug knew conceptually where he was (on my treatment table, reporting for Rosen duty, being a good client, wanting to tell me about his troubles with Jack) but that he could not feel my hands at all. I might as well have been touching a wall for the lack of response I was feeling.

After a while, I moved my hands to the sides of his abdomen where the muscles were softer, aiming to find a more responsive part of his body, and a way to contact Doug in the subjective emotional present.

"Can you feel my hands here?" I said, after a few minutes of gently holding his sides.

"Yes."

OK, I thought, here's an opening to embodied self-awareness. "What do they feel like?"

There was a long pause, the first pause in his lengthy monologue about Jack.

"Warm." Another pause. "OK, I can feel you now, thanks for bringing me back," he said, relaxing a bit and taking a deep breath.

This was a recognition not only of his accepting the opportunity, right in this moment, to be in the subjective emotional present, it also acknowledged that as being the reason why he continued to come back to see me: an embodied rather than a conceptual reason for being there. Doug's breathing continued to become easier and I could see that his shoulders were starting to relax, but I kept my hands gently on the sides of his abdomen because this was clearly working to reach him. His shoulders would continue to relax as his awareness grew, as he settled into himself, and as his breath got deeper. This would happen even if I did not touch his shoulders.

"You got really caught up in that encounter with Jack," I said, pointing out what I had observed in his behavior.

"Yeah, wow, it takes me over. I can't help it. I get so. . . ."

"What?"

Another long pause. "I don't know. I don't know," he said and I could hear the desperation in his voice as his shoulders began to tense up again and his breath became shorter.

About half the session had passed, so I asked him to turn over on his back. I wanted to put my hands on the front of his abdomen, where I sensed some movement but also unrest. Once he got resettled and I had my hands on his belly, I said, "You don't know . . . is that what's still going on?"

Apparently, in turning over, he was able to find more clarity. "I'm frustrated with myself. I hate getting caught up in the same old pattern of giving in to people, getting taken advantage of, getting tense. I'm sick of it." He said, "same old," with disgust and also a bit of anger, which I could feel in my own face and gut.

Hoping for him to further explore his embodied feelings, and not wanting to put words in his mouth, I suggested, "It feels to me like there's more than frustration here."

He was silent, as his face began to tense up with a scowl and I could feel his belly tightening. I thought that this is what he does, tense up his belly to suppress his anger at being used by others, or maybe anger at his "same old" pattern of giving more of himself away than he really wanted to. But in this state of tension, Doug was losing touch with his embodied self-awareness. He could not have felt any of the words I was thinking about saying. I needed to bring him back to the present moment.

"Doug," I said softly, "can you still feel my hands on your belly?" Silence, but his belly began to soften a bit, the muscles trying to "find" my hand. "What's going on here, Doug, in your belly?"

"I'm angry," he said very quietly, almost to himself, but his face and mouth were tight, like it was hard for him to say that.

"I could hardly hear that." I wasn't asking him to speak louder so I could hear him. I was asking him to hear himself, to encourage more self-awareness.

"I'm angry," this time louder and more forcefully.

"Stay with it Doug, feel my hand." I was thinking, yes, now he's getting closer to the feeling, but I also knew that reminding him to feel my hands could keep him in the subjective emotional present.

He started breathing heavily, his arms and legs thrashing, his face red with fury, growling loudly, shaking. I got scared—Doug was much bigger and stronger than me and I was right next to his body—but I used the awareness of my own fear to link to what I thought might be his fear. I needed to stay still and keep my hands softly contacting his belly.

He began to settle a bit, and I also calmed down realizing that Doug had suppressed his anger because he didn't want to hurt anyone. I said, "You never had a chance to feel angry, did you?"

He began to cry with a sense of deep recognition of the effort it had taken to hold back his anger all these years. "I had no idea I was so angry," he said through his tears.

This was followed by a renewed tension and build-up of the anger that recurred several times in the remainder of the session, as if he were discovering how good it felt to be angry, to let it come, to not suffer retaliation, and to not hurt anyone else (including me!). The theme of suppressed anger was a turning point in his treatment, coming and going over the next several months, with increased conceptual and embodied self-awareness about its origins: having to be compliant with a feared father and the resulting anger at having to give himself away without recognition by his father.

Doug learned to feel his anger and welcome it into his embodied self-awareness. He never stopped being gentle and caring with others but he learned to use his felt experience to warn him when people were stepping over the line in abusing his largesse. He learned to say no when necessary and to establish his boundaries with others.

Psychophysiology of Self-Awareness

Notice how this case follows the basic steps of regaining embodied self-awareness listed in Table 1.1.

- *Resources* were found in the felt experience of my soft hand and voice during the session, and in Doug's memory of the benefits of our ongoing work together.
- *Slowing down* to enter the subjective emotional present was encouraged by my finding ways to contact Doug so that he could feel my hands, pause, and breathe.
- *Coregulation* occurred in the dialogue of touch and talk that sustained our contact during the session. Embodied self-awareness treatments access the relatively chaotic subjective emotional present in which the feelings and emotions may arise spontaneously and in unpredictable ways. This means that the therapist must be open to changes of course, following the client, adapting to his or her own embodied self-awareness, in order to find a way to maintain and enhance the interpersonal connection with the client.
- *Verbalization* occurred throughout. I avoided putting a label on the anger until after Doug had named it, even though I sensed it was there. I felt that Doug needed to come to this himself, if not in this session then perhaps in another.
- *Links and boundaries* came up as Doug began to sense how the anger was his, had come from his childhood, how it got triggered in current life situations, and how he could use it to choose to set boundaries in relation to others.
- *Self-regulation* began as Doug learned to feel and manage his anger, using it as an internal signal to avoid partnerships in which he felt used.
- *Reengagement* happened gradually over time, as Doug entered relationships more freely and with more enjoyment, knowing that he could regulate the process.
- *Letting go* takes a long time. When Doug decided to end his Rosen treatments with me, I felt that he was moving in this direction but he still felt somewhat guarded in his approach to others, perhaps a result of unacknowledged fear that he might get caught again in someone else's web.

Interoception is the technical term for the ability to feel one's own body states and emotions. Doug's ability to feel the sensation of my hand (or not) and to feel his anger (or not) are part of interoception. Anger, in particular, presents challenges to embodied self-awareness practitioners. Many angry people are not aware of their own anger. Somatic psychotherapeutic approaches to enhance anger awareness have included having people record and listen to their own speech and expressions using videos, mirrors, and role play. These approaches must also be coupled with helping the person "own" their anger as an acceptable emotion and learning that they can feel it without having to act on it (Lambie & Marcel, 2002).

The terms *feeling* and *emotion* are similar yet different. A **feeling** is any sensation that is experienced as coming from our own bodies. Feelings can be tingly, warm, soft, calm, jumpy, "butterflies," and so on. **Emotion** is the embodied evaluation of those feelings, reflecting how good or bad something feels to us (called its *hedonic value*) accompanied by a motivation or urge to act in a particular manner in relation to that sensation, thing, or being that seems to be causing the emotion. In Doug's case, the anger felt tight, constraining, limiting. In someone else, anger might feel liberating. It was also, for Doug, accompanied by the sense that it was a "bad" feeling, not permitted, which led to the motivation to repress it.

Typically, feelings and emotions go together. The felt sense of being hot or cold, for example, is not a simple absolute measure of temperature as might be judged by a thermometer. Hot or cold sensations are usually coupled with an emotional meaning in our awareness. "Thus, the cool glass of water that feels wonderful if you are overheated feels gnawingly unpleasant if you are chilled. Conversely, if you are chilled, then a hot shower feels wonderful, even if it is stinging and prickly, but would be called painful if you were too warm" (Craig, 2008, p. 274). We don't just have the "pure" interoceptive feeling of stinging and prickly in the shower, we *relate* to the sensation by embracing it or cringing from it. Even if there is not an overt action, emotion is always accompanied by an urge to act, or an action tendency (Frijda, 1986).

Emotions are also coupled with feelings. We can feel our heart racing when we are afraid, our cheeks getting hot when we are ashamed, or our arms and legs thrashing when we are angry. It is not a contradiction to talk about "feeling our emotions." An emotion requires sensing the body feelings as well as whether those feelings are liked or disliked, and what those feelings make one want to do. If I feel my cheeks getting warm I don't know I'm ashamed unless I also notice that I am uncomfortable with a social situation and that I feel exposed (hedonically negative). At that point, I might close down, hide, cover my face, or cry. Or I might smile and laugh at myself. This is all part of the interoceptive awareness of the emotion of shame.

Interoception is so fundamental to what most people experience living in their bodies that it is easy to take it for granted. As we walk, for instance, we hardly notice that we have to monitor our muscle contractions in relation to the surface on which we are walking and the reason why we are walking. Being late to catch a train in a busy station demands a different kind of walk than a leisurely stroll in a park on a warm sunny day. Walking on a paved surface is different from walking on a steep and rocky hiking trail. While most of this monitoring of movement takes few of our attentional resources, we can, at any moment, deliberately focus our attention on these movements in order to take special care not to trip or fall, not to bump into someone, not to get too tired, or even to enjoy the feeling of exertion and accomplishment.

The more honest interoception behind the student's excuse that, "The dog ate my homework," could be "I had my period and was feeling miserable," or "I am an emotional wreck because my parents never stop arguing," or "My girlfriend came over and. . . ." If we go too long without actually feeling our emotions, or without sharing our true experiences with another person who we can trust, as in the case of Doug, we may "forget" that we have emotions. Those excuses, part of our conceptual self-awareness, come to dominate our self-focused attention, eventually suppressing or eliminating embodied self-awareness.

Another example of embracing or avoiding interoceptive self-awareness is grief over the death or loss of a person close to us. Working through a loss successfully is a lengthy process that can take weeks, months, or even years. Research shows that the effective resolution of the loss progresses through a series of emotional stages: Denial (This can't happen; It's not right), anger (Why did you die and leave me? Where is God now?), depression-sadness (I can't go on alone; She deserved to live longer), acceptance (It's all for the best; Time to let go) (Kübler-Ross, 2005). Reaching the final level of acceptance is essential for the survivor's psychological well-being and to arrive there requires mourners to go through the steps of regaining embodied self-awareness listed in Table 1.1.

The example of getting in touch with one's emotions throughout the grieving process shows the importance of interoceptive embodied self-awareness for personal well-being. Recent neurophysiological research helps us to explain how this happens. The neural pathways that allow us to sense the internal condition of our bodies—sensations and emotions—are intimately linked to neural pathways for the regulation of the body processes that maintain mental and physical health. Interoception is a way of monitoring ourselves so that we can ease the felt pain, expand the felt joy, and make sure that we get the resources needed in any given moment.

Neurophysiology of Interoception and Self-Regulation

In everyday life and in the embodied self-awareness treatments and interventions discussed in this book, it is often the case that attending to one part of the body leads to an awareness of "referred" sensation or pain in some other part of the body, or that relaxation of a tight muscle is accompanied by the awareness of a long-forgotten memory or a strong emotion, or that massage therapy can make one feel more alive, happy, and connected. These apparently paradoxical effects can all be understood with respect to the systemic nature of the body and how we become aware of our bodies. Clinically, we shall see that there are multiple entry routes to embodied self-awareness—through movement, or touch, or music, or talk—and that almost any connection to an embodied experience can lead, creatively and spontaneously, to opening, transformation, and self-repair in multiple domains of physical and mental health.

The Body Is a Complex System

These phenomena occur because the body is a complex **dynamic system**. A dynamic systems perspective on the body acknowledges that there is a coregulating and interdependent linkage between neural, hormonal, circulatory, digestive, and immune pathways (Dehaene & Naccache, 2001; Thompson & Varela, 2001; Tucker, 2001). Instead of thinking of the body as a *structure* of cells and organs, it makes more sense to think of it as a *process*. Cells are always alive and changing, fluids and electrical impulses are always moving within and between cells, and the body as a whole is never completely at rest with its breathing, heartbeat, and other organic movements: we are complexity and flow.

I introduce this dynamic systems conception of the body before introducing the neurophysiological research because a good deal of that research is not systemic. Neuroscientists are able to localize a particular brain area that becomes active during a behavioral task given to research subjects. This encourages neuroscientists to think in terms of **modularity**, the assumption that those particular areas of the brain that are activated are "responsible" for causing and therefore explaining the particular behaviors to which they have been associated in the experiment.

The modularity view is antisystemic for two reasons. First, it suggests that one particular brain area is more important than another brain area. Second, it suggests that the brain is the origin, source, and controller of the body, neither of which is ever true. One brain area *always* works together with others. The brain *always* works together with the rest of the body, both sending signals (**efferent** pathways) to and receiving signals (**afferent** pathways) from the rest of the body.

In the brain, as elsewhere in the body, it takes a whole community of coactivating regions and cells to create a working body function. One could say that respiration is "located" in the lungs but that is not even close to being the case. Respiration involves muscles in the chest and diaphragm, the autonomic and skeletal nervous systems, the blood, the heart, and the brain. Take any one of these out of the loop, and you no longer have respiration that will sustain life.

It is conceptually much easier to use modularity. We can talk about one or two brain areas as if they explained everything and leave it at that. A lot of applied neuroscience in clinical domains does this, in part because the scientists are thinking in terms of modularity, and in part because it is easier for practitioners to say something to their clients like, "Your body is tense because your hypothalamus is overactive."

As a clinician, I can see the appeal of this simplicity. As a scientist, however, I can see how it quickly leads to misconceptions and eventually to clinical assumptions that obscure rather than illuminate practice. Clinicians and educators who work with embodied self-awareness often talk about "mind" and "body." This is an oversimplification that leads to misconceptions: the "mind" is in the head and the "body" is below the neck. The problem is that *the mind is part of the body and the body has a mind of its own* in its peripheral nerve cells and receptors and in its bath of circulating fluids rich in neurotransmitters and neurohormones.

What people generally mean when they say "mind" is what I call **conceptual self-awareness**, while "body" is for me **embodied self-awareness**. To avoid misconceptions, it is important to realize that *both of these forms of self-awareness depend on connections between the brain and the rest of the body, and as we shall see, utilize very similar neural processes.* Both of these are forms of *awareness* and thus are equally "mental" but also equally "embodied."

So, as fair warning to readers, I will be looking at the body as a dynamic system. I will suggest that there are different and distinguishable **networks** of related areas in the brain and elsewhere in the body, networks that create different kind of self-awareness and that also explain dysfunctional self-awareness. This means that I will be roaming around the body linking up its various related parts and using technical language for those parts. There are forests to be seen, the networks, but we will be walking in the dense undergrowth of the linking vines and branches of those networks from time to time. Stop and take a breath if you need to, or skip to the end for the big-picture network story.

A Note on Neuroscience Research Methods

The past 10 years has seen a rapid increase in neurophysiological research because of the availability of newly powerful methods for brain imaging. In the past, brain research was done primarily on animals. The scientist gave one group of animals a particular experience like learning a maze, and then after "sacrificing" the animals, compared the anatomy and chemistry of particular regions of their dissected brains with those who did not get exposed to the maze. Online learning studies have been conducted in animals by surgically implanting electrodes into particular brain regions during learning trials.

These techniques are not applicable to studies with humans. Until recently, human brain research could only be done by using sensors on the scalp that recorded the electrical activity on the surface of the brain. The electrical activity, however, needed to be averaged over time, and it is impossible with this method to localize the activity to a particular site in the brain. The other method of brain research in humans involved patients with brain damage known to be localized to a particular region—such as from a head injury or stroke—who could be studied for how their behavior deviated from normal. The limitation with this approach is that brain lesions are often not strictly localized and the injury or stroke may have other side effects.

The recent development of functional neuroimaging, widely used today, monitors brain temperature and blood flow. The resolution is rather precise so that particular groups of cells can be localized if activated anywhere within the brain and 3-D maps can be made of the entire brain. The advantage of these methods—positron emission tomography (PET) or functional magnetic resonance imaging (fMRI)—is that a person can be engaging in a social or cognitive task while the brain is being monitored. The disadvantage is that the person needs to lie perfectly still in a body-shaped (claustrophobic) tube immersed in the relatively loud sound of the machine at work. It also takes a bit of time for blood flows to change in the brain so these methods are not precise at measuring the time course of activation.

The localization potential of neuroimaging can easily lead to modular thinking. To take a single example, consider the dorsomedial prefrontal cortex (DMPFC). The DMPFC is important in conceptual self-awareness. It becomes activated when people think about, judge, and evaluate themselves. The modularity view would take this as evidence that conceptual self-awareness is "in" the DMPFC. Why is this modularity conclusion a problem?

In research studies of the DMPFC, people are asked to make judgments about how closely a particular sentence (I'm easygoing most of the time) or words (*happy, outgoing, depressed*) fits their self-image. Neuroimaging during these self-reflection tasks shows that not only the DMPFC is activated, but other nearby and distant brain regions—to be named later—are also activated. So, how can a researcher make a claim for the modularity of conceptual self-awareness in the DMPFC? Because when people are asked to feel their embodied experience, those other areas of the brain are also activated but the DMPFC activity is suppressed. It seems reasonable to scientists working from this perspective to conclude that the DMPFC is maybe not the only brain region involved in conceptual self-awareness, but it must be the crucial one.

Modularity is a kind of shorthand for saying that a region like the DMPFC is the most important region for some functions, in this case, conceptual self-awareness. Modularity makes it easy to talk about "where" conceptual self-awareness is "located." The problem, however, is if there is damage to one or

Embodied Self-Awareness

more of those other areas of the brain that are coactivated with the DMPFC, it can also impair conceptual self-awareness or eliminate it entirely. The DMPFC is important, but only as part of a larger cross-body network that supports self-awareness.

Where Self-Awareness Begins: Receptors, Spinal Cord, and Brain Stem

Just to emphasize the point about dynamic systems and neural networks, we'll start our journey through the body at its periphery rather than in the brain. Interoception begins with receptors, in different body tissues, for sensing internal state—**ergoreceptors**. These receptors are designed to convert different forms of chemical and physical stimulation into neural signals for transmission to the spinal cord and brain. Muscles have receptors for stretching (mechanoreceptors) and for fatigue (chemoreceptors). The circulatory system has receptors for pressure (baroreceptors) and blood nutrients (metaboreceptors). The skin has receptors for movement at the base of the hair follicle (mechanoreceptors), for pressure on the skin (mechanoreceptors), for vibration (vibroreceptors), for heat and cold (thermoreceptors), and for pain (nociceptors) (see Figure 2.1 and Table 2.2).

Figure 2.1
The skin has many different types of receptors

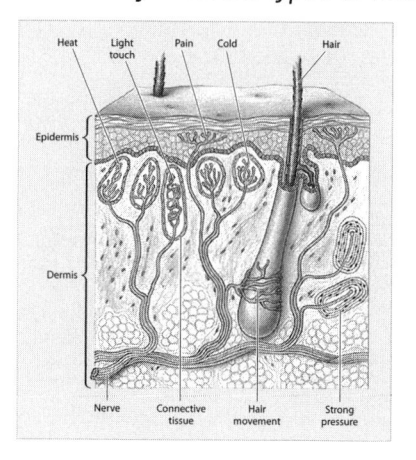

Psychophysiology of Self-Awareness

All neural information that flows from the body toward the brain is referred to as **afferent** information, the body **aff**ecting the brain. Interoception is one form of afferent information in which the signals specify sensation within the body. **Exteroception** is another form of afferent information in which the signals specify sensation that impinges on the body but where it becomes important for the individual to identify the source of that information as external to the body. Exteroception includes receptors for sound, light, taste, and smell. Interoception and exteroception rely on different sets of receptors and different neural pathways to and through the brain (Craig, 2002; Critchley, Wiens, Rotshtein, Ohman, & Dolan, 2004; Damasio et al., 2000).

Table 2.2
Felt senses in embodied self-awareness

Interoception: Sensations interpreted as coming from one's own body (originating in specific ergoreceptors that assess the condition of the skin, muscles, joints, teeth, bones, fluid electrolytes and water, and viscera).	**Exteroception**: Sensations interpreted as coming from outside of one's body, i.e., characteristics of living and nonliving things in the world (The five sense organs)
Heat/cold	Touch: Vibration, pressure, texture
Itch/tickle/pinch	Vision: Color, movement speed and direction of objects, size and shape recognition
Sensual/other touch	Smell
State of contraction/tension/ache/burn in striated muscles of face, neck, trunk, and limbs	Taste
Thirst/hunger	Audition: Quality of sound, movement and location, pitch
Dull/sharp pain	
Cramping	
Air hunger, difficulty/ease breathing	
Visceral urgency, gut & bladder	
Tension/relaxation	
Cell rupture	
Allergens and noxious chemicals	
Immune system invasion	Sources: Craig (2002, 2008).

Embodied Self-Awareness

Receptors convert the chemical or mechanical or temperature information into electrical and neurochemical impulses in the nerve cells to which they are connected. Nerve cells have long fibers that extend outward from their compact cell bodies. These fibers connect, via synapses (junctions between nerve cells), to the fibers from other nerve cells. In some cases, the fibers from a single nerve cell can be very long, extending from the receptor at the periphery of the body all the way to the spinal cord. The afferent nerve cell fibers that originate in the ergoreceptors (called $A\delta$ and C fibers) are small and unmyelinated. Myelin is a protective coating around nerve cell fibers that speeds transmission. Unmyelinated fibers, therefore, conduct more slowly which partly explains why it often takes several minutes or even longer to feel particular embodied sensations and sense their source within the body.

It also helps to explain why, in educational and therapeutic interventions for embodied self-awareness, multiple sessions with intervening practice and rehearsal is needed in order to clarify and expand our embodied self-awareness. *Expanding embodied self-awareness is slow and deliberate in comparison to the rapid and instantaneous generation of ideas and thoughts in conceptual self-awareness.* The faculty of conceptual reasoning, because it is so powerful and rapid in humans, can hinder the growth of embodied self-awareness. Embodied self-awareness requires our conceptual mind to slow down and take a rest from its continual stream of evaluations and "to-dos." This is step no. 2 of the guidelines for enhancing embodied self-awareness, Table 1.1. We need to learn to trust the physiology of interoception in spite, or maybe even because of, its slowness (see Box 2.1).

BOX 2.1
Slowing Down

Take a moment when you can be quiet and alone. Sit, stand, or lie down in a comfortable place. Check in with what you are aware of in this moment. It might be "out there," like light coming in a window, or rain drops tinkling, or a barking dog. Or, it might be your conceptual mind running through a string of thoughts, plans, or worries. It does not

continued

Psychophysiology of Self-Awareness

> **BOX 2.1** (continued)
>
> really matter. You can start from either of these places and attempt to enter into the **subjective emotional present** of interoceptive self-awareness.
>
> Suppose you focus on what is "out there," outside of your body, like the light coming in the window. Gradually begin to notice how the light affects you. This could be in the form of a passing emotion, like happiness or sadness, or a little memory that flashes and disappears. It could also be a feeling of warmth, or a desire to move toward it, or to stretch out and take a nap. Notice how these feelings and sensations come and go, appear and disappear.
>
> If the light doesn't bring you into your embodied self awareness—if you keep thinking about things—you have a couple of choices. Focus on something else out there that may serve you better as a route into your felt body sense. Move to a different location where you can find something you know, from experience, will calm your mind a bit and "bring you back." Just move, walk, dance, wiggle, or do something that makes you feel your body. Or, work with the thoughts.
>
> If the latter, try to latch onto a single thought by slowing down the flood of ideas. Suppose the thought you choose to explore is: "I forgot to stop at the grocery store." Repeat that thought to yourself several times but now observe your sensations and emotions. Because the body is a complex system, all thought is tied to an interoceptive body state, and we can choose, at any moment, to "sink in" and pay attention to this link. Maybe you picture the pasta or the pudding or the pickles that you forgot. Another moment of lingering on these images might lead you to feeling hungry for that food, or nostalgic. You've reached pay dirt. Dig into those feelings of hunger or nostalgia and see where they take you.
>
> Maybe, instead, you picture a family member who has asked you to buy that food. Stay with this image a moment. Where does it lead? It could lead to more thoughts: "She'll be disappointed in me if I don't
>
> *continued*

Embodied Self-Awareness

> **BOX 2.1** (continued)
>
> stop at the store," or "I keep failing her," and so on. Fine. That's your conceptual self-awareness making self-evaluative judgments. You are actually getting closer. Start from there and slow down to see if any sensations and emotions come up: sadness, anger, guilt, love?
>
> This is the process: Slowing thought, waiting, being patient, letting those embodied sensations and emotions emerge spontaneously and in their "I'll-take-my-own-time-thank-you" way. You'll find that you can't command yourself to feel something but you can ask yourself to wait, pay attention, and keep coming back.
>
> What if none of this works for you? You keep returning to what is "out there" or to those thoughts. You're already more aware of yourself for noticing that, right now, this is all you can do. That in itself is a small victory in expanding your self-awareness. Try again another time or place. It may take a while to find the right moment. Or find someone who can help guide you. Don't expect to stay in the subjective emotional present for very long in any case. What happens there is not under your control but each time you can "find yourself," it makes it just a little easier to return on subsequent occasions.

All of the interoceptive neural pathways are these small, slow Aδ and C fibers. All these interoceptive fibers go to the same place in the spinal cord, from whence they project to a common location in the brain stem, and from there to a common set of brain regions. Exteroceptive fibers are larger and faster (apparently, we need to have a faster response to the external environment) and they project to a different set of spinal and brain pathways than the interoceptive fibers. *This means that there is an anatomical basis to our ability to differentiate between interoception (the sensations coming from inside the body) and exteroception (the sensations coming from outside the body)*, and that difference begins all the way out at the receptors (Craig, 2008).

Following the afferent (toward the brain) pathway from the ergoreceptors and the Aδ and C fibers, they all connect in the most superficial layer of the grey matter at the back of the spinal cord (in lamina 1 of the dorsal horn of

Psychophysiology of Self-Awareness

the spinal cord; see Figure 2.2). Staying together as a package of interoceptive neural information—yet sorted into the different types of sensations that the receptors detect—the impulses from this region of the spinal cord move together toward localized regions of the brain stem.

Figure 2.2

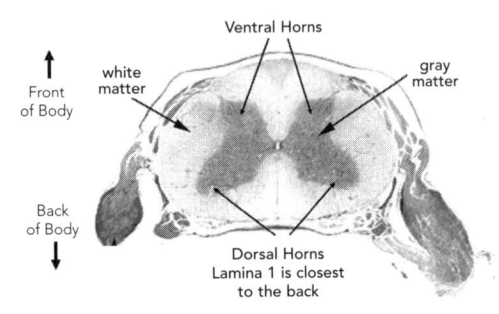

White and grey matter in a cross-section of the spinal cord. The grey matter has two dorsal "horns" (facing the back of the body), and two ventral horns (facing the front of the body). Interoceptive pathways travel in lamina 1 of the dorsal horns.

These regions of the brain stem are specifically responsible for what is called **homeostasis** (*homeo*=equal, *stasis*=to stand or stay), a term that refers to the regulation of all the functional systems of the body. From these same brain stem centers, there are **efferent** (back to the body) pathways that alter body systems to assist in this regulatory process, including such entities as heart rate, blood flow, respiration, digestion, and movement,. If, for example, I have an itch on my left forearm, it is sensed by the ergoreceptors, sent via lamina 1 to these homeostatic areas of the brain stem. If I scratch my itch without being aware of doing it, this is because my brain stem, with the help of the motor regions of the brain, sent a signal to the appropriate muscles that got me scratching. Even without awareness, my body "knows" how to regulate the itch and restore homeostasis just as it "knows" how to adjust my breathing and heart rate when I exercise.

This anatomical link between interoception and the brain stem centers for maintaining homeostasis is crucial for our understanding of why we need to feel into our bodies. Simply put, interoception—with or without our awareness—is essential for staying alive and well. Interoceptive afferent information is linked, via the brain stem and other parts of the brain to be discussed momentarily, to efferent pathways for altering, adjusting, compensating, and regulating our breathing, digestion, level of comfort, food and drink intake, blood pressure, muscle tension. and fatigue.

There are limits to what our brain stem can accomplish (it's not particularly smart and we share it with all vertebrate animals). Humans can add embodied self-awareness into the homeostatic self-regulation system to make it more powerful as a tool for homeostasis. Embodied self-awareness can help us avoid eating or drinking too much (our brain stem can be greedy on its own). We also need self-awareness to do something about muscle strain or else it may lead to back ache and chronic fatigue, or to prevent addictions. But we need to expand the network to get that awareness.

The Second Level in the Formation of Self-Awareness: Emotion, the Limbic System, and the Insula

So, let's continue our journey from the receptors through the brain stem and up to the brain. There are a lot of additional possible links in the neural network once in the brain, and each of these links provide different types of information for homeostatic regulation. The bundle of interoceptive nerve fibers leaves the homeostatic areas of the brain stem and connects to the central part of the brain (the limbic system) and then to the outer layers of the brain (the cortex). This is where the story gets more complex (my apologies), so before going on, it may be helpful to review some basic brain anatomy and anatomical terminology.

Figure 2.3 shows the directional labeling for the brain: **rostral** (toward the head, in this case toward the forehead) and **caudal** (toward the tail, or spinal cord); **ventral** (toward the front; anterior and inferior) and **dorsal** (toward the back, superior and posterior); and (not shown) **lateral** (toward the outside, left or right) and **medial** (toward the center). Figure 2.4 shows the basic divisions of the cortex into **lobes**, so named because these regions are separated by deep fissures (or sulci; singular is sulcus). Each of the cortical (pertaining to the cortex) lobes has a different function which will be discussed later.

Psychophysiology of Self-Awareness

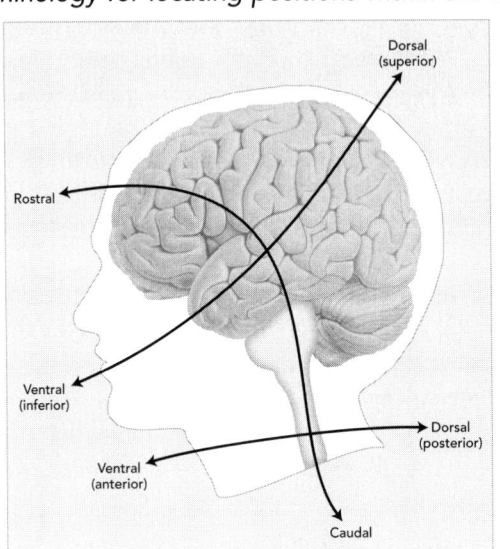

Figure 2.3
Terminology for locating positions within the brain

Figure 2.4
The lobes of the cerebral cortex

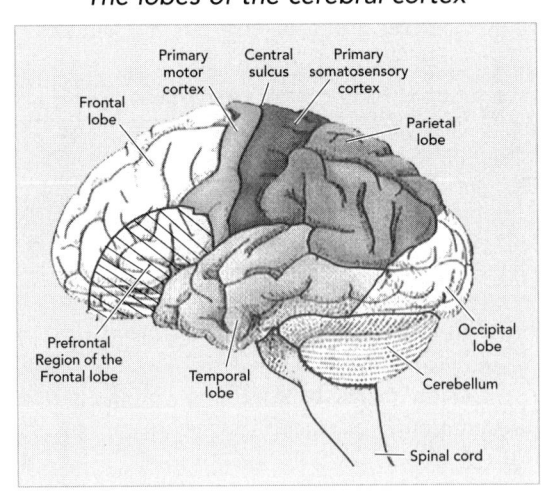

Embodied Self-Awareness

Where is the dorsomedial prefrontal cortex (DMPFC), the part of the brain we discussed earlier that plays an important role in conceptual self-awareness? This is actually very difficult to show in a 2-D picture because the brain is 3-D, and because the DMPFC is medial (closer to the center of the brain). The prefrontal cortex (PFC), of which the dorsomedial-PFC is a part, lies on the caudal (toward the brain stem) section of the frontal lobe, adjacent to the temporal lobe, and positioned roughly above the eyes (Figure 2.4). The DMPFC is in the dorsal (toward the top of the head) and medial (toward the center of the head) section of the PFC. The location of the medial prefrontal cortex (MPFC) as a whole is roughly indicated in Figures 2.5 and 2.6. I include all these different 2-D views to provide different perspectives on locations.

The DMPFC has a partner, the ventromedial PFC (VMPFC), which lies just below (inferior to) the DMPFC. The VMPFC, it turns out, is related to embodied self-awareness while the DMPFC is related to conceptual self-awareness. Thus, the dorsal and ventral sections of the MPFC are central to shifting between embodied and conceptual forms of self-awareness. This aspect of the role of the MPFC will be elaborated more in Chapter 3.

Coming back to our journey from ergoreceptors to the brain, the interoceptive pathways from the brain stem make their first connections in the center of the brain with the hypothalamus and thalamus (see Figures 2.5 and 2.6). These structures lie within what is called the **limbic** system, which also includes the amygdala, hippocampus, and cingulate cortex.

The **hypothalamus** (*hypo*=under) is an extremely important and complex part of the brain. It works with the brain stem to regulate homeostasis in the body and it does this in two ways. One of these ways is through efferent neural links back to the brain stem. This is the efferent pathway of the **autonomic nervous system** (ANS) that is responsible for the homeostatic regulation of all the important internal organs of the body including heart, lungs, and gut. The other link from the hypothalamus to the body is through the secretion of a wide array of neuroendochrine hormones that work on both the body and the brain through the bloodstream.

Psychophysiology of Self-Awareness

Figure 2.5
Vertical section of the brain, through the ears

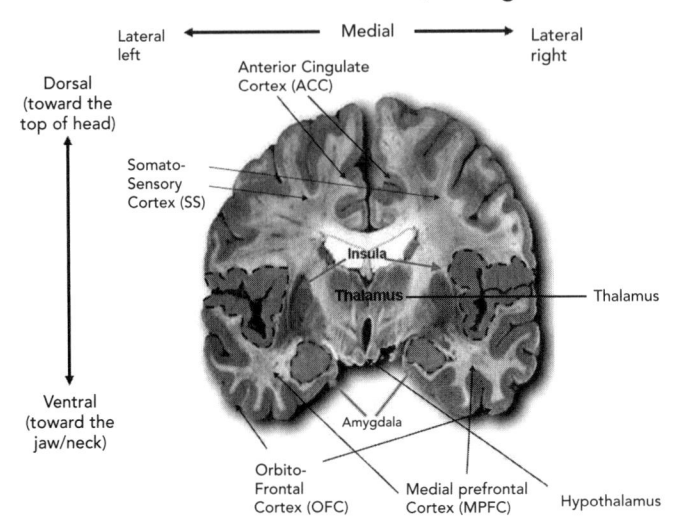

Figure 2.6
Limbic System and related structures

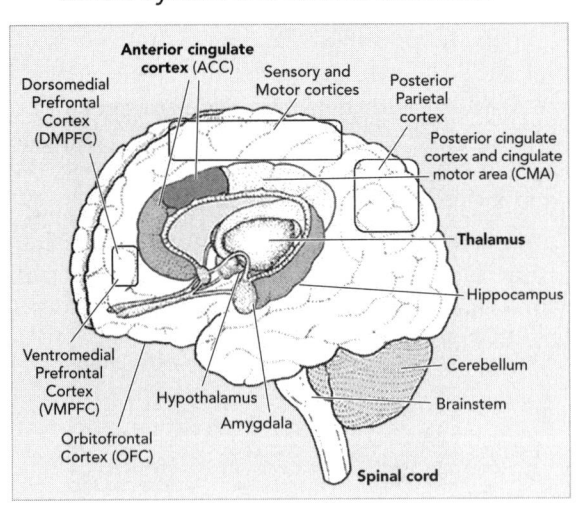

The next step is the connection of the interoceptive pathway from the hypothalamus to the thalamus, in particular the ventromedial (VM) portion of the thalamus. Lying virtually in the center of the limbic system in the center of the head, the **thalamus** is a relay station where inputs from different parts of the body, spinal cord, and brain stem get sorted out and sent to regions of the cortex for further processing. The thalamus also plays a role in organizing the efferent connections back to the body. The itch sensation mentioned earlier goes up through the thalamus, and the commands to and from the motor cortices (Figure 2.7) to locate that part of the body and move the appropriate muscles to scratch it are sorted out in the thalamus.

From the VM thalamus, the interoceptive pathway goes to the posterior (toward the back of the head) region of the **insula**, located in the interior of the temporal lobe, adjacent to the thalamus and other limbic structures such as the amygdala (Figure 2.5). The posterior insula is designed to sort out the different feeling quality of each of the different receptors (Craig, 2008). The neural pattern of activation in the posterior insula is not the same as the original neural activity at the receptor site but it is analogous to that receptor activity. We can say that the posterior insula creates a *representation* of the receptor activation. Itchy feels different from soft, hot different from cold, tingly different from numb: thank the neural representations in your insula for keeping it all straight.

Our network so far is not quite ready for self-awareness. The neural representations in my insula help me to identify itchiness, the thalamus relays the information of the appropriate motor centers for scratching it, the hypothalamus sends alert signals that something is wrong. I scratch, but I don't need to be aware of it for all this to happen. Whew! That's a relief. If we had to be aware of everything our body does to regulate itself, it would be exhausting and overwhelming. We need a way to select, out of all the possible homeostatic tasks which are mostly handled without our self-awareness, which ones actually require our attention.

Fortunately, we have a very effective method for sorting internal sensations into order of importance for deciding how to allocate awareness. This method has a long evolutionary history across different vertebrate species and appears to have evolved specifically because it gets our attention. This method is our emotions, our sense of whether something is good or bad for us and the accompanying motivation or urge to approach or avoid.

How is emotion created in the brain? We saw how the thalamus sends the interoceptive information to the posterior insula, just lateral to the thalamus. There is also another interoceptive pathway from the thalamus to the anterior (toward the front of the head) portion of the cingulate cortex (**anterior cingulate cortex, ACC**) which lies just dorsal to (above) the thalamus. That thalamic-ACC connection continues with a pathway from the ACC to the insula.

The ACC is located adjacent to the brain's cortical motor areas (see Figures 2.5 and 2.6) and has connections to them, including the motor cortex, the premotor cortex (PMC) and the **supplementary motor area** (SMA). Research shows that *this link between the ACC and the motor areas creates the motivational aspect of emotion, what the body wants to do (intentions and urges), what the body does (emotion related behavior, including expressions and vocalizations)*. In addition to coordinating messages about urges and actions to the skeletal muscles, the ACC can also motivate internal actions via the autonomic nervous system (ANS) back through the hypothalamus, brain stem, and then to the internal organs (heart racing, breathing changes, flushing, sweating).

Premotor (urges to act) and motor (actions) areas of the cortex are typically activated via the ACC (Cohen, Kaplan, et al., 1999; Hajcak et al., 2007). Just as the representations in the insula sort out different sensory feelings, representations in the ACC sort out different types of actions that are emotion-specific (Frijda, 1986). So, shame may result in hiding or covering the face, anger in making a fist, while joy may result in laughter (Coombes, Janelle, & Duley, 2005).

You can thank your ACC for this because lesions in the ACC lead to lack of spontaneity and indifference, suggesting that the ACC is crucial in the task of mobilizing one's actions in relation to emotion. Schizophrenics, who have trouble monitoring their own actions and often confuse them with a presumed external agent, have impaired function in the ACC (Carter, MacDonald, Ross, & Stenger, 2001; Northoff & Bermpohl, 2004).

Embodied Self-Awareness

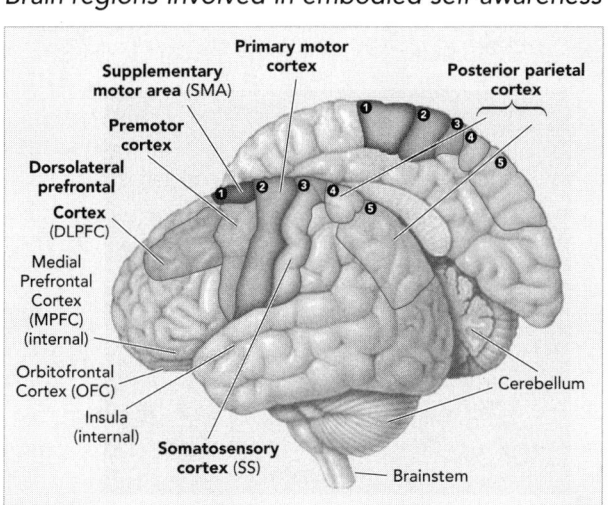

Figure 2.7
Brain regions involved in embodied self-awareness

The other part of the brain involved in emotion is in the lower section of the prefrontal cortex, just above the eyes, the **orbitofrontal cortex (OFC)**, see Figures 2.5, 2.6, and 2.7. The OFC helps in the appraisal of body states as positive or negative, the hedonic tone of the feeling. It works together with the ACC to regulate whether to take approach (good) or withdrawal (not so good) action. People with lesions in the OFC show signs of impaired ability to make decisions for long-term benefit. They have difficulty interpreting when sensations are helpful or harmful to their bodies, often choosing immediate rewards in spite of later consequences, a course of action that occurs in addictions (see Chapter 4).

Impairment in the connection between the ACC and the OFC can lead to obsessive-compulsive disorder and the uncontrollable tics and obscenities of Tourette's syndrome (Barrett, Pike, & Paus, 2004; Devinsky, Morrell, & Vogt, 1995; Paus, 2001). In these cases, the body has difficulty regulating and slowing down actions, even when those actions are not useful or helpful. It is as if the person feels the need to act when no need is present.

Psychophysiology of Self-Awareness

Finally: Neural Integration and the Emergence of Interoceptive Self-Awareness

Even with all the complexity of the neural processes reviewed thus far, we may not be aware of the emotions created in the ACC-OFC-posterior insula network. This was the case for Doug's anger (Case Report 2.1). He had made decisions that were not in his best interest by acting on the basis of suppressing the anger of which he was not aware. Through treatment, he learned to be aware of his anger which ultimately led to improved homeostatic self-regulation. So, we are now ready to ask: where does awareness come from? How does it emerge?

Awareness—in our case, the embodied awareness of interoceptive feelings and emotions—is not "in" the OFC, or "in" the insula. Rather, *awareness emerges as a whole systems phenomenon, a consequence of the coactivation across these and other regions of the brain and body in the interoceptive network*. This coactivation encompasses the whole body, all the way from the ergoreceptors to the ACC and sensorimotor cortices. Emergent properties are not uncommon in nature. The solidness of physical objects, for example, is not "in" its component atoms and molecules which are mostly empty space at the subatomic level. Rather, hardness (and other naked-eye physical properties) emerges in the dynamic interplay of networks of dynamically interacting molecular bonds.

Complex dynamic systems have the property of **emergence**, in which a pattern of activity—like the solidity of an object—is created across all the elements of the system and is not contained in any single element. Water can exist in three different states—ice, liquid, and vapor—depending upon the temperature. It's all the same H_2O but the coactivity of the water molecules changes the way they link together as a function of temperature. The solid, liquid, and gaseous states are emergent properties of this ensemble, properties not contained in the molecules themselves. The same could be said for the patterns that form in a river—eddies and rapids—as a function of water pressure and volume.

The patterns that emerge in dynamic systems may "hold together" for a particular period of time. These relatively stable patterns, the eddies and whirlpools, are called **attractors** because the elements of the system appear to be attracted to each other in a particular way. Waves, eddies, and rapids are all different attractors in a system of moving water.

Similarly, different states of awareness—sleep, wake, attentive, distracted—are emergent attractors of coregulating **neural networks** in the brain and the rest of the body (Dehaene & Naccache, 2001; Thompson & Varela, 2001; Tucker, 2001). How does this neural integration and emergence happen? We need the anterior portion of the insula to bring it all together.

The representations of receptor information in the posterior insula and the representations of motivational information from the ACC, as well as representations coming from the other parts of the interoceptive network, join together in the anterior portion of the insula. The anterior insula integrates all this information and represents it in its own neural language. The activity in the anterior insula has therefore been called a **rerepresentation**, yet another transformation of the receptor and motivational information (Craig, 2008; Damasio et al., 2000; Panksepp, 1998; Tucker et al., 2003).

Rerepresentation is the ability of the brain—in particular the interoceptive neural network that includes the anterior insula—to form feelings and emotions—fashioned out of the original sensations of the receptors. Rerepresentation is the brain communicating with itself in its own language of electrochemical and energetic vibrations. These vibrations form attractors, exactly like eddies in a river. The energy that supports this oscillation comes from the cellular consumption of metabolites that is converted into electrochemical energy that can be observed at the surface of the brain as coordinated brain wave rhythms (Ward, 2003).

In addition to the anterior insula, we also need the **dorsolateral PFC (DLPFC)**, which serves to take sensory impressions from the interoceptive and exteroceptive networks and to "hold" them temporarily. Note that earlier we discussed the **dorsomedial PFC** (DMPFC). The DLPFC is located just laterally to the DMPFC, and on the surface of the brain near the center of the PFC (see Figures 2.4 and 2.7). The DLPFC is activated when people have to hold something in mind, like a math problem, while they think about it, a skill called "working memory" (Barch et al., 1997). The DLPFC, in other words, provides an opportunity for the rapid neural signals to slow down long enough for us to feel and process them. *Awareness, then, is an emergent pattern of neural integration across all the levels of the interoceptive network.* The three levels of the interoceptive network are summarized in Table 2.4.

Psychophysiology of Self-Awareness

Table 2.4
Self-awareness at different levels of the body

Level of the body	Level of Awareness
Level I: Brain stem (homeostasis of heart, respiration) and hypothalamus (homeostasis of blood pressure, body temperature, body fluid and electrolyte balance (thirst), and body weight (hunger)	Coarse, typically not directly accessible to awareness.
Level II: Thalamus, posterior insula, motor areas, OFC and ACC create sensations, evaluations, and motivations that form emotions	These patterns direct our behavior (approach and withdrawal) alone and with others but we may not be aware of the emotions that organize these patterns.
Level III: Neural integration and emergence of attractors of embodied self-awareness across particular patterns of activation within the specific neural networks that include the previous levels and also the anterior insula and DLPFC.	Awareness of specific emotion-feeling states and an awareness of self in the act of feeling those states. This is embodied self-awareness.

Sources: Critchley, Mathias & Dolan, (2001), Critchley, Wiens et al. (2004), Damasio, (1999), Damasio et al. (2000)

Embodied self-awareness in the **subjective emotional present** (Craig, 2008) is the time during which these rerepresentations remain activated across the entire neural network. During the subjective emotional present, there is a suspension of the sense of time and an amplification of feelings and emotions that "fill up" our awareness.

There are many different attractors that can form in this network of vibrational metabolic energy that converges in the anterior insula. On the field of embodied self-awareness, these different attractors are the qualitatively different ways in which we can feel our bodies (Posner & Rothbart, 1998; Ward, 2003). The "draggy feeling," mentioned earlier, is one such attractor. Feelings of elation, sadness, anger, bone-weariness, or bracing cold are other attractors. While all these interoceptive states of embodied self-awareness partake of the same general neural network, they are distinguished by the differences that originated in the receptors, all of which the brain can identify, represent, and then bring into awareness as a particular type of felt sensation and emotion (rerepresentation).

This explains why embodied self-awareness can't be commanded to happen. Embodied self-awareness emerges suddenly, apparently without warning. It just happens when rerepresentations emerge across the entire neural network. Embodied self-awareness practitioners can facilitate the process of emergence using the means listed in Table 1.1 and as illustrated in Case Report 2.1, and all the other case reports in this book. Although we can't make it happen, no more than we can make a plant grow, we can provide the supportive context—the soil, water, light, and nutrients for the plant—that best encourages its growth.

The more we actively practice creating opportunities for embodied self-awareness to emerge, however, the more we have the ability to stay longer in the subjective emotional present and the ability to choose to tune into particular sensations in particular parts of the body. This practice effect happens because the brain learns from each experience of embodied self-awareness. Neural learning is reflected in physiological changes in the nerve cells and their connections. Practice leads to the growth of an increasing number of interconnecting fibers that can synapse between cells. The more synapses between adjoining cells, the more likely there will be a direct communication between them, and the stronger the neural network.

It is exactly like walking across a grassy field. The first person bends the blades of grass a little bit. The next person sees this indentation in the grass and follows it, making the grass more bent. As this goes on over time, all the grass is gone and a dirt path "appears," easy to see and easy to follow.

The growth of neural pathways through practice and repeated experience is called **experience dependent brain development**. These increasingly entrenched pathways make it easier for information to travel along the same routes in the future. This neural attractor for the pattern of activation and its link to the body's receptors and effectors is how we form memories and habits.

When it comes to embodied self-awareness, practice is crucial in expanding it and giving us opportunities to make choices for our own benefit. Our body also has some built-in ways to jolt us into awareness. Yawning, of course, helps us to wake up from drowsy or sleepy states. Yawning, it turns out, has all the right physiology for starting the process of waking us up to ourselves (see Box 2.2).

BOX 2.2
Yawning: Waking Up the Body to Itself

Yawning is a powerful and pleasurable action, the experience of which can reach deep into our bodies and activate an emergent awareness of how we feel. Yawning is typically not voluntary but rather a spontaneous and more-or-less automatic response. Yawning is usually initiated by feelings of boredom and drowsiness which are accompanied by hypoxia (reduced oxygen intake), reduced metabolic rate, and slowed activity (Askenasy, 2001; Guggisberg, Mathis, Herrman, & Hess, 2007). If observed during the day, yawning is associated with higher rates of body activity, like stretching and deeper breathing, suggesting that yawning may signal the body to wake up to itself (Baenninger, Binkley, & Baenninger, 1996).

During a yawn, the movements of the neck, mouth, and jaw are tightly coordinated. The yawn is a neurobehavioral attractor that shows a similar form on each repetition. It seems to be fundamentally important to our well-being since it appears in most vertebrate animals and can be seen via ultrasound images to begin around the third prenatal month (Walusinski, 2006; Zafar, Nordh, & Eriksson, 2000).

As can be seen in Table 2.3, yawning activates many muscles, stimulates breathing, enhances the flow of hormones such as oxytocin and neurotransmitters like serotonin that increase feelings of well-being and pleasure. Because of this flood of physiological activity, it is hard not to become aware of how good it feels to yawn.

In addition to these biochemical wake-up calls, the act of yawning itself stimulates the afferent pathways (back to the brain) of the parasympathetic nervous system. The parasympathetic is one branch of the autonomic nervous system (ANS) that regulates the internal organs. The other branch is the sympathetic nervous system. In general, parasympathetic pathways promote relaxation while sympathetic pathways promote arousal (see Chapter 5).

continued

Table 2.3
Yawning enhances embodied self-awareness

Respiration	Long inspiration at the start stretches muscles of the respiratory tract (diaphragm and intercostals)
Throat	Pharynx diameter expands by 4-fold Larynx opens Maximal stretching of vocal cords Stimulates vagus nerve in throat which stimulates blood flow
Face and neck	Stretching of muscles around the cheeks, jaw, neck, and upper chest; may cause tears and partial obstruction of hearing
Hypothalamus	Oxytocin enhances relaxation Serotonin enhances feelings of pleasure and well-being ANS parasympathetic activation leads also to relaxation
Brain stem (reticular activating system) and thalamus	Facilitates shift of alertness and attention from waking to sleeping and vice versa by activating muscles and increasing oxygen to body from inspiration; also affects brain stem centers for inducing respiration and stimulating the phrenic nerve to the diaphragm and the nerves to the intercostal muscles
Cranial parasympathetic nerves coming directly from face and neck into the brain stem (nucleus of the solitary tract, NTS) intercept the interoceptive pathways coming through lamina 1 of the dorsal horn of the spinal cord from the body, especially from the skeletal muscles, joints, and diaphragm	Feelings of losing consciousness (falling asleep) or coming back to oneself (waking); also feeling the body through deeper breathing and stretching; resets the rerepresentation of the body configuration

Sources: Argiolas and Melis (1998), Askenasy (2001), Askenasy and Askenasy (1996), Kasuya, Murakami, Oshima, & Dohi (2005), Walusinski (2006).

Psychophysiology of Self-Awareness

> **BOX 2.2** (continued)
>
> These parasympathetic afferents do not enter the brain through the spinal cord but rather go directly to the brain stem from the body regions, in this case from the face, throat, and neck muscles via the vagus nerve and from the diaphragm via the phrenic nerve. What is especially important here is that these afferents meet up, in the brain stem, with the interoceptive afferents from the ergoreceptors through lamina 1 of the dorsal horn of the spinal cord. From there, the parasympathetic and interoceptive afferents travel the same pathways through the hypothalamus—which regulates the ANS via neurotransmitters and neurohormones (see Table 2.3)—the thalamus, insula, and ACC. These can also signal the body to move, breathe, and ultimately to feel.
>
> The spontaneity of the yawn and its activation of the interoceptive neural network creates the conditions for the emergence of embodied self-awareness. It is like rebooting your internal computer. Because yawning is such a stable attractor across species and across ages, it is as if our physiology has a built-in mechanism to bring us back to ourselves. So, the next time you yawn, notice not only how it feels good and stimulating, but also that it draws your attention to become more fully present in your body.

Finding and Losing Embodied Self-Awareness

When in the subjective emotional present, we are fully engaged in the embodied experience whatever that may be. We lose any sense of time passing. We are totally caught up in the experience as it fills our entire field of awareness. We are not observers of ourselves, not seeing ourselves objectively, as in conceptual self-awareness. Instead, we are fully ourselves. There is no third person point of view or even a first person point of view. We simply are, in that subjective emotional present, fully alive. As in the quote at the beginning of the chapter, we do not have a body in that moment—we are our bodies.

Catch Me If You Can:
The Impermanence of Embodied Self-Awareness

In spite of the intensity of this lived experience in the subjective emotional present, it does not last long. Any particular feeling or emotion is temporary. We can feel our sadness when appropriate, but it is likely that we may suddenly switch to joy or gratitude. The rerepresentation attractors in the neural network for interoception are highly dynamic and distributed across the entire neural network, including the receptors at the periphery of the body. Thus, particular emotional states, while stable enough for us to fully appreciate them while they last, can easily transform into other states as information across the network dynamically shifts and changes in response to changes anywhere in the network.

In the same way, we can suddenly shift from not being aware of emotion into an emotional awareness in the subjective emotional present. The feeling of sadness, for example, may arise in a conversation as the other's empathy and willingness to wait for the person's feeling to come in self-awareness. In this **coregulating** open link between people, the oscillations in the neural network may have an opportunity to coalesce into an identifiable emotion. In general, coregulating with another person encourages the interoceptive neural network to crystallize into a state of embodied awareness (Table 1.1). The emergence of a neural process into awareness is sudden and spontaneous.

In dynamic systems language, this is called a **nonlinear transition**. There is not a gradual transformation from thinking and talking into an embodied feeling of sadness, but rather an abrupt and surprising shift. This suddenness is typical of our experience in the subjective emotional present. Put another way, *when we lurch into the subjective emotional present of embodied self-awareness, we no longer have the ability to control what we feel. Spontaneity, non-predictability, and even uncertainty—what has been called* **chaos**—*reign in this subjective world; quite the opposite of the relatively "safer" world of felt control and logical progressions in conceptual self-awareness.*

Chaos is actually a sign of health. In a resting state, the beat-to-beat intervals of the heart form a fairly steady heart rate and pulse. In actuality, however, the intervals between heart beats are never exactly alike. There is always some small variability and uncertainty involved in healthy heart function. **Chaos**, in the lexicon of dynamic systems theory, is variability within stability, a recognizable pattern but one that never precisely and exactly repeats itself in the same way. We may cycle through feelings of sadness and joy in the subjective emotional present but we can never really predict when one or the other will come and how long it will last.

Part of what is learned by entering and reentering embodied self-awareness, then, is the ability to "stay present" for longer periods in the face of chaotic sensations and suddenly strong emotions. This is why we often need someone else to guide us in and out of this state. With practice, we become better able to maintain ourselves there, but ultimately the full exploration of new emotional territory requires help from a coregulating other.

Because embodied self-awareness is systemic, dynamic, and subject to sudden transitions, there is always new emotional territory. *The subjective emotional present is the place of our creativity, our inspiration, and our personal growth.* Once an emotion emerges in awareness, however, it serves as a kind of glue that holds the awareness together for some finite period of time.

Freud was one of the first to point out that new learning and the formation of lasting memories crystallize around salient emotional experiences, what he called *cathexes*. Cognitive processing and memory formation in the visual areas of the brain (the occipital lobe), for example, is heightened when people view more emotionally intense pictures (victims of violent death, erotica) than for less arousing images (happy families or angry faces) or neutral objects (household items).

Emotions ensure our survival by informing us that whatever is happening right now deserves our attention. When emotion is present, it allows us to assess whether the information is self-relevant and how (emotions are about the hedonic evaluation of harms or benefits) (Bradley, 2003; Schupp, Junghofer, Weike, & Hamm, 2003). This means that emotional salience activates awareness and that leads eventually to the formation of learned patterns of response, experience dependent neural connections, and thus memories for the salient events and the actions that were involved.

A Ship Without a Wheel:
How Can We Have an Emotion and Not Be Aware of It?

Given the importance of emotional self-awareness, one might think that we would and should be aware of all our emotions. This is not the case. For Doug

(Case Report 2.1), he had likely been angry for many years and yet only in his Rosen session with me was he able to actually become aware of his angry feelings. If Doug was angry even though he was not aware of it, where was that anger hiding? If he could not feel it, did that mean it had no effect on him?

These questions raise an issue that has been discussed for many centuries. It is usually framed in terms of the concept of the "unconscious." In this view, the unconscious is any thought, sensation, or emotion that is presumed to be lurking somewhere inside of us but we are not aware of it. In Freud's theory, the unconscious contained emotions and feelings that had been repressed in early childhood because of painful and threatening situations. Repressed, unconscious emotions were thought to be toxic, creating distorted thought patterns, physical symptoms with no medical diagnosis, and disturbed interpersonal relationships.

As we shall see in this book, the deleterious effects of emotional suppression have been borne out by recent research. But the word *unconscious* is not used in this book. This is partly because it is a confusing term with many possible meanings. One can become "unconscious" (in ordinary language) by having a head trauma, by fainting, by being in a coma, or by being in a deep sleep state. Scientists like me can take a word, like *unconscious* and define it as a technical term for their purposes. For technical terms, I prefer to choose words that are not already laden with the baggage of multiple meanings and possible misinterpretations because of that baggage. I'm using the concept of **embodied self-awareness**, which I have defined and contrasted with **conceptual self-awareness**. So, what some readers may call or think about as "unconscious," most likely related to the sensory and emotional processing that occurs at Levels I and II (Table 2.4), in the absence of embodied self-awareness.

So, coming back to the questions above—in what sense can one "have" an emotion and not be aware of it?—we already have an answer. Efferent feedback to the body for self-regulation and homeostasis requires afferent information from the body. Some of that information is directed back to the body at Level I from the spinal cord and brain stem, and some from the Level II neural network (Table 2.4) including the hypothalamus, thalamus, insula, OFC, and ACC. At each of the three levels of the neural network, there are different types of neural representation. The representation in the Level II network is emotional in the sense that it takes information from the receptors, evaluates it for harm or benefit, and translates that information into a motivation to act. All this can happen without our being aware of it. It is absolutely necessary for self-regulation and survival.

Anger is an emotion that arises when our desires are thwarted. For some people who are unaware of their anger, that motivation to act may translate into violence, assault, rape, and other acts to harm persons or things. The person who does these things may not be aware of the feeling of anger, or of any particular feeling or emotion that may have provoked the act. They may act in very cold-blooded ways, using conceptual justifications for their actions. Many perpetrators continue to act in part because they have not been able to feel their anger (or sadness, or other emotions), and the likely accompanying feelings of loss or abandonment in childhood, an inability to form a **secure attachment** with a parent figure, that sparked the anger.

For Doug (Case Report 2.1), his *unfelt* anger led to passivity and self-denial. Doug's motivation to retaliate against his demanding father was interpreted by the OFC in the emotional neural network as potentially harmful to Doug. He not only had to suppress the awareness of the anger, but also the awareness of his urge to retaliate, the consequences of which were described in the case report. **Suppression** of embodied self-awareness occurs whenever there is a sense of threat that prevents us from finding resources, slowing down, and coregulating with another person. The root of Doug's suppressed anger was also a lack of secure attachment.

These examples make clear that *unfelt* emotion is not the same as *felt* emotion, of which Doug became aware in treatment. His felt anger was not retaliatory. It was, ultimately, comforting. Once the emotional evaluations and motivations are rerepresented in embodied self-awareness, the actual experience of that emotion depends upon the circumstances of its emergence, and emergence, as we have seen, is not predictable. My presence with Doug, and the particular approach I was taking with him (using Rosen Method as opposed to a more movement oriented treatment, or me as the practitioner as opposed to another Rosen practitioner) also play a role in the way in which the Level III networks become activated.

People who might talk about Doug's unconscious anger are likely thinking that it is the same as the felt and expressed anger but is just hidden from view. This is certainly not how the neural networks function. Emotions originating in the Level II neural network of which we are not aware help us to self-regulate and regain homeostasis. They act automatically to adjust behavior and body states and set in motion experience dependent developmental pathways like the two types of anger suppression described above. Once we do become aware of a body feeling or emotion at Level III, however, that awareness transforms the representations from Level II (the rerepresentation) and as a result we can gain some additional degree of self-regulatory control over what happens to us and how we use that emotion in the future. We can make choices such as, "I've had enough to drink," or "I'm going to avoid this person because I know if someone makes me feel angry, they are likely not acting in my best interests." This is because self-awareness is a neural integration in the entire network, and also because the dorsolateral PFC (DLPFC), can hold the emotion in mind so that it can be evaluated by higher cognitive centers in the prefrontal cortex responsible for decision making and self-regulation.

As often happens in interventions to enhance embodied self-awareness, what may have initially seemed too painful to feel becomes less so and perhaps even a desirable state to visit because it ultimately leads to a lessening of pain and an improvement in outcomes. Doug's (Case Report 2.1) growing comfort with feeling (and not acting out) his anger was crucial to his ability to self-regulate in interpersonal situations.

Also at Level III the prefrontal areas of the DLPFC and OFC can, to some extent, slow the speed of processing and lower the level of intensity of an embodied experience (see Box 2.1) further transforming the Level II representations. Confronting memories of trauma is especially painful and in **posttraumatic stress disorder** (PTSD) the person's experience is that these memories come on without warning, like an unstoppable freight train. A veteran of the Iraqi war, for example, may be driving down a busy street in the United States and all of a sudden have a fully alive and present experience of being under attack by snipers. Treatments involve helping the individual gain some measure of control about how long to stay with and how intense one experiences the remembered emotions. After a while, the prefrontal areas develop sufficient experience dependent connections to the other interoceptive areas that they can be more effective in self-regulating while in the subjective emotional present of embodied self-awareness.

So, after treatment, when driving down the street, the veteran can interoceptively feel the frightening memory coming on and take steps to modulate it (slow it down) so it does not become overwhelming. Such treatments are not cures in the sense of eliminating all traces of the traumatic memory at Levels I and II, but rather work by bringing some measure of self-regulatory confidence that one can "handle" being in the subjective emotional present at Level III with such memories.

In summary, *the goal of enhancing embodied self-awareness is to arrive at this third level of expansive presence coupled with the ability to choose a course of action for self-benefit.* If any of these abilities is impaired, it takes a long time in the company of coregulating others to regrow the pathways that lead back to the subjective emotional present, back home to our bodies. If we are plagued by a history of self-avoidance and suppression or intrusive traumatic memories, we will never completely lose those patterns. That is just the way our brain and body grew given the opportunities and tragedies of our life history.

We can, however, learn to embrace those experiences. We can welcome them home and accept them as part of who we are and who we were. We can choose not to ignore them, to let them arise in our awareness whenever and however they come to us: in dreams or in situations that trigger those feelings. By honoring these experiences, owning them, and feeling them, we can detoxify them. They lose their ability to overpower, hurt, and overwhelm. We can come to feel more complete, more alive—and like our own guides and teachers who have helped us safely explore the territory of our own subjective emotional present—more empathic and more generous with those who have similarly suffered.

3

Links and Boundaries: Locating Ourselves

"Now move your right leg forward."

I try but nothing happens. I look down at my foot. Move, please. Nothing happens. Come on, move. Move, damn you! Sweat drips onto my foot. There must be some terrible neurological damage. Nancy bends down and moves my right foot forward a few inches.

"Now put your weight on it," she says, gripping my elbow. Figuring out how to do that is the hardest mental task I've ever performed.

(Weimer, 1994, p. 52)

This quote is a description of the author's first physical therapy session following surgery to repair damaged vertebrae in her lower back. After months of intensive and physically difficult work, she was able to regain the ability to stand and to take some steps with help. Fortunately, she was able eventually to regain complete function. Her emotions—shock, fear, and anger—result from the inability to feel a once familiar part of her body and to command it to move. Sensing the linkages of one part of ourselves to another, and feeling the boundaries of our bodies in relation to others and to the environment, is the topic of this chapter.

Most of us can get a drink when we feel thirsty. We have to know that the arm and hand reaching for the drink belong to us, that we can make them move in this particular way or do most other ordinary tasks upon our command, that we can feel those movements in a way that guides them to the target, finds it, and brings it to the mouth without spilling. We also sense the length of our arms, so that getting a drink container may require leaning to put us in reach of the desired object. We have to maintain a reasonably steady **posture** as all this occurs and to be aware of how our reaching links to our postural stability. The **body schema** is the part of embodied self-awareness that senses that our body belongs to us and to no one else, as well as our sense of movement and balance, our ability to locate particular parts of ourselves, our sense of our body size and shape, and the awareness that our body has boundaries that separate us from objects and other bodies.

The sense of thirst is an interoceptive feeling, and the desire to obtain a particular kind of liquid is a felt emotion, but the implicit understanding of our body's ability (or lack of ability) to actually satisfy the thirst is part of the body schema. The body schema is related to the skeletomotor system and the parts of the nervous system that are responsible for making movements intentional (meaning that the movements are in response to our interoceptive needs and desires), coordinated (smooth linkages), and comfortable (without excessive effort, pain, or fatigue).

The body schema is a schema-in-relation, with linkages and boundaries. Movement always occurs in space and that space always contains some elements that do not belong to the self. Even in a completely empty terrestrial environment, we have to relate to the pull of gravity and the way it brings us into contact with the ground. In any conceivable posture—lying, sitting, standing—and any conceivable movement—walking, reaching, or changing postures—our body needs to adapt to the fact of having a surface below us with textures and obstacles, and the weight of our limbs and torso being pulled toward that surface (see Box 3.1).

BOX 3.1
The Unbearable Heaviness of Being

We spend most of our time working to resist the force of gravity. Staying upright, whether sitting or standing, takes muscular effort. This could be in our larger postural muscles of the upper legs and lower back, or it could be the tiny muscles of our face that tend to stay active to keep up appearances. Neck and shoulder muscles are also involved to keep our big-brained heavy heads afloat. Babies have a much harder time with this. While the ratio of head to body length in adults is 1:8, in a newborn it is 1:4!

continued

BOX 3.1 (continued)

All these antigravitational efforts—especially as they are coupled with social expectations for posture, movement, and facial expression—become habitual. We do them even when no one else is around and even when we are trying to rest. These expectations lead many people to show persistent motor activity at low levels of muscular contraction 24 hours a day, 7 days a week. This low-level activity is energetically costly over the long run. Like a slowly leaking faucet, it can drain our metabolic resources and leave us more fatigued and less healthy than we might if we could find a way to stop the leak during rest periods.

You can feel this for yourself in your interoceptive and body schema self-awareness. Lie down on your back in a comfortable place. Prop some cushions or pillows under your knees and neck as needed to relieve any undue strain. If you are too uncomfortable on your back, try lying on your side with a pillow under your head and one between your knees. Cover yourself if you feel cold. Make sure, in other words, that you have done everything you can to find the perfect resting state for your body.

Once you finally lie down, take a few moments to "settle in." Now check to see where your muscles continue to work even now, when they do not really need to do anything. You can sense this interoceptively with feelings of tightness, shortness of breath, or perhaps some slight pain in the area of the overworked muscles. Persistent thoughts of having things to do and reasons why you should not be taking this time to lie here can also mask interoceptive feelings. Use your body schema sense to locate the places where you most notice the muscular effort: your jaw, or neck, or chest, or hips, or even in the small muscles of your hands or face.

Ask those places to slow down and rest. You can also ask them to "give" their weight to the earth or bed or whatever you are lying on. Here you are using private speech and conceptual self-awareness to guide yourself into embodied self-awareness. You can also do this with

continued

Psychophysiology of Self-Awareness

> **BOX 3.1** (continued)
>
> the help of a teacher in a class on Restorative Yoga, a practice that focuses on deep relaxation into supported poses using your awareness of your body to help it rest into the pull of gravity (http://www.wikihealth.com/Restorative_yoga_poses).
>
> Most of the time, however, you are likely to find that any letting go of these muscles is at best temporary. A few places may let go, but when you turn your attention to other places, the earlier ones are already tightening up again.
>
> You can go more deeply into your interoceptive awareness. Is there a persistent feeling of having to do something? Is there an expectation you are not meeting? Is there anger or fear? Emotional self-awareness can help to relax some muscles but again, don't expect too much of yourself the first few times you try this. Maybe the best you can do is to notice that you are tired and let yourself take a little snooze. And don't forget that it is a valuable expansion of your embodied self-awareness to notice that your body probably doesn't like to lose control, even to the inevitability of a force much bigger than itself.

When our feet strike the ground in walking, we are exteroceptively aware of hardness or softness, smoothness or roughness of the surface, and interoceptively aware of whether the surface feels comfortable or not. The body schema part of embodied self-awareness has the role of adjusting our movements according to the emotional evaluation of why we are doing this activity. Walking over hot coals seems like the right thing to do if one is a Yogi. Having made that choice, careful attention must be paid to a host of receptors that monitor pain and movement. Most of us, however, would rather just avoid those burning coals. The sense of what aspects of the environment fit best with our body and how to negotiate threatening or dangerous environments is also part of the body schema.

The body schema can be expanded or contracted in our relationship with objects in the world. The class of objects we use as tools is a good example. The vehicle we drive, in our embodied self-awareness, becomes an extension of our body schema. We can "feel" the boundaries of the vehicle as if they were the boundaries of our bodies. This allows us to change lanes, follow at appropriate distances, and park. We may conceptually be aware that the vehicle is not actually part of our body, but in the act of driving, we sense it as an extension of self. The same is true of a tennis racket, skis, hammers and screwdrivers, and pencils (Ihde, 2002).

We can also extend this thinking into the realm of computers, such as entering into the space and movements of virtual characters in a virtual reality (Ihde, 2002). Virtual reality (VR) therapy is being used to help veterans overcome the symptoms of **posttraumatic stress disorder** (PTSD). Developers of these VR programs have created different scenarios: walking alone on patrol down an Iraqi street, patrolling with companions, at a checkpoint, inside a building looking for terrorists, riding in a Humvee or in a helicopter (Rizzo et al., 2005).

The therapist can vary details of the scenes, such as whether or not the avatar (the client's onscreen alter ego) has a weapon, according to what the veteran remembers. He or she can also adjust the intensity and timing of the encounter to help the veteran enter into the subjective emotional present of the combat memories with resources, coregulation of the therapist, and opportunities for enhancing self-regulation (see Table 1.1). The purpose of the VR treatment is to immerse the veteran in the movements and postures, the body schema sensations, that occurred at the time of the trauma. It helps that the young men and women who suffer from PTSD have experience with video and computer VR games, allowing them to put themselves in the place of the avatar and thus work through their emotions via the body schema. These treatments work because during the therapeutic session the veteran actually becomes—in body and mind—the virtual soldier in the virtual war zone (Gerardi, Rotlbaum, Ressler, Heekin, & Rizza, 2008; Rizzo et al., 2005).

Our body schema comes into play in our dealings with other living beings. This could range from avoiding contact to seeking close contact, from friendly to combative. In either case, we are typically in a situation in which both individuals need to make adjustive responses of their bodies in relation to the other. This process of mutual coordination is called **coregulation**, the ability to be and move with another individual in relation to a shared set of interoceptive sensations and emotions and in relation to the linkages and boundaries of each person's body schema.

Psychophysiology of Self-Awareness

In these situations, we implicitly know where our body leaves off and where the other's begins, how to coordinate muscular or mental effort, all the while preserving our sense of body ownership and cohesion (see Figures 1.2 and 1.3). Boundaries may be rigid or permeable. There are many ways to lose oneself in the other. In loving relationships characterized by secure attachments, we may have temporary feelings of being lost in the other's eyes or arms, experiences in which the self and all its cares melt away into a blissful and timeless state of cobeing. In these situations, each person still retains a cohesive self to which they may return at any time.

As illustrated in the opening quote, loss of body schema boundaries can occur in people who suffer physical or emotional abuse, injury, violent assault, war, torture, captivity, slavery, and forced labor. People can lose their boundaries when they are victims of a controlling or charismatic other, an other who preys on the vulnerabilities and weaknesses in the boundaries of the body schema. Children who suffer an invasion of their body boundaries never have the opportunity to completely define the borders and limits of the body schema. Infants and children who have difficulties establishing a secure attachment relationship with parents may also develop problems with body schema, the formation of linkages and boundaries with others.

This is illustrated in Case Report 3.1, in which a toddler and mother who are insecurely attached are treated with an embodied self-awareness approach called **dance movement psychotherapy**.

Dance movement psychotherapy is a creative arts therapy that uses movement and dance as a communication tool, as a diagnostic tool, and as a therapeutic intervention. The basic premises of dance movement psychotherapy are these:

- An individual's characteristic style of natural movement shows personality traits and attitudes.
- A significant change in clients' dance/movement affects their total functioning and behavior outside of therapy.
- Therapeutic rapport between therapist and client is established on both verbal and nonverbal levels. A trusting rapport fosters a client's development and growth toward independent living. Clients develop themselves emotionally, socially, mentally, and physically. (DiPalma, 1996)

Case Report 3.1
Dance Movement Psychotherapy Treatment of Josh, A Toddler with Attachment Difficulties

[1]Suzi Tortora

Josh, age 20 months, is brought to dance movement psychotherapy by his parents for they feel he is overly anxious. He cries easily, does not sleep well and clings to Dad. Both parents speak of a difficult birth experience, the sorrow of it lingering in the air as it is described. Mom mentions postpartum depression and Dad speaks of a traumatic event that occurred in his extended family that caused them to uproot themselves to move closer to relatives. I ask them to not give me any more details. With this outline in mind, I want to now attend to the nonverbal dialogue between baby and parent, and my own reactions—in thought, emotion, and somatically felt. I am both observer and participant. As I witness my own multisensory responses I aim to glean the "essence in the air, " revealed through the underlying qualitative elements of their interactional exchange (for more details on the method, see Tortora, 2006).

Mom, Josh and I are sitting on the floor playing together. Mom sits cross-legged, hands clasped at her center, across from Josh and me. I assist Josh to roll over a small egg-shaped physio-ball. This is difficult for him to do. He does not easily shape his body to the contours of the pliable surface. Holding his head, neck, shoulders and upper chest as one extended piece he slides off the egg from the left side of his body, moaning, with his head down on the mat. The containment in his posturing, the lack of coordinated flow in his movements, and a deep sense of sadness strike me. Is this a cry of physical discomfort or something more, I wonder? The quality of the moan resonates deeply in my abdomen.

I adjust my physical presence, making sure my actions are slow and contained. As I assist him I embody a more coordinated posturing, shaping my body over his, and gently stroke his spine in a downward motion, as I support his belly from underneath with a firm cupped palm. Through my close proximity and the quality of my touch, I hope to communicate a kinesthetic sense of stability and fluidity through his body center. Simultaneously I softly coo, "Woah... yeah... Beautiful job" to the rhythm of his moans. Josh drops his head to the mat and lifts his buttocks upward as if attempting to stand up, but ultimately folds his legs underneath him, sitting up within the crescent shaped space my folded legs and leaning torso create.

Josh looks towards Mommy and begins to moan. Arms stretch out, extending to the farthest reaches of his range, his body does not move. His cry heightens into a deep sighing whimper that takes on a rhythmic quality, yet he still does not mobilize forward. "You can find Mommy" I hear myself gently saying. Mom claps with a quick beat, stating "Yeah, you did it." But Josh seems to be stuck. Though she is only a foot or two away, I am overtaken by a sensation that she is miles away—I am possessed with a feeling of anguish at her distance. I note my word choice that has come so instantly: "You can find Mommy." I experience an intangible barrier between Mommy and baby.

Though at this moment I could easily lift Josh up and place him in Mommy's arms, I am hesitant to do so. Through my somatic attunement to his actions, I sense it is much more important for him to know he can reach his mom through his own physical efforts. "Oh, I know… you see your Mommy and you can't get to her," I say with deep empathy as I stroke his extended back. I cup my hands on his hips. "Let's find her, let's get to her," I utter, "I know, I know… ." I shape my body around him as Josh pivots into my arms, still whimpering, momentarily dropping his body into mine. Rocking side to side he shifts his weight back up and turns to face Mom again, pointing at her with extended arms as he moans, "Da…da…da." Again using the quality of my touch as my communication I assist Josh, rocking his pelvis side-to-side, sliding forward to Mom.

But again, I am struck by a somatic sensation, this time to my heart. When Josh reaches Mom, he drops his head down folding his body over his legs, forming a closed ball, at her crossed legs. Mom does not move, her face is still and silent, her arms remain clasped at her center, with her elbows resting on her folded knees. She is contained in her own private space. My breath is taken away as I attune to the "essence in the air" exuded by this couple. The depth of sadness is palpable; the intangible wall between them is almost visible. Through embodied resonance, I sense the sadness of this moment, fleeting as it is, as the core issue that plagues their relationship.

Both Mom and baby are in deep pain. Both feel immobilized, unable to reach each other, literally and figuratively. I realize at this moment that I must "hold" both mom and baby through my actions, my words, and the activities we create in the session. Josh must experience that he can successfully reach his mom and Mom must be able to experience that she is a capable mother, and her boy needs and wants her. She must learn that she is capable of being emotionally present for him. We must strive to repair the pain they both hold from those months of her depression, when she was oversleeping and emotionally not available as she had hoped to be.

Again through careful placement of my hands as our communicator, I support Josh to climb into Mom's arms without doing all the work for him. Mom caresses him, but Josh does not mold into her hug, but instead, steps away walking out of her lap. They stay connected by holding hands. Mom holds and firmly rubs his fingers, as Josh walks further and further away, until their arms are stretched out as far they can extend.

The famous Michelangelo painting (*The Creation of Adam*), two fingers almost touching, arises in my mind. How can I help this couple come together? I ask myself. I note the quality of their lingering fingers, and Mom's firm hold before they separated and feel a sense of calm encouragement. I remark out loud again to Josh, poised quietly alone a few feet from Mom, "You found Mommy, you did." A warm smile emerges across his face and he circles around back to Mom, tapping her back. We continue to play variations of this game, coming to and going away from Mommy. Always culminating with a warm embrace, and this time Josh cuddles into Mom as they gaze into each other's eyes. As Josh molds his body into Mom I cover them both with a soft sheer large blue scarf. I pause this moment for Mom and baby to frame it for them both; and to give them a sense of privacy. I want Mom to experience her baby's love, as he settles into her arms, and Josh to feel the safety and undivided attention of Mom. Images of a precious womb containing them both, comes to mind. A warmth spreads inside of me, feeling honored to be witness to their intimate reunion.

Case Report 3.1 is reproduced with the author's permission.

[1]Suzi Tortora, EdD, ADTR, CMA, LCAT, LMHC, is a dance movement psychotherapist with over 23 years experience working with individuals of all ages.

Psychophysiology of Self-Awareness

Like the other cases reported in this book, this case follows the basic steps of regaining embodied self-awareness listed in Table 1.1.

- *Resources* were found in the therapist's guiding presence and in the props she used (physio-ball, scarf).
- *Slowing down* occurred in this case for the therapist as she stopped herself from putting Josh into his mother's arms, affirming instead Josh's incipient feelings of longing to be with his mother and his inability to find a way to do that in his still unformed body schema.
- *Coregulation* occurred in the dialogue of touch and talk between Josh, his mother, and the therapist.
- *Verbalization* was salient because Josh could not voice his desires even though he likely had enough linguistic skill to do so. Instead, he resorted to grunts and moans which the therapist translated into words for him (and for his mother).
- *Links and boundaries* are the salient feature of this case report. The emotional importance of the at-first unbreachable distance between mother and baby, followed by the therapist-facilitated emergence of increasingly closer and more intimate contact. The session begins with rigid boundaries and ends with linkages that accentuate a more permeable boundary giving opportunities for both closeness and separation.
- *Self-regulation* began as soon as Josh smiled, realizing that he could indeed approach and withdraw as needed, that his mother welcomed him when he came, that he could mobilize his body schema to move and to find postures of connection. There was also a dyadic regulation, as mother began to understand her child's needs for approach and withdrawal, and as she found ways to show her own needs and feelings to her child.
- *Reengagement* had begun, clearly, by the end of the session. One can imagine that this opening of the body schema in both mother and child will lead to opportunities to share and play together as well as to establish a more secure attachment relationship.
- *Letting go* did not completely occur in this single session, but it did seem that the pain Josh had suffered from his inability to approach his mother and to feel welcomed by her was already on the mend.

Variations in the Body Schema

The case of Josh and his mother illustrates how body schema impairment (the closed postures of the mother and the rigid and helpless postures of the baby) can lead to emotional difficulties in close relationships with other people. Impairment of the body schema can also influence relationships within the self and between the self and environment. Oliver Sacks, the popular neurologist, has written a great deal about alterations of the sense of the body and self under extremely devastating conditions of neurological disorder. One of his first books, *A Leg to Stand On* (1990), however, was about a leg injury he suffered while hiking in the pristine mountains above Hardanger Fjørd in Norway. An accidental fall tore part of his quadriceps muscle. He managed to drag himself painfully down the mountain until he found a person who could seek help.

He only became aware of a change in his body schema once he became a patient in a local hospital, which for a doctor was a radical shift of perspective. His biggest surprise, however, came after the surgery to repair the torn muscles. Like the author in the opening quote, his leg muscles no longer responded to the will to move.

> What I did *not* expect, and what struck me as exceedingly strange and disquieting, was to find the muscle completely limp—most horribly and unnaturally limp—in a way one would never find with disuse alone. . . . I had a qualm of absolute horror, and shuddered; and then the emotion was immediately repressed or suppressed. (Sachs, 1990, p. 54)

We can assume that the horror was a spontaneous and emergent emotion as Sacks connected—in the subjective emotional present of embodied self-awareness—his change in body schema to his interoceptive self-awareness. He graciously admits to us that he could not stay in that emotional present: the horror was too disturbing. It is much easier to shift into conceptual self-awareness. If people fill up their awareness with thoughts of trying to understand or explain why the muscle is limp, or with thoughts like, "It will get better soon," or "I'll ask the doctors," they no longer have to face the pain and horror head-on.

Psychophysiology of Self-Awareness

Shifts in body schema can come about in many different ways. Those with **dysmorphophobia** (*dys*=disturbance, *morph*=form, *phobia*=fear) become obsessed with real or imagined physical flaws like the size or shape of their nose, breast, or penis. These individuals often seek surgical correction or suffer from self-inflicted injuries against the offending part. In milder forms, this, along with cultural proscriptions for body size, shape, and appearance, keeps alive a large industry of cosmetic surgery and treatments to enhance the "beauty" of skin, hair, and nails. Of course, what counts as beautiful varies between cultures.

In certain psychiatric illnesses there is a distortion of both interoception and body schema. In depression, for example, the person interoceptively experiences the body as heavy (a lump in the throat, immobility), rigid (tension in the chest). Even simple actions may feel as if they take great effort which seems so big that the person simply gives up. Appetites and desires are lost. In the realm of the body schema, the person's body becomes a prison from which there is no escape. In some cases, severe depression may transform into **depersonalization syndrome**, a feeling of living outside one's body and outside the world. Nothing seems real, everything feels empty and bleak (Fuchs, 2005).

People with spinal cord damage (paraplegics or quadriplegics) report a loss of both feeling and a sense of ownership of the paralyzed limbs. Robert Murphy was an anthropology professor who suffered from a tumor of the spinal cord that left him paralyzed. He details the growing loss of feeling and the changes of his sense of himself as he became confined to a wheelchair and subjected to being lifted and moved around by other people. He reports that one of his coping strategies was a "radical dissociation from the body, a kind of etherealization of identity" (Murphy, 1990, p. 101), and that he became "rather emotionally detached from my body, often referring to one of my limbs as the leg or the arm" (p. 100).

The Neurophysiology of Body Schema Awareness

One of the clever ways in which the neurophysiology of the body schema has been studied is by creating experiments in which the sensation of body ownership or nonownership is manipulated via an illusion. In one type of study, for example, researchers had participants place one of their hands under a table while the other hand was placed on the table. Standing in for their real hand under the table, the researchers placed a rubber hand that was oriented the same way, and with the thumb on the same side, as their hand under the table.

The experiment takes advantage of the fact that sense of body schema is an integration between at least two different sensory modalities: in this case, proprioception and vision (Graziano, 1999). **Proprioception** is the felt sense of the location and relative position of different parts of the body in relation to objects and to individuals. Proprioception relies on **proprioceptors** at the periphery of the body: the sense of touch, the sense of muscle and tendon stretch, and the sense of balance in the middle ear. Synchronizing the stroking, with a small brush, of the rubber hand *in view* on the table and the subject's own hand (*out of view*, under the table) leads to the felt sensation that the subject's own hand is in fact receiving the touch from the brush.

In the experiment, the rubber hand was oriented at 0, 90, and 180 degrees to the subject's own (hidden) hand, and the brush strokes on the rubber and subject's hand were either in or out of synchrony. The illusion of ownership of the rubber hand occurs only in the case when the rubber hand is oriented in the same direction as the subject's (0 degree) and the brush strokes are in synchrony between the real hand and rubber hand. Setting up the other experimental conditions allows the researchers to compare brain activation in situations when the postural and visual situation is roughly the same but differs with respect to whether or not the condition is illusory or nonillusory.

In the synchronous condition (in which people perceive the illusion of ownership), the proprioceptive pathways from touch receptors in the skin match the visual information of the rubber hand being oriented in the same direction as the real hand. This means that the sense of body ownership (this hand belongs to me) is due to the integration of synchronously timed inputs to the brain across these two sensory modalities.

Studies using the rubber hand illusion have found that this intersensory integration, and therefore the sense of body ownership, occurs in a neural network that includes the premotor area of the motor cortex, the posterior (toward the top of the head) parietal cortex, the **somatosensory cortex** (SS), along with the ventrolateral (VL) thalamus, the brain stem, and cerebellum motor regulation areas (Ehrsson, Holmes, & Passingham, 2005; Graziano, 1999; see Figures 2.4–2.7). This network is the same even when the hand is moved to a different location, suggesting that the network registers ownership in a body-centered frame of reference. A similar network is also activated when participants experienced an illusion that their waist was shrinking, which was created by wearing a vibrating belt (Ehrsson, Kito et al., 2005).

This is a different neural network from the one responsible for interoceptive self-awareness (see Figure 3.1). Aside from involving different brain regions, the proprioceptive regions have a different cellular structure and links to the rest of the body than those in the interoceptive system. The motor and SS cortex, as well as the cerebellum and brain stem motor areas are organized somatotopically. **Somatotopic organization** means that specific cells in those areas are linked to specific groups of muscles. There are a series of representational maps in the brain, in other words, that directly link to and correspond to specific muscles in the body.

These brain regions have neural connections to the proprioceptors that sense muscle and tendon stretch and also to the motor neurons that activate the muscles. The somatotopic representation of the muscles of the arm and hand in the motor cortex, for example, is located next to the somatotopic representation of the muscles of the neck and upper chest.

In one case study, an amputee learned to move a prosthetic hand and arm by being trained to activate the efferent nerves of the muscles of the neck and chest which stimulated electrical sensors that were linked to the motor gears of the prosthesis (Kuikan et al., 2007). This and other research has revealed that the somatotopic organization of the brain is plastic. In neuroscience, **plasticity** refers to the ability of the brain to develop new experience dependent pathways in the case of impairment or damage. The somatotopic brain cells that were formerly devoted entirely to sensing and moving the neck and chest, in the case of the amputee, began to take over the functions of the adjacent "arm" cells, appropriating some of those cells for the job of moving the prosthetic arm via the neck and chest muscles.

One advantage of somatotopy is that links between area-specific cells can lead to a sense of the cohesiveness of the body, the connection between one body part and another, which is also part of the body schema. The ability to hold a piece of paper in place on a desk with one hand, and to write on that paper with the other hand, requires this sense of body cohesiveness. Virtually all motor skills, in addition to needing to relate to environmental conditions, require a coordinated relationship between different parts of the body. The importance of interbody and body–other relationships in the formation of the body schema was also seen in the case of Josh and his mother (Case Report 3.1).

Acquiring body schema awareness begins prenatally via a spontaneous motor discharge, twitching. Twitching continues to occur throughout life and seems to serve a similar function of helping one body part "find" another (see Box 3.2).

BOX 3.2
Twitching: Initial Integration of the Body Schema

Most vertebrates during the prenatal and newborn period show spontaneous muscle contractions called myoclonic twitches (myo=muscle, clonus=contraction). Fetal twitches create electrical and chemical discharges in the not-yet-innervated peripheral muscles. These discharges help the nerves growing from the brain stem and spinal cord to find their targets in the muscle proprioceptors and motor neurons, linking brain and body. Once the neural connections are made, twitching continues to help calibrate the body schema by detecting limb weight and distance from other parts of the body (Khazipov et al., 2004; Petersson, Waidenstrom, Fahraens, & Schauenborg, 2003).

These twitches tend to occur when the fetus or newborn is in a completely relaxed state during sleep. They are often synchronized across different body regions so that an arm and a leg may twitch at the same time. Twitching appears to be generated by different regions of the spinal cord, brain stem, and brain working in synchrony. This synchrony between different parts of the nervous system and different parts of the body may be a built-in process that allows one's body schema to develop via somatotopic experience dependent connections. Twitching can induce activation in the SS and motor cortices in the somatotopic areas where the moving body part is represented (Kohyama & Iwakada, 1991).

continued

> **BOX 3.2** (continued)
>
> After the newborn period, twitches decrease in frequency because voluntary motor exploration of the world during waking states plays an increasingly important role in the body schema formation. If infants have brain stem immaturity, however, twitching will continue for several months longer, apparently allowing the infant to use the built-in spontaneous movements to catch up from any delays in voluntary movement control (Kohyama & Iwakawa, 1991). Twitching, in other words, seems to be an essential mechanism to start the development of neuromotor links that introduce one body part to another and serve to integrate the body schema.
>
> Is twitching important for older infants, children, and adults? Typically, twitching after the newborn period is inhibited by centers in the brain and brain stem because it can interfere with experience dependent learning from normal, and preferred, voluntary movement. When there is brain damage, however, twitching may be one of the symptoms observed. On the other hand, if there is damage to the peripheral nervous system, electromagnetic stimulation to the peripheral nerve to induce twitching has been used as a treatment to assist the cortex to find, remap, and thus reintegrate, the body (Turton, McCabe, Harris, & Filipovic, 2007).
>
> One patient described in the literature had lost sensations of touch and muscular proprioception due to damage in the brain from a viral infection. Stimulating a twitch in the patient's forefinger allowed him to eventually move the finger voluntarily (Cole & Paillard, 1998). In normally functioning adults, active sleep, which includes rapid eye movements and occasional twitches, is responsible for "physiological restoration" and integration across neural circuits (Blumberg & Lucas, 1996).
>
> I have observed twitching in some of my clients during Rosen Method Bodywork sessions. These clients in particular report that they have little felt awareness of particular parts of their bodies. Chronic
>
> *continued*

> **BOX 3.2** (continued)
>
> tension in those muscles damp sensation from the proprioceptors so that the person may not be able to feel my hand touching their upper back or their legs. These impairments in the body schema often result from prior trauma leading to the muscle tension (habitual defensive postures) and thus a suppression of self-awareness.
>
> As their muscles begin to relax during treatment and as they report increasing awareness of those "missing" body regions, they sometimes twitch involuntarily. This does not appear to be a random discharge since, at least in my experience, it only occurs as the body is shifting to a relatively novel (for that client) state of relaxation and as awareness is increasing.
>
> My guess is that the neural pathways normally responsible for proprioception, having been neglected from disuse, are once again sending signals out to other parts of the body to help "find" the lost connections. Reconstruction of the body schema following disorders of embodied self-awareness, then, may reactivate the same spontaneous prenatal and neonatal nervous discharges that were used to construct the body schema in the first place. Embodied interventions work best when they can activate the body's own intrinsic neuromotor growth processes.

By the 7th prenatal month, as involuntary twitching is replaced by more voluntary movements, fetuses can find their hand in relation to their mouth (see Figure 1.1). This early learning of the body schema is made possible by the specific neuroanatomy of proprioception. The nerves from the spinal cord to the proprioceptors for stretch and to the spinal cord from the motor neurons used to activate muscle contractions—compared to the small, slow and unmyelinated interoceptive neurons—are fast, large, and myelinated. This means that it is easier and quicker to tell whether something is part of the self or not, and to sense the links between one part of the self and another, than to detect the interoceptive sensations related to that body part.

Another difference between proprioceptive and interoceptive networks is that they travel through different spinal cord pathways. The interoceptive

Psychophysiology of Self-Awareness

pathways are in the dorsal horn of the spinal cord while the proprioceptive pathways are in the ventral horn of the spinal cord (see Figure 2.2). Thus, the entire network for sensing the body schema, including brain and body receptors and pathways, is anatomically different from that involved in interoception. This difference is summarized in Figure 3.1.

Figure 3.1

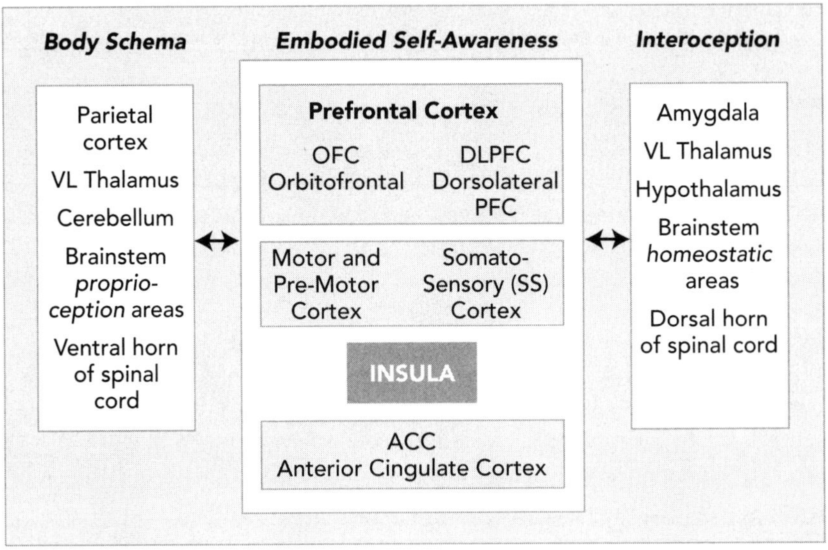

Body Schema	Embodied Self-Awareness	Interoception
Parietal cortex VL Thalamus Cerebellum Brainstem *proprioception* areas Ventral horn of spinal cord	**Prefrontal Cortex** OFC — Orbitofrontal	DLPFC — Dorsolateral PFC Motor and Pre-Motor Cortex	Somato-Sensory (SS) Cortex **INSULA** ACC Anterior Cingulate Cortex	Amygdala VL Thalamus Hypothalamus Brainstem *homeostatic* areas Dorsal horn of spinal cord

Links and differences between interoceptive and body schematic embodied self-awareness (VL=ventrolateral, PFC=prefrontal cortex, OFC=orbitofrontal cortex, ACC=anterior cingulate cortex)

The proprioception network becomes activated when research participants are asked to identify the boundaries of the body, by noticing visually and by touch when their body makes contact with an object. This also means that the sense of body ownership is relational, the stimulating object is perceived as being *nonbody* (Ehrsson, Spence, & Passingham, 2005). The physical object itself becomes part of embodied self-awareness in several ways. First, the object is perceived as "not-me," meaning that its existence in awareness depends crucially on the fact that it does not belong to the person. Additionally, the object takes on a purpose or a reason to exist because it is sensed in embodied self-awareness in relation to the body schema and the body's emotional goals and actions (Gallese, 2000).

When someone strokes the newborn's cheek near the mouth, the baby will turn to the side where the touch was felt. This is called the rooting reflex and is believed to assist the newborn in finding the nipple. Researchers made videos of infants while being touched on the cheek by an adult, and compared them to videos of times when the infant's own hand moved across the face and touched the cheek. The babies only rooted when touched by another person (Rochat & Hespos, 1997).

By 4 months, infants prefer to look at a video image, taken from above, or their own legs but with the left and right leg reversed, compared to a video image of their own legs in the usual position, showing that they noticed the discrepancy (Morgan & Rochat, 1997). Before infants learn to reach and grasp objects, around the age of 4 months, they often swipe toward an object unsuccessfully. Electromyographic recordings of specific muscle movements showed that in the weeks before they learned to reach, infants used primarily their biceps and triceps (upper arms) while after learning to reach they also included their trapezius and deltoid muscles of the upper back. Infants who can reach also show the ability to change their posture to lean toward the object and compensate for gravity (Rochat, Goubet, & Senders, 1999; Savelsbergh & van der Kamp, 1994; Spencer & Thelen, 2000). This shows that the babies have developed a more complete sense of their body schema in relation to the objects in space. As babies learn to crawl and walk later in the first year, similar alterations of whole-body patterns of movement coordination are observed (Adolph, Vereijken, & Denny, 1998; Ledebt, 2000).

Integration of Interoception, Emotion and Body Schema in Embodied Self-Awareness

Body schema self-awareness is rarely felt on its own. Typically, it is accompanied by an emotional component; what the person wants or needs to do. In Case Report 3.1, Josh's initial inability to mold to the physio-ball, and the rigidity of his body as he tried to reach for his mother was linked to his sense of sadness and helplessness when it came to satisfying his needs for closeness to Mom.

Psychophysiology of Self-Awareness

The location of my arm at a particular moment does not attract my attention unless I need my arm for some purpose: to get a drink, scratch an itch, or whatever. The body schema neural network, like the interoceptive neural network, links up with the anterior cingulate cortex (ACC), orbitofrontal cortex (OFC), and dorsolateral prefrontal cortex (DLPFC) (see Chapter 2) for the purpose of enlivening the body location and boundary information with some kind of emotional color.

One of the ways in which the neurophysiology of the emotional aspects of the body schema has been studied is through the experimental application of pain. Perception of pain in particular parts of the body integrates interoception, emotion, and body schema because pain perception can be divided into *attention to location* (body schema) and *attention to unpleasantness* (interoception).

In one study, subjects experienced laser-induced painful vs. nonpainful stimulation to the back of the hand. The control condition of a nonpainful laser stimulation was necessary to factor out the effects of the tactile sensation per se. When asked to attend to the *location of the pain*, there was activation in the somatosensory (SS) and parietal cortices; that is, areas in the body schema neural network (Figure 3.1). When subjects were asked instead to *attend to the unpleasantness*, there was additional activation in the ACC, OFC, amygdala, hypothalamus, and posterior insula: the interoceptive network (Kulkami et al., 2005).

A similar type of study has been done using the rubber hand illusion. When there is a painful stimulus (a needle) observed approaching the rubber hand, there is activity in both the interoceptive network and the body schema network, but only in the synchronous condition when the rubber hand is oriented in the direction of real hand (Lloyd, Morrison, & Roberts, 2006). The stronger the feeling of ownership of the rubber hand, as judged by self-report, the stronger the sense of threat and corresponding activation of the ACC and insula (Ehrsson, Wiech, Weiskopf, Dolan, & Passingham, 2007).

Pain integrates location (body schema), an interoceptively felt sensation (burning, sharpness), and a motivational–emotional component (withdrawal, escape, fear). This accounts for the sense that the pain is penetrating the body at a particular location along with a sense of what needs to be done to stop or avoid it. Linking the body schema network with the emotional and interoceptive networks, in other words, gives the homeostatic regulatory system more versatility. This could mean moving a specific body part away from something hot, squeezing and compressing a particular area that has been struck or stung, running away from (flight *away* rather than *toward* the source of pain), or attempting to resist (fight) against the source of the pain.

We can assume that any activation of this complex network will coactivate all the other parts of it in some way. Under some conditions, I may primarily be aware of interoception, or of emotion, or of my body schema. Hearing of a loved one's death, I may feel the emotion of grief as the primary experience, while my body goes numb (with interoception in the background) and I lose any sense of where I am at that moment (with body schema in the background). I may even collapse, losing control of my body schema's ability to maintain an upright posture. This was similar to Josh's posturing and movement patterns at the beginning of the session described in Case Report 3.1

I could, alternatively, be skiing down a mountain, noticing primarily my balance and direction (body schema) and my excitement (emotion) but completely unaware of my muscle pain, fatigue, and sense of feeling cold (interoception in the background). Or all three aspects of embodied self-awareness may be active, as during an especially rewarding musical performance, when my body movements in relation to the instrument (body schema), emotion (awesome!), and interoception (the feeling of a deep resonance between myself and the instrument and the audience, like a swelling or enlarging of my being, and a pervasive warmth) all unite in a transformational experience of being fully in the present, fully embodied, and fully connected to self and others.

Impairment in Body Schema Awareness Occurring with Brain Lesions Shows Links to Specific Brain Networks

The field of neurology is filled with cases of disturbances in body schema as a result of brain damage. These cases are poignant because of the resulting inabilities of the person to feel themselves as a complete individual. Most of the impairments of the body schema result from lesions in the parietal and premotor cortices, the areas responsible for integrating the information from proprioception and other senses, like vision, into a coherent sense of the relationship among parts of the body and of the body in space.

Psychophysiology of Self-Awareness

People with right posterior parietal lesions may not be able to identify their limbs as part of their self. Some individuals have feelings of hatred for body parts and may try to push the disowned limb out of bed, a condition called **misoplegia** (*miso*=hatred, *plegia*=paralysis) (Pearce, 2007). Some patients report extra hands and feet that do not belong to them (Berlucchi & Aglioti, 1997). Lesions of the right posterior parietal and of the right posterior insula produce **anosognosia** (*a*=without, *nosos*=disease, *gnosis*=knowledge). These individuals may have severe motor deficits, paralysis, or even blindness from their stroke but they deny the existence of the condition (Baier & Karnath, 2008). Patients with paralysis and an awareness of that paralysis have intact insulas. This suggests that the insula, in connection with the parietal cortex, provides a sense of agency about one's own movements, that is, one feels that he or she is the author of those movements (Farrer & Firth, 2002; Karnath, Baier, & Nagele, 2005).

Asomatognosia (*somato*=body) is when parts of the body are reported as missing or have disappeared from awareness and a lack of feeling that a part of the body belongs to the self. This is associated with damage to the right posterior parietal and the right premotor cortex (Arzy, Overney, Landis, & Blanke, 2006). **Somatoparaphrenia** (*para*=beside, *phrenia*=mental disorder) is denial of ownership of a body part, as if it belonged to someone else or that someone else left it behind, is also associated with parietal lesions.

A 73-year-old woman with a large right hemisphere stroke that included the parietal lobe was unaware of her left arm paralysis and believed her left hand belonged to someone else. She could see and identify the rings on her hand that she had worn for years, but denied ownership of the hand and rings. When the rings were on her right hand, she saw them as her own. There was a memory of her left hand and its rings but that memory was no longer associated with self-awareness (Berlucchi & Aglioti, 1997).

Schizophrenics who report being controlled by an alien agent, or god, have a dysfunction in the right parietal lobe and posterior insula. Because these areas are connected to visual and auditory portions of the SS cortex, abnormal insula activity may lead to the creation of sensory hallucinations. People with schizophrenia may become convinced that their hands are not theirs and that those hands need to be watched and cannot be trusted. Some patients report a sense of alienation and a loss of body ownership. This often leads to a deliberately calculating style, where every move is watched and studied. One patient reported that, "When I am looking into a mirror, I do not know any more

Locating Ourselves

whether I am here looking at me there in the mirror, or whether I am there in the mirror looking at me here" (Fuchs, 2005, p. 104).

Out of body experiences (OBE), imagining the self from a distant location, are associated with disturbances of the posterior parietal lobe (Blanke et al., 2005). In the normal self-awareness of the body schema, the sense of location of the body is coupled with the sense of perceiving the world from inside that same body. In OBEs, the sense of the unity of the body and self is changed because the self is not experienced as located within the body. It is often the case that the self seems located in another body, one's own, hovering over the physical body.

Many amputees have so-called "phantom limbs," the very real sense that their limb is still attached and that it belongs to them. There can also be phantoms from missing jaws, breasts, and penises. Phantom sensations include interoceptive touch and pain, and proprioceptive feelings of movement. This is not due to stimulation of sensory nerves in the scar, but has a central origin: the persistent coactivity of the neural network of the SS cortex, parietal cortex, ACC, and insula (Berlucchi & Aglioti, 1997).

This shows the importance of a complex neural network and that this network attributes—based on prior experience dependent learning when the limb was still attached—its own self-generated activity (rerepresentations) to the missing body part (Berlucchi & Aglioti, 1997). Phantom limb sensations, however, are reduced if the unfortunate individual has, in addition, posterior parietal lesions. Apparently even phantom limbs require the parietal cortex to maintain their existence in embodied self-awareness. Under certain conditions, new experience dependent pathways can be learned that eliminate phantom limb sensations (see Box 3.3).

BOX 3.3
Amputating a Phantom Limb

The neurologist V. S. Ramachandran devised a simple procedure for treating phantom limb sensations. The procedure relies on a similar strategy as the rubber hand illusion, the association between vision and

continued

> **BOX 3.3** (continued)
>
> proprioception. Amputees saw a reflection of their existing limb in a mirror. The mirror was oriented so that the actual limb appeared to be in the place where the missing limb was located. The visual sensations interacted with the proprioceptive neural network, so the people felt a touch on the existing limb as if it came from the missing one. Therapeutically, this method also reduced phantom pain (Ramachandran & Blakeslee, 1999).
>
> The first patient that Ramachandran treated with this device had complained of pain in the phantom limb and also that he could not "move" it. When "Philip" saw his reflected limb in the place of the phantom, he was elated and said, "My left arm is plugged in again. It's as if I'm in the past. All these movements from many years ago are flooding back into my mind. I can move my arm again. I can feel my elbow moving, my wrist moving" (Ramachandran & Blakeslee, 1998, p. 48). When Philip closed his eyes or looked away, he could not feel the phantom limb move.
>
> Ramachandran suggested that Philip take the device with him and practice at home, hoping Philip would get to a point where he could feel the phantom without looking, but something else happened instead. One day, the phantom simply disappeared and took the pain with it. Ramachandran reports that he "realized that this was probably the first example in medical history of a successful 'amputation' of a phantom limb!" (p. 49). Philip's brain, in trying to connect with the missing limb, eventually decided that it was not there after all and created a new somatotopic map of the body, creating a body schema without the missing limb.

Box 3.3 shows that the emotional connection between the person and the missing limb was a crucial part in the treatment of phantom limb pain. This emphasizes the links shown in Figure 3.1, between the sense of location and boundaries and the sense of an emotional connection to the body and its relation to other bodies.

The Neurophysiological Links between Conceptual and Embodied Self-Awareness

Now that we have covered the entire neural network of embodied self-awareness including proprioception, interoception, and emotion, we can return to the topic of conceptual vs. embodied self-awareness and understand the differences from a physiological perspective. Suppose that you feel a pain in your right knee as you are walking. Your brain "knows" that this needs your attention because you have to make the choice to continue walking or to stop. All the limbic homeostatic areas can do on their own, without self-awareness, is perhaps supply more blood to the area or change your respiration, allowing you to "breathe through" the pain. If you become interoceptively aware of the pain, you may also access conceptual self-awareness to make a decision to stop walking. You sit down and start to move your knee, feeling what actions make it hurt and which ones do not, maybe rubbing the knee in the spot where the pain is felt.

This ability to access the feelings of pain in embodied self-awareness, alternating with the ability to conceptually think about the options to relieve the pain or seek help, are made possible when a different part of the PFC enters the self-awareness network, the medial prefrontal cortex (MPFC). The MPFC is divided into ventral (toward the face/neck) and dorsal (toward the top of the head) portions (see Figures 2.6 and 2.7). The ability to conceptually reflect on, interpret, judge and make a decision about an embodied sensation occurs when the **dorsomedial PFC (DMPFC)** is activated along with the interoceptive and body schema neural networks. The DMPFC works together with the thought and language areas of the brain "above" it, and with the embodied self-awareness areas "below" it (see Figure 3.2) to create conceptual self-awareness about the body and conceptually-mediated decision making.

Psychophysiology of Self-Awareness

Figure 3.2

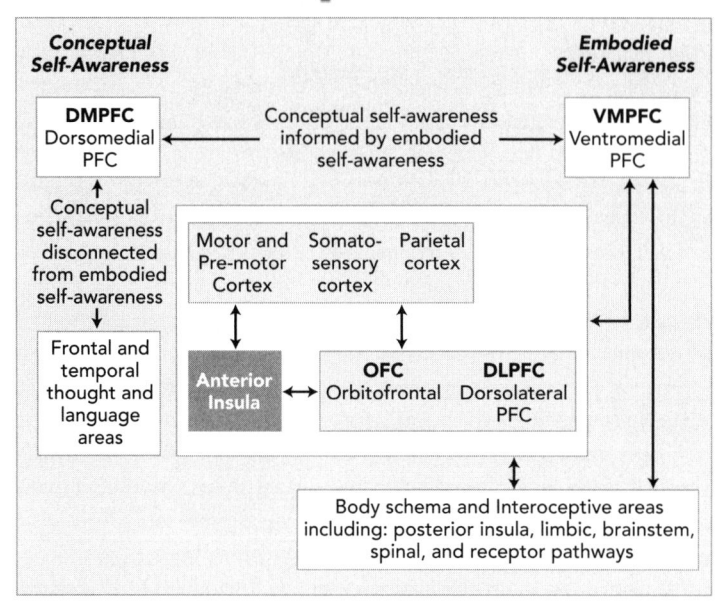

Conceptual Self-Awareness		Embodied Self-Awareness
DMPFC Dorsomedial PFC ←	Conceptual self-awareness informed by embodied self-awareness →	**VMPFC** Ventromedial PFC

Conceptual self-awareness disconnected from embodied self-awareness

- Motor and Pre-motor Cortex
- Somato-sensory cortex
- Parietal cortex

- Frontal and temporal thought and language areas
- **Anterior Insula** ↔ **OFC** Orbitofrontal
- **DLPFC** Dorsolateral PFC

Body schema and Interoceptive areas including: posterior insula, limbic, brainstem, spinal, and receptor pathways

Different neural networks for conceptual and embodied self-awareness (VM=ventromedial, DM=dorsomedial, PFC=prefrontal cortex, DL=dorsolateral, OFC=orbitofrontal cortex.)

The DMPFC is activated when research subjects are asked to describe themselves in words or to endorse a verbal/conceptual description about themselves given to them by the experimenter, such as, "I forget important things," or "I'm a good friend." In these studies, other coactivated areas include the ACC and the posterior parietal lobe (M. K. Johnson, Raye, 2006; S. C. Johnson, Baxter et al., 2002; Kelley et al., 2002; Moran, Macrae, Heatherton, Wyland, & Kelley, 2006; Northoff & Bermpohl, 2004). The DMPFC is active when people monitor their own self-generated thoughts, or what they intend to say, or when they are thinking about a past emotional state (rather than directly experiencing the emotion). The DMPFC, then, is related to thinking and making decisions specifically about one's own thoughts and to thoughts about one's own feelings.

In neuroimaging studies, the DMPFC has been observed to be continuously active during waking states. This has led some neuroscientists to speculate that the DMPFC may be involved in the stream of thought that most people have running in their heads most of the time (Gusnard, Akbudak, Shulman, & Raichle, 2001). This running internal monologue is extremely useful and important for what it means to be human. It helps keep the brain active, to rehearse future action, to spontaneously generate ideas that guide the person's future, and to make self-relevant decisions. I get a lot of ideas for writing when I'm not directly involved in writing. This happens, for example, at the end of the day when I go for a walk or swim. I'm not paying direct attention to my body at these moments. I am occupied with thoughts about myself, revisiting my progress in writing earlier, and hopefully deciding about future plans.

The running stream of thought is also clinically valuable. While thinking precludes feeling in embodied self-awareness, the neuroanatomy in Figure 3.2 shows that thinking is directly linked to the interoceptive and body schema neural networks. *Just as emotions of which we are not aware can show up in our actions and expressions, thoughts may reveal embodied experiences of which we may not be aware.* Doug's thoughts about his business partner, Jack, in Case Report 2.1 (Jack takes advantage of me, I am always giving in to Jack) were ultimately related to a sense of unfelt anger which later become part of embodied self-awareness.

The client's verbalizations of his or her thoughts in embodied self-awareness treatments can be clues to find openings into embodied self-awareness. *Verbalized thoughts that reflect judgments and evaluations of others generally reflect feelings of longing, fear, anger, abandonment, or other interpersonal emotions that have not yet been brought into the client's embodied self-awareness.* It is also worth noting that the decisions one makes from the perspective of a disembodied conceptual self-awareness are not always in one's best interest. Once Doug became aware of his anger, he was less likely to decide to act simply in order to please someone else. *Conceptual self-awareness informed by embodied self-awareness is the best source for making decisions beneficial to both self and others.*

Thus, the thoughts in the neural network involving the DMPFC region are linked to our socially regulated and constructed autobiographical narratives, the stories by which we describe ourselves to other people. As you are sitting there and reflecting on your hurt knee, you are not only deciding what to do next, but you may also be rehearsing what to say to your friends or to your doctors. Damage to the DMPFC results in a lack of self-reflection and introspection (Wheeler, Stuss, & Tulving, 1997).

The partner of the DMPFC in the MPFC is the **ventromedial prefrontal cortex (VMPFC)**. Anatomically adjacent to the DMPFC, the VMPFC also helps with decision making but in a radically different way. The decisions that the VMPFC facilitates are on-line; they occur when one is in the subjective emotional present. This might be a decision to stop walking because the pain is too intense, a decision made prior to any thought about the pain. As shown in Figure 3.2, the VMPFC is part of a neural network that includes the prefrontal and cortex areas related to embodied self-awareness, including direct links to the body via the interoceptive and body schema neural networks that extend out to the periphery of the body (Gusnard et al., 2001; Moran et al., 2006).

In one research study, subjects were asked to imagine an emotional situation, such as, "Imagine that someone tells you that one of your friends died in a car accident." Then the subjects were given sentences that reflect possible emotional reactions and asked to imagine that these were their own thoughts and feelings. Some sentences described a spontaneous emotional experience, such as, "Everything collapses around me." In this condition, the VMPFC showed the most activity.

In another experimental condition, the same subjects were asked to evaluate or think about the situation of their friend's death, such as "Is this situation important for me?" In this case, activity in the VMPFC activity was suppressed and activity in the adjacent DMPFC was activated (Schaefer et al., 2003). In general, if attention is directed toward thought and away from emotion, the DMPFC is more likely to be activated (Gusnard et al., 2001). Put another way, the DMPFC is related to *judgments* about the self while the VMPFC is related to *choices* about how to experience the self (Banfield, Wyland, MacRae, Münte, & Heatherton. 2007; Bar-on, Tranel, Denburg, & Bechara, 2003; Damasio, 1996).

Activation in the MPFC is like a switch: it is either ventral or dorsal but not both. In Chapter 2, we described this kind of on-off, either-or process in the brain as a nonlinear transition. **Nonlinear transitions** occur when there is an abrupt shift from one state to another rather than a smooth transition. If you are pouring water from one container into another, the water gradually empties out of the one and into the other. This is a smooth, linear change of location of the water. Imagine, instead, that the water suddenly jumps from one container to the other without any noticeable time spent in pouring.

This is impossible for moving water but the analogy to the brain shows how radical the shift between VMPFC and DMPFC, and between embodied and conceptual self-awareness, can be. Like water, the flows of energy across the neural networks have a fluid quality. As a psychologically experienced entity, awareness can feel very substantial, the very substance of our existence. Yet unlike water, the fluid of neural network activity does not have mass. It is in a sense, insubstantial as a physical entity.

Any way you want to look at it, the fact is that we cannot be in conceptual and embodied states of self-awareness at the same time. The dorsal–ventral movement of activation in the MPFC is the neural switch that activates one, or another, neural network for self-awareness. Although you cannot have both forms of self-awareness at the same time, you can under certain circumstances, self-regulate the switch. Thoughts, judgments, and decisions about the self (DMPFC) might be instantly "checked" or "verified" for their interoceptive and proprioceptive accuracy by switching over to the VMPFC (see Figure 3.2). The VMPFC-guided embodied self-awareness can also change thought patterns that do not fit with the data of felt embodied experience. In addition, the VMPFC can help with embodied decision making, such as choosing to direct one's awareness to the specific body schema location of the unease or pain (Schooler, 2002).

Coming back to the example of feeling a pain in the knee while walking, sitting down in order to move, sense, feel, and make choices about that activity partakes of this network that may include both the DMPFC and the VMPFC. While you are doing this self-examination of your injury with awareness and presence, you can allow yourself some conceptual thoughts (switching over the DMPFC network) like, "Maybe I should rest here a while," or "It must be my old injury here acting up again," or even "I'm really hurt and I don't know what to do." Yet, you can continue to verify the veracity of those conceptual judgments by "checking in" with your embodied self-awareness using the VMPFC network. Coming back across to the conceptual side, you might now think, "OK, it's not as bad as I thought and I'll try to stand and walk back home," or "It's worse than I thought and I better locate my cell phone and call for help."

In this way, your can mobilize all of your body's impressive resources for self-awareness and harness them for the purpose of making decisions that affect the safety and health of your body. In the same manner, getting in touch in embodied self-awareness with a persistent pain, or the grief of a loss, or the previously suppressed anger at a business partner or boss, can mobilize the body's regulatory and healing processes—including our conceptual powers to make sweeping changes in our lives.

Thoughts can be generated to bring us back to embodied self-awareness. We can ask ourselves to slow down and feel, to rest, to nourish ourselves, to drink fluids. Actions can be planned in thought that mobilize the body to act in its own best interest: "If I feel uneasy, I can go talk to someone who will listen," "If my back is hurting while I'm sitting, I can shift my position in the chair to become more comfortable."

If the back hurts there are limits to what the autonomic homeostatic mechanisms can do without self-awareness and if we rely entirely on them we will eventually overtax and potentially damage the cellular pathways that make the autonomic system work in the first place. This failure or inability to consult our embodied self-awareness is one of the pathways for the emergence of physical disease in the body. It is essential, then, for us to be sufficiently aware of our bodies to remind ourselves to change postures when we hurt, to eat when hungry, or to rest when tired. It is much easier for homeostatic and immune systems to tackle their more-or-less automated jobs of cell repair and rejuvenation if we take an active role in assisting them to do that.

The longer we stay in thought, the more difficult it becomes to shift back over to the direct experiencing of the subjective emotional present. How does this happen? **Experience dependent brain development** allows your awareness to "get used to" thinking and not feeling and it does not take too long for there to be a perceived barrier to coming back to embodied self-awareness. Your conceptual self-awareness will make up a convenient autobiographical narrative, a just-so story, in which you become convinced that thinking is enough to hold it together ("I don't have time to just sit," or "Leave me alone, I can manage on my own," or "I know what I'm doing"). Thought regulation becomes substituted in awareness for embodied self-regulation. These thoughts get compounded with the imagined dangers of crossing over to the side of embodied self-awareness (chaotic uncertainty, fear of feeling our "true" selves).

How do we get back to ourselves, to find the MPFC switch to access our present embodied states? Experience dependent brain development etches brain pathways in both directions. You have to practice finding yourself, again and again, in order for those pathways to regrow. If you are too far gone into the land of thinking yourself out of situations, you are going to need help finding your embodied self and plenty of time, months or years. Neural networks don't grow overnight. Remember that the pathways that grew to convince you that you can figure it all out in thought took many years to form and so may the new ones that bring you back to yourself.

4

Out of Touch with Ourselves: Suppression and Absorption

> . . . the False Self sets up as real and it is this that observers tend to think is the real person. In living relationships, work relationships, and friendships, however, the False Self begins to fail . . . . At this extreme the True Self is hidden.
> (Winnicott, 1960, pp. 142–143)

Joan was a middle-aged professional who came to see me some years ago as a client in my Rosen Method Bodywork practice. She wanted bodywork because of persistent abdominal pain, pain that did not have a clear connection to a gastrointestinal disorder. Her pain had come and gone over the years but it went back as far as she could remember into childhood. She had tried the medical route—endless tests and misdiagnoses—and had visited a psychotherapist on several occasions, but neither of these methods had provided lasting relief.

As we will see in this chapter, when we are unable or unwilling to stay in the subjective emotional present with a feeling, and if that pattern of avoidance goes on for too long, we will develop neuromotor pathways that amplify and reinforce our ability in the future to suppress our body states from reaching self-awareness. Our muscles play a role in literally holding ourselves together and clamping down on **ergoreceptors** and **proprioceptors** to block sensations from entering into embodied self-awareness, diverting our attention to conceptual self-awareness.

Joan was intensely physically active, with a muscular and trim body, and she ran regularly in marathons and other distance races. She had a pixielike face. She liked to laugh and her dark eyes sparkled when she smiled. She had a mysterious quality when we first met that I experienced as both captivating and disturbing. The captivating part made me curious about her, and I suspected that many people would be drawn to her because of this and because of her sense of humor. She did especially well in her position in management for a midsized corporation that sold outdoor products (Salt Lake City, where she worked, is a hub for outdoor recreation) and clearly loved her job. The disturbing part of Joan made me aware of something hidden from view, as if her humor and all of her activity allowed her to keep a distance from her embodied self-awareness.

The opening quote of this chapter is from a work by Donald Winnicott (1896–1971), a London physician and psychoanalyst who is among the writers that have most deeply influenced my thinking. Winnicott saw embodied self-awareness as the basis of psychological and physical well-being. He also postulated that embodied self-awareness develops over time in close interpersonal relationships starting from infancy.

According to Winnicott, *the **True Self** is our embodied self-awareness, our ability to stay comfortably in the chaos of the subjective emotional present, and to use that to inform, verify, and update our conceptual self-awareness.* "The True Self comes from the aliveness of the body tissues and the working of body-functions, including the heart's action and breathing" (1960, p. 148). *The **False Self** is our conceptual self-awareness in the condition that it becomes divorced from the regulating reassurance of embodied self-awareness.* It is the story we tell about ourselves that is not based in the "reality" and "truth" of our sensations and emotions in the subjective emotional present, when "there develops a dissociation between intellectual activity and psychosomatic existence" (1960, p. 144).

Winnicott used the data from his many patients to show how the True Self and the False Self develops from early relationships with significant others. To the extent that parents recognize, honor, and respect their children's inner experiences and emotions as real, the child will accordingly learn to recognize, honor, and respect being in the subjective emotional present. True Self development arises from "highly particular transactions that constitute love between two imperfect people" (Nussbaum, 2003), meaning that life is chaotic and unpredictable and we do our best to stay present with the flow of experience. To the extent that the child's body sensations and emotions are denied, devalued, ignored, or punished by parents, the child will find ways to avoid sharing them with others and eventually to avoid feeling them entirely.

Joan, I thought, was not her True Self. I did not know why or how, I did not know what she was hiding, but I could sense that there was something missing, something that the humor and gregariousness and muscularity was covering up. There will be a case report about the early phases of Joan's treatment in this chapter, with later phases appearing in subsequent chapters.

There are many forms of hiding from the True Self, and they will be discussed in this chapter. These include all forms of *suppressing* the experience and expression of emotion, cutting off interoceptive awareness, and in general denying and dissociating from one's embodied self-awareness. Some methods of being out of touch with embodied self-awareness, however, seem like just the opposite. The person fixates on embodied experiences in such a way as to become totally *absorbed* by them. Such methods include **somatization** in which the person feels "eaten up" by a body state and sees it as a disease. Some eating disorders involve a hypersensitivity to digestive feelings and body size and shape. Addictions involve out of control urges. Absorption's unitary focus results in a lack of a more general and flexible embodied self-awareness, one that can "go with the flow" and shift in a dynamic and adaptive way to changing circumstances and body states.

Suppression and Expression

Suppressing our awareness of feelings is not always bad for us. We can't expect to act on every urge to satisfy ourselves. The demands of living in a lawful and safe society require our ability to self-regulate on a daily basis. Our neurophysiology is especially well designed for this task. Our nervous system has the exquisite ability to feel deeply into ourselves and to adjust our actions to enhance embodied self-awareness. We also have a rather powerful ability to control and regulate that process, to put the brakes on experience for the sake of fitting in and adapting to social and environmental demands. A state of psychological and physical well-being requires us to suppress our feelings when needed be but then to find safe opportunities to access them more freely. Problems arise when suppression continues without respite.

In some experimental studies of suppression, people are shown emotionally arousing videos, for example, and then asked to behave so that someone else could not know that they are feeling something. This request invariably results in increased internal arousal as measured by activation of the **sympathetic nervous system**, that part of the **autonomic nervous system (ANS)** that increases preparation for action and defense. Specifically, during the experiment people sweat more, their body temperature rises, they have higher heart rates, and higher blood pressure. People also show impairment in their short-term memory, being less able to concentrate on a list of words they are asked to later remember.

Of particular interest is that following this experimentally induced period of suppression, people seem distracted and unable to concentrate (Gross & Levenson, 1993; Polivy, 1998; Richards & Gross, 1999). They are also more avoidant of arousal or pain (Cioffi & Holloway, 1993). This means that even a brief period of suppression sets the stage for more suppression because people are less able to focus their attention interoceptively and less able to tolerate mildly aversive stimuli.

Higher sympathetic nervous system activation is important in the short run because it helps us rise to challenges and mobilize our resources. If we can return to a more relaxed state soon after, allowing our **parasympathetic nervous system** to slow down our hearts and cool our bodies, normal recovery and restoration of our metabolic energetic resources will result in an ability to think clearly and to be more in touch with our embodied self-awareness. This demonstrates the importance of providing **resources** in embodied self-awareness enhancement treatments: to access a sense of safety and relaxation.

In another neuroscience experiment, men were allowed to feel and enjoy their sexual arousal when watching erotic videos. Their interoceptive neural network was fully activated including the anterior cingulate cortex (ACC) (motivation to engage and enjoy), the orbitofrontal cortex (OFC) (evaluation of stimulation as pleasurable or not), the insula (integration of interoceptive feelings from the body), and the dorsolateral prefrontal cortex (DLPFC) (working memory in the subjective emotional present).

In another part of this experiment, the same erotica-watching men were asked to *inhibit* their sexual arousal. In this suppression condition, there was activation in the DLPFC and the ACC but in none of the other areas of the interoceptive neural network. Normally, the DLPFC works to hold sensory representations in working memory to enhance embodied self-awareness in the subjective emotional present. In this case, however, the DLPFC was active in holding in working memory the feeling of *inhibition* of the interoceptive neural network leading to a suppression of felt sexual arousal. The activation of the ACC suggests that there is some type of motivation to engage with the erotic material, an urge to act that needed also to be suppressed (Beauregard, Lévesque, & Bourgouin, 2001).

Holding It In: Suppressing Our Urges to Act

Activity in the neural network for embodied self-awareness is linked to activation of the premotor and motor areas to send efferent signals back to the body in order to direct movement. Activation in the ACC makes us want to move according to how we feel. If there is an itch, it wants to be scratched. If someone invades personal space, the body wants to move away. If there is a feeling of happiness, a smile or laugh wants to arise and be expressed.

What if the person who is experiencing the interoceptive feeling is unable to make adjustive and regulatory movements? This could occur, for example, if one is holding a baby while being stung by a bee. Even though the body "wants" to deal with the sting, the first consideration is to put the baby down safely. It also happens routinely when people sit in classrooms or meetings and feel a cramp or muscle spasm, need to urinate, have a headache, or want to laugh or cry out loud. Politeness and propriety dictate sitting still and holding onto or bearing the urge to act. Somehow we know how to do this but how does it work physiologically?

An answer to the question about what happens in the brain to urges to act that are not transformed into action arose almost by accident in neuroimaging studies of the effects of intense pain on the brain. In the study of pain using the needle approaching the rubber hand (see Chapter 3), while researchers expected and found activations in the emotion, body schema, and interoception areas, they also noticed corresponding activation in an area of the brain known to be related to the preparation for action, the **supplementary motor area (SMA)** (see Figure 2.7) (Ehrsson, Wiech et al., 2007).

The researchers reasoned that the observed SMA activation might have been because of the subjects' inability to move during the experiment. Under normal circumstances, the subject might have withdrawn the hand or arm from the painful stimulus. In follow-up studies, researchers compared brain activity when the subject was allowed to retract the hand from the approaching needle with a condition in which they were asked to remain still, finding more activity in the SMA in the latter condition (Ehrsson, Wiech et al., 2007). Activation in the SMA, in the **cingulate motor area (CMA)**, adjacent to the ACC, and in the ACC, is known to increase just before a voluntary movement (Cunnington et al., 2005), and thus reflects the anticipation of that movement.

The CMA is located in the middle section of the cingulate cortex (also called the cingulate gyrus), just in back of the ACC and just underneath the SMA (see Figure 2.6). The CMA has connections to the SMA and also to the motor and posterior parietal cortices above it, and to the amygdala below. The posterior parietal cortex is where information from different senses, such as vision and proprioception, are integrated to create the body schema.

The SMA and CMA are also activated—along with the insula, posterior parietal, and prefrontal areas—when people have an urge to void the bladder, again suggesting a relationship between these areas and the urge to move under conditions of even mild urgency, threat, or anxiety (Kuhtz-Buschbeck et al., 2007). Similar results have been found when heat rather than a needle is used to induce pain (Farrell, Laird, & Egan, 2005; Kwan, Crawley, Mikulis, & Davis, 2000). The CMA is particularly activated when the urge to move involves a threat, while the SMA is activated in most other kinds of preparations to move. The SMA plays a role in preparing for and encoding actions, "whether or not those actions are subsequently executed," and the SMA "holds such plans or representations in readiness for action prior to movement initiation" (Cunnington, Windischberger, & Moser, 2005, p. 651).

When the urge to act cannot be realized, the representations in the SMA have to "go" somewhere. The SMA activation follows the usual pathways and induces low level activation in the somatotopic areas of the motor cortex, which in turn creates low level contractions—via the efferent pathways—in the related skeletal muscles. When there is an urge but not the possibility to urinate, for example, the urine has to be prevented from escaping so the sphincter muscles that hold back the flow need to remain contracted at some low level, just enough to avoid an accident.

In the suppression of urges, then, it is not just the brain but the neuromuscular system that is activated to contain the urge. If one is threatened but cannot fight or escape, the skeletal muscles in the arms, legs, and trunk that might have become fully active instead become tensed at a low level of contraction. If you've ever witnessed a cat (or for that matter any animal including human) preparing to pounce on its prey, you can get a sense of what this looks or feels like.

In this way—using the neuromotor system—we can suppress many different types of urges including the urge to express an emotion, hunger, thirst, sleepiness, sexual arousal, needs for elimination, cravings food, drink, drugs, possessions, and gambling. In a study of college students' embodied experience, it was found that uncomfortable classroom settings, the need to sit still for long periods, and negative emotional climate created the need to distract themselves from their body feelings. One student said,

> It's an evening class so I'm aware I'm hungry. I'm aware I'm thirsty. I cough a lot more. . . . A lot of times I have itchy ears so I realize I'm touching my face, scratching my head, scratching my ears. A lot of times my throat bothers me, so I sit with my hand on my neck. So I'm a lot more fidgety. (McClelland, Dahlberg, & Plihal, 2002, p. 6)

Like suppression of feelings, suppression of urges has consequences, especially if the need for suppression of the urge is in conflict with one's desires. In addition to the chronic muscle tension and possible pain, these consequences include feelings of discomfort and longing, distracted and impaired thought processes, obsessive thoughts about what one is being denied, and possibly the transformation of the suppression into excess, which happens for example in binge eating and addictive behavior (see below, Polivy, 1998).

Victims of childhood physical and sexual abuse, or of criminal acts, generally cannot act appropriately (running, screaming, hiding, fighting) in response to the attack. The suppressed urges create sympathetic nervous system arousal, which leads to smooth and skeletal muscle tension which in turn creates more sympathetic arousal, maintaining the suppression-tension network for possibly many years. *Self-awareness treatments for such individuals need to work with awareness of thought processes, suppressed emotions, and suppressed body movements encased in chronic muscle tension* (like the symptoms of Doug's suppressed childhood anger, Case Report 2.1).

Cultural Demands for Suppression

Over the course of normal development, children learn to suppress emotion by crying less, speaking more softly and without screaming, moderating their levels of enthusiasm and excitement, and in general "miniaturizing" their expressions (Holodynski, 2004). This need to learn about the suppression of urges and emotions appears to have been the case for millennia. The !Kung bushmen are a hunter-gatherer group living in the Kalahari desert in Africa. !Kung infants are indulged completely, as if embodied self-awareness was the most important early life lesson (see Chapter 1). !Kung women carry their infants in a sling so the infants are next to their bodies. The infants are breast-fed on demand, sometimes as many as 60 times in a 24-hour period.

By the time infants are ready to be weaned, however, they are required to learn the art of suppression. Nisa, a !Kung woman who collaborated with an anthropologist to write an autobiography, remembers her own weaning in this way.

> When mother was pregnant with Kumsa, I was always crying, wasn't I? One day I said, "Mommy, won't you let me have just a little milk? Please, let me nurse." She cried, "Mother! My breasts are things of shit! Shit! Yes, the milk is like vomit and smells terrible. You can't drink it. If you do, you'll go 'Whaagh..whaagh..' and throw up." I said, "No, I won't throw up, I'll just nurse." But she refused and said, "Tomorrow, Daddy will trap a springhare, just for you to eat." When I heard that, my heart was happy again. (Shostak, 1983, p. 53)

Some other indulgence may have been substituted for the longed-for breast, but Nisa nevertheless faced the ancient requirement of the human child to "grow up" and "become less childish," adapting to social demands by suppressing her feelings and wants.

The earliest written narratives of human experience reveal themes of the need for suppression and self-regulation in society as well as the need to find ways to come back to one's embodied self-awareness. Odysseus—in the *Odyssey*, the model for all later heroic epics—suffered many trials through which he had to conquer his immediate desires, only after which could he return home to indulge his desires as a father and husband.

People in Europe and the Americas today are taught that emotions and the body are less valued than conceptual thinking and conceptual self-awareness (see Chapter 1). This need for suppression conflicts with the cultural value of independence. It is permitted to show justifiable anger if one's "unalienable rights" are curtailed (Fischer & Jansz, 1995). Road rage is acceptable, even rational and fitting, if another driver behaves in a way that seems selfish or arrogant, thus taking some perceived "right" of self-expression away from the enraged driver. Never mind that the offender may feel the same way, precipitating a duel of "I got here first," or "You don't own the road."

In many Asian cultures, suppression of overt emotion expression is considered to be a sign of maturity and stability. Autonomy, in many Asian cultures, means the ability to self-regulate while at the same time fitting in with the demands of the group to conform and behave as expected. Studies asking people to suppress their emotions in the laboratory, such as those described earlier, reveal that Asians are less likely to suffer from undue activation of consequent sympathetic arousal compared to North Americans (Butler, Lee, & Gross, 2007).

Suppression, in general, occurs when we feel the need to protect ourselves by not exposing our feelings and urges to others. *Suppression, then is a response to some kind of perceived threat to our ability to be in the **subjective emotional present**.* People may have the need to cry, for example, but feel that it is not permitted in a social situation. Even when crying does occur, it is not always fully experienced in the subjective emotional present, partly as a result of current social demands and partly as a result of how significant others responded to the person's cries as a child (see Box 4.1).

BOX 4.1
Crying: Expression or Suppression?

A good cry is restorative, creative, and cleansing. It can help us heal and regain a sense of hope. However, a good cry is paradoxical: it is about pain *and* relief, despair *and* hope, loss *and* gain. (Nelson, 2005, p. 104)

A "good" cry is connected deeply to the interoceptive sensations of warm tears, blurry vision, a sense of vulnerability, feelings of relief, and

continued

BOX 4.1 (continued)

the emotions mentioned in the quote above. A good cry resonates in sound and feeling with embodied self-awareness and it can thereby activate the homeostatic systems of the body that restore optimal function.

Cries of this type have been shown in experimental studies to activate the **parasympathetic nervous system (PNS)**, that part of the autonomic nervous system (ANS) that stimulates relaxation responses to the internal organs such that breathing and heart rate slow and digestion can resume in a normal way. The parasympathetic nervous system activates the lachrymal glands of the eyes to stimulate tears, and it also stimulates the production of saliva and digestive fluids (Ding, Walcott, & Keyser, 2003). Before the start of a good cry, there may be a build-up of **sympathetic nervous system** (arousal) activation as a result of a perceived need to suppress the crying. As the need to cry outweighs the risk of exposure, sympathetic activation changes over to parasympathetic as the cry unfolds in time (Gross, Fredrickson, & Levenson, 1994; Hendriks, Rottenberg, & Vingerhoets, 2007; Rottenberg, Gross, & Gotlib, 2003).

Tears that arise from a good cry have a different composition from tears that normally lubricate the eye in response to irritants like dust. Emotionally induced tears contain the hormones of prolactin, **adrenocorticotropic hormone (ACTH)**, and the natural opiate (pain reliever) leucine enkephalin. Prolactin stimulates breast feeding in women but also plays a role in feelings of sexual gratification and interpersonal connection in both genders, similar to that of **oxytocin**. ACTH is a stress hormone and a precursor to cortisol. This means that good crying releases and flushes toxic stress hormones from the body, calms and soothes, and creates fellow feelings (Sullivan, Block, & Pena, 1996; Walter, 2006). Females produce more prolactin than males, which may partially explain their tendency to cry more frequently.

Clinical observations also suggest that good crying, and other forms of release/relaxation during therapy, is sometimes accompanied by **psychoperistalsis**, involuntary noises of relaxation from the gut—gurgles,

continued

Psychophysiology of Self-Awareness

> **BOX 4.1** (continued)
>
> tummy rumbles—that are not related to digestion. Whenever the gut or the breathing relaxes, and the heart rate slows, it is a sign of parasympathetic activation. Good cries also enhance body-resonant conceptual self-awareness about what might have been troubling the person and provide an emotional sense of relief (Kennedy-Moore & Watson, 2001).
>
> The good cry is clearly a form of embodied self-awareness in the subjective emotional present. Not all cries, however, are experienced by the crier or the listener as good. Such cries show evidence of voluntary or involuntary suppression. One can begin to observe these differences even in newborn infants. A good newborn cry begins almost immediately following a disturbance: the cry develops into an intense and highly rhythmical series of vocalizations and body movements, and then is rapidly soothed. Other types of infant cries take longer to begin following the disturbance, are irregular in rhythm, last much longer, and are less likely to be easily soothed (Chen, 1985).
>
> **Table 4.1**
> *Symptoms of inhibited or suppressed crying*
>
> | Type of cry | Features | Response by others |
> | --- | --- | --- |
> | "Good" crying | Connected to embodied self-awareness of emotions and interoception, restorative, cleansing, calming, full but relatively brief, readily soothed, most likely to have tears | Nurture, affection, empathy |
> | Protest crying | Intense, loud, sobbing, angry, helpless, unsoothable, exhaustion, possible unresolved grief or situations that are felt as "too much" | Apathy, irritation, feeling blamed, pushed away, or guilty |
>
> *continued*

	Table 4.1 (continued)	
Infantile crying	Infantlike sounds and behaviors (e.g., lip quivering, trembling), may be tearless, repetitive stereotypical movements, possible link to infantile attachment trauma	Sensing that the person is unreachable, "lost" inside themselves, feeing of helplessness to reach them
Unprovoked or prolonged crying	Not preceded by any obvious thought or feeling, may be related to neurological damage and to psychiatric disorders such as depressions; possible unacknowledged grief or unfulfilled attachment needs	Confusion, tendency to "find" an explanation for why the person keeps crying
Dramatic crying	Not clearly connected to an emotion, needy without knowing why, socially inappropriate, "dead" feeling inside, "narcissistic," possible links to early childhood rejection and the need to act out to get attention	Manipulated, avoidance of person's apparent attention seeking, urge to be rid of the person

Sources: Alexander (2003), Mills and Wooster (1987), Nelson (2000), Rydé, Friedrichsen, and Strang (2007).

Table 4.1 shows a list of some of the cries that have been identified by clinicians during counseling and psychotherapy sessions. Suppressive crying may alert the therapist to earlier trauma or disappointment with significant others. Dramatic crying, for example, may develop as a strategy to get attention from a distant or uninvolved parent. Protest crying, on the other hand, can become habitual in cases where the parent willfully ignores the child's needs or responds to them with anger and resentment.

Suppressed forms of expression have also been found for smiling. So-called felt smiles tend to involve the full face with a raising of the cheeks and a crinkling around the eye corners. "False" smiles involve primarily the mouth, with lip corners upturned, but not the rest of the face. False smiles occur in social situations where politeness or deference is called for (Ekman & Friesen, 1982).

Psychophysiology of Self-Awareness

In embodied self-awareness treatments, the goal is to help people to become comfortable with the whole range of their emotional experience, including negative emotions like anger (see Case Report 2.1) and the need for good crying. According to one psychotherapy client,

> [When] your sad emotion is your enemy . . . you react to it with distance and you are like, "I don't want to cry, . . . I want to get away from it . . ." [but if] you make friends with your emotions, then you are like, "Crying is okay." . . . It just has this really remarkable effect, in the sense that, you know, you are not running away from it. You are not angry at yourself for doing it. You are not trying to stop yourself and trying to hold back because that is *who you are* at the moment. . . . I am happy to be with the crying cause that's what I need to do right now. (Levitt, Butler, & Hill, 2006, p. 321)

Alexithymic (*a*=lack, *lexi*=words, *thymic*=mood, emotion) individuals have difficulty experiencing and naming their emotional states. They may not be able to connect a racing heart with excitement, or burning cheeks with shame. This is not the same as being aware of feelings but being unwilling or reluctant to talk about them, a pattern that often distinguishes males from females. Alexithymics seem to not be able to fully sense the internal sensations from the body and they tend to focus on concrete things, like their work, which are external to their bodies (Sifneos, 1973).

Suppression of interoception and emotion can take other surprising forms. Novice parachute jumpers who were monitored in a study of fear and anxiety often claimed to be feeling completely calm prior to their first jump. One novice, however, was astounded when asked to look down and saw his legs shaking and knees knocking together. Experienced jumpers were much more aware of their body states, knew that they felt fear but accepted it, after which those feelings passed away prior to their jumps (Fenz & Epstein, 1967). The threat to the novice's safety was too great for that person to face.

Freudian psychoanalytic theory was among the first to recognize and name **defense mechanisms**, the forms of suppression having the goal of avoiding what is unpleasant or threatening to the self. Although some lists of defenses can have 30 different categories, for our purposes the main types are denial, repression, intellectualization, and projection (Lambie & Marcel, 2002). **Denial** is the suppression of self-awareness of the possibly difficult and painful *outcomes* of one's embodied experience, an experience of which one is aware. An example would be telling oneself that even though one feels hurt and abandoned, one "doesn't need" a significant other who has decided to end a long-term relationship. **Repression** is the covering up of the feeling itself so that it does not enter embodied self-awareness, such as flirting for fun but not feeling or acknowledging an underlying sexual attraction.

Intellectualization and projection are different forms of our old friend, conceptual self-awareness, activated in a way that it leaves little or no room for embodied self-awareness. Both of these defenses transform the underlying feeling into an autobiographical narrative that reflects a False Self, not honestly accepting the embodied feelings. **Intellectualization** is a judgment or reinterpretation while **projection** imputes the problem to someone else. For the flirt, the former is "Hey, I'm just having some fun," while the latter may be, "It's his fault; he's trying to lead me on; I'm just being friendly." Table 4.2 summarizes these defenses.

Curiously, those suppressive thoughts have an attraction all their own. *These thoughts are about the most important thing in the world for the thinker: maintaining one's protections against the threatening world. We can easily get lost in spinning out self-justifications, finding reasons to promote ourselves and our interests. Conceptual self-awareness is, fundamentally, about preserving the self.* This self-conscious and self-promoting aspect of conceptual self-awareness is sometimes called the "ego."

Because of the need to self-regulate in social situations, people are often reluctant to talk about their bodies and their diseases with others. People with migraines refer to the headache as "*it*." "Why is *it* happening now?" This is partly a way to suppress the negative emotions surrounding "owning" such a condition, and partly a form of depersonalization and repression. Research shows that owning the migraine condition and also learning to pay attention to the muscle tension in the neck and shoulders that precedes the onset of an attack, can lead to reduction of pain and stress (Bakal, 1999).

Psychophysiology of Self-Awareness

Table 4.2
Forms of suppression

Type of suppression	Characteristics	Physiology
Substitution of embodied experience with conceptual thought; *some contact with* embodied self-awareness	Defenses of intellectualization and projection; conceptual self-awareness of judgment, explanation, justification but without making the link to embodied states	DMPFC with thought and language areas of the cortex, disconnected from direct sensations from the body; occasional access to to interoceptive and emotion network via the VMPFC (see Chapter 3)
Active suppression using low-level muscle tension and sympathetic arousal; *some contact with* embodied self-awareness	Defense of denial; some awareness of effort from muscle tension, elevated blood pressure and heart rate, compromised gut function, lowered ability to concentrate and remember, but without ability to identify the denied feelings	DLPFC with OFC activate ACC, SMA, CMA and cortical motor areas along with hypothalamus, (ANS and hormones) that put body on alert and hold back urges
Active muscular and sympathetic arousal *without* embodied self-awareness	Defense of repression; muscular and sympathetic arousal, but no awareness of these effects nor of the repressed feelings but possible awareness of pain or disease	Same as above

Sources: Lambie and Marcel (2002), Mendolia (2002).

Similarly, the pain of childbirth can be reduced by paying attention to the interoceptive feelings of the muscle contractions. Researchers compared a group of women who were instructed to feel the sensations of each contraction as it came and went with a group who were given methods to distract themselves from the sensations. The women who were asked to attend to the sensations (embodied self-awareness) had less self-reported pain than the women in the distraction group (Leventhal, Leventhal, Shacham, & Easterling, 1989).

Consequences of Long-Term Suppression of Emotions and Actions

In the short term, suppression can be an effective means of homeostatic self-regulation because it alerts the body to activate defensive and protective means against the perceived stressor. Over the longer term, however, it is not an effective strategy and its continued use can begin to erode the very psychophysiology that makes normal self-regulation possible. The same mechanisms that allow for suppression in the short term are those that remain "on" for the long term: habitual activation of judgmental and negative thought patterns, overactivation of the hypothalamus leading to high sympathetic arousal and tension in smooth muscles, and suppression of urges in the ACC and SMA leading to persistent tension in skeletal muscles. As a consequence of these physiological effects, long-term suppression is related to higher levels of cardiovascular disease, high blood pressure, gastrointestinal diseases such as colitis and ulcers, and respiratory diseases such as asthma (King, Taylor, Albright, & Haskell, 1990; Sifneos, 1973).

Many types of **myalgia** (*myo*=muscle, *algia*=pain), or muscle weakness and pain, can be traced to stressful working conditions in which people are not encouraged to move, to focus on themselves, or to take rest breaks. Stress-related myalgia is more likely to be caused by sympathetic overarousal and suppression of urges than by specific injuries (Burns, 2006a).

The psychophysiological processes related to long-term suppression may eventually impact immune system function and may lead to more serious autoimmune disorders. **Neoplastic diseases**, the growth of some types of non-malignant and malignant tumors, has been linked to suppression of emotions (Jamner, Schwartz, & Leigh, 1988; Kneier & Temoshok, 1984). Rheumatoid arthritis, a chronic inflammation of the joints, is an autoimmune disorder that has also been linked in part to avoidance of body symptoms and emotions when under stress (Sifneos, 1973).

Another autoimmune disorder is **fibromyalgia**, in which musculoskeletal pain is not localized to one or two areas, distributed instead across different regions of the body. There may also be highly tender places that hurt when touched, chronic fatigue, problems with sleep, and negative mood. A study of women with fibromyalgia showed that they were considerably higher on measures of avoiding emotional feelings and expression than women without the disease. The women with fibromyalgia were more likely to endorse statements such as, "I do not take the time to figure out what I am feeling," or "I do not usually let my feelings come out," or "If I think I'm going to feel sad, I change what I'm thinking about" (van Middendorp et al., 2008).

Long-term psychological effects of suppression have also been found in research studies. Suppression results in higher levels of negative mood including anxiety and depression, and a decreased sense of well-being (Campbell-Sills, Barlow, Brown, & Hofmann, 2006). Often people who are habitual in their suppression of emotion, like the novice parachutists mentioned earlier, report little anxiety or negative mood but when given laboratory tests show higher levels of sympathetic arousal (heart rate, sweating, muscle tension) compared to nonsuppressors who report feeling anxiety (Gillath, Bunge, Shaver, Wendelken, & Mikulincer, 2005; Lambie & Marcel, 2002; Weinberger, Schwart, & Davidson, 1979).

As if all this were not enough, people who habitually suppress their emotions and feelings report less satisfying interpersonal relationships, including less rapport with others and reduced ability to form lasting relationships (Butler et al., 2003; Campbell-Sills et al., 2006). The creation of intimacy in interpersonal relationships requires participants to talk openly about their emotions and to be responsive to their partner's emotions. Conflict avoidance and low emotional disclosure in marriages is related to low levels of satisfaction within the relationship and is one of the salient predictors of divorce (Gottman & Levenson, 1992). Premature ejaculation in males and orgasmic dysfunction in females also correlates with higher levels of perceived stress and lower levels of emotional expression and self-awareness (Michetti et al., 2007; Seal & Meston, 2007) suggesting that open and healthy sexual communication requires awareness of and emotional engagement with one's own body sensations.

As might be expected from this discussion, feeling, expressing, and disclosing emotions and body sensations has long-term benefits. Although the suppressor believes that holding onto emotions can reduce their intensity, in fact, the opposite is true. As in the case of good crying (Box 4.1), opening up our emotions with others yields a sense of relief and relaxation. All those muscles that were holding on with sympathetic activation can relax because there is no longer a need to suppress the urge to cry or speak (Kennedy-Moore & Watson, 2001). This leads to less stress on the cardiovascular and respiratory systems in the long run (Pollatos & Schandry, 2008).

Out of Touch with Ourselves

Another related benefit of expression is that with experience at communicating what one is feeling, it becomes easier over time to tolerate negative emotions and pain. Instead of trying to rid oneself of a bad mood by suppression, one can actually enjoy it by probing deeper interoceptively for what might have caused it, ultimately bringing the regulation of negative mood under self-control. Being able to "stay with" emotional states in the subjective emotional present expands embodied self-awareness and creates an opportunity, via the link between the dorsomedial and ventromedial prefrontal cortices (DMPFC, VMPFC, see Figure 3.2), to conceptually reflect on and understand the self without judgment while remaining aware of body experience (Lischetzke & Eid, 2003).

Eating Disorders as One Common Symptom of Suppression

By all measures, eating disorders are epidemic in industrialized nations. The rise of the middle class in North America, Europe, India, China, and Japan has apparently brought with it conditions that create opportunities for the overuse and misuse of food. On the one hand, there is the year-round worldwide availability of a huge diversity of food, including highly processed foods. There is increased pressure on families to work more to maintain their middle-class standard of living that leads to less free time and an increasing reliance on fast food and processed foods containing high levels of salts, sugars, fats, and carbohydrates (Lee, 2007; Rosenbaum, 2007).

The consumption of consumer appliances, computers, televisions, and video games means that recreation has turned increasingly indoors, become sedentary, and has the effect of numbing the body and its sensations as one is engaged in these activities. Electronic media also has the effect of amplifying the distribution of notions about ideal body size and type, leading to eating disorders related to weight loss, and distributing messages about the desirability of potentially unhealthy food products that may contribute to obesity. This sociocultural process has been especially hard on youth with a dramatic worldwide rise in pediatric obesity and adolescent eating disorders. Pediatric obesity can lead to early onset type 2 diabetes, cardiovascular disease, and predispose the individual to adult obesity (Lee, 2007; Rosenbaum, 2007).

For optimal health and rejuvenation, we all need exercise, rest, time to feel deeply into ourselves, and meaningful and emotionally expressive human contact. Under stress, however, these "needs" can be easily ignored. We do, however, have to eat. It's required. When done with embodied self-awareness, eating not only satisfies hunger and nutritional needs, it can become a highly pleasurable and renewing experience (see Box 4.2). Eating becomes disordered when it is done without embodied self-awareness.

BOX 4.2
Slow Food

Slow Food is a non-profit, eco-gastronomic member-supported organization . . . to counteract fast food and fast life, the disappearance of local food traditions and people's dwindling interest in the food they eat, where it comes from, how it tastes and how our food choices affect the rest of the world. . . . By reawakening and training their senses, Slow Food helps people rediscover the joys of eating and understand the importance of caring where their food comes from, who makes it and how it's made. (http://www.slowfood.com)

The Slow Food movement was founded in the 1980s in France and Italy, countries known to have a long history of savory and nutritional cuisine made from local products and ingredients. As they witnessed the rise in a more fast-paced life and the opening of American fast food restaurants in their neighborhoods, the founders sought to preserve their gastronomic traditions though "taste education" and funding for local and natural agricultural and food distribution services.

If you live a fast-paced life with little time to enjoy food, you might be thinking that the Slow Food movement is a luxury for people with time and money on their hands. Slow Food members believe that their approach should be part of everyday life, not only for the leisure class, but for everyone.

Let's follow the food chain in embodied self-awareness. Growing food takes labor and exposure to the whims of climate fluctuation. What would

continued

> **BOX 4.2** (continued)
>
> it feel like to arise early and tend to animals before breakfast? What if it is cold and snowy or hot and humid? What does the weariness of farm work feel like: pointless or satisfying? How do you relate to the insects and birds that want to share in your crops? Think of the disappointment of animals dying from disease or predators, of drought or floods, of low prices paid for what you produce, for rising gasoline and other costs.
>
> Who does the labor of shipping and distributing food? Do they care about the products in their warehouses, trucks, railcars, and airplanes? And on the receiving end, in the food markets, do the grocers take pride in the product and its display? Do they have a personal relationship with their customers? Are they choosing to sell products that nourish and enrich people's lives?
>
> How do you go about buying food? Are you looking for something prepared, easy, quick, and cheap? Is your shopping for food in-and-out? If you take a few extra minutes, you can have a wonderfully sensual experience in the market and later at home when you prepare the food. Fresh fruits and vegetables come in great varieties of colors, tastes, textures, and smells. Can you let your choices be guided by all your senses, not just your economic sense of value or your conceptual thoughts about what seems easiest? (Pollan, 2008).
>
> Buying and preparing food with embodied self-awareness can be restorative: the zen of shopping and chopping. You have to eat, right? Maybe you don't have time to meditate or exercise or get a massage but you can use this necessity of eating to pull you back into your body and its senses. This connection to and through food can be expanded if you share foraging, cooking, and eating with friends and family. Food brings people together like nothing else, especially if your life is otherwise spent away from these cherished people. Research shows that having regular family mealtimes increases child health and promotes social and cognitive development, in part because of the shared activity that accompanies eating slowly and with others watching (Fiese & Schwartz, 2008).
>
> *continued*

> **BOX 4.2** (continued)
>
> Like all forms of embodied self-awareness in the subjective emotional present, practicing Slow Food techniques will nourish your senses with pleasure and purpose sending cascades of mood elevating neurotransmitters and hormones through your system. So, what may seem like an unnecessary break from your chores will actually recharge your batteries so you can go back to work with more energy and enthusiasm than before.

There is no simple solution to the massive epidemic of disordered eating. It is beyond the control of the individual and to mediate the situation will take large-scale public health efforts over a long period. People need access to safe play and recreation areas in schools, workplaces, and communities. Municipalities also can create footpaths and bike lanes, provide more public transportation that encourages walking, and create walkable communities in which housing is distributed with shops and pedestrian streets. Governments need better standards for food producers to regulate unhealthy ingredients and healthier foods should be available in schools, workplaces, shops, and restaurants. We can count on increasing medical approaches including appetite reduction medication and surgery (Lee, 2007).

These approaches are important but they work by protecting people from themselves, as if the person was his own worst enemy. Embodied self-awareness approaches, in addition to what the community can do, can change a person's relationship to food, their embodied self-awareness with regard to food consumption, and replace the use of food as a way to regulate stress. In eating disorders, food is used as a way to suppress underlying emotions and levels of stress. There are two basic strategies: either to eat too much or eat too little.

In the case of those who eat too little, they are focused more on external images of the ideal body or they are behaving in accordance with peer group expectations (Hart & Kenny, 1997). They are excessively preoccupied with being negatively evaluated because of the way they look, and the stress of performance suppresses their own embodied self-awareness (Beales & Dolton, 2000; Gilbert & Meyer, 2005; Mann & Ward, 2004). Eating too little can become chronic in the case of anorexia nervosa (self-starvation). Anorexic teens show a typical profile of emotional suppression, in which higher levels of sympathetic arousal occur in the body with the person showing little or no awareness of their interoceptive state (Zonnevylle-Bender et al., 2005).

Those who eat too much focus on the food itself. If food is present, no matter what type of food, they are likely to indulge in eating it. They suppress interoceptive awareness required for homeostatic regulation of food intake, such as the feeling of satiety, or gastrointestinal distress and indigestion (Spoor et al., 2005). Individuals who suffer from obesity are also less able to feel pleasurable sensations from the taste of food compared to others, due to a possible genetically linked impairment of dopamine receptors in the brain, resulting in overconsumption of foods high in fats and sugars in order to be able to feel satisfied (Stice, 2008). Eating food in quantities that surpass the body's capacity to process it is referred to as **binge eating**. Binge eating has been linked to life stress coupled with suppression of interoception and emotion, and negative mood in a wide range of populations and in many different research studies (Barker, Williams, & Galambos, 2006; Kessler, Schwarze, Filipic, Traue, & von Wietersheim, 2006; Talleyrand, 2006; Wheeler, Greiner, & Boulton, 2005).

The cases of eating too little and those of eating too much are highly similar from the perspective of suppression of embodied self-awareness: both groups are focused on external rather than internal cues to guide their behavior. Either filling up with too much food or entering a state of semistarvation creates changes in the peripheral receptors of the homeostatic body systems that lead to particular interoceptive states. These may feel soporific or energizing, depressive or anxious. Clinical case reports reveal that these interoceptive states suppress the underlying feelings of loneliness, loss, and trauma from which the food or starvation "high" becomes a palliative (Goodsitt, 1983; Harrington, Crowther, Payne Henrickson, & Mickelson, 2006). Adolescents with higher reported stress eat more fatty foods, fewer vegetables, more unhealthy snacks, and fail to eat breakfast (Cartwright et al., 2003).

Women are especially vulnerable to the effects of body image on their eating behavior. When men and women were presented with illusions in which their body size appeared to change, women were more likely to show activation in the interoceptive and emotional areas of the brain (Kurosaki, Shirao, Yamashita, Okamoto, & Yamawaki, 2006), meaning that women had strong emotional reactions even to what they knew to be a temporary illusion of a change in the way they looked. Women prone to overeating compared to those who were not, for example, were more likely to order dessert at a restaurant following a filling meal if other people in the group were planning to order dessert (Antoniazzi, Zivian, & Hynie, 2005). In women, depression is often an accompaniment to body dissatisfaction and disordered eating (Stice & Bearman, 2001).

Girls as young as 5 years old were more likely to endorse statements showing dissatisfaction with their own bodies after experimental exposure to thin Barbie dolls and to thin female images in the media (Dittmar, Halliwell, & Ive, 2000; Dohnt & Tiggemann, 2006). As girls reach adolescence, body dissatisfaction can be exacerbated or lessened, depending upon whether the peer group and family is focused on external ideals and criticism or supporting an embodied awareness sense of personal well-being (Clark & Tiggemann, 2006; Davison & Birch, 2002; Jones, 2004; McKinley, 1999; Stice & Whitenton, 2002).

Some forms of binge eating reflect suppressed urges to eat that accompany attempts to diet in order to please others. Not only has the individual suppressed normal nutritional needs but they also have suppressed negative emotions surrounding the stressful demands from others (Blackburn, Johnston, Blampied, Popp, & Kallen, 2006; Heatherton & Baumeister, 1991). The same pattern of a female thinness ideal and eating disorders has been found even in Japan, where people are typically thinner than Westerners (Nishizawa et al., 2003).

Women are also vulnerable to negative feelings and images about other aspects of their bodies besides their weight and girth. When women exercise in environments with mirrors, for example, they actually feel less positive about themselves, offsetting any mood improvement benefits of exercise per se (Martin-Ginis et al., 2003). Women who feel less satisfied with their breast size, their facial attractiveness, and their sex appeal are less likely to express their opinion in public. They are less confident in their ability to succeed, feel more self-conscious and more ashamed of their bodies. They are also less likely to feel satisfied in their sexual relationships and show less assertiveness regarding their own sexual needs (Arndt & Goldenberg, 2004; Harter, Waters, & Whitesell, 1997; Koff & Benavage, 1998; Nezlek, 1999; Wiederman, 2000). These effects, by the way, are not related to how the woman looks to others but are entirely based on how she feels about herself.

Embodied Self-Awareness Treatments for Eating Disorders

Given the link between eating disorders, body image concerns, and lack of interoceptive self-awareness, one might think that enhancing self-awareness of body sensations and emotions around issues related to body size, shape, and food intake would be helpful. This is indeed the case. Cognitive-emotional-behavior therapy (CEBT) has been successful in helping individuals become aware that their eating behaviors are linked to an attempt to suppress an emotion that they did not want to feel. Treatment centers around diary keeping of feeling states before binges, food avoidance, or purges, with an emphasis on understanding both the precipitating emotion (sadness, for example) and the reasons why they did not want to feel it (belief that they may lose control of themselves, or that emotions are not socially acceptable to reveal) (Corstorphine, 2006).

In cases in which individuals believe they are too fat or too thin, a form of **dysmorphophobia** (*dys*=disturbance, *morph*=form, *phobia*=fear), mirror images and video images of the person have been used to begin the process of reinterpretation of how and why they have been led to distort their body schema (Delinsky & Wilson, 2006; Garner & Garfinkel, 1981–1982). One client said, "When I try to estimate my own dimensions, I am like a color-blind person trying to coordinate her own wardrobe. I will have to rely on objective data or someone I can trust to determine my actual size" (Garner et al., 1981, p. 279). Psychotherapeutic approaches of any type that help the client become more self-aware of the link between emotion suppression and eating patterns have shown success (Goodsitt, 1983; Harrington et al., 2006; Sella, 2003).

Somatic psychotherapy (sometimes called body psychotherapy) also focuses on enhancing embodied self-awareness. Therapists call attention to their client's postures and gestures, patterns of muscle holding and tensions, movement patterns and movement limitations, the breath and other body rhythms, and forms of suppression of emotion and sensation. A somatic psychotherapeutic approach to eating disorder treatment begins with the client's experience of distorted body schema and suppressed interoception and emotion: the feelings of being lost, empty, and without form (see Case Report 4.1).

> ### Case Report 4.1
> ### Somatic Psychotherapy Treatment of Jennifer's Eating Disorder
>
> Jennifer was a college senior who had suffered from bingeing and purging for the past four years. At the start of treatment, Jennifer was aware that she turned to food when she felt depressed. She also knew that bingeing was accompanied by a feeling of anxiety and having to eat quickly, that this resulted in stomach cramps and feeling "fat," which led to immediate purging.
>
> Jennifer was fortunate to have this much self-awareness, allowing the therapist to help refine her awareness of her interoceptive and emotional states as well as linking those to the online function and a more realistic appraisal of the appearance of her body. With the help of the therapist, Jennifer began to be aware of more details about her feelings and sensations during bingeing and purging.
>
> She first discovered that, "When I felt empty and lonely as a girl, I would wish something really bad would happen to me, so then I would have a real reason for feeling really terrible." Weeks later, she said, "Recently, when I binge, and feel fat, and see my distended stomach—it is something for me to feel bad about. I created it." Here, she is discovering that she has suppressed the memory of parental criticism during childhood—something she could not understand and could not control as a child—and replaced it with something similar as an adult that she could control.
>
> Later, Jennifer becomes more self-aware regarding this theme. "I feel helpless, worthless that I can't control how someone responds to me. That's what brings me back to my body—to be destructive at least—to binge. It's a substitute for the things I can't get and want." And then, "I can eat my way into feeling better—at least for a little while. Then I'm back to where I was before. Miserable." She now gets that the reason she is creating this uncomfortable body state and that she has a sense of worthlessness is because she could not control how her parents responded to her.
>
> Her therapist pointed out that at least Jennifer was now the one controlling her own misery. Jennifer replied, "At least I'm in control of something." Jennifer also began to realize that bingeing and purging calms her anxiety, and makes her feel "slowed down," "blanked out," and tired, so she doesn't have to think about how bad she feels. *Finally,*

> *she is entering into the domain of the subjective emotional present by identifying her body states in relation to the eating pattern.* This awareness is considerably more refined than the earlier sense of anxiety and stomachaches.
>
> This new awareness was not the magic cure for which Jennifer had been searching. Her therapist began to help her see how her "blanked out" state was a way of not taking responsibility, and helped her move on from there to a conceptual self-awareness of how she had used her bingeing to self-soothe. This was an opening into her awareness of the links between her perception of her body schema, her emotions of feeling worthless, and the body sensations of bingeing and purging. These seeds of awareness, with the support of the therapist and the eventual ability to tolerate feeling her helplessness and loneliness in the subjective emotional present, helped her to reestablish a healthy and satisfying relationship with food and with her body.
>
> Case report 4.1 was adapted from Krueger (1989, pp. 80–82).

Finally, there has been some success using nonpsychotherapeutic methods that focus on enhancing embodied self-awareness. In one study, young women with eating disorders were randomly assigned to one of three groups: a yoga class, an aerobic exercise class, and no class. Yoga practice, which focuses on self-awareness as one moves through various postures and meditations, was the most successful at enhancing a more realistic appraisal of body schema (size, shape, attractiveness), satisfaction with one's body, and reducing the symptoms of eating disorders. Exercise alone, in spite of its long-proven health benefits, was not sufficient to alter behavior. Yoga has the advantage of encouraging people to focus on their breathing, muscle stretch, body position, pain, and emotion, thus enhancing both interoceptive and body schema self-awareness (Daubenmier, 2005).

Normal and Pathological Absorption

One method of suppression is distraction, in which attentional focus is turned away from an undesirable feeling to another feeling that seems to be more under the control of the person. In eating disorders, the body sensations of

Psychophysiology of Self-Awareness

bingeing or purging or starvation, which are under the person's control—fullness, spaced out, "drunk," or lethargic—replace the unwanted and uncontrolled feelings (loneliness, abandonment). What began as a suppression of one embodied form of awareness becomes a total absorption into another one.

During normal states of attention there is a central focus but one can be aware, peripherally, of other states and events going on at the same time. Visual attention has both focal and peripheral elements to it so that one can easily shift attention to a new focus noticed in the periphery. **Absorption** is a way to exaggerate and amplify attention, the effect of which is the sense of getting "lost in" and "fully engaged with" experience so that the periphery is eliminated. In this chapter, we'll review four forms of absorption: **normal absorption, pathological dissociation, rumination,** and **addiction**. These are summarized in Table 4.3.

Table 4.3
Forms of absorption

Type of absorption	Characteristics	Physiology
Normal	A sense of pleasure or "high," attention is totally focused on an activity, a loss of self-consciousness (but not necessarily self-awareness), and an expansion of the felt sense of time.	Likely an amplification of resonant activity in the relationship between the interoceptive and exteroceptive neural networks (Figure 3.1)
Dissociative	A sense of separation (or "detachment") from certain aspects of everyday experience, such as the body (as in out-of-body experiences), the sense of self (as in depersonalization), or the external world (as in derealization); can also occur as undiagnosed physical disorders (somatization).	Likely a failure of the body schema neural network to integrate a sense of a unified self in the posterior parietal lobe and its links with proprioception and interoception (Figure 3.1) and a possible accentuation of the negative evaluations in the OFC looping with the interoceptive network

continued

Type of absorption	Characteristics	Physiology
Ruminative	The tendency to repetitively focus on symptoms of distress and possible causes and consequences of those symptoms without engaging in active problem solving.	Likely a looping between the DMPFC and negative evaluations from the OFC (see Figure 3.2)
Addictive	Addiction is when the behavior cannot be restrained and it is ultimately self-injurious in spite of the "high" period.	Looping of unrealistic positive evaluations from the OFC to the ACC to create intense urges, held in awareness by the insula and DLPFC (Figure 3.1 & 4.1)

Normal Absorption

Imagine being fully engaged in an activity that you love. It could be listening to or making music, watching or participating in sports, gardening, reading a good book, playing with a child, watching a film, a religious experience, or a romantic or sexual encounter. **Normal absorption** is a state of relating to activities in such a way that they capture all of your attention. You lose contact with the rest of the world. You may not hear the phone ring and you don't have another thought in your head.

On the surface, this sounds pathological, and in fact it may seem pathological to someone who walks up and wants your attention. You may not be at all aware of your body if your focus is outside of yourself, or you may be acutely aware of your body in one particular way that is required to carry out the activity in which you are engaged. Daydreaming and fantasizing are also forms of normal absorption. As one loses awareness of the current surroundings there is a corresponding focus on reliving or reshaping past events, rehearsing or making up intended future events, and problem solving. These are times for using intuition, creativity, and dreamlike associations that are not possible during more deliberate conceptual thinking (Butler, 2006; Holmes et al., 2005).

The most highly creative form of normal absorption has been called flow. Flow occurs when one's skills perfectly match the challenge of a task, when there is a sense of pleasure or "high," when attention is totally focused on one's activity, a loss of self-consciousness (but not necessarily self-awareness), and an expansion of the felt sense of time. One recreational modern dancer said, "I get a feeling that I don't get anywhere else . . . I have more confidence in myself than any other time. Maybe an effort to forget my problems. Dance is like therapy. If I am troubled about something, I leave it out of the door as I go in the dance studio" (Csikszentmihalyi, 1990, p. 59).

Normal absorption has been described as the primary aesthetic state of awareness. John Dewey (see Chapter 2) described our engagement with works of art—either as makers of the art or as appreciators of it—as an experience of "being a whole and of belonging to the larger, all inclusive, whole which is the universe in which we live" (Dewey, 1934, p. 195).

Dewey's description of the experience of art is similar to William James's writings in the late 1800s about religious experience. Writing about James, psychologist and philosopher Ciarán Benson (1993) says,

> Such states of mind are ineffable in the way they defy expression in words; are transient and cannot be sustained for long, yielding insights beyond the reach of discursive thought; and perhaps, after a period of active preparation, the subject of such experience feels him- or herself as though "held by a higher power." (p. 25)

In observations done by myself and colleagues, we noticed normal absorption in infants beginning around 4 months of age. Prior to this age, most infants engage in emotionally charged and lively games of face-to-face play with adults including mutual cooing and smiling. Once infants learn to reach for objects, they become absorbed in mouthing the object, drastically reducing their gazing and smiling at their mothers. Mother may try to distract the infant from the toy, but she is typically unsuccessful (Fogel, Garvey, Hsu, & West-Stroming, 2006). In fact, infants are absorbed in learning to coordinate mouth, hand, and eye in object exploration but from the perspective of the adult, the infant seems "lost" in her own world (Juberg, Alfano, Coughlin, & Thompson, 2001).

Pathological Dissociation: The Absorption into Negative Body States

Pathological forms of absorption are less common than the normal ones but more problematic. There are so many distinctions and definitions of dissociation in the psychological and psychiatric literature that they are impossible to summarize. I will follow the lead of Holmes et al. (2005) in defining **pathological dissociation** as having two basic forms: **detachment** and **compartmentalization** (see Table 4.3).

Detachment is "characterized by a sense of separation (or 'detachment') from certain aspects of everyday experience, be it their body (as in out-of-body experiences), their sense of self (as in depersonalization), or the external world (as in derealization)" (Holmes et al., 2005, p. 5). Detachment may also be seen in the form of entering a trancelike state in which the person seems to be frozen and immobilized, falling asleep, or creating a "pretend" persona (happy, rich, playful, sexy) which is different from the more troubled "real" person (see Case Report 4.2).

Out-of-body experience (OBE) is a type of detachment, as the perception of the self but from a distant location; the perceiver is often experienced as floating above their detached body and sees their body as if it was that of another person (Blanke et al., 2005). **Depersonalization syndrome** is a feeling of living outside one's body and outside the world. There is a feeling of separation from the self and a sense of emptiness (Fuchs, 2005).

While recreational dancing (see previous section) can be a way to induce normal absorption and relieve stress, professional dancers, especially females, may suffer from dissociative detachment. Standing on the toes in ballet shoes is a painful experience. The rigors of conditioning, training, and rehearsing can be emotionally and physically draining. Many dancers suffer from eating disorders in order to maintain their ultra-thinness.

> When you are dancing, you do not feel any pain. Once, during a rehearsal one of my *pointe* shoe ribbons broke. I put it together with a safety pin and while I was dancing the pin started to bend and the point of it went through my foot. This had been going on for some time and the bleeding was heavy. But I did not feel a thing! Because I had been dancing and concentrating on the dancing. Therefore you do not feel pain in that situation. (Aalten, 2007, p. 116)

This description of dissociative detachment reveals both the similarities and the differences between normal absorption (flow) and dissociation. In both cases, there is a total focus on the activity and a loss of peripheral awareness. While normal absorption is inherently pleasurable, however, dissociation is a loss of body sensation so as to avoid pain.

Compartmentalization, the other form of dissociation besides detachment, "incorporates dissociative amnesia and the 'unexplained' neurological symptoms characteristic of the conversion disorders, such as conversion paralysis, sensory loss, seizures, gait disturbance, and pseudo-hallucinations" (Holmes et al., 2005, p. 7). **Conversion disorder** is the contemporary name for what Freud called "hysteria," the substitution of a painful traumatic memory for a somatic symptom; basically, a psychosomatic disorder having no physical cause or diagnosis (Hurwitz, 2004; Kozlowska, 2005). Self-injurious behavior, such as cutting, also falls into this category.

Some of the trancelike body feelings of eating disorders such as lethargy, being "spaced out," or "drunk" on food are examples of compartmentalization (Waller et al., 2003). In most cases, by getting absorbed in these intoxications, the individual attempts to suppress negative feelings and sometimes even the pain and discomfort of the eating disorder. When the symptoms of the eating disorder become ends in themselves, to be recreated and amplified to the point of absorption, they become pathologically dissociative.

Conversion disorder is a form of somatization, sometimes called somatoform disorder. **Somatization** occurs when people become absorbed in, dwell on, and amplify their inner experiences to the point of exaggerating their importance. They may interpret otherwise benign sensations in the chest as a heart condition and seek medical attention. They have a tendency toward hypochondriasis (unnecessary use or overuse of medication and medical testing) and they exhibit symptomatic conditions like chest pain without known medical explanation.

What seems to be a focus on *health* in somatization is in fact a focus on illness. In Freud's cases, and many subsequent examples, the somatic symptom is often used as a way of getting sympathy, love, and attention that was not forthcoming in the person's childhood (Kirmayer, Robbins, & Paris, 1994). Observations of children with mothers who have a somatization disorder show that the mothers are overly focused on their child's health and safety, to the exclusion of the child's psychological and emotional needs. As a result of this unwanted attention, these children develop a pattern of ignoring their mother's offers of care and suppressing their own emotional needs (Bialas & Craig, 2007).

It is decidedly not healthy to amplify illness states at the expense of other more positive resources. People who somatisize have been shown to have more complicated postoperative recoveries compared to those who do not (Cohen & Lazarus, 1973). They also are predisposed to develop chronic fatigue syndrome, fibromyalgia, chronic sensitivity to environmental substances, and other long-term autoimmune disorders. Research suggests that the continued suppression of interoceptive information that could potentially lead the body back to a state of health via homeostatic regulation begins to drain metabolic resources. If the body thinks it is sick, it will induce the immune system to generate **proinflammatory cytokines** that stimulate neurotransmitters and alter brain states to maintain "sickness" behavior that includes muscle weakness, fatigue, fever, and depressed moods (Dantzer, 2005; Gendolla, Abele, Andrei, Spurk, & Richter, 2005; Jones, 2008; Rief & Barsky, 2005; Wilhelmsen, 2005).

Case Report 4.2
The Beginning of Joan's Rosen Method Bodywork Treatment

Given Joan's apparently normal absorption in physical and social activities in spite of her abdominal pain (described at the beginning of this chapter), I had assumed that her pain was likely due to a simple case of suppressing some emotion or early childhood experience. For the first few months of weekly Rosen treatments, nothing occurred to disconfirm this initial impression. Joan would spend a good part of the session talking conceptually about herself and her life, mostly staying on the surface of things and not in touch with embodied self-awareness except for her abdominal discomfort.

Her muscles were indeed tense to my touch, especially in her upper back and chest, shoulders, and neck. Her belly was taut but her hips and legs were loose, almost limp. Even in athletes, if they are not working their muscles should ideally come to rest. Rosen practitioners typically do not follow and interpret the thought processes in the client's running autobiographical narrative. We wait for small "openings" in that narrative when there is a connection between words and a change in body state. We notice if there is a longer breath or a sigh, a reddening of the skin indicating that sensation is returning, or sensations of muscles relaxing under our hands.

Often, the client is not aware of these initial openings. I may ask the client first to notice them and then to take a little longer with them, slow their thoughts so that they might begin to feel their bodies. "Did you notice that change in your breathing?" "No." And then waiting a bit, "There it is again. It happens when you talk about X." These are baby steps of interoceptive awareness, typically not accompanied by any emotions.

As Joan began to notice some of these links, she started to feel like she was learning something from our sessions that encouraged her to notice more and to feel safe enough to explore possible links between body symptoms and emotion. When Joan talked of her family, her body became tense and her breathing shallow. At first she was able to notice this pattern of tenseness, but as she attempted to feel her body in relationship to the words she spoke about her family she began to "disappear" into sleeplike states in which she did not speak or move. It was at this point that I became aware of her tendency toward dissociative detachment. This was surprising to me. I did not expect it.

After several more weeks, the pattern repeated itself again and again, and I wanted to find a way to help Joan become aware of what was happening to her. Because dissociative detachment is a way of "leaving" the present reality to become absorbed in another type of experience, helping someone to be aware of themselves in the present moment is a challenge. Because I could feel the subtle shifts of muscle relaxation and breathing that occurred just prior to her body going into the trance state, I tried to point this out to her, hoping that I could get her to become aware of herself in the process of making the transition into the dissociative state.

The result was that she found a way to escape even more quickly. Her reaction told me that I was trying too hard to connect with her. After she disappeared into herself, I felt useless, like it was my fault that I "lost" her. I remembered Rosen basic principles: to follow the client rather than lead them. It's not about where I want them to go, but about staying with where they are going. With that conceptual self-awareness, I could feel my shoulders relaxing and my breathing becoming easier. I made sure I could feel my feet touching the floor and that

Out of Touch with Ourselves

my hands were soft and receptive. This was accompanied by the emotions of relief that I didn't have to work so hard and gratitude that I, at least, could come back to my own embodied self-awareness.

I suggested to Joan that she just go into the drifting off without trying to fight it. This freed her. She began to show myoclonic twitches (see Chapter 3) and instead of going completely away, she became "dreamy" as she described it. She entered a trancelike state she seemed to enjoy, and she spoke in a "tiny" and liltingly playful voice, like a 5-year-old child during a game of pretend. As that small child, she could converse with me but she did not want to feel her body and she did not want to leave the dreamy playful state.

Over the next few sessions we explored this territory together. She began to feel that it was safe to visit this place with me, a kind of hiding place she had kept secret from everyone else. She began to have random memorylike images in this state: her mother, her brother, an overturned chair, a feeling of anxiety. I repeated these back to her in a soft voice, talking to the scared child, as if to confirm the veracity of these memories for her. As I did this, her skeletal and gut muscles began to relax: I could feel the former and both feel and hear the latter via **psychoperistalsis**, the involuntary noises of relaxation from the gut.

This was the beginning of my sensing the link between Joan's childhood experiences, her gastrointestinal symptoms, her suppression of embodied self-awareness, and her dissociative detachment. For the adult Joan, however, these links were not yet part of her conceptual or embodied self-awareness.

The early sessions of this case illustrate some of the basic steps of regaining embodied self-awareness listed in Table 1.1. Further developments in Joan's case will be reported in the next two chapters.

- *Resources* were found for Joan in different ways. At first, she began to feel comfortable with the routine of coming for her sessions. When she began to dissociate, I needed to reassess what kind of resources she needed. This turned out to be permission to indulge in her dissociative hiding place.
- *Slowing down* and being able to stay in the subjective emotional present occurred only briefly, as opening moves, in these early sessions. Mostly,

it was a challenge for me to remain self-aware when confronted with the client's withdrawal.
- *Coregulation* was part of the mutual adjustment process as the two of us discovered a way to welcome the "little girl" voice into the treatment room. This shift was not something initiated by the client or by me, but rather an emergent "dyadic state of consciousness," (Tronick, 2007) shared between the two of us.
- *Verbalization* on the client's part was a surprising mixture of "adult" and "child" voices. Joan seemed very calmed and pleased to be talking like a young child and I needed to learn how to talk with this part of her.
- *Links and boundaries* came up as Joan decided it was safe enough to come out of her "sleep" state and begin to cross over into the embodied feelings and behaviors of a child.
- *Self-regulation* in the sense of the adult Joan managing her emotions in the subjective emotional present as a way to calm herself and soothe her gut did not occur in these early sessions. The increasing confidence of the child voice, and the relaxation in her body that occurred along with it, was an incipient form of self-regulation but not part of her embodied self-awareness.
- *Reengagement* and letting go were not part of this phase of treatment. Stay tuned.

Entering into a client's dissociative state during a treatment session has been called **therapeutic dissociation**. Therapeutic dissociation is a shared awareness, coregulated between the client and the practitioner by which the client can come to better understand the dissociated part, where it came from, and what it needs from the adult (Davies, 1996). It can become therapeutic and lead to increased self-awareness because of **resources** provided by the presence of the practitioner. Even though Joan was speaking from the perspective of her "little girl," there is a shared awareness that the adult client is also present in the room, called "double consciousness" (Bosnak, 2003).

This is illustrated in a description of a craniosacral therapy session in which the therapist was both a craniosacral practitioner and a psychotherapist. Craniosacral therapists use gentle touch to feel the flow of cerebrospinal fluid. When stuck flows are felt, it can indicate emotional and other holding in the system. Although not typically focused on client self-awareness, this example shows how craniosacral therapy can be combined with self-awareness approaches, much like what occurs in Rosen Method Bodywork. In the session, while being touched in the hip and sacral area, the client, Jane, experienced a 6-year-old dissociative state and was invited by the therapist to explore it. Speaking of "double consciousness," the therapist wrote,

> I believe that the same phenomenon occurs by virtue of the physical contact between Jane and myself, which establishes a grounding in and reminder of the existence of the adult Jane who is lying on my table. . . . While we are explicitly involved with the experience of the 6-year-old, staying in relationship to her and tracking her experience through the movements of Jane's body. . .we are also implicitly in relationship to the adult Jane whose voice is being used by the child. By my staying in relationship to both Janes simultaneously, we are creating a possibility for both Janes, 6-year-old and adult, to come into relationship with each other in a new way. (Bass, 2007, pp. 159–160)

Rumination: The Absorption into Negative Thought Patterns

Thinking about the self, **conceptual self-awareness**, can take several forms. One form is the ability to think about the self and be simultaneously aware of embodied experiences. This occurs as the dorsomedial and ventromedial prefrontal cortices (DMPFC and VMPFC) partner with the interoceptive and emotional neural networks. The other form is thinking about the self without an awareness of body state, thoughts that occur primarily in the brain without a link to body receptors, mediated by the DMPFC (see Figure 3.2). This typically involves generalized judgments and evaluations of the self ("I'm too fat." "I'm not worthy of love.") that are disconnected with the lived condition of the body.

In some cases, the latter pattern of thoughts becomes like a broken record: the same thoughts keep repeating over and over again. **Rumination** is defined as "the tendency to repetitively focus on symptoms of distress and possible causes and consequences of those symptoms without engaging in active problem solving" (Nolen-Hoeksema, Stice, Wade, & Bohon, 2007, p. 198).

Psychophysiology of Self-Awareness

Rumination is one form of suppression of the underlying feelings and emotions that precipitate the distress but rumination works by creating a highly stable and distressingly absorbing series of negative thoughts (see Table 4.3).

Rumination as absorption in negative thoughts may serve as a guard against negative feelings but ultimately, like all pathological forms of absorption, it serves also to maintain the underlying negative state. Like somatization, which is a kind of ruminative focus on negative body feelings, rumination affects the immune, cardiovascular, and neuroendocrine systems in a way that maintains illness: depressed thoughts and negative self-evaluations lead to depressed moods and vice versa in a self-sustaining cycle (Brosschot, Pieper, & Thayer, 2005; Ciesla & Roberts, 2007; Gendolla et al., 2005; M. D. Lewis, 2008; Muraven, 2005; Pyszczynski & Greeberg, 1987; Tronick, 2007; Watkins, 2004). In addition to depression, rumination also occurs in eating disorders and some somatization disorders (see above) in which people have difficulty disengaging from the felt pain (van Damme et al., 2004), and addictions (see below) (Brown, 2004; Nolen-Hoeksema et al., 2007).

Accessing the negative feelings that may underlie the ruminative thoughts, via embodied self-awareness, clears the way to ending the negative cycle by using conceptual self-awareness to help assist in the healing process. Attention to feelings as opposed to attention to thoughts leads to a decline in rumination and depressed moods (Lischetzke & Eid, 2003; Watkins & Moulds, 2005). Nonruminative conceptual self-awareness is correlated with high self-esteem and empathic concerns for others (Joireman, Parrott, & Hammerslea, 2002). *The clinical implications are very clear and have been substantiated by research: teaching clients to pay attention to embodied self-awareness can assist them in changing their thought patterns to more positive and self-consistent ones, to elevating their moods, and enhancing the ability of their prefrontal cortex to link thought and feeling based in homeostatic self-regulation* (Lischetzke & Eid, 2003).

Addiction: The Absorption into Intoxication

The final form of pathological absorption that we will cover here is the intoxication of addiction (see Table 4.3). Addictions can take many forms. Addictive substances include alcohol, tobacco, caffeine, opiates, and sedatives. There is growing acceptance of the idea that people can also be addicted to pornography, to sex (compulsive promiscuity), to sugar- and fat-containing foods, to the Internet, to video games, and to watching television. The point at which normal absorption in these activities becomes an addiction is a matter of degree. Typically, one is considered addicted if the behavior cannot be restrained and it is ultimately self-injurious in spite of the "high" period. As many as 50 to 90% of addicts relapse within 6 months after treatment (Polivy, 1998). A newspaper in Detroit offered $500 to 120 families if they would give up watching TV for a month. Only 30 of them agreed, and all of these people described how difficult it was to do this (Berger, 1981).

Links between the OFC and ACC-SMA create the ability to suppress urges. Impairments in the communication between the OFC and the ACC can create an unrestrained urge to use or obtain an addictive substance. The ACC is responsible for the feeling of craving and the related actions of seeking, obtaining, and consuming (Verdejo-García, Perez-García, & Bechara, 2006).

The OFC works with thoughts and memories of the pleasurable body states of addiction and in conjunction with the DLPFC, can hold them in mind in order to make decisions related to action. These areas, together with the insula, bring the urges into the realm of self-awareness. When the insula highlights the euphoria of addictive substances in embodied self-awareness, there is a tendency toward the "forgetting" of the negative consequences of the addiction (social stigma, cost, withdrawal) (Bechara, Damasio, & Damasio, 2000; Verdejo-García et al., 2006).

In addictions as well as panic/anxiety attacks and some binge eating disorders, the insula runs unchecked, in a way, by activating the neural network to create constant cravings or fears that cannot be fully satisfied. Brain injury or stroke lesions of the insula have been shown to reduce craving associated with addictions. One insula lesioned patient said that he stopped smoking because his "body forgot the urge to smoke" and he said, "I forgot that I was a smoker" (Naqvi, Rudrauf, Damasio, & Bechara, 2007, p. 534).

This inability to remember the negative consequences, leading the OFC to focus more on the pleasure, is also due to increased concentrations of particular neurotransmitters. The primary neurotransmitter in addiction and pleasure is **dopamine** (Panksepp, Knutson, & Burgdorf, 2002). Dopamine is related to the activation of feelings of pleasure, enjoyment, and the motivation to perform activities that contribute to those feelings. This neurotransmitter is produced in the brain stem homeostatic sites and can be transmitted throughout the brain. All of the interoceptive brain areas—thalamus, ACC, and insula—contain **dopaminergic receptors** (Cohen & Carlezon, 2007), meaning that when dopamine is present, these receptors activate the cells in that area of the brain.

Dopamine is released during naturally rewarding activities like sex and eating. These are some of the "natural highs." Drugs, sugars, and other substances may become additive because they overstimulate dopamine release. When there is too much dopamine, it diminishes the activity of dopaminergic cell receptors in the interoceptive network, meaning that more of the substance is required in order for the interoceptive cells to feel "satisfied," as we saw in the reduced taste sensations of some obese individuals. And, paradoxically, even small amounts of the substance will activate the entire interoceptive network, including links between the insula and the motivational ACC, and thus produce craving for more of that substance.

As a general rule, abnormal alteration of receptors in any brain region can alter and even damage the ability of that region to effectively communicate with other regions. This helps to explain the defects in self-regulation in addiction, particularly in the inability of the brain to maintain homeostatic regulatory circuits in the prefrontal areas, and a corresponding amplification of desire in the insula-ACC circuit. Behaviorally, this means that urges cannot be controlled resulting in continued use of the substance but compromising the health of the rest of the body systems in the process.

In summary, pathological absorption in all its forms (Table 4.3) is an amplification of awareness on one particular focus to the exclusion of all others. Pathological absorption results in increasingly negative interoceptive states with a momentum that draws the person into them and makes it difficult for the person to escape. My client, Joan, did not want to leave her "little girl" dream world. People with somatization disorders are emotionally attached to the created identification with their "illness." Depressed people seem unable to climb out of the "black hole" of ruminative hopelessness and negativity. Addicts can destroy their bodies and ruin their relationships because of their inability to give up their cravings. Tapping into embodied self-awareness in any form has been proven to be therapeutically useful. It is not the particular treatment approach that matters, but rather the activation of some or all of the basic treatment processes for enhancing embodied self-awareness (Table 1.1).

5

Shelter from the Storm: The Effects of Safety and Threat on Embodied Self-Awareness

> *When the world was half a thousand years younger, the outlines of all things seemed more clearly marked than to us. The contrast between suffering and joy, between adversity and happiness, appeared more striking. All experience had yet to the minds of men the directness and absoluteness of the pleasure and pain of child-life. . . . Calamities and indigence were more afflicting than at present; it was more difficult to guard against them and to find solace. Illness and health present a more striking contrast; the cold and darkness of winter were more real evils.*
>
> (Huizinga, 1998, p. 1).

The above description of European life at the end of the Middle Ages sounds distant and foreign. Life in the 21st century is equally calamitous, however, in both similar and different ways. Today's afflictions are from interpersonal loss and strife, family violence, illness and death, automobile accidents, crime, warfare, and natural disasters. Poverty, hunger, displacement of persons from their homes, human trafficking, slavery, and genocide are occurring somewhere in the world today and perhaps very close to home.

Apart from these environmental and social forces, there are many other ways in which stress and trauma can enter people's lives. Most Americans feel that their well-being is threatened by stress and much of this worry is related to their jobs and finances. Less than a quarter of a sample of over 1,800 people surveyed believe they are handling the stress well and the rest admit to suppression via overeating, drinking too much, watching too much TV, not getting enough exercise, and the like (http://www.apahelpcenter.org).

Estimates vary but of the more than 1.5 million troops sent to Afghanistan and Iraq between 2001 and 2008, over 300,000, or about 20%, have returned

Psychophysiology of Self-Awareness

home with posttraumatic stress disorder (PTSD) or depression, and physical wounds accompanied by emotional trauma also afflict a substantial number of veterans (http://www.msnbc.com). Every year in the United States, there are about 3 million motor vehicle injuries (http://www-nrd.nhtsa.dot.gov), 1.5 million violent crimes (http://www.fbi.gov/ucr), 5 million victims of child abuse and neglect (Lambie, 2005), 4 million reported cases of nonfatal occupational injuries (http://www.bls.gov), and 1.5 million new cases of cancer (http://www.cancer.org). By any estimate, every single year, a substantial number of people are added to the tally of the wounded. The families and caregivers of these individuals are also affected.

No matter one's country of residence, in some way, at some time in our lives, we or someone close to us has been a victim of something that felt extremely threatening. The topic is important in this book because threatening events, especially if they are chronic, can fundamentally alter our embodied self-awareness. In fact, the forms of suppression and absorption reviewed in the previous chapter arise in humans as a way to protect against a sense of threat.

Threat, Stress, and Trauma

The ability to recognize and respond to threats to our safety is a fundamental design feature of our physiology. **Threat** is the felt sense of fear that a person or her or his property or significant others are under attack and in danger of physical or psychological harm. The threat may originate from outside of ourselves or from inside our bodies. One can be threatened by an attacker, and also threatened by the physical wound caused by the attacker. If the threat is personal, persistent, and sudden, there is no time to think about and plan for it. Our bodies, as we shall see in this chapter, have a rapid response system that is linked to the pathways for interoception, emotion, proprioception, and the body schema.

Stress is the condition that results when the body is unable to achieve homeostatic balance. Hans Selye, who first studied the effects of stress on the organism (1950), suggested that the stress response goes through three phases: the sense of threat or alarm, the body's attempt to adapt or cope, and either resolution and return to normal function or exhaustion of the body's resources. **Trauma** is the condition that results from prolonged exhaustion of resources, a condition in which the person becomes unable to integrate the resulting interoceptive experiences, emotions, changes in body schema, and thoughts thus creating another level of stress on the system. Both stress and trauma depend upon how a particular person responds to events. In the same situation, one person may be affected while another not at all.

Suppose that you work in front of a computer screen for many hours each day. You like your work, and you enjoy doing a good job and getting recognition for it. Your working conditions are not stressful but your desire for good performance leads you to forget your body. After 2, or 5, or 10 years, you discover that you are developing chronic lower back pain. You go to the doctor or the chiropractor and the analgesics and adjustments help for a while, but the condition persists. Soon you can't concentrate on your work very well, you become grouchy with coworkers and companions, you can't do gardening, which you love, you can't lift up and hug your kids, which you love even more, and most days you don't feel like getting out of bed.

Most likely, you had been sitting for many years in a way that put stress on your lower back. This posture was related to the emotions around work achievement and being a valued employee. These emotions were in the background since your focus was conceptual: deadlines, judgments about your own performance, expectations from others that kept you thinking even after work and into the night. Your interoceptions were even more buried: you didn't even notice the muscle strain in your back, hips, and thighs except maybe to feel a bit stiff after standing up. Your body schema was also distorted: you imagined yourself as a social player in a larger organization but you could not see yourself as sedentary and immobile most of the time.

You did notice the pain once it began, the body's wake-up call to pay attention to yourself. It is to be hoped that it was not too late to use relatively simple self-awareness remedies like adjusting your posture, standing up and stretching from time to time, going to the gym to cleanse the body of toxins, getting a massage, or meditating to clear the mind of your compelling thoughts or to make friends with your pain (see Box 5.1).

Paradoxically, even though pain is meant to be a wake-up call, it is often treated like an unwelcome guest. All we want to do is get away from it or to have that guest leave as soon as possible. Pain often leads to suppression and absorption. Continuing to suppress pain in the absence of embodied self-

Psychophysiology of Self-Awareness

awareness that leads to self-care, therefore, can predispose us to even more suffering (see Figure 5.1).

If you continue to ignore the pain, you may develop tissue damage like tendonitis, or loss of cartilage, or bone compression in the vertebra, or a pinched nerve. Your body was under stress the whole time and you did not become aware of that until it had progressed into the stage of depleting your body's resources to cope with it: literally destroying cells that maintain your ability to function. The pain, which seemed to come from nowhere since you had not been paying attention to yourself, is now compounded by multiple threats: the threat of disability, the threat of losing work productivity and even your job, the threat of a compromised family life, and perhaps other threats as well.

You have passed from stress into trauma, the condition of being overwhelmed by the suddenness of a series of threatening, compounding, and chaotic changes over which you have no control. Now, to get better, you not only have to treat the tissue damage but you also have to treat the trauma, your psychological sense of helplessness as the ground on which you thought you had been safely standing is no longer solid and supportive.

Trauma is an example of the formation of an **attractor** in a dynamic system (M. D. Lewis, 2005). Figure 5.1 shows how this happens. A threat from outside the body (an infection, an assault, work stress, exposure to an environmental toxin, warfare, etc.) creates an interoceptive and motivational reaction in the body (arousal, irritation, immune system response, protective reaction, etc.). The body will keep doing this so long as it perceives the threat, which, as in the example of work-induced lower back pain, could go on for many years. **Shock trauma** is the effect of a relatively brief and sudden event like an assault or a drug overdose. **Developmental trauma** results when exposure occurs over a longer period of time. Eventually, the tissues around the interoceptive receptor sites may become physically threatened, at which point the person begins to feel pain.

Now what happens is that the threat, in addition to coming from the external sources, also begins to come from within the body. This amplifies the sense of threat and further exacerbates the body's attempts to cope with it. The typical way to cope with pain that seems to get in the way of our completing our goals (which were to avoid the threat of poor work performance or the threat of an attack) is to avoid it by suppression and absorption. This may ultimately lead to a disease state that drains even more resources and ups the level

Safety and Threat

of threat once again (see Figure 5.1). This is an attractor: an apparently never-ending looping cycle of dysfunction and avoidance.

Figure 5.1

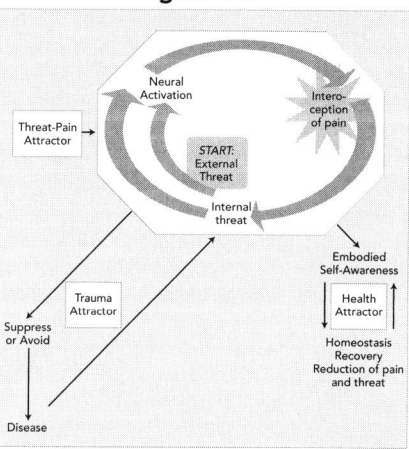

The pain-threat cycle starts with an external threat, leading to the activation of ergoreceptors, proprioceptors, and possibly nociceptors for pain. That information gets sent to the brain where it is re-represented as the embodied self-awareness of threat. A second threat arises from the pain itself, the fear of what might be wrong with the body. The cycle may persist even after the external threat has disappeared. If the pain is persistently suppressed, it may lead to a traumatic disease state. If the pain is experienced directly and allowed to be felt, it can return the body to homeostasis and reduce the pain.

Some individuals, those who become absorbed in somatization, are more likely than others to amplify body feelings. These individuals are prone to anxiety and irritability. By a self-perpetuating attractor in self-awareness, they become absorbed in worry over benign symptoms, zoom in on those symptoms to the exclusion of other forms of embodied self-awareness, and feel that they are abnormal and ill (Bakal, 1999).

Research on people with muscle pain—lower back and neck-shoulder pain as well as tension-type headache—shows that the muscles around the site of the pain tense up as a way of suppressing the pain and the neurophysiological connections between the muscles and the sensorimotor cortices becomes altered in a way that limits both sensation and movement. The muscle tension actually helps to suppress the pain (think of squeezing your arm or leg if it gets bumped) but that only works for a short time. People come to fear movement of those muscles and avoid using them, the "pain–stress–pain" cycle. Eventually, the person may begin to distrust the body and to feel despair, hopelessness, and grief, as well as higher **sympathetic nervous system** activation under stress and sensory sensitivity in the area of the pain. Relaxation and other treatments for chronic muscle tension have proved useful (Ashina et al., 2005; Burns, 2006; Flor, Birbaumer, Schugens, & Lutzenberger, 1992; Knardahl, 2002; Knost, Flor, Birbaumer, & Schugens, 1999; Lund, Donga, Widmer, & Stohler, 1991; Nederhand, Hermans, Ijzerman, Groothuis, & Turic, 2006; Sterling, Jull, & Kenarely, 2006; van Dieën, Selen, & Cholewicki 2003; Vlaeyen & Crombez, 1999; Zautra, Smith, Affleck, & Tennen, 2001).

In this example, even a work injury in an otherwise happy life with lots of support at home and at the office can lead to serious consequences if unattended. If the trauma is precipitated by more severe conditions such as those mentioned in the opening paragraph of this chapter, and if no immediate treatment is forthcoming, it can lead to posttraumatic stress disorder (PTSD). **Posttraumatic stress disorder** is a condition precipitated by an extremely threatening event or series of events that is characterized by persistently high arousal, flashbacks of parts of the trauma event, memory loss for other parts of that event, lack of ability to concentrate, and impairment of social functioning (see Table 5.1).

Table 5.1
Symptoms of posttraumatic stress disorder (PTSD)

1. Exposure to an event involving a serious threat to life, health, or personal integrity that produces intense fear and helplessness.
2. Persistent reexperiencing of the traumatic event in the form of flashbacks, nightmares, or feeling that the traumatic event continues to recur.
3. Persistent avoidance of anything related to the traumatic event, such as being in similar situations, talking about the event, inability to recall aspects of the event, and feelings of detachment from others.
4. Persistently high arousal such that the person is easily "triggered" by current situations that resemble the traumatic event, persistent anger, difficulty resting or sleeping, difficulty concentrating.
5. Disturbances in social, occupational, or other roles that may lead to job loss, family dissolution, and loss of support systems.

Source: American Psychiatric Association. (1994). *Diagnostic and Statistical Manual of Mental Disorders* (4th ed.). Washington DC: Author, pp. 467–468.

Safety and Threat

There have been many and varied approaches to the study and treatment of PTSD. The goal of this chapter is to show how all forms of threat, from the simple everyday ones to those that precipitate PTSD, fall on a continuum. They are all disturbances of embodied self-awareness and they can all, if we fail to pay attention to ourselves, lead to disease states.

Biobehavioral Responses to Safety and Threat

Responding to threat, and its accompanying physical and psychological pain, is a fundamental aspect of survival. Seeking safety is also essential to give the individual an opportunity to recover and to heal the physical and emotional trauma that may have arisen from the sense of threat. *The ability to respond to threat and to seek safety is the most important job of our nervous system.*

In addition to the interoceptive and body schema neural networks, there is a neural network dedicated to assessing and responding to threat and seeking safety (Fields, 2004) and it occupies virtually all of the core parts of our brain: neural cells and pathways in the brain stem, limbic system, prefrontal, sensorimotor and parietal cortices. This core architecture of the brain is virtually identical in all vertebrate animals. As humans, we have more extensively developed cortical areas for the kind of brain-based rerepresentations that allow for embodied and conceptual self-awareness. This, however, is just the icing. The cake has the same ingredients across species (Tucker, 2001).

In response to threat and safety, there are six major **biobehavioral response patterns**: vigilance, threat mobilization, threat immobilization, restoration, engagement, and normal absorption. There are other ways of conceptualizing the body's responses to threat and safety but I have chosen this schema of six categories because it seems to me the best fit with the wide ranging themes of embodied self-awareness across the spectrum of threat vs. safety. These categories are summarized in Table 5.2. Because these response patterns are so essential to survival, they can operate automatically, without the need to bring them into self-awareness. With practice and therapeutic intervention, however, we can access these patterns in embodied self-awareness to assist in recovery.

In a state of safety, the individual is capable of creative and flexible **engagement** in the **subjective emotional present** with self and others (Cell 2, Table 5.2). This includes all forms of embodied self-awareness. Normal attentive awareness requires a balance between the two parts of the **autonomic nervous**

Psychophysiology of Self-Awareness

Table 5.2
Biobehavioral responses to safety and threat

	Primarily parasympathetic nervous system (PNS)	PNS-SNS homeostasis	Primarily sympathetic nervous system (SNS)
Safety or concern	1 **Restoration** Rest, meditate	2 **Engagement** Engagement in the subjective emotional present; Embodied self-awareness *Attachment:* Secure *Significant other:* Consistently available and loving	3 **Vigilance** Alerting, arousal, attention *Attachment:* anxious-resistant *Significant other:* Inconsistently available but loving
Threat	4 Threat **Immobilization** Freeze, faint, dissociation, somatization *Attachment:* Disorganized-disoriented *Significant other:* Frightening	5 **Normal absorption** Flow	6 Threat **Mobilization** Fight, Flight Suppression *Attachment:* Avoidant-dismissive *Significant other:* Angry or intolerant

system (ANS): the **parasympathetic nervous system** (PNS, rest and relaxation), and the **sympathetic nervous system** (SNS, arousal and action). If there is a PNS–SNS balance, we can feel and express our emotions while at the same time being able to empathize with and relate to others. The ANS, which is connected to the hypothalamus and brain stem autonomic areas, regulates the cardiovascular, respiratory, and digestive systems as well as the activation of the salivary and lachrymal (tears) glands, and the medulla of the adrenal glands (see Table 5.3).

The adrenal cortex secretes **cortisol** when stimulated by the cascade of blood-borne hormones (ACTH) along the **HPA axis** to increase blood glucose and heart function in response to stress and threat (See Figure 5.5).

Because of this cascade of hormones along the HPA axis, it could take up to 30 minutes for cortisol to show up in the bloodstream in amounts large enough to affect the body. The adrenal medulla is directly and rapidly innervated by the ANS and when there is stress, the sympathetic branch induces the adrenal medulla to secrete **epinephrine** (also known as adrenaline). Epinephrine has similar arousing affects on the body as cortisol. There is an important difference between the two hormones related to the long-term impact of threat and stress on the body. As part of the HPA axis, cortisol has receptors in the hypothalamus, amygdala, and prefrontal cortex and too much cortisol can damage these receptors with effects on mood, memory, and hyperreactivity to stress. Epinephrine finds most of its receptors in the liver and muscle cells, to trigger glucose production and vasodilation, ultimately being less toxic to the body and to the neural networks regulating safety and threat.

The PNS is connected with relaxation of the internal organs while the SNS generates a state of heightened arousal. We need both the arousal and the relaxation in order to orient to and attend to the environment and to ourselves in the subjective emotional present. As the sense of threat increases, there can still be a balance of the PNS and SNS. This occurs during some forms of **normal absorption** (see **absorption**), the so-called **flow** experiences (Cell 5, Table 5.2).

Table 5.3
Autonomic nervous system

Body area	Sympathetic nervous system	Parasympathetic nervous system
Digestion	Inhibits secretion of saliva and digestiveive enzymes as well as intestinal muscle movements, contracts sphincters	Enhances secretory and motor aspects of digestion, relaxes sphincters
Respiration	Dilates bronchial passages, increases respiration rate, more forced expiration	Constricts bronchial passages, slows respiration rate, leads to relaxed breathing
Eyes	Dilates pupils	Constricts pupils, stimulates lachrymal gland to produce tears
Cardiovascular	Increases heart rate and blood pressure, dilates blood vessels	Decreases heart rate and blood pressure, contracts blood vessels
Sweat glands	Stimulates secretion	No effect

Psychophysiology of Self-Awareness

Flow occurs when one is fully and totally immersed in an activity in the subjective emotional present and when that activity is potentially risky. An artistic or athletic performance brings with it threats such as strain or injury (pulled muscles and tendons, broken bones), death (in activities like circus performance, extreme skiing, race-car driving), stage fright, and performance anxiety. Flow occurs in the face of these threats as the individual gives in to the feeling of safety in their level of skill and then lets go of worry and fear in order to enter the flow state. The normal absorption of flow may also occur in emotionally risky interpersonal encounters, such as presenting one's deepest feelings or one's naked body to another person.

On either side of the PNS–SNS balance, one or the other is the primary mode of ANS function. On the parasympathetic side, there are two modes of operation. One is **restoration**, and the other is **threat immobilization**. The parasympathetic **vagus nerve** is a cranial nerve, originating in the middle brain stem and traveling directly to all the internal organ systems mentioned here without passing through the spinal cord (see Figure 5.2). Restoration is regulated by the ventral (toward the front of the body) portion of the vagus nerve while immobilization is regulated by the dorsal (toward the back of the body) portion of the vagus nerve (Porges, 2001, 2004).

Restoration (Cell 1, Table 5.2) is a quiescent state—often following threat or intense engagement—that involves self-care, resting, sleeping, and recovering. In humans, restoration can take the form of being with embodied self-awareness in the subjective emotional present, meditation, soothing baths or massages, or being held or touched by another person in a nondemanding manner. Restoration involves relaxed breathing, normal heart rate, and regularized digestive function. If it follows severe stress, restoration may have characteristics similar to "sickness" behavior—feelings of muscle weakness, fatigue, and perhaps inflammation—that encourage the body to rest and recover.

During threat **immobilization** many of the basic life functions are slowed or shut down (Cell 4, Table 5.2). It can take the form of *freezing* or *fainting* and includes decreased responsiveness to the environment, slowing of heart rate (brachycardia), and slowing of breathing, digestion, and metabolic activity. Typically, threat immobilization occurs as a biobehavioral response to threats that are perceived as *inescapable*. These may be threats such as traumatic physical injury, repeated experiences of defeat in encounters with the environment, or confrontation with a clearly more powerful adversary (Bandler, Keay, Floyd, & Price, 2000; Porges, 2004).

The SNS, in contrast to PNS relaxation, creates a state of arousal in the body. When the individual encounters a cause for concern, it activates attention toward that cause. When there is the possibility that the concern may be threatening, attention shifts into a state of **vigilance**, a slowing or cessation of movement except for head and eye scanning accompanied by autonomic changes such as a slowing of heart rate (brachycardia), short, quiet, and shallow breathing, and skeletal muscle tension and possible tremors. This can be described as an anticipatory fear state (Cell 3, Table 5.2; Bradley et al., 2003; Duan et al., 1996).

If, as a result of this vigilance, the individual feels that there is no reason for alarm, there can be a return to engagement, restoration, or absorption. If threat is perceived, however, this may engender a **threat mobilization** response: active **defensive** strategies, in particular, *fight and flight*. Fight and flight are outward-directed forms of engagement with the source of the threat and they are accompanied by specific behavior patterns such as crouching, attack, running, and autonomic responses of increased heart rate (tachycardia) and rapid respiration rate, increased blood flow to the peripheral muscles and away from the digestive system (Cell 6; Table 5.2). Mobilization occurs when the threat is perceived as *potentially escapable*. When the threat seems inescapable, the system may shift into immobilization.

In the same encounter, there may be changes between perceptions of escapability and inescapability. If a prey animal sees a predator approaching, the prey will become quiet and vigilant. If there is an opportunity to escape, the prey will begin to run and seek safety (flight). If caught, the prey may decide to resist by kicking, screaming, or biting (fight). If the prey senses, however, that resistance is futile (or if a serious wound has already been inflicted) there will be a rapid (nonlinear transition) shutdown of activity (freeze). In either case, this "playing dead" is adaptive because many predators only pursue the prey if it is alive and moving. The predator gets aroused by flight and fight even in the absence of hunger. If the animal escapes the incident alive and finds safety, it can enter into a restoration state followed by a return to normal engagement states.

Psychophysiology of Self-Awareness

These biobehavioral responses occur automatically and out of our awareness. This has been called **neuroception**, the ability of our nervous system to assess safety and threat and make appropriate adjustments to prepare our bodies to survive (Porges, 2004). As humans, we can later come to feel and remember these responses either in embodied or conceptual self-awareness.

The "choices" our bodies make on their own, without our awareness, when we are under threat are not always the choices we might have made in a calmer state of mind. Sexual assault victims, for example, may become immobilized if the attacker threatens to kill or disfigure them. Part of the resulting traumatic impact of the assault is guilt for not resisting and self-blaming thoughts for "giving in." *The simple physiological fact, however, is that under threat embodied and conceptual self-awareness go off-line as the more primal parts of the brain activate an ancient trove of wisdom that has assured the continuation of life on earth for millions of years.* "You," the one who can sometimes become self-aware, had no role at all in that response, and you can credit your ancestors for your ability to survive at all.

The Neural Networks for Automatic Biobehavioral Responses to Safety and Threat

Fear is an emotion engendered by the threat of actual, imagined, or anticipated injury and its accompanying pain. Pain perception can begin in the periphery or in imagination and memory. Pain is sensed in the peripheral areas of the body by **nociceptors** that send signals to the brain when the mechanoreceptors, thermoreceptors, and other ergoreceptors sense a *threat* of injury to the body tissues (they may be burned, torn, crushed, starved, infected, or poisoned).

Nociceptor signals travel on unmyelinated, slow Aδ and C nerve fibers in the dorsal horn of the spinal cord (in lamina I and other neighboring laminae, Figure 2.2). These pain fibers are anatomically similar to the lamina I Aδ and C nerve fibers from the ergoreceptors (Chapter 2) and travel on parallel tracks with them. Pain *sensations* ultimately enter the limbic and prefrontal areas of the interoceptive neural network while pain *location* ultimately enters the body schema neural network.

Pain and threat sensations first pass through the homeostatic areas of the brain stem, alongside the signals from the ergoreceptors (interoception) and

Safety and Threat

proprioceptors (body schema). From there, unlike the ergoreceptor and proprioceptor signals which pass directly to the thalamus and hypothalamus, pain signals take a detour through the **periaqueductal grey (PAG)**. The PAG is located at the very top of the brain stem (most rostral portion; see Figure 5.2), just behind (dorsal to) the hypothalamus and the other limbic system structures.

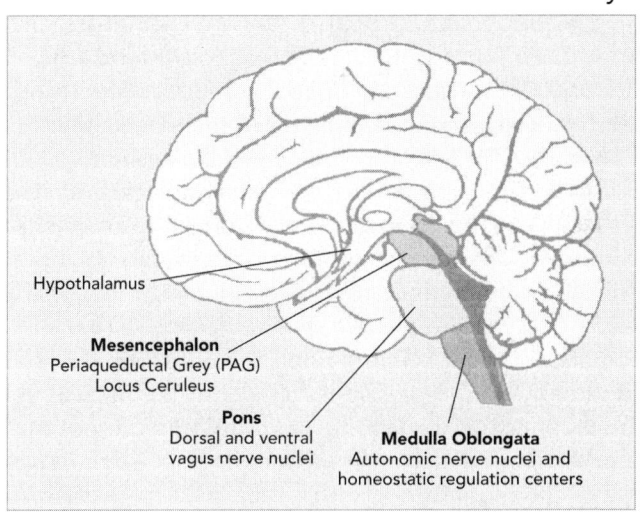

Figure 5.2
Brain stem structures related to threat and safety

- Hypothalamus
- **Mesencephalon**
  Periaqueductal Grey (PAG)
  Locus Ceruleus
- **Pons**
  Dorsal and ventral vagus nerve nuclei
- **Medulla Oblongata**
  Autonomic nerve nuclei and homeostatic regulation centers

The PAG helps to locate pain signals in the body and to select one or more of the biobehavioral response patterns described in the previous section. The cylindrically shaped PAG runs vertically through the center of the upper brain stem and surrounds a tube called the cerebral aqueduct, a cavity in the neural tissue through which **cerebrospinal fluid (CSF)** is conducted between the spinal cord and the cerebral cortex. CSF serves as a cushion for the brain, protecting it from injury inside the skull and also affording some immunological protection for the brain. Craniosacral therapy works on enhancing the flow of CSF through the spinal column and into the brain and may play some role in modulating the pain signals in the PAG.

Even though there are body-based treatments that are effective for many types of conditions, craniosacral therapy and most types of massage do not typ-

Psychophysiology of Self-Awareness

ically require clients to enhance their embodied self-awareness, and thus will not be covered in this book. For that matter, most medical interventions are body-based treatments. As noted elsewhere in this book, adding an embodied self-awareness component to these interventions can enhance their effectiveness.

The PAG is organized into columnar bundles of nerve cells on its dorsal (back), lateral (sides), and ventral (front) areas. Research has shown that different columns and different regions of the columns regulate different biobehavioral responses. **Mobilization** is organized in the lateral columns of the PAG, while **immobilization** and **restoration** are coordinated by the ventrolateral columns of the PAG. The PAG has a **somatotopic** organization, meaning that its specific regions are linked to specific somatotopic regions of the sensory and motor cortices, the cerebellum, and to specific sites at the periphery of the body. The PAG can thus direct the biobehavioral responses to and from specific body locations and also communicate with the rest of the brain (Bandler & Keay, 1996; Bandler et al., 2000). We are typically not aware of how the brain stem affects the body unless it is joined by limbic and cortical branches of the interoceptive neural network to activate rerepresentations.

The PAG also links into the ANS centers lower in the spinal cord. The immobilization area of the PAG in the upper brain stem, for example, is connected to the dorsal vagal (parasympathetic) output nucleus in the middle brain stem (see previous section), while the restoration area of the PAG is connected to the ventral vagal nucleus in the middle brain stem (parasympathetic) (see Figure 5.2). The mobilization area of the PAG is linked into the sympathetic ANS nuclei in the lower brain stem (see Figure 5.2; Fields, 2004; Tucker, 2001).

Input to the PAG, in addition to coming directly from the body via nociceptive pathways, can also come from the central nervous system. The central neural structure for the processing of the threat-related emotion of fear is the **amygdala** (see Figure 5.3). The left and right amygdala are part of the limbic system, located on either side of the hypothalamus and just at the end of the horseshoe shaped structure called the hippocampus. The amygdala is part of the neural network by which threat is detected quickly by the brain to activate the biobehavioral responses without the need for embodied self-awareness (Amorapanth, LeDoux, & Nader, 2000; Grove et al., 2007; Kim & Forman, 2005; Roozendaal, Koolhaas, & Bohns, 1997).

Safety and Threat

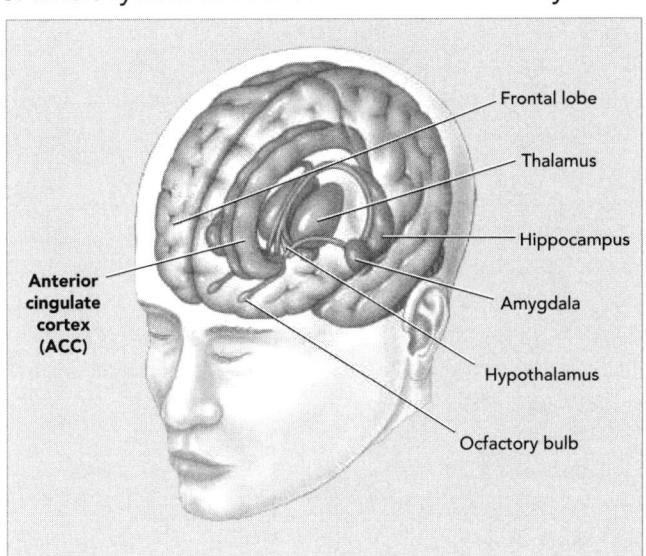

Figure 5.3
3-D view of limbic system structures related to the safety-threat network

The amygdala is linked, via the thalamus, to the sensory cortices of the brain, and these cortices are linked to the **exteroceptors**, the sense organs in the visual, auditory, olfactory, gustatory, and tactile systems of the body. This allows for multisensory recognizing of fearful situations and also, acting with the SNS, to directing attention toward and increasing **vigilance** regarding possible sources of threat (Bradley et al., 2003; LeDoux, 1989). The amygdala has direct inputs to the PAG that, like the nociceptive inputs from below, can trigger the neuroception of the automatic biobehavioral response patterns (Grove, Coplan, & Hollander, 1997).

The amygdala also plays a role in the activation of the biobehavioral response patterns not only through the neural links to the PAG and ANS, but also via a neurochemical system that includes endogenous opiates, hormones, neurotransmitters, and immune cells (see Figure 5.4). This system is highly complex and massively interconnected in ways that are not completely understood. The following paragraphs give a brief overview of some of the clinically relevant aspects of this system.

Psychophysiology of Self-Awareness

Figure 5.4
Neurochemical network connected with the activation of biobehavioral responses to safety and threat

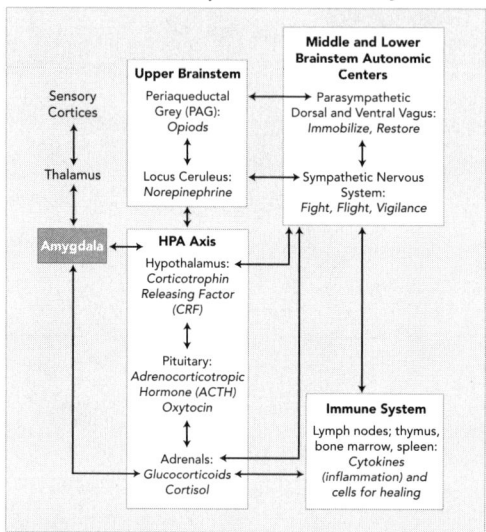

```
                    Upper Brainstem          Middle and Lower
                                             Brainstem Autonomic
                                             Centers
   Sensory          Periaqueductal      ←→   Parasympathetic
   Cortices         Grey (PAG):              Dorsal and Ventral Vagus:
        ↑           Opiods                   Immobilize, Restore
        ↓              ↕                            ↕
   Thalamus         Locus Ceruleus:      ←→   Sympathetic Nervous
        ↑           Norepinephrine            System:
        ↓              ↕                     Fight, Flight, Vigilance
   [Amygdala] ←→    HPA Axis                      ↑
                    Hypothalamus: ←
                    Corticotrophin
                    Releasing Factor
                    (CRF)
                       ↕
                    Pituitary:
                    Adrenocorticotropic
                    Hormone (ACTH)
                    Oxytocin                 Immune System
                       ↕                     Lymph nodes; thymus,
                    Adrenals:                bone marrow, spleen:
                  → Glucocorticoids ←→       Cytokines
                    Cortisol                 (inflammation) and
                                             cells for healing
```

Studies have shown that in situations of threat, stress, and pain when the individual must continue to attend to the demands of the situation, such as during fight or flight (as when a prey animal is being attacked by a predator), the PAG-amygdala system can induce the secretion of powerful endogenous opiates (morphinelike substances) that have an analgesic effect. The opiates reenter the brain and have receptors in most of the brain areas related to pain perception and interoception.

While these opiates are essential to short-term coping, continued suppression of the pain is not advantageous in the long run. *Individuals need to switch to more active forms of coping using their embodied self-awareness as an aid to homeostatic recovery, such as resting, relaxing, and paying direct attention to the wound or hurt* (Drolet et al., 2001; Fields, 2004). Opiates are also secreted to help keep the individual relatively sedated during periods of restoration.

There are two different hormonal pathways related to threat and safety: one through the hypothalamus (the HPA axis) and the other through a region of the upper brain stem adjacent to the PAG called the locus ceruleus. The **HPA axis** refers to the vertical arrangement and linkages between the hypo-

Safety and Threat

thalamus, pituitary gland (located in the base of the brain just below the hypothalamus, see Figure 5.4 and Figure 5.5), and the cortex of the adrenal glands (located above the kidneys).

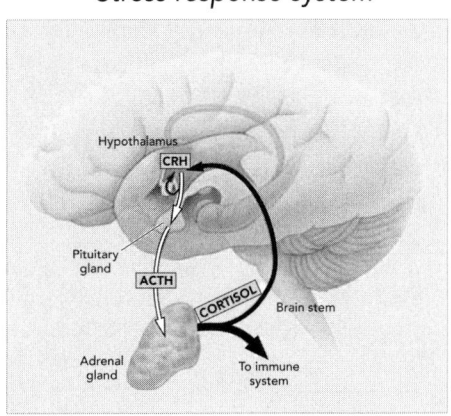

Figure 5.5
Stress response system

The HPA axis (hypothalamus-pituitary-adrenal). The hypothalamus secretes CRF (corticotrophin releasing factor; sometimes called CRH, corticotrophin releasing hormone) that stimulates the pituitary to secrete ACTH (adrenocorticotropic hormone), that stimulates the adrenal glands located above the kidneys to secrete cortisol. The hypothalamus and pituitary also secrete oxytocin directly into the blood stream. CRF also re-enters the brain directly from the hypothalamus.

The hypothalamus produces, among other hormones, **CRF** (corticotrophin releasing factor; sometimes called CRH, corticotrophin releasing hormone) which stimulates the pituitary to secrete **ACTH** (adrenocorticotropic hormone), which in turn stimulates the cortex of the adrenal glands to secrete **cortisol**, one of the substances in the glucocorticoid family of steroids. Cortisol is carried in the blood and in response to threat increases blood pressure, blood glucose, and also suppresses the activity of the immune system. This allows the metabolic energy systems of the body to be directed to the skeletal muscles for threat **mobilization** and normal **engagement** (Duan et al., 1996; Pecoraro et al., 2006).

In addition to stimulating the secretion of ACTH, CRF also circulates directly back to the brain where it finds multiple receptor sites. CRF receptors in the amygdala, for example, heighten its sensitivity to similar threat-related stimulation, a learning and remembering process that will be discussed more below. CRF also travels to the brain stem where, via the locus ceruleus and PAG, it activates the ANS and biobehavioral response patterns (Dunn, Swiergiel, & Palamarchouk, 2004; see Figure 5.4 and Figure 5.5).

The hypothalamus, in addition to responding to threat, also adjusts activity and energy levels in the body in response to daily and seasonal cycles. Normally, cortisol increases in the morning and then falls during the day and is lowest at night. Cortisol is essential for normal forms of engagement with the environment.

Cortisol, like CRF, has multiple receptor sites in the brain. Under normal conditions, these receptors create a feedback system that tells the hypothalamus to slow or stop secretion of CRF to regulate energy and activity. *If threat is persistent, more cortisol is secreted, which ultimately makes the individual more sensitive to even minor forms of threat or stress, and creates the feeling of threat in the prefrontal areas even when threat is not present in the environment.* This is the physiological origin of trauma in the body.

These changes in the blood chemistry in response to threat pair up with the neurological and neurochemical changes coming from the amygdala and hypothalamus and passing through the PAG and locus ceruleus on the way to the brain stem autonomic areas. The sympathetic pathway inhibits the action of the digestive system, increases heart rate and respiration, and along with the hormone-induced increased blood flow and blood glucose, energizes the muscles for action.

The **locus ceruleus**, located next to the PAG, secretes norepinephrine (NE), considered both a hormone and a neurotransmitter. **Norepinephrine (NE)** is a stress hormone that activates the brain stem sympathetic nerve centers and also feeds back to the hypothalamus to increase the secretion of CRF which ultimately becomes cortisol (Dunn et al., 2004; see Figure 5.2 and Figure 5.4).

If there is a sense of safety, the hypothalamus suppresses the secretion of CRF which in turn suppresses the activation of the locus ceruleus, sympathetic nervous system, and cortisol. In the case of safety, the hypothalamus begins instead to secrete hormones that lead the pituitary to secrete oxytocin, which enters the blood stream directly. **Oxytocin**, also a hormone and a neurotransmitter, stimulates maternal behavior and female reproductive function (see Figure 5.4). It also plays a role in affiliation, attachment, and the reduction of anxiety in both males and females (see Chapter 6).

Oxytocin works together with the endogenous opiods and the parasympathetic nervous system to engender states of normal **engagement** and **restoration**. In some situations, oxytocin can stimulate affilitive responses even in the face of threat by lowering blood pressure and heart rate. Partly, this system evolved to facilitate maternal behavior following the extreme stress of childbirth, and the effects of oxytocin are enhanced in the presence of estrogen (Light et al., 2000). One might expect, because of the link between oxytocin and maternal behavior, that women would be more likely than men to be affiliative under stress. There is no conclusive evidence to support this (Taylor, 2006). Both men and women, it turns out, secrete oxytocin in multiple affiliative situations (Uvnäs-Moberg, 2003). Affiliative engagement under stress can also help explain why some people can come to the aid of others during an attack or natural disaster.

Finally, the hypothalamus plays a role in the regulation of the immune system (see Figure 5.4). The higher incidence of disease states following a period of severe stress—including autoimmune disorders, tumor formation, cardiovascular disease, obesity, diabetes, depression, anxiety disorder, addiction, and infections—is due to this link. Higher levels of cortisol, norepinephrine, stress-induced opioids, and persistent activation of the sympathetic nervous system in response to ongoing threats suppress some of the tissue repair functions of the immune system (Dobbs, Vasquez, Glaser, & Sheridan, 1993; Moynihan, 2003; O'Leary, 1990).

On the other hand, these neurochemicals increase the production of **proinflammatory cytokines**. These are the immune cells that initiate the inflammatory response to tissue injury and psychosocial stressors. The inflammatory response leads to redness, pain, swelling, fever, and "sickness behavior." Proinflammatory cytokines reduce physical activity and food intake and promote a withdrawal from the environment that is part of the biobehavioral response of **restoration** (Dickerson, Gruenewald, & Kemeny, 2004; Larson & Dunn, 2001).

Inflammation in turn stimulates the HPA axis to help the body respond to the threat of that inflammation. In the case of long term threat, the inflammation response and the HPA axis are activated. The state of threat, however, has suppressed the production of other immune cells, those that initiate tissue repair, from the lymph nodes, thymus, and spleen that can actually promote healing. The result is a downward cycle of increasing stress on the body with increasing inflammation. This makes the body more prone to the diseases mentioned above (Webster, Tonelli, & Sternberg, 2002).

The Neural Networks for the Embodied Self-Awareness of Biobehavioral Responses to Safety and Threat

Now we are ready to integrate the above information on threat and safety processing with that of embodied self-awareness. There are four networks related to self-awareness, all of which can interact with each other: the **embodied self-awareness network** (rerepresentations in the VMPFC, DLPFC, the ACC, and the anterior insula), the **interoceptive network**, the **body schema network**, and the **threat and safety network** (refer to Figures 3.1 and 5.4). This is summarized in Figure 5.6.

Figure 5.6
Body sensation and memory networks that are linked to the self-awareness network

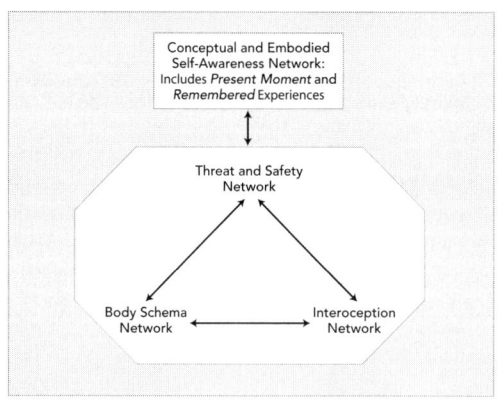

```
Conceptual and Embodied
Self-Awareness Network:
Includes Present Moment and
Remembered Experiences
         ↕
    Threat and Safety
        Network
        ╱    ╲
       ╱      ╲
Body Schema ←→ Interoception
  Network        Network
```

The embodied self-awareness network, therefore, plays the same role for the threat and safety network as it does for the interoceptive network and the body schema network. The embodied self-awareness network can allow us to feel our sense of threat or safety and make decisions about appropriate actions, or it can actively suppress our fear and become involved in conceptual thought processes, or become pathologically absorbed into the sense of threat or safety via dissociation, somatization, and rumination (de Gelder, Snyder, Greve, Gerard, & Hadjikhani 2004; Fellous, 1999).

In experiments in which individuals are allowed to become aware of a fearful stimulus (the subjects are given time to consider how they might respond), the ventromedial prefrontal cortex (VMPFC, embodied self-awareness) becomes activated while amygdala activity (sense of immediate fear) is lessened (Amat et al., 2005; Carlsson et al., 2004; Hariri, Mattay, Tessitore, Fera, & Weinberger, 2003; Urry et al., 2006). This means that when people are given an opportunity to actually feel their fear but are also told that they can safely take the time to consider the options, they can stay in embodied self-awareness and at the same time access conceptual self-awareness. This, in fact, is the state of healthy and balanced self-awareness discussed in Chapter 3. What is new here is the application of these concepts to the sense of threat. The ability to feel, sense, and appropriately act in relation to pain and threat allows the individual to discover the resources needed to recover.

It may seem counterintuitive since pain is not a very pleasant sensation, but *feeling one's pain or fear in the subjective emotional present activates the homeostatic recovery system of the body so that it has the opportunity to take care of itself.* In humans, this could mean not only rest and self-care but also knowing whether to contact a loved one, a psychotherapist, an embodied self-awareness practitioner, or a physician.

These social contacts, as well as warm baths and rest, drinking lots of water, going on vacation, or whatever contributes to restoration, can be counted among one's **resources** (see Box 5.1; Ogden et al., 2006). Accessing resources activates the endogenous opiate system connected with the neurochemical threat and safety network (Figure 5.4). *Accessing resources allows us to feel pain with more clarity and attention in the subjective emotional present.*

Crying infants who are given mild solutions of sucrose, who are held by their mothers, or who can engage in positive social interactions are more rapidly soothed and physiologically calmed (Bazhenova, Plonskaia, & Porges, 2001; Gormally et al., 2001). During the first two years of life, infants are primarily dependent upon adults for calming, soothing, and restoration. Even pacifiers, bottles, and toys that can calm an infant need to be monitored and regulated by an adult.

Donald Winnicott, who, as noted earlier, developed the concepts of the True Self and False Self, observed that by 2 years of age, infants begin to rely on blankets, teddy bears, and other soft objects for soothing. These can be carried around independently by the child and are under the child's control. Winnicott called these "transitional objects" because they represent a set of resources for the child that are used developmentally in between total dependence on parents and the more autonomous self-regulatory and self-soothing abilities of the preschool age and older child (Winnicott, 1971).

If adults are experimentally given a painful or fearful stimulation and told that they can expect the stimulation to be decreased soon, the activation in the threat neural network and the perceived sense of threat diminishes, *even before the actual pain stimulation has been removed* (Hunt, Keogh, & French, 2006; Koyama, McHaffie, Laurienti, & Coghill, 2005). Anticipation of reward, even in the face of current fear, leads to more regulated activation of the HPA axis such that sufficient cortisol is secreted to address the threat but not so much as to keep the individual in a persistent state of fear (Pecoraro et al., 2006; Putman, Hermans, Koppeschaar, van Schijndel, & van Honk, 2007). Box 5.1 suggests ways of working with, rather than against, pain and fear.

BOX 5.1
Making Friends with Pain

It may not seem like it at the time, but pain exists in our bodies as a way of getting our attention back to ourselves. Like yawning (Box 2.1), myoclonic twitching (Box 3.2), and good crying (Box 4.1), pain is one of the ways the body can spontaneously and automatically remind us to notice a physical or emotional threat we may have been avoiding.

This leads to a paradox. The only way out of the suffering is to jump back into it. The only way to ease the pain *and at the same time to heal the body* is to attend to and feel the pain in embodied self-awareness. Analgesics and opiates, alcohol and psychoactive drugs—like the endogenous opiates—can only temporarily blunt the pain.

continued

BOX 5.1 (continued)

Box 3.3 shows how a simple alteration of body schema self-awareness can eliminate phantom pain sensation. It is not as simple as merely seeing the real limb's mirror reflection in the place where the missing limb used to be attached. The amputee must "go into" the experience of feeling the mirror image as if it were the missing limb, must emotionally reconnect with that missing limb in order for the brain to let it go and to recalibrate the body schema.

The sensations from the nociceptors at the periphery of the body are not pain. Nor are the nerve impulses that travel up the **neuraxis** and are represented in the brain stem, hypothalamus, thalamus, anterior cingulate cortex (ACC), and insula. Pain is the emergent state of embodied self-awareness across the entire threat and interoceptive neural networks that is the rerepresentation of all these earlier transformations and representations of the nociceptive information. *This means that pain is not a concrete thing, but a state of self-awareness and that self-awareness can alter and possibly extinguish the sense of pain* (Chapman & Nakamura, 1999). Back at the nociceptors, there may be the same input signal coming into the brain, but how it is felt and how we relate to it emotionally (fear or acceptance) can be changed, perhaps permanently, by becoming more aware of it.

First time sexual intercourse may be experienced as painful or frightening but after some period of practice, patience, tenderness, love, and encouragement, if all goes well, it begins to feel pleasurable. This is exactly what it takes to make friends with pain. You can make progress on your own with some forms of pain, although you may also find that you want and need a helper.

Find a quiet place to sit or lie down, inside or outside, wherever you feel completely safe and comfortable. As best you can, come to rest inside yourself. Let your body sink into gravity (Box 3.1) as much as you are able.

continued

Psychophysiology of Self-Awareness

> **BOX 5.1** (continued)
>
> Now, use your body schema self-awareness to locate the painful area (your head, neck, back, leg, or wherever). If you can, feel the boundaries of the pain: is it the whole leg, just in the thigh, or localized to just above the knee on the inside of your leg, etc. Your headache may be just behind your right eye, or just over your left ear. Shift your awareness between painful areas and adjacent nonpainful areas. Notice the differences. Let the nonpainful parts "talk to" the painful parts. This is often enough to start the pain "moving," or "softening."
>
> Now forget the pain and focus on your breathing, your sense of your body connecting with the surface on which you are sitting or lying, or on some other constant and reliable presence in your body or your surroundings that feels safe, stable, and supportive: These are your **resources**. Other resources could be the nonpainful parts of your body, the trees over your head, a clock ticking, someone's hand that you are holding for support, a stuffed animal, a mental image of a person you love, or even your sense of God's presence. Make sure you can locate these resources reliably because you'll need to come back to them anytime that the pain becomes "too much."
>
> Now localize the pain again. Find your resource again. Practice going back and forth between them. Finally, with your resources in mind, come back to the pain and this time "go into" it. Really try to feel it. You may not be able to do this at first. Your pulse may quicken, your breathing may become short and gaspy. This is your sympathetic biobehavioral response to feeling threatened. Come back to your resources. See if you can let your parasympathetic system help you to settle down. Try again. This is the process. It may take multiple tries and multiple sessions. If your resource stops working for you, try a different one. You can have a whole collection of resources—no limit—if that helps.
>
> In this process, you are working through the threat of the pain, rather than the pain itself. You first have to convince your body that it is safe to go in there and feel it. Having accomplished that, you can begin to
>
> *continued*

Safety and Threat

> **BOX 5.1** (continued)
>
> deepen your interoceptive, emotional and body schema self-awareness of that pain. You may be surprised that the pain morphs into different forms—from physical to emotional (sadness, anger, fear) and back again. It may even change locations or be felt at multiple locations in your body.
>
> When you really know the pain and all its forms and faces, because you have fully felt it and followed its movements in your embodied self-awareness, it may eventually lessen in intensity and perhaps even disappear completely. Some pain, however, may not be soothed in this way. Even if you need to take pain medications and other medical treatments to alleviate your pain, embodied self-awareness can play an important role in your recovery.
>
> You will have begun to make the pain your friend. It can now objectively inform you of when you need to pay attention to yourself, just like any good friend who will tell you the truth about yourself. You don't have to be afraid of that friend's advice because you know it is given in your best interests and because you are absolutely certain that friend totally loves you.

Pathologies of Embodied Self-Awareness of Threat

Unfortunately, finding safety, accessing resources, and recovering from threat is not easy for humans. Because of all the demands and expectations heaped upon us as members of a complex social and cultural network, we somehow find it more expedient to ignore the ancient wisdom of our bodies. Oddly, but for reasons we can all recognize, millions of years of embodied education that is woven into the fabric of our tissues seems less compelling than deadlines and social appointments only days or weeks old. In situations of more severe threat, the demand is even more compelling.

Threat and fear are the primary reasons why people avoid coming back to their embodied self-awareness and its restorative potential. Conversely, a sense of safety is an essential ingredient for allowing our attention to leave the environment and to come back to ourselves. The neuroception of threat, by activating the body systems that shut down self-regenerative function and amp up the systems that help us respond to danger, literally takes us away from ourselves (Kozlowska, 2005).

We saw in the previous section how the ventromedial prefrontal cortex (VMPFC) can assist with paying attention to embodied sensations of fear, pain, and threat by partially inhibiting the amygdala so we can attend to our hurting body without being afraid of it. Individuals who have suffered severe trauma or who have been diagnosed with PTSD have a corresponding *inability* to suppress amygdala activity and a reduced ability to access the VMPFC and other prefrontal regulatory areas (Bremner et al., 1999; Centonze et al., 2005; Kolassa et al., 2007; Milad et al., 2005). Relative lack of ability or inability to activate the VMPFC and OFC—the circuits used to make embodied emotional sense of a situation—and a hyperactivation of the amygdala has been found in many different neuroimaging studies across a very wide range of disorders related to threat, trauma, anxiety, and panic (Francati, Vermetten, & Bremner, 2006).

In addition to impairments in the function of the VMPFC, people with PTSD, anxiety, and panic disorder show a hyperreactivity in the network involving the amygdala, insula, and the anterior cingulate cortex (ACC). These are part of the neural network for the interoception of fear and they lead to a pathological absorption in fearfulness including high anxiety, easily triggered fears, hypervigilance toward potentially fearful aspects of the environment, a tendency to compulsively avoid fearful situations, higher baseline heart rates, mental confusion, sleep disturbance, muscle tension, digestive upset, and suppressed activation of the parasympathetic nervous system (Lipp & Waters, 2007; MacLeod, Mathews, & Tata, 1986; Miltner, Krieschel, Hecht, Trippe, & Weiss, 2004; Nagai, Kishi, & Kato, 2007; Pillay, Gruber, Rogowska, Simpson, & Yurgelun-Todd, 2006; Quirk & Gilbert, 2003; Simpson, Drevets, Snyder, Gusnard, & Raichle, 2001; Stein, Simmons, Feinstein, & Paulus, 2007; Thayer & Brosschot, 2005). These people are also more likely to avoid talking about emotions and interoceptive sensations and to suppress them, and they are more likely to become pathologically absorbed in **rumination** on catastrophic thoughts (Brosschot et al., 2005; de Berardis et al., 2007; Frewen et al., 2008; Richards, Cooper, & Winkelman, 2003; van der Kolk, Roth, Pelcovitz, Sunday, & Spinazzola, 2005).

People with chronic musculoskeletal pain, fibromyalgia, migraine, asthma, and cardiovascular disease, for example, are more likely to have a history of psychosocial or tissue trauma than people without these disorders. These individuals also are more likely to show a pattern of ongoing pain, postural and movement disorders, muscle tension or muscle flaccidity, a lowered ability for interoceptive awareness and hypervigilance to pain (Crombez, Van Damme, 2005; Flor, Turk, & Birbaumer, 1989; Kamarck & Jennings, 1991; Haugstad et al., 2006; Hinz, Seibt, & Scheuch, 2001). They are, in a real sense, living in a body that threatens them.

Individuals who are prone to pathological **dissociation** are also likely to have suffered a severe trauma. Dissociative states such as frozen postures, trances, sleeping, loss of connection to one's body or to others and are forms of biobehavioral **immobilization** responses. Research has consistently found connections between dissociation, trauma, immobilization, and related physiological factors. The more severe the threat, the more the likelihood of dissociation (Näring & Nijenhuis, 2005; Nijenhuis, Vanderlinden, & Spinhoven, 1998). Dissociative states in individuals with PTSD are connected with increased activation in the dorsal vagal system and the secretion of endogenous opioids (Scaer, 2001; van der Hart, Nijenhuis, Steele, & Brown, 2004; Figure 5.4, and Table 5.2).

While dissociation is often listed as a symptom of stress and trauma disorders, it is considerably more prevalent as a symptom if the trauma event itself provoked dissociation at the time it happened. In fact, dissociation during the trauma is one of the main predictors of PTSD. This is especially the case for children who experience trauma, and dissociation, along with all the other related functional impairments associated with trauma is more likely in younger rather than older children (Eisen, Goodman, Qin, Davis, & Crayton, 2007).

Children have relatively few emotional resources outside of the significant others in their lives. If the trauma is caused by one of these individuals—as in physical or sexual abuse or other serious maltreatment by a close family member—dissociation is very likely to occur during the assault. This predisposes those children to a lifelong susceptibility to be "kindled" by any later threats into states of dissociative immobilization and freezing (Scaer, 2001; Tucker, 2001). Case Report 5.1, a continuation of the case of Joan from the previous chapter (Case Report 4.2), gives an example of dissociation from childhood abuse trauma.

Psychophysiology of Self-Awareness

Case Report 5.1
Continuation of Joan's Rosen Method
Bodywork Treatment (From Chapter 4)

Joan's "little girl" state, which she visited for both long and short periods of time over several months of weekly sessions, was a haven of safety, a resource inside of herself that she had invented as a 5-year old child. She was unable to feel my touch in that state. If I pressed a bit harder into her tense muscles, she writhed and groaned in a kind of "pretend" agony and turned her head away. I asked her what she liked about her special place:

"I can do anything here, anything I want. I can go anywhere," she would say in a taunting, childlike tone of voice.

Yes, I thought, anywhere to get away, but from what? What was so threatening to Joan when she was a child? In one session, I simply held her shoulder and upper arm gently to provide a sense of support. She turned her head toward me with her eyes closed, and her face showed a mixture of confusion and frustration. After a moment, she touched my hand with hers, held my hand gently for a moment, and then let go and went back into herself. This was a heartening change: she had become aware of my hand and of a wanting to touch it, a small fissure in her immobilizing dissociation.

In the next session, Joan went again to her special place but appeared to be more aware of my hands touching her. For some moments, I could feel her muscles soften and her breathing become easier. It was as if her body was "coming out" to meet me, non-verbally, silently, with her eyes closed. A bit later in the session, she opened her eyes and looked at me. Her eyes became teary.

"Are you OK?" she asked me in her adult voice.

I said that I had been waiting there for some time, waiting for her to make contact. "It's important," I said, "that you are starting to become aware of going away and coming back." It was also a sign of her willingness to coregulate with me.

In the next sessions, Joan more consistently was able to connect with my hands. Every time she "went away," I would now say, "Joan, I lost you. I don't know where to find you," in a playful tone that matched hers. She was more ready now to accept this for what it was: a simple observation—information for her embodied self-awareness—

rather than as a judgment or interpretation. During this period of her treatment, I also mentioned to her—in that same nonjudgmental manner that is part of Rosen Method practice—that her body from the back seemed split at the diaphragm: the part above the diaphragm was tense and raised up, and below it felt lifeless.

Her body had been this way since we started working together but Joan was only now able to let this into her embodied self-awareness. I could tell that her awareness was growing because she became curious.

"How did I get this way?" the adult Joan inquired about the split in the middle of her body.

"Probably something that happened in your childhood, when you were 4 or 5 years old. Something that your body is still holding onto." Mentioning the probable age of a probable trauma was based on my observation of the likely age of the "little girl." There was a long sigh, almost relief but not quite.

Although I had suggested on a few occasions that something might have happened to her when she was little, she had not been able to really hear it in an embodied way. This time, more present in her adult self, she began spontaneously to relate memories, memories not connected in time or space, but images and impressions. She talked about being afraid of her brother, who was 7 years older. She mentioned feeling alone, not having anyone to talk to about her feelings. I could hear the fear and loneliness in her voice.

Then she stopped and asked, "Why do I have to remember all this?"

I said, "You don't have to remember, only if it helps, and only if you feel comfortable doing it."

Her body, now fully awake, became tense and her face became contorted with pain and effort. This too was progress. She was frightened but now she could feel the fear in the subjective emotional present. After 6 months of weekly treatments, she left my office not wanting to reschedule another session. As she left, I told her that she was at a crossroads, that old feelings and images were coming into her awareness, that these might be helpful to her but that they were also scary to her.

Several weeks later, she phoned to say that she had a dream convincing her to continue with the Rosen sessions. In the dream, she heard a voice saying that she did not have to suffer anymore, that she did not have to hold back her feelings. This was a sign that she had some other **resources** that might be useful to her continued progress. In the next session, she was able to stay more fully in the subjective emotional present of what she was feeling at that moment in time.

Near the end of the session, without any prior mention of the subject of her childhood, Joan said—in an adult tone of voice—"My little girl got hurt so she had to run away." This voice was full of emotion, not pretending to be happy.

I said, "That's what you have been doing all your life, running away."

She nodded silently as I asked her to pay attention if she could to my hands, which I had placed under both of her shoulders as she was lying on her back. I again wanted to give her a sense of the presence of a supportive resource to help sustain her embodied self-awareness in the subjective emotional present.

Her tense upper body began to soften. "What happened?" I asked.

"I'm relaxing some," she said.

This was an amazing leap in embodied self-awareness, one that I decided to take one step further. "Right now, you aren't running away," I suggested. "You are allowing yourself to be held and comforted." For the first time in her treatment, tears flowed effortlessly down her cheeks: it was a deeply felt "good" cry.

Over the next 3 or 4 months, Joan made more progress in her embodied self awareness. Sometimes, she could stay with her feelings and memories, mostly memories not related to a trauma. Other times, however, as she came close to an old memory of feeling fear or anger, she would retreat into her special place. At this point in her treatment, she could feel herself going there and expressed a genuine desire to come back, a way of accessing resources by asking for help. Also during this period, Joan would repeat her "stopping" of her weekly treatments and then return several weeks later with statements like "I know I have to feel my pain." This was an important way of self-regulating the balance between the avoidant fear of threat and the sense of safety required to feel the threat.

By the end of this phase of treatment, Joan was able to access some of the memories of terror when being physically abused, as it turned out, by her older brother, beginning when she was about 5 years old. When no one was watching, he would hit and kick at her. Sometimes, he came silently into a room where she sat playing and smacked her on her back, knocking her over in pain. He threatened retaliation if she told anyone.

Safety and Threat

> Her growing awareness of these memories and emotions led, gradually, to a reduction of her skeletal muscle tension and a disappearance of the gut muscle tension and stomachaches that had caused her to come to see me in the first place. Joan's case will conclude in the next chapter, in which we discuss the role of muscle tension and relaxation in embodied self-awareness.

The middle sessions of Joan's case again illustrate some of the basic therapeutic steps of regaining embodied self-awareness listed in Table 1.1.

- *Resources* occurred as Joan discovered that she could find me by touching my hand and by feeling me touching her. This represented a major step in her sense of safety in the therapeutic situation.
- *Slowing down* to be in the subjective emotional present occurred increasingly more often as she became aware of the importance of feeling her hurt and pain.
- *Coregulation* happened in different ways during these sessions. Perhaps most striking was her growing ability to "find" where my hand was touching her body—in her interoceptive and body schema self-awareness—which was an active coregulation with the sensations in my hand. Her asking me if I was "OK," also shows an ability to take another person into account and to adjust her behavior accordingly.
- *Verbalization* began to shift between childlike and adultlike voices ("double consciousness"), with an increasing ability to name and accept her feelings and her history.
- *Links and boundaries* came up in Joan's exploration of my hand with hers, finding where her body left off and mine began.
- *Self-regulation* was seen, paradoxically, in Joan's temporary terminations of her treatments. It was a way of gaining control and deciding for herself what she needed.
- *Reengagement* was seen in her ability to find my hand and feel it, in letting herself be comforted, and in coming back to the Rosen sessions after temporarily leaving treatment.
- *Letting go* began in small ways, but especially in letting herself cry in a good way, with relief.

Psychophysiology of Self-Awareness

Joan's opening to her embodied self-awareness during her treatment is similar to that of other trauma victims who receive treatments to enhance embodied self-awareness. In one study of adult victims of childhood incest and sexual abuse, the subjects were randomly assigned to receive either massage-therapy or awareness-based somatic psychotherapy using both touch and talk. While people in both groups improved, those in the awareness-based therapy group were better able to feel and express their interoceptions and emotions. Here is what some of the individuals in the self-awareness group wrote about their experience.

> "I relaxed those deep abdominal muscles and I just started to weep. I was shocked that this 'weeping and sadness' was in me."
> "I learned to relax my muscles from the inside. I was able to stay inside parts of my body rather than just looking at them from the outside."
> "This [treatment] strategy has really opened me up to ways that I can stay in my body more often without fearing for my life. I am learning that being inside my body can be empowering and enjoyable." (Price, 2005, pp.53–54)

There have been many excellent works published on the treatment of trauma and PTSD using awareness based practices such as somatic psychotherapy and **somatic experiencing,** a method developed by Peter Levine that focuses on awareness of embodied sensations and titrating the traumatic memories with an ongoing sense of safety to help the person find a way out of the "trauma vortex" (Levine, 1997).

Across these different clinical approaches, the basic principles for treating trauma are those listed in Table 1.1. *Confronting trauma memories in the subjective emotional present is required in order to integrate the dissociated parts into a more integrated embodied and conceptual self-awareness of accepting and letting go of symptoms. This can only be done, however, in the context of supportive resources, client–therapist coregulation, ability to verbalize and at the same time feel, and therapeutic support for a gradual return to re-engagement and self-regulation* (Levine, 1997; Ogden et al., 2006; Scaer, 2000; Solomon & Siegel, 2003; van der Hart et al., 2006).

Confronting trauma memories means making friends with the physical and psychological pain that co-occur. Research on writing about trauma shows that while participants experience higher blood pressure and more negative moods after writing, they expressed fewer symptoms and had fewer doctor's visits six months later (Pennebaker & Beall, 1986). Similarly, Holocaust survivors who disclosed their traumatic experiences in a clinical interview had better long-term health outcomes than a control group of nondisclosers (Pennebaker, Barger, & Tiebout, 1989). Disclosure also reverses the immunosuppressive effects of threat and activates tissue repair and immunological resistance to infection (O'Leary, 1990). The importance of sharing emotions with others in the trauma recovery process is most salient in infancy and early childhood, and especially in the negotiation of threat and safety in the child's first attachments.

The Formation of Attachments

As the case of Joan illustrates, our neurophysiology and the accompanying biobehavioral response modes are especially sensitive to safety and threat in interpersonal encounters. This is primarily because, from birth, we are dependent upon other people to provide all of our basic needs. *The primary function of the infant nervous system is to evaluate and respond to safety and threat in interpersonal encounters* (Main, 1999; Schore, 2003).

Infants in the first two months of life have a relatively immature nervous system and are faced with the demands of adapting to the extrauterine environment with its changing patterns of stimulation. This means that their primary biobehavioral response state is **restoration**. During this period, infants sleep on average 15 hours per day, although this can vary considerably between infants (Parmelee, Schulz, & Disbrow, 1961; St. James-Roberts & Plewis, 1996). While animals find restorative shelter in the safety of a burrow or den, for human infants the primary haven of safety is being in direct physical contact with the body of the primary parental figure, most typically the mother (Main, 1999).

Finding safety in the arms of another individual is not the same as finding safety in a den or other fixed location. Access into the personal space of another person, especially the space involving touch and physical contact between the exposed skin surfaces of two different bodies, requires a complex

Psychophysiology of Self-Awareness

process of interpersonal **coregulation**. People must be able to signal the desire to be next to or apart from each other, and they must be able to regulate together the duration and closeness of that encounter. Coregulation is a dynamic mutual adjustment of comovements in time and space, done in a way that each person can interoceptively and proprioceptively sense their own sensations, emotions, and body schemas in relation to the other.

Because infants are not able to communicate in words, much of this communication is via movement and touch. Nonverbal coregulation is commonplace as we accommodate to other's movements in public spaces like elevators and athletic events and in private encounters like sharing cooking in a small kitchen space or sharing a bed. Similar concepts include mutual entrainment (Sander, 1962) and mutual regulation (Gianino & Tronick, 1988; Tronick, 2007).

As coregulation continues over several minutes or longer, each round of successful communication creates an emotional attunement in which positive facial expressions and mutual gaze amplify feelings of interpersonal connection, mutual affirmation, safety in being able to "let go" into the softness and vulnerability of the other person's body (see Table 1.1; Beebe & Lachman, 2002; Stern, 1985). To take the example of pull-to-sit shown in Figures 1.2 and 1.3, imagine that it becomes a game in which each person is smiling at and looking at the other. With each repetition there may be escalating vocal contours of excitement in the parent's voice that mirror the infant's widening eyes and broadening smile as well as an increasing susceptibility of each to be emotionally and physically touched by the other. This amplification of emotion in coregulated encounters is called **resonance** (Schore, 1997; Wooten, 1995).

The urge to find safety with other people, the need for coregulatory communication of movement and touch for close proximity, and the resulting resonant states of positive emotion for and with the other person leads to the formation of a long-term emotional tie, an **attachment**, between two individuals. In humans, attachment bonds between children and parents formed in early childhood—because they are so fundamental to survival in terms of the regulation of safety and threat—can last a lifetime.

The Psychobiology of Attachment

Feelings of attachment are linked to the experience-dependent neurochemical

Safety and Threat

pathways that form the basic biobehavioral responses to safety and threat. If the attachment relationship feels safe because of consistent positive emotional resonance, then the attachment figure (the parent of the infant, for example) is a haven of safety in addition to being someone with whom the infant seeks closeness. This is the case for **secure attachment**, a type of a attachment relationship in which the infant who feels threatened will seek proximity and comfort from the parent, be easily calmed, and then be able to return to normal patterns of **engagement** (Table 5.2, cell 2).

Insecure anxious-resistant attachment is a type of relationship characterized by **vigilance**. The threatened child will seem ambivalent, sometimes approaching the parent and sometimes hesitant. These children will have a difficult time calming, are watchful of the environment and of the parent, and do not readily return to states of engagement (Table 5.2, cell 3). Infants with this type of attachment are either temperamentally susceptible to stress or have parents who are inconsistent in terms of emotional availability in times of stress (Cassidy, 1994; Cassidy & Berlin, 1994).

Insecure avoidant-dismissive attachment occurs when infants do not outwardly shown signs of distress under threat. Measures of their physiology, however, show high activation of the sympathetic nervous system and cortisol indicative of high emotional arousal coupled with active suppression (Cassidy, 1994; Spangler & Grossman, 1993). These infants will resist attempts to pick them up or comfort them, by turning away or squirming to get down (Table 5.2, cell 6). These flight-and-fight **mobilization** reactions, and the accompanying emotional suppression, typically occur when parents are intolerant of the child's feelings of distress, threat, and anger, or when parents become angry at the child in response to the child's distress.

Finally, **disorganized-disoriented attachment** is connected with the biobehavioral response mode of **immobilization** and dissociation (Table 5.2, cell 4). This type of attachment occurs when the infant suffers from extreme and consistent threat from the attachment figure such as from physical or sexual abuse, maltreatment, parental psychopathology, and parental substance abuse. Infants may show frozen postures such as staring at a wall. They may self-comfort by rocking or thumb-sucking for extended periods. They may also show contradictory behavior such as approaching the parent by crawling backwards (Forbes, Evans, Moran & Pederson, 2007; Madigan, Moran, & Pederson, 2006).

Psychophysiology of Self-Awareness

Similar attachment patterns can be found throughout the life course. Adults may have attachment relationships with their living parents and also with romantic partners. Romantic relationships are almost always attachment relationships. This is because of the development of attachment feelings in the context of the coregulation of close physical proximity and the intense sensory and emotional interoceptions typically connected with sexual coactivity.

The attachment style of adults with their romantic partners may depend in part on their style of attachment to their parents, in part on the communication process in the adult relationship, and in part of current life circumstances. People who routinely suppress emotion are likely to have adult attachments that are avoidant-dismissive. Those who are absorbed in anxiety and anxious rumination are likely to have anxious-resistant attachments. Individuals who suffered interpersonal trauma from either past or current attachment figures are more likely to show the dissociative absorption characteristic of disorganized-disoriented attachment (Edelstein, 2006; Lyons-Ruth, Dutra, Schuder, & Bianchi, 2006; Mikulincer & Orbach, 1995; Roisman, Tsai, & Chiang, 2004; Shaver & Mikulicer, 2002; Stovall-McClough & Cloitre, 2006; Waters, Merrick, Treboux, Crowell, & Albersheim, 2000).

As shown in Table 5.2, because the different types of attachment are directly related to the different biobehavioral response patterns, *the physiology of attachment is in fact the same as the physiology of the threat and stress component of embodied self-awareness, linked with the interoception and body schema networks*. In terms of attachment in infancy, these neural linkages are more strongly developed on the right side of the brain (Diamond, 2001; Schore, 2000, 2002, 2003).

Why the right brain? In adults, the left brain is connected primarily with thought and language, abstract and conceptual reasoning. The right brain is more connected with nonverbal sensations and emotions (T. Lewis, Amini, & Lannon, 2000; Schore, 2003). It is not actually that simple because language used to describe embodied self-awareness, via the ventromedial prefrontal cortex (see Chapters 3 and 7), is more connected to right brain prefrontal and insula activity. And, because expressive motor movements of the body are controlled by neural pathways on the opposite side, all activity combines both left and right brain functions. As usual, the brain and body act together as a complex dynamic system. So, right and left is not either–or but rather a matter of relative levels of activation in whole brain states.

The right brain, however, is more developed at birth and the nonverbal dialogues with others, including emotions, sensations, and the impressions of safety and threat, activate experience dependent connections primarily in the right brain. The infant's left brain is more attuned to objective perceptual processing, category formation, and later, the onset of conceptual language and autobiographical remembering related to conceptual self-awareness (Schore, 2003).

We also know that *early experiences of communicating with others—because of their emotional salience and relevance for safety vs. threat—are the most important experiences around which early brain development occurs.* These experiences, therefore, will have long-term impacts on self-regulation and self-awareness because they are biobehavioral.

Effects of Relationship Threat and Stress in Early Childhood

The period between approximately the 5th prenatal month up until the child's 4th birthday is one of the critical periods for brain development. A **critical period** is a relatively circumscribed period of the life course in which particular forms of environmental input are required to sustain psychobiological development. The other major critical period for the brain's development is during puberty and adolescence. Both infancy and adolescence are characterized by rapid brain development, major changes in body size, shape, and composition, major shifts in emotional and cognitive abilities, and important changes in interpersonal relationships (Webb, Monk, & Nelson, 2001).

During these critical periods, threat and safety can play a central role in shaping the neurobiology, psychology, and behavior of the individual. This is partly due to what we have reviewed in this chapter: that the main job of the nervous system is to assess safety and threat and prepare appropriate responses. *Humans come to decide from an early age whether the world is a safe or a threatening place and much of their subsequent behavior is based on that early assessment, made primarily on the basis of neuroception in the absence of self-awareness* (Panksepp, 2001; Porges, 2004).

The other reason why threat and safety during infancy and adolescence have a lasting impact is because brain growth during these periods is extremely rapid and extremely sensitive to environmentally induced **experience dependent brain development**. During these periods, the brain has a great deal of **plasticity**, meaning it can quickly form long-term connections within the neural networks for homeostasis and self-regulation.

Psychophysiology of Self-Awareness

The effects of stress/threat on brain development can begin before birth. Maternal stress and anxiety during pregnancy predisposes fetuses to higher activity levels and higher circulating cortisol than fetuses of nonstressed mothers. After birth, infants who experienced more prenatal maternal stress cry more and are less likely to calm when soothed. As children and adolescents they have more symptoms of impulsivity and anxiety, lower attentional ability, and socioemotional problems. As adults, these individuals are more likely to be diagnosed with mental illnesses such as schizophrenia, depression, and anxiety (DiPietro, Hilton, Hawkins, Costigan, & Pressman, 2002; Khashan et al., 2008; Lapante, Zelazo, Brunet, & King, 2007; Phillips, 2007; Schneider et al., 2008; van den Bergh, Mulder, Mennew, & Glover, 2004).

If the relationship threat occurs postnatally during infancy and early childhood, there are multiple and lasting effects on physiology, emotion, attention, self-awareness and self-regulation. Children with a history of maltreatment (neglect, physical abuse, severe verbal abuse, or sexual abuse), for example, are more vigilant toward possible sources of threat in the environment and more prone to show symptoms of anxiety, panic, depression, withdrawal, substance abuse, somatization complaints, thought and memory impairments, early onset sexual promiscuity, or aggression. They are also more likely to show insecure attachments and difficulties establishing intimate adult relationships (Anda et al., 2006; Bifulco, Moran, Baines, Bunn, & Stanford, 2002; Collman & Widom, 2004; Eisenberg et al., 2001; Éthie, Lemelin, & Lacharité, 2004; Gershoff, 2002; Pollak, Vardi, Bechner, & Curtin, 2005; Shackman et al., 2007; Vigil, Geary, Byrd-Craven, 2005). In one study it was found that children who were physically abused were 3 times as likely as nonabused children to have panic attacks as adults, while children who were sexually abused were 4 times as likely to have such attacks (Goodwin, Fergusson, & Horwood, 2005).

These effects of threat on neurobiological development are in part due to the toxicity of excess cortisol to developing neural structures. Children who live with parents having marital difficulties or who have insecure attachment relationships with their parents, for example, show elevated cortisol levels (Pendry & Adam, 2007). These effects involve a chronic dysregulation of the HPA axis, including the direct feedback of CRF from the hypothalamus to the brain (see Figure 5.4; Bugental, Martorell, & Barraza, 2003; Goel & Bale, 2007; Goodyer, Park, Netherton, & Herbert, 2001; Gunnar & Cheatham,

Safety and Threat

2003; Gunnar & Donzella, 2002; S. Levine, 2005; Shea, Walsh, MacMillan, & Steiner, 2004).

Chronic activation of the sympathetic nervous system and underactivation of the vagal parasympathetic system also contributes to the long-term effects of stress (Hastings et al., 2008). If infants and parents have interactive difficulties in the first 3 months of life, the infant's ability to activate the ventral vagal parasympathetic (relaxation) system is impaired (Feldman, 2006; Haley & Stansbury, 2003; Moore & Calkins, 2004). This includes an inability of parents to help the infant to regulate arousal and engagement and a breakdown of coregulation. This typically results in **vigilance**, **mobilization**, and **immobilization** biobehavioral responses that can be observed early in the first year of life (Beebe & Lachman, 2002). Because attention is so focused on the source of threat, over the long term this impairs the child's ability to sustain attention for positive engagement and normal absorption (NICHD Early child care research network, 2004). This is seen in Case Report 5.2.

Case Report 5.2
Peter (6–10 months) and His Mother: Flight, Freeze, Engagement

About 22 years ago, my students and I made videotapes of 13 mothers as they interacted in free play with their infants. Beginning at the age of 1 month, each of these couples came to a university laboratory playroom equipped with three wall-mounted video cameras from which any two could be chosen to provide the best views of both mother and infant. The mother was told simply to, "Play with your infant in the way you might typically do at home." Following that first visit, each dyad came back to the lab once each week, with occasional missed weeks for illness or vacation, until the infant was 1 year old. No further instructions were given, so that we had a video record of how their relationship, at least in this situation, changed over the first year of life. We also continued to videotape 11 of these families every 2 weeks in the second year, and for 3 consecutive weeks around the child's third birthday.

My students, colleagues, and I have published many research articles and books using these videotapes. The research focuses on changes in the communication over time between mothers and infants, the study of developmental transformations of movement, emotion, and attention over time within the relationship (e.g., Fogel, 1993; Fogel, Garvey et al., 2006; and also http://www.psych.utah.edu/lab/somatics/index.php for free downloads of research articles).

Here I report, for the first time, the case of one mother–infant pair from this study who, in the second half of the first year, developed some problems in their ability to coregulate. This led the infant, over a 4-month period, through a series of biobehavioral reactions from engagement, to vigilance, to flight, to freeze, and back to engagement.

One of the notable features of this developmental change in the infant is that the mother was not in any way abusive or negligent. During this period, however, the family was under considerable stress due to her husband's loss of employment. Peter, her infant son described here, was the fifth child in the family. This case illustrates how everyday forms of stress become traumatic and can nevertheless have an impact on people's ability to engage with each other, with particularly severe effects on infants. Given the relative plasticity of the infant brain, these stressful circumstances and the resulting withdrawal from the interaction led Peter into a relatively long-term pattern of emotional suppression and hypervigilance.

Period 1: Peter, up until six months of age, was very sensitive to his mother's interventions, easy to smile on the one hand and ready to turn away from her if she became too demanding. Peter's mother was able to restrain her demands as she observed and attuned to Peter's withdrawal. When Peter is around 6 months of age, at the onset of the family financial stress, his mother seems to become less able to stay in the subjective emotional present with Peter. She seems impatient and more demanding.

(26 weeks) During the first 6 minutes of this session the mother's attempts to engage Peter were unceasing. She comes in close, gets "in his face," calls his name and sometimes pokes and prods. Peter guards himself from these actions (flight). They develop a routine that has been called "chase-and-dodge," with the mother chasing harder to get the attention of the infant who is withdrawing progressively more (Beebe & Lachman, 2002).

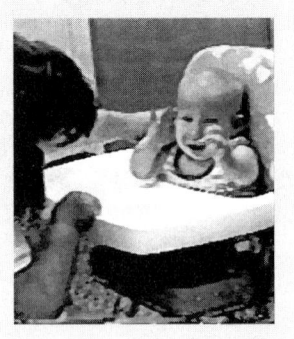

Safety and Threat

(28 weeks) Mother is less demanding today. She sits back in her chair, waits for Peter to look at her, and then smiles or shows a toy. Peter responds to the introduction of a toy. He seems much more willing to engage when given space but he seems to keep his distance. His smiles are accompanied by some facial muscle tension in the cheeks and around the eyes, as if he does not want to let go of his feelings. In general, he seems vigilant.

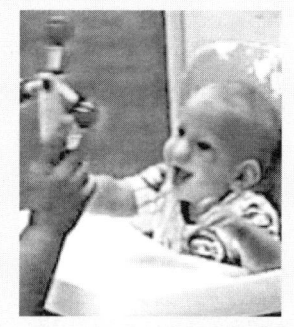

(33 weeks) Now Peter's gaze aversion begins to take on a hypnotic quality as the mother persists in her attempts to engage him. This is the first sign of a shift from flight into immobility. In the first minute of this session, Peter's mother poked, tickled, or prodded him 16 times, asked him to say "da-da" 9 times, asked him to make a "raspberry" sound 2 times, and asked him 4 times "does that tickle?"

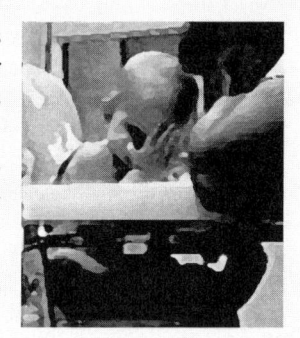

Period 2: Peter begins to slip into an unfocused, flat, emotionless gaze, away from the mother, as she seems even more desperate to make contact with him. He is now more consistently in this immobilized freeze state.

(38 weeks) During a "stretch" game, which lasted 26 seconds, Peter gazes blankly away as his mother pulls his arms up in the air. He offers no resistance to the mother's manipulation of his arms. This passive response suggests that there is a whole body immobilization.

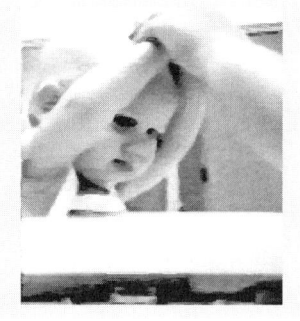

Psychophysiology of Self-Awareness

(40 weeks) Peter has been independently and intentionally rocking his high chair back and forth for much of these first 4 minutes. This type of behavior is often seen in autistic children and is a form of self-soothing. It is Peter's attempt to block out the stress of avoiding his mother and to establish a state of self-restoration.

Period 3: Peter sporadically begins to engage with his mother once again, by participating in those games the mother initiates. Peter wants to engage but he seems not fully in the subjective emotional present. His facial expressions are tense, his gaze is vigilant, but he shows little attempt to resist (fight) or turn away (flight).

(41 weeks) Peter claps his hands after repeated demonstrations and pleas from his mother to do so. With a beaming face the mother says, "There you go! Good boy!" Peter, clearly enjoying his mother's enthusiasm, which has been lacking for the past few months, looks directly at her and smiles tensely with his eyes squinting. In this and subsequent sessions, this couple finds ways to engage with each other but Peter continues to show muscle tension in his face, shoulders and neck, as if he is ready to pull back and turn away at any moment.

By the time Peter's mother begins to engage again in a less demanding way, Peter's ability to express positive emotion has been curtailed. Although he clearly wants to engage and enjoy, he is still vigilant and tense. Their communication continued to have both more open and more demanding moments so that even at the age of 3 years, the last time we observed this couple, Peter seemed to be holding back his emotions with muscle tension in different parts of his face and upper body.

In this case, one can observe the progressive shutdown of embodied self-awareness in the infant. Peter's facial expressions showing muscle tension around the mouth and eyes are notable in light of recent research showing that facial expressions affect sensory awareness. Fear expressions, for example, open the nasal passages and widen the eyes to take in more information. Disgust expressions do the opposite, close down receptivity to offensive smells and sights (Whalen & Kleck, 2008). Our impression is that Peter is not only withholding his emotions from his mother, but he is also shielding his vision and indeed, his whole body from her.

We have published a description of another case—Susan and her mother—across this same age period in which shared positive emotion and coregulated communication led to an expansion of the infant's interoceptive and body schema self-awareness. By the same age of 41 weeks (about 10 months) Susan had developed a wide range of facial and body expressions of emotion which were spontaneous and effortless. Susan also was aware of her effect on her mother because her mother easily adapted to Susan's actions. Unlike Peter who had to become mobilized or immobilized to avoid interacting, Susan by this age could shake her head "no" and smile slyly at her mother to openly indicate unwillingness to go along. Her mother's response was typically laughter and celebration of Susan's achievements in self-awareness and links and boundaries (Fogel & DeKoeyer-Laros, 2007; http://www.psych.utah.edu/lab/somatics/index.php). This use of humor in the case of Susan is presented in Case Report 8.1.

One of the pioneers of infant-parent communication research, Louis Sander, noted that infants' ability to become aware of their own feelings, intentions, and emotions depended upon the adult's ability to "recognize" that feeling in the infant and to respond appropriately to it. The parent's "recognition" of the infant can "facilitate a more accurate inner perception—again fostering self-recognition" (Sander, 1965, p. 11). Through these exchanges—coregulated, animated, enjoyable, accepting—the child can come to recognize "his inner experience as his own" (Lyons-Ruth, 2000, p. 87).

In spite of the large amount of research on the deleterious effects of early trauma, some children appear to be more resilient than others, seemingly faring well in the long run. One study looked at the incidence of symptoms of PTSD in 65 Palestinian families between 1993, when the children were 10 to 11 years old, and 2000. All the families had suffered some form of trauma, including death or imprisonment of family members, military violence, night raids, or beatings. Those families who had the most resources (personal insight, strong family relationships, creativity, humor, life satisfaction, belief in their ability to improve the situation) had the fewest symptoms of PTSD (see Table 5.1; Helminen & Punamäki, 2008; Punamäki et al., 2006).

Another study looked at children living in lower Manhattan who had direct exposure to the attacks on September 11, 2001 including witnessing the collapse of the towers, seeing injured or dead people, or people jumping out of buildings. Children with the most lasting impacts of the attack were those who in addition had experienced other trauma in their lives including accidents, severe illness, natural disasters, or witnessing other violence (Chemtob, Nomura, & Abramovitz, 2008).

On the other hand, it appears that some children are born with a propensity to be more temperamentally fearful, so that even given normal childrearing and relatively nonstressful environments, they show lasting physiological and behavior patterns of high anxiety and withdrawal similar to children who have been traumatized (Fox, 2004).

These findings suggest that some fearful children may not have been abused or deliberately threatened. And, conversely, those who had been victims of violence or maltreatment will not necessarily develop pathological symptoms. We can think of fearfulness as resulting from multiple causes including actual physical threat, genetic predisposition to anxiety, hypersensitivity to phobias such as fear of certain animals or situations, life events, other uncontrollable stressors and the availability of resources including nonabusive family members and early intervention programs (Cicchetti, 2002; Dybdahl, 2001; Heim & Nemeroff, 2001; Muris, 2006; Osofsky, 1999). Although there are individual differences, children who grow up in the midst of endemic street violence (an inner city neighborhood in Chicago or a hillside favela in Rio de Janeiro), or continuing terrorist attacks (the Middle East), or war (Africa, the Middle East) or ethnic hatred (just about anywhere in the world) will suffer in some way (Belsky, 2008; Quota, Punamäki, & Sarraj, 2008).

Secure attachment and the cultivation of a sense of safety in early childhood, as one might expect, creates opportunities for the enhancement of the biobehavioral responses of **engagement** and **normal absorption** in both social and nonsocial situations. Securely attached individuals, in both infancy and adulthood, are more likely to show positive emotions, maintain interpersonal states of **engagement** and emotional openness, are more self-aware of their emotions and can communicate them more effectively with others, are more likely to make and keep friends, and more likely to establish healthy adult romantic partnerships (Bates, Maslin, & Frankel, 1985; Berlin, Cassidy, &

Belsky, 1995; Erickson, Sroufe, & Egeland, 1985; Fagot, 1997; Main & Cassidy, 1988; Steele, Steele, Croft, & Fonagy, 1999).

These individuals are also more likely to show a balanced activation of the sympathetic and parasympathetic nervous systems, higher levels of circulating oxytocin and endogenous opiates, and a greater activation in the orbitofrontal cortex and anterior cingulate cortex (responsible for the evaluation and maintenance of positive emotion and engagement) (Aron et al., 2005; Esch & Stefano, 2005; Feldman, Weller, Zagoory-Sharon, & Levine, 2007; Fries, Ziegler, Kurian, Jacoris, & Pollak, 2005; Kramer, Choe, Carter, & Cushing, 2006; Noriuchi, Kikuchi, & Senoo, 2008; Uvnäs-Moberg, 2003). This balanced functioning of the neural networks associated with attachment, health, and self-awareness is called **neural integration** (Siegel, 2001)

And, fortunately for people who suffer from being disconnected from their embodied self-awareness—a condition that always stems from a neurodevelopmental response to threat—there are a wide variety of effective treatments available today that were not widely used or recognized until 15 or 20 years ago. Also fortunately, our neurochemical response systems continue to retain the possibility for plasticity throughout life. There is hope that old patterns of self-avoidance can be changed, that new neurochemical pathways will grow, that intrusive memories can be attenuated, and that chronic disease states can be slowed or reversed. The information presented in this chapter shows that because psychological wounds related to threat are accompanied by tissue damage throughout the neuraxis, regeneration can be slow, frustrating, and sometimes painful.

One resource that can help everyone is a broader understanding of the complex network of connections in our bodies that create states of health and disease, awareness and avoidance. This understanding may make the long and sometimes bumpy journey back toward health a little bit more hopeful. This resource is the knowledge that our bodies ache for a reason, that it's not "all in our heads," that if we can find the right embodied self-awareness practice we will change, that healing from trauma is essentially no different from healing from major surgery—requiring safety, rest and restoration—and that there are people out there who themselves have been on this journey and who have devoted themselves to helping others find their way.

6

In the Flesh: Moving and Touching

> *Desire is movement, it is the body in movement. How can there be movement without desire, when every desire implies a moving toward and any movement implies a desire to move?*
>
> (Manning, 2007, p. 36)

Moving and touching are words with multiple meanings. There are the overt acts of moving one's body through space and of making a physical contact between a part of one's body and some other animate or inanimate object. In this sense, they are different and imply different organs: movement is muscle, touch is skin. Moving and touching can also converge in a single meaning: to stir the emotions. To say one is moved emotionally by something is the same as saying that one is touched by something. The acts of moving and touching also imply each other. Touching is never a passive act: one must move by stroking, patting, fingering, brushing against, fondling, caressing, vibrating, or holding. Moving requires one to touch something at all times: the earth and the air at the very least. Moving and touching imply emotion, a *desire* to reach toward or away.

Moving and touching are not solitary acts. One moves in relation to something: from or towards, in or out, up or down. One touches the other. They can be relational acts for and within oneself although this may go unnoticed in embodied self-awareness. Reaching or stepping—acts of the arms and legs primarily—can't be done without adjusting the stance and posture of the trunk, head, and other limbs. We touch our own bodies frequently and in many cases, without awareness.

The linguistic connection between moving and touching, acting and feeling, is a reflection of the reality of our psychophysiology. As we have seen, the sense of threat limits our ability to act and to feel. Threat creates muscle tension that limits spontaneous movement, makes us less flexible and more rigid, both physically and mentally. When we feel safe, our movements and our emotions can be more spontaneous and we can be more free to realize our fullest potential as those terrestrial beings with the most articulate hands, the most agile minds, and the most subtle range of emotional feelings (Feldenkrais, 1985; Johnson, 1992; Rosen, 2003).

In this chapter, we examine the psychophysiology of the organs of movement and touch: the muscles and the skin. The second aspect of movement and touch to be covered is how our moving and touching in relation to others help us to form a unique pattern of embodied and conceptual self-awareness. We will also see how this ability to coordinate movement and touch leads to a sense of linkages and boundaries, of being different from the other and also a sense of being connected to the other.

The Flesh: Muscle and Skin

Under conditions of threat, biobehavioral response modes become activated automatically, sending a cascade of stress hormones, immunosuppressants, and sympathetic neurotransmitters into the body to activate the skeletal muscles and inhibit the activation of the gut muscles during states of **vigilance, mobilization**, and **immobilization**. Long-term threat and stress is associated with muscle tension and muscle pain, resulting from the chronic activation of the threat response neural networks.

Skeletal Muscles: Physiology, Tension, Pain, and Stress

There are three types of muscles in the body: skeletal, smooth, and cardiac. Cardiac muscle will not be covered in this book. **Skeletal muscles** control the physical movements of the body by attaching to bone and contracting to move body parts across the joints. **Smooth muscles** are found in most of the internal organs including the gut, respiratory tract, arteries and veins, bladder, reproductive tracts, and uterus.

Skeletal muscles are more structurally complex than smooth muscles. Skeletal muscles are composed of bundles of muscle cells (also called muscle fibers) that form a single motor unit. Each motor unit is regulated by a single neuron that contracts all the cells in that motor unit at the same time. Neurons from the ventral (toward the front of the body) horn of the spinal cord that

Psychophysiology of Self-Awareness

activate motor units are called α - **motor neurons** (α–**MN**), large, myelinated neurons with fast conduction speeds. These α - **motor neurons** are connected somatotopically to the motor cortex of the brain via the cerebellum and brain stem and are responsible for all voluntary movements of the body (see Figure 6.1; Ramnani, 2006).

Figure 6.1

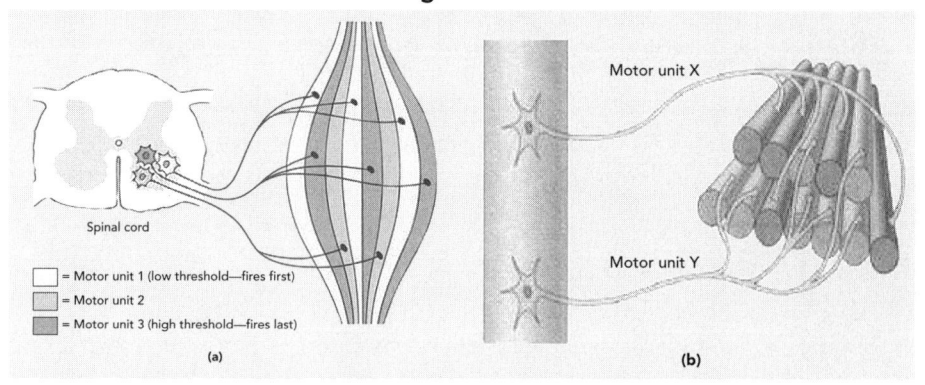

(a) Organization of skeletal muscle cells into motor units. Each motor unit is regulated by a single α - motor neuron located in the ventral horn of the spinal cord. (b) Each motor unit is made up of multiple muscle cells (fibers) distributed throughout the muscle. Activation of the α - motor neuron contracts all the fibers in that unit at the same time.

Motor units are organized according to how much force they exert to contract a muscle and how quickly they "fire" (activate a contraction of the cells in the unit via an electro-chemical discharge at the nerve endings) upon receiving input from the brain stem and brain. Low-threshold motor units fire the most quickly and exert relatively little force. These units are often involved in isometric contractions, in which the motor unit becomes stiff or tense but the length of the muscle does not change and therefore no actual movement occurs. Higher threshold motor units are slower to fire and exert more force, resulting in actual length contraction of the muscle and movement across a joint. Typically, the motor units discharge (relax) in reverse order (see Figure 6.1; Binder, Bawa, Ruenzel, & Henneman, 1983; Hägg, 1991; Hennig & Lømo, 1985; Henneman, Somjen, & Carpenter, 1965).

Within the belly of a skeletal muscle is a structure called the muscle spindle. **Muscle spindles** are fatter in the middle and narrower at the ends. They contain the **proprioceptors** that sense the extent and speed of stretch (mechanoreceptors) and tension of the muscle as a whole, and they are regulated by **γ–motor neurons (γ–MN)**. Muscle spindles are called intrafusal muscle fibers, while the muscle fibers in the motor units that actually contact the muscle as a whole are called extrafusal fibers (see Figure 6.2).

Figure 6.2

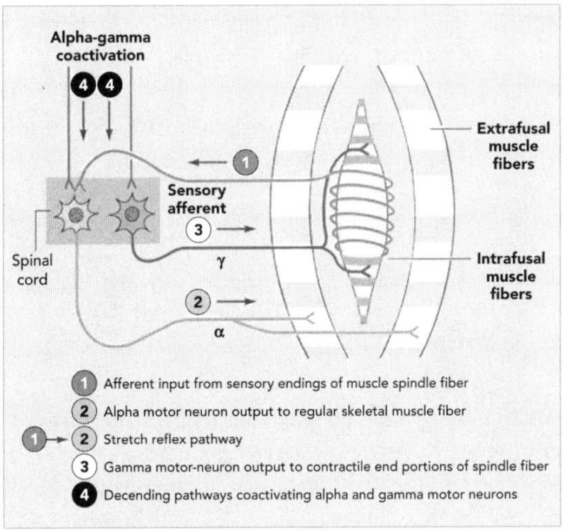

① Afferent input from sensory endings of muscle spindle fiber
② Alpha motor neuron output to regular skeletal muscle fiber
①→② Stretch reflex pathway
③ Gamma motor-neuron output to contractile end portions of spindle fiber
④ Decending pathways coactivating alpha and gamma motor neurons

Muscle spindles (intrafusal muscle fibers) sense stretching in the extrafusal skeletal muscle. More stretch sends signals to spinal cord and brain via sensory afferent pathways leading to making the spindle more receptive via γ – motor neurons and/or contracting the extrafusal fibers via α - motor neurons.

These γ –MN are myelinated but have a slower conduction speed than the α – MN fibers. They do not contract the extrafusal muscle fibers in the motor units. Rather, they stretch the muscle spindle slightly from the ends to make it more receptive, that is, to better sense the amount of stretch in the muscle as a whole (see Figure 6.2). Tendons, the tissues that link the muscle body to the bone, also have proprioceptors that sense stretch called Golgi tendon organs.

Afferent sensations of muscle stretch from the muscle spindles can activate centers in the brain stem, cerebellum, and motor cortex for the voluntary regulation of muscle activity. This results in the coactivation of both α - MNs and γ –MNs, the former to control the muscle contraction and the latter to make the muscle more sensitive to voluntary control. If the stretch occurs very rapidly, however, the afferent signal triggers the activation of the α–MNs at the spinal cord, the so-called stretch reflex, contracting the muscle to protect it against overstretching and therefore tearing.

Slow, deep pressure from touch directed at the belly of a tense (contracted) muscle will slow the firing of the afferent stretch pathways which in turn lowers the firing rate of the α – and γ – MNs, causing the muscle to relax. This is one of the ways in which massage therapy has an effect on relaxation (Johansson, 1962). Pinching or any sudden deep pressure will cause a muscle to contract via the stretch reflex.

Chronic muscle tension occurs when the muscles contract but are not doing any work to move body parts across a joint. As noted elsewhere in this book, muscle tension is a symptom in a variety of musculoskeletal and stress-related disorders. What is the origin of this stress-induced muscle tension? One of the pathways is the anticipation of the possibility of needing to move or act which creates an urge to act. The other pathway is the activation of the **sympathetic nervous system** (SNS) and the neurochemical threat response network including the **HPA-axis**.

Urges to act originate in the **cingulate motor area** (CMA) and the **supplementary motor area** (SMA). As explained in Chapter 4, suppression of the urge to act in the SMA and CMA occurs in cooperation with the regulatory prefrontal cortex. Often, however, this urge does not disappear but sends signals to the motor cortex to activate the muscles in a way that *prevents the body from moving*. This results in the contraction of the *low-threshold motor units*, keeping the muscle stiff but immobile.

The urge to act can come from the body, as in needing to urinate, and the need to suppress that urge likely comes from social expectations that don't permit one to get up and go to the toilet. It may also happen that social expectations create both the urge to act and the need to suppress that action. Thus, in addition to normal anticipation of movement, there is the added effect of the threat of meeting or not meeting those social expectations. If the threat is perceived as physically dangerous—as during assault or child abuse—and the person is not able to activate mobilization (fight, flight) biobehavioral response because of additional threats to *not move*, this leads to trauma and potentially to post-traumatic stress disorder (PTSD). Particular patterns of muscle contraction in preparation for fight or flight have been linked to activation of the fight or flight areas in the **periaqueductal grey** (PAG) (see Chapter 5; Li & Mitchell, 2000).

This has been demonstrated in the laboratory in several different ways. Experimental subjects shown threatening pictures of mutilation displayed freezinglike postures that included muscle tension and body stiffness (Azevedo et al., 2005). Muscles contract faster and with more intensity if people are experimentally exposed to unpleasant as compared to pleasant images (Coombes, Cauraugh, & Janelle, 2007). *These studies reveal the importance of enhancing embodied self-awareness of muscle tension as a component, in addition to the awareness of thoughts and emotions, in the treatment of stress and PTSD.*

Muscle tension can also come from working conditions in which particular postures are maintained for long periods but the amount of muscle force required is relatively low. This occurs, for example, in computer work when the forearms and wrists are held in an elevated, contracted posture while the fingers do light work against the keyboard. Ergonomic adjustments of chair height and keyboard position may help here, as well as pads on which to rest the wrist so that wrist and forearm can be relaxed. Tension in the neck and shoulders may be helped by adjusting the screen size, height, and distance from the head to the screen. *Embodied self-awareness interventions can also help by teaching people to reduce unnecessary tension in the arms and wrists, neck and shoulder and by taking regular breaks for moving and stretching* (Hägg, 1991; Sjøgaard & Sjøgaard, 1998).

A final source of muscle tension is related to psychological demands that create mental stress. Even simple laboratory tasks that demand attention while a person is sitting in front of a computer screen activate low-threshold motor units in the neck, forehead, and trapezius muscles of the upper back (Lundberg et al., 2002; Waersted, Elen, & Westgaard, 1996; Waersted & Westgaard, 1996). The chronic contraction of these muscles is typically associated with a sense of responsibility to perform (see Case Report 2.1).

This muscle tension induced by the stress of performance demands in experimental situations has also been shown to be accompanied by SNS and HPA responses such as higher blood pressure, heart rate, and cortisol (von Boxtel, Damen, & Brunia, 1996; Hanson, Schellekens, Veldman, & Mulder, 1993; Krantz, Forsman, & Lundberg, 2004). Similar muscular, autonomic, and hormonal responses have been observed in response to work-related time pressure demands and low perceived control (Bongers, de Winter, Kompier, & Hildebrandt, 1993). SNS activation contracts smooth muscles, but it can also indirectly activate skeletal muscles. This occurs partly because the SNS can contract blood vessels in the muscles and also because it can increase stress hormones in the blood that may induce the α–MNs to contract by activating the stretch reflex in the muscle spindles (Grassi et al., 1996; Hjortskov, Skotte, Hye-Knudsen, & Fallentin, 2005).

Individuals who report more stress, hostility, irritability, and anger also show more muscle tension in work situations. They also have more chronic back, shoulder, and neck pain (see Case Report 2.1; Bru, Mykletun, & Svebak, 1993; Burns, 2006a; Flodmark & Aase, 1992; Flor, Turk, & Birbaumer, 1985; Freeman & Katzoff, 1930; Gonge, Jensen, 7 Bonde, 2002; Jabusch, Müller, & Altenmüller, 2004; Lundberg, Dohns et al., 1999). Chronic muscle tension is higher in people who are rated as anxious or having an anxiety disorder, most likely from the chronic activation of the biobehavioral responses of vigilance and mobilization of the SNS (see Table 5.2; Fridlund, Hatfield, Cottam, & Fowler, 1986; Hoehn-Saric & McLeod, 2000; Osborne & Swenson, 1978; Sainsbury & Gibson, 1954).

One early research study used electromyography (EMG) to monitor muscle tension in the forehead, neck, forearm, and leg during weekly clinical interviews with psychiatric patients diagnosed with anxiety disorder. Each week, the researchers noted the average level of muscle tension and how it related to the predominant emotional content of the patient's talk as rated by the psychiatrist (Shagass & Malmo, 1954). In spite of the fact that the study was done more than half a century ago, it is still one of the few studies to show correlated changes in muscle tension over time with respect to changes in emotional state (see Figure 6.3).

The pain from tense muscles comes in part because the chronic low-threshold motor unit activation creates a build-up of metabolic waste, depletion of oxygen and increase in $CO2$, and a depletion of nutrients such as glucose which are sensed by chemoreceptors and nociceptors (for pain) in the body of the muscle, sending signals of discomfort to the interoceptive and body schema neural networks (Longhurst & Mitchell, 1979). In addition, the SNS induces dilation of the smooth muscles of the blood vessels in the skeletal

Moving and Touching

muscle tissue as well as increased cardiac output and blood pressure. These SNS responses are intended to bring more blood-borne nutrients to the skeletal muscles for mobilization responses. When the skeletal muscles are not executing high energy movements—as in situations of forced immobility during threat or from social constraints including sedentary working conditions—this swelling of the blood vessels activates nociceptors in the relatively tense skeletal muscle (Dodt, Wallen, Fehm, & Elam, 1998; Knardahl, 2002).

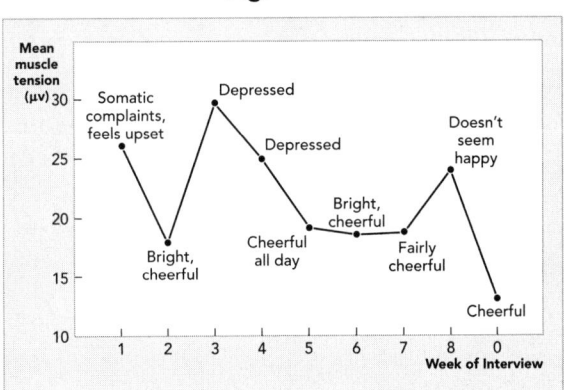

Figure 6.3

Muscle tension (in microvolts from the EMG recording) and psychiatrist-rated predominant emotional state during weekly interviews with an anxiety disordered patient.

Interoceptively, muscle pain may have different qualities depending upon the receptors involved. Chemoreceptors produce sensations of burning, aching, or fatigue. Mechanoreceptors in the muscle spindles create the sensation of cramping. Nociceptors detect pinching, cutting, and tearing (Schwellnus, Derman, & Noakes, 1997; Simone, Marchettini, Caputi, & Ochou, 1994).

Muscle pain from tension can actually increase tension in the pain–stress–pain cycle (Figure 5.1). Muscle pain is sensed as a threat causing low threshold tension and a fear of moving painful muscles. Muscle tension also continues to activate regions of the motor cortex, which replies by continuing to send signals for more contraction (Kaelin-Lang et al., 2002). These vicious cycles become **attractors** that create ongoing and chronic patterns of tension even when the body is resting or sleeping. Women with chronic pelvic pain, for example, show higher muscle tension, guarded posture in the pelvic area, higher anxiety, and a history of sexual abuse or dysfunction (Haugstad et al., 2006).

This has important implications for people with chronic pain from injuries, stress, fibromyalgia, or chronic fatigue (Biedermann & Forrest, 1991; Flor, Birbaumer, Schugens, & Lutzenberger, 1992; Kanbara et al., 2004). *Treatments need to be geared to break this cycle, addressing the sense of threat in the body by finding resources and working through the embodied self-awareness of the pain and its links to the past as they may be revealed in the subjective emotional present.*

Another line of evidence linking psychological state with the muscles is that people with mental disorders often also have muscle tension and movement disorders. In one study, 86% of patients hospitalized with a psychiatric disorder had motor, postural, and gait disorders. When walking, patients kept their arms stiff, had an exaggerated curve in their backs, and their high muscle tension limited movement flexibility including clenched fists, jaws, "folded up" postures when sitting and lying, tremors, and spasms. Other patients had difficulty initiating movements and lack of voluntary control over movements (Malmo & Shagass, 1949; Mittal et al., 2007; Özekmekçi, Apaydin, Ekinci, & Yalçinkayce, 2003; Rogers, 1992; Thomas & Jankovic, 2004).

Dystonia is the technical term for a movement disorder characterized by sustained contractions of the muscles, sometimes located in particular regions of the body. Dystonia is often associated with abnormally high activity in the premotor areas of the brain, including the SMA and CMA, suggesting a trauma-induced inhibition of an unrealized urge to act under conditions of threat (Gilio et al., 2003).

The Smooth Muscles: The Vascular and Gastrointestinal System

Smooth muscle does not have the same structure as skeletal muscle. The cells (fibers) of smooth muscle are smaller and they do not form into motor units. Instead the entire sheet or tube of the muscle contracts as a whole. Many smooth muscles have rhythmic waves of contraction, such as to move blood through a vessel or food through the gut. Smooth muscles are activated by the autonomic sympathetic and parasympathetic nervous systems, for contraction and relaxation respectively. In addition, smooth muscle can be made to contract or relax from hormones circulating in the blood, in particular hormones in the safety-threat network including cortisol and its precursors (ACTH and CRF), oxytocin, and hormones specific to vasodilation and vasocontraction from the hypothalamus (Anton et al., 2004; Taché & Bonaz, 2007).

The gastrointestinal system, in addition to its link with the autonomic nervous system (ANS), has its own local nervous system. **The enteric nervous system (ENS)** is embedded in the lining of the tissues of the gastrointestinal system. Sometimes called the "brain in the gut," the ENS has more neurons than the spinal cord and about 1/100th of the number of neurons in the brain. In addition to acting on information from the ANS, the ENS can act independently to control contraction and relaxation of the gut muscles and to secrete digestive enzymes in response to enteric mechanoreceptors and chemoreceptors in the interior of the gut (Wilson, 2004). Like the ANS, the ENS also plays a role in regulating immune function (Gross & Pothoulakis, 2007).

In both children and adults, anxiety, stress, and some types of psychopathology are associated with stomachaches and gastrointestinal dysfunction that go along with skeletal muscle tension (Egger, Costello, Erkanli, & Angold, 1999). In addition, gastrointestinal dysfunction is quickly detected by the interoceptive neural network, including the ACC and insula, which means that it can easily lead—via the pain–stress–pain cycle—to increased anxiety and a subsequent suppression of sensation (Mayer, Naliboff, & Craig, 2006).

Armoring

The research we have reviewed in the previous two sections clearly shows that psychological state can induce muscle tension in both skeletal and smooth muscles, tension that leads to pain, functional limitations, and postural dysfunction. Once a person has assumed a particular muscle pattern, however, that pattern can itself induce an alteration in psychological state (Ginsburg, 1999). Experimental subjects who were placed in hunched and threatened physical postures reported feeling greater stress, and subjects placed in slumped postures reported feeling more depressed (Riskind & Gotay, 1982). This means that *thought patterns, emotions, forms of embodied self-awareness, muscle tension and relaxation act together as a dynamic system, each element of which influences and maintains the others to form characteristic postures of relat-*

ing to the world. It also means that embodied self-awareness treatments can have multiple entry points into that system including body-oriented talk therapy, therapies based in movement, and therapies based in touch.

Posture can be submissive, defiant, depressed, bouncy, open, or relaxed. Posture is our way of expressing the basic biobehavioral response modes (see Table 5.2). Posture can be used to take a stance toward (engagement) or against (fight mobilization) or away from (flight mobilization) the world. Restoration is shown in postures of openness, reclining and sleeping, vigilance in postures of hesitation, and immobilization in rigid and inflexible postures.

Posture, in other words, is the neuromotor system's expression of emotion and attitude about and orientation toward or away from the world (Cacioppo et al., 1993; Maxwell & Davidson, 2007; Wallbott, 1998). Muscles are—along with the symptoms of autonomic nervous system function such as sweat, tears, trembling, body temperature, heart rate, and skin color changes—the main avenues that your brain and nervous system uses to express itself in the world. All facial expressions, for example, are made by movements of the muscles under the skin of the face.

The way that emotion and stress affects muscle tension and tension in turn affects feelings of stress and emotional state creates an attractor that can stabilize into each individual's characteristic postural appearance and attitude. Clinicians who have observed this link between muscle tension and emotional state refer to the skeletal musculature as a kind of armor. **Armoring** is the experience- dependent development of a protective shell of muscle tension grown over time in response to a history of threat, anxiety, and trauma (Reich, 1972).

Armoring is a form of suppression that results in the shutting down of sensory receptors and a corresponding lessening of activation in the interoceptive and body schema areas of the brain related to that part of the person (Mangan, Murphy, & Farmer, 1980). Just as the skeletal muscle armor protects the person from threat impinging on the outside of the body, smooth muscle tension in the gut is a protection against threats that are physically or metaphorically brought inside the body (Wilson, 2004).

It makes good sense that the muscles play an essential role in self-protection since they are potentially under voluntary control. Muscle tension armoring is especially useful to infants and children who do not have the mental resources to understand or to cope with what is happening to them during situations of maltreatment and trauma. They can, however, use their muscles for self-protection and self-comfort. If the threat is ongoing in childhood, the muscle tension becomes a habitual way of suppressing unpleasant feelings. As it stabilizes into an attractor, the armoring remains while the reasons for it, the memories of the threat situation, may have been forgotten in autobiographical memory (Boadella, 1987; MacNaughton, 2004; Rosen, 2003).

This link between armoring and embodied self-awareness or suppression of embodied self-awareness, is at the heart of Freud's theoretical premise that relationships with significant others in early childhood can lead to repression of awareness of body feelings and the resulting somatic symptoms of hysteria. Freud's ideas inspired Wilhelm Reich (1972) and Alexander Lowen (1958) to map the links between musculoskeletal systems and personality as the basis for psychoanalytic treatment practices. Lowen's "objective during therapy sessions was to help patients learn to understand how tensions in various regions of their bodies were associated with repressed fears and hostilities" (Bakal, 1999, p. 11). These founders created what is now called bioenergetic therapy, which was one of the precursors to somatic psychotherapy that uses talk, movement, breathwork, and touch to address client symptoms.

Marion Rosen, the founder of Rosen Method Bodywork, describes one case of a tall man who habitually rounded his shoulders, pulled in his chest and belly, and arched his head forward and down. Using the listening touch of Rosen's bodywork method to help him interoceptively feel the tension in his shoulders and chest, this man came to remember that he began to hide himself as a teen because he was gay and afraid of being attacked by other boys. While one might think he could use his height to give himself a sense of empowerment, the neuroception of threat took over his ability to make logical choices. He learned instead to make himself invisible. Rosen relates that she also learned to hide inside her body as a way to minimize her felt sense of threat as a Jewish teen growing up in Nazi Germany (Rosen, 2003).

Making a person aware of the location of muscle tension through touch and verbal reminders is typically not sufficient to alter the entrenched attractor pattern.

> Once the self-imposed restraint that protects us from an immediately threatening situation becomes converted to the security of

> armoring, it takes an act of daring to break out and expand against our confines. If we lack the courage, we are caught and the imprisonment perpetuates itself. (Herskowitz, 1997, p. 35)

This means that the relaxation of muscle armor requires some or all of the basic principles of treatment for loss of embodied self-awareness (Table 1.1). The ability to access and remain in the subjective emotional present requires the availability of supportive resources, slowing down in order to feel, coregulation with a therapist, sensing the location of the tension and its links with associated emotions, and verbalization of the connection between past events and the armoring.

> G.H. developed writer's cramp between the ages of 10 and 13, after two forearm fractures of her dominant arm and during a period that she was being sexually abused by her father. The writer's cramp then disappeared but reappeared when she was 35, when her father's impending death from an incurable lymphoma created ambivalent feelings of grief and hatred towards him because of the previous abuse. The writer's cramp persisted after her father's death for 3 years until, with counseling about her feelings towards her father over a period of 12 months, it completely resolved. (Rogers, 1992, p. 19)

This case shows the link between movement disorders and unresolved emotions as these link to the potential effectiveness of embodied self-awareness based psychotherapy for their resolution. Somatic psychotherapy, dance movement therapy, awareness-based exercise therapy, Feldenkrais, massage, relaxation techniques, and yoga breathing awareness have all been found in research studies to alleviate the movement disorders connected with psychiatric conditions as well as some of the mental and emotional problems that were salient in those conditions (Deutsch, 1950; Junker, Oberwittler, Jackson, & Berger, 2004; Reich, 1972; Rick, 2001; Schofield & Abbuhl, 1975; Tinazzi et al., 2002; Tkachuk & Martin, 1999).

Since armoring and chronic muscle tension is typically connected to suppressed emotions and feelings of threat, the relaxation of those muscles is sometimes accompanied by a release of spontaneous emotion or a personally vivid **participatory memory** in embodied self-awareness.

> When a muscular block is definitely resolved, it is frequently claimed by the subject that there occurs a vivid, spontaneous recall of typical situations, perhaps dating back to childhood, where he learned to tense in this particular manner. (Hefferline, 1958, p. 748)

This is illustrated in the continuing case of Joan's treatment for gastrointestinal pain (see Case Report 6.1).

Case Report 6.1
Completion of Joan's Rosen Method Bodywork Treatment

As Joan's sense of safety during the Rosen Method Bodywork sessions increased, she stopped retreating into the "safety" of her "playful little girl" dissociative state (see Case Report 5.1). On the other hand, she did dissociate when she felt stress from her current life coupled with the onset of participatory memories of her sibling abuse—full of fear and pain—during a session. Instead of retreating into the little girl, however, she would become drowsy. This was a minidissociation and it did not last more than a minute or two. Joan became better at catching herself drifting off. She also continued her pattern of "terminating" her treatments every month or two, after which she would return with renewed commitment.

Rebuilding the neural network for embodied self-awareness and for staying in the subjective emotional present following long-term and previously unresolved early trauma takes a long time and requires the full spectrum of self-awareness therapeutic principles (Table 1.1). Joan's case also shows that the treatment path is not direct. My sense was that Joan's retreats into her drowsy state and into withdrawal from her regular weekly sessions were in fact positive acts of **self-regulation** and **restoration**, to help her maintain her metabolic reserves for her athletics, her work, her social life, and her continuing Rosen treatment.

During the remaining 5 months of Joan's work with me, the focus became more related to her gastrointestinal dysfunction, the symptoms that had originally brought her to see me. She was increasingly capable of bringing her attention to her gut and I brought my hands there more frequently. She began to make the connection that this part of her tensed when she thought about or talked about situations of conflict: either remembered conflicts from childhood or conflicts in her everyday life.

The internal smooth muscles of the gut are not protected by a bony structure. The heart and lungs are sheathed by the rib cage and the reproductive organs and bladder by the pelvis. If there are gut problems, they are often accompanied by tension in the abdominal wall and lower back skeletal muscles in addition to smooth muscle tension in the gut itself. It is as if those muscles become an exoskeleton (armor) to keep the gut from losing control or from feeling pain.

As Joan's awareness grew about the link between conflict and muscle tension, her abdominal wall muscles began to relax. My hand could then feel more deeply into her belly. This does not require additional pressure but rather a focusing of the practitioner's intention on "touching" the gut muscles. Her gut organs felt hard, almost like rocks inside her belly.

When she was lying face up, she became more aware of a new sense of vulnerability to my more penetrating contact. She could feel her abdominal wall muscles tightening up as a result, and she reported feeling anxiety, fear, and sometimes sadness. I felt she was pushing me away from that area and, as much as I wanted to stay there and investigate, I would take my hand off after a short while. I did not want to accentuate the fear beyond her ability to tolerate it, allowing her to maintain homeostasis through her **coregulation** with me (Table 1.1).

During the session on which this case report is focused, there was an increased relaxation, softening, and opening to my touch as I worked on her back and neck when she was lying face down. As a result of this relaxation, I thought she may have felt safe enough to attempt another exploration of the guarding in the abdominal area. It occurred to me to coregulate an alliance around this issue. I said, "I'd like to touch your belly but I want you to really pay attention and let me know if it feels comfortable or not." Could Joan's increased ability to self-regulate serve as her own **resource**?

Joan acquiesced but not wholeheartedly. My very gentle touch precipitated an immediate tensing of the abdominal wall muscles and a shift to a more panting breath. She didn't say anything, as if she had to stay still and bear it no matter what. I said, "It feels like you are tensing up."

Moving and Touching

She agreed but could not bring herself to ask me to back off. I said I was going to move my hand to her hip and that she should observe what occurred. She began to breathe easier and I could feel relaxation coming in again. I asked if she noticed anything and she was able to clearly describe the unpleasant/pleasant difference in sensation between the belly and hip.

I said that I could put my hand back on her belly or move somewhere else.

She said, "Well it's uncomfortable but maybe it's good if you touched there again."

I said, "Check in with your body right now and see if what you just said feels right." There was a deeper breath and a tentative nod. Talking softly, I described that I would move my hand slowly back to where it was on her belly and I asked her to notice what happened as I did that. This time, I could feel some small degree of receptivity. I continued to ask how it felt, whether I should move my hand or not, or about the pressure (she said "heavy," although my touch was very light, slow, gentle, and not penetrating).

This process continued, shifting my touch from her belly to her hip, all the while asking her to pay attention and let me know what she wanted and felt.

Finally, she invited me back verbally. "Can you touch me here?" She pointed to a particular area, between her sternum and navel, and her body responded receptively to my touch. That was the first time she actually made a deliberate choice about this part of her body to say "yes" or even "no."

"I can feel you accepting this touch rather than pushing me away."

"Is that what it felt like to you, that I was pushing you away?"

"Yes," I said, "and that makes sense to me because this is a part of your body that has suffered some trauma." (Her brother would sometime punch her there.) She took a very deep breath and relaxed more.

A few minutes later she said she was remembering the thrill of making her first goal in a soccer match, a **participatory memory**. She went on to say that she felt the only way to combat her abusive brother was to become athletic. She started playing girls' soccer in elementary school and later took up gymnastics. Even by age 9, her body was strong and quick. She fed off the adulation of teammates and peers and

> she learned to use humor to avoid or defuse conflict. She began to feel more confidence in herself.
>
> During the session, she realized that thinking about, avoiding, and defusing conflict were all connected to her gut muscle tension. Her terror of her brother's retaliation had ultimately kept her from any chance of direct confrontation with him and from telling her parents. She learned to adopt a posture of sticking out her chest and holding in her gut to make herself feel stronger, taller, and invincible. In this session, the new awareness resulted in her abdominal wall and her gut muscles softening considerably.
>
> Her stomachaches took months more to completely disappear, all the while attenuating in frequency and intensity as she amplified her awareness of the links between the gut and conflict in her life. Paradoxically, her increased awareness of the gut became her barometer of conflicting feelings and of a rising threat of a potential interpersonal conflict. This "early warning signal" eventually allowed her to actually feel the conflicting feelings on-line, without suppression, and to become more assertive and less evasive with her friends and co-workers.

Only much later, when writing this book, did I discover that Joan's case was similar to that of one of Freud's early patients, Frau Emmy. Emmy's most persistent symptom was gastrointestinal pain. In the course of Freud's treatment of Emmy with a combination of massage, hypnosis, and emotional release (and until writing this book, I did not know that Freud used touch in his work), Emmy recalled some of her childhood trauma.

> . . . how her siblings used to throw dead animals at her; how she unexpectedly saw her sister in a coffin; how her brother terrified her by dressing up in a sheet like a ghost; and how she saw her aunt in a coffin and her aunt's jaw suddenly dropped. (Wilson, 2004, p. 31)

And, just to finish up this section on a more positive note, also in preparing this book I was fascinated to read a study of the views of female college athletes about their body experiences. Unlike many women of their age who exemplify the soft smooth bodies of the "ideal" female, these women were highly muscular: large leg muscles for soccer, for example, and large upper body and arm muscles for basketball, compact breasts and little curvature above the hips because of strong transverse abdominal muscles. While some of the women were embarrassed about their muscles in mixed company, many of them were proud of their bodies. One woman, talking about her relationships with men, said,

> He told me, "Oh, I thought you had the best body when you came to school, then you started lifting and bulking up. I wish you wouldn't lift as much. All my buddies give me shit, saying that you're stronger than me. I have to stick up for you all the time." It bothers me that he didn't like my muscles, but I do—so forget him! Other boys tell me my body is hot. (George, 2005, p. 335)

As a result, I was able to watch Dara Torres, Kerri Walsh, Misti May-Trainor, Nastia Liukin, and many other athletes during the Beijing Summer Olympics, 2008, in an entirely different way. These women show courage in breaking boundaries and finding new linkages both inside and outside of the competitive arena; their physical prowess translates into a sense of personal power and integrity.

Interpersonal Movement and Touch in the Development of the Distinction between Self and Nonself

How do we come to know that our body and our feelings belong to us? It is very common for young children, for example, to confuse their feelings with those of the people around them. A 2-year-old, upon witnessing his mother stub her toe and scream in pain, may offer to let the mother use his bottle or blanket or teddy bear. The child feels that the parent's pain is "like mine" and that "what comforts me will also comfort my mom."

Marital conflict can have a long-term traumatic effect on children partly because of the sense of threat to their own well-being and safety if the parents break up or if the anger turns on the child. In addition, however, the children's and adolescents' sense of threat is exacerbated because they sometimes feel that they are the cause of the parental conflict. They do not know about or

Psychophysiology of Self-Awareness

understand the adult issues between the parents, but they interpret a parent's normal disappointment or anger at them for their childish "transgressions" as the cause of the parental conflict.

Table 6.1
Erik Erickson's Eight Ages of Man.
Stages from Erickson, 1950. All other material by author.

Age (years)	Stage	Self vs. Other
0–1½	Trust vs. mistrust	The development of secure vs. insecure attachment, safety and threat. Security allows for the ability to engage with the sensations and emotions of self and others; threat leads to suppression and dissociation.
1½–3	Autonomy vs. shame/doubt	Self-assertiveness and self-control over body functions including walking and running, fine motor control, toilet training, speech and autobiographical memory. Uncertainty and lack of emotional support can lead to feelings of self-doubt and shame and suppression of these emotions.
3–6	Initiative vs. guilt	Independent activity is approached with either a sense of purpose (initiative) or self-blame (guilt). Initiative includes trying out adult roles through play, becoming assertive with peers, and asking questions about self and others. Guilt refers to the feeling that the person's initiatives are not appreciated and therefore do not "belong" to the self, leading to inhibition.
6–11	Industry vs. inferiority	Interest in learning and skill development or a sense of inadequacy and loss of motivation. The former is connected to achievements in peer groups and school and the growth of new knowledge and abilities that provide a sense of being uniquely different from others. The latter comes from criticism by peers, teachers, and parents that lower self-esteem and prevent the development of a person's unique resources.
11–20	Identity vs. role confusion	Perception of self as a unique individual; development of personal values or confusion about identity and role in life. The former results from an examination of moral and ethical issues, and the start of seeing how the person might fit into

continued

Table 6.1 (continued)

Age (years)	Stage	Self vs. Other
11–20	Identity vs. role confusion	the larger society in terms of career, devotion to a cause, and religion. The latter results from lack of support to explore, either because of rigid family and school pressures for moral behavior or because of threats that lead to being pulled into criminal or promiscuous alliances. The former is a sense of making informed choices and the latter is the sense of having no choice.
20–40	Intimacy vs. isolation	This is the stage of establishing romantic relationships, mentee-mentor relationships in advanced schooling or the workplace. Issues of attachment security or insecurity, safety and threat, arise once again except now they can affect success or failure at sustaining long-term partnerships and having emotional fulfillment or suppression.
20–65	Generativity vs. self-absorption	Generativity is the ability to go outside the self to give to others: such as children or students or employees to help them to realize their own self-development. It is also the creation of financial security for self and family. Self-absorption is the suppression of other's needs and the pathological absorption into rumination and dissociation. Once again, the self fails to be distinguished from others as absorption may lead to blaming others for one's failures or manipulating others to achieve one's goals.
55–death	Integrity vs. despair	Integrity is the development of wisdom, the sense that life has meaning and purpose in spite of difficulties, heightened awareness of a larger universe of which the self is merely one part, no more important than others. Despair can be either the loss of faith and meaning in life, a sense of life as worthless, or continuing self-absorption leading to dogmatic and rigid beliefs and an inability to see oneself as human, vulnerable, and subject to death.

Psychophysiology of Self-Awareness

Developmental psychologists have charted the changes with age in our ability to distinguish between self and other, and to fully experience the sense of self across the life course. The best description of this developmental process, in my opinion, is that of Erik Erikson in his classic book, *Childhood and Society* (1950). Rather than seeing development as cumulative and progressive, Erikson saw that we could either enhance or inhibit self-awareness and other-awareness at different times in life, and that the ways of doing this changed with age (see Table 6.1). Erikson also clearly acknowledged that our sense of self develops in relation to others and to the encouragement, or lack of it, that we get from people to *be ourselves and feel ourselves.*

Self and Other

Oddly enough, the ability to distinguish self from other in early childhood in part derives from the ability to recognize how we are similar to others, or rather, how others are "like me" (Meltzoff, 2007). From a very young age, infants are capable of imitating other people. In fact, imitation is one of the quickest routes to connecting with a small, nonverbal infant. Infants like to imitate and they like to be imitated.

Observers of these early imitations have wondered how it is possible that an infant of several months of age, who likely is not aware of the links between many parts of her own body, could possibly see someone else make a facial expression—like repeated mouth opening—and reproduce the same expression in the correct part of her own face. Even more mysterious are findings showing that newborns, who have never seen someone else's face, can under certain conditions reproduce what that face is doing. Mouth opening or tongue protrusion are commonly used behaviors in such research (Meltzoff & Moore, 1997). And, surprisingly, infants from the first months of life can apparently tell the difference between people and objects. Infants look longer at animate human faces compared with inanimate faces and also compared with animated dolls (Legerstee, 1997), presumably because the human faces are more "like them."

One explanation of these phenomena is that infants have a rudimentary body schema that they can match with another person's movements. This seems unlikely, however, because the body schema of very young infants is still in the process of development. It takes a while for the infant to learn to guide her hand to her own mouth, for example. It is actually more likely, given the many hours that infants spend in the company of others, that their own body schema develops from experience dependent interactions and observations of people. Infants do not recognize that their image in a mirror is themselves until they are at least 18 months. This developmental milestone is accompanied by higher levels of activation in the parietal cortex, the part of the brain connected with body schema awareness (Lewis & Carmody, 2008).

If the body schema in fact develops partly from observing others, how do babies seem to "know" how to use their observations of others to make the links between observing other's bodies and identifying the relevant similar parts of their own bodies? Recent discoveries in the neuroscience of the body schema have provided at least a partial answer to this question.

When humans perceive actions made by other people, it automatically activates the same brain regions that regulate one's own similar actions (Decety & Chaminade, 2003; Montagna, Cerri, Borroni, & Baldissera 2005). Neurons in a monkey's body schema neural network (the sensory, motor, and parietal cortices) that were activated when it performed an action were also activated when it observed another monkey do that same action. Scientists have dubbed the specific neurons in these motor areas that get activated during observation of others as **mirror neurons** (Ferrari, Gallese, Rizzolatti, & Fogassi, 2003; Gallese, Fadiga, Fogassi, & Rizzolatti, 1996; Rizzolatti, Fagita, Gallese, & Fogassi, 1996).

The existence of mirror neurons, which fire when we observe other people doing actions similar to ones we ourselves can do, helps us to understand the findings on infant imitation and on how infants and adults learn about their own body schema from watching others. The mirror neurons that relate to our own similar movements will fire automatically upon observation. That neural activity will in turn generate efferent signals to the muscles that lead us to make similar, imitative movements. Via practice and continued observation, body schema self-awareness can expand.

Interpersonal Movement

The concept of mirror neurons in the neural networks for embodied self-awareness is therapeutically very important because it suggests an embodied approach to working with people who show body schema and interoceptive deficits. The implication is extremely simple: *let a person observe or move with someone else, or highlight their interoceptive and body schema self-awareness through comovement and touch, and then allow the person's nervous system to "take over" by creating experience dependent neural pathways that help the person to "find themselves."*

To help a newborn find a nipple, all that is necessary is to let the nipple or an adult finger touch the infant's cheek near the mouth or to gently touch the lips. The baby can take over from there. Want to help a toddler to walk? Just hold their body by the hands or under the arms in such a way as to let their feet touch the ground but not with so much weight on their legs that they collapse. Babies actually have the ability to cycle their legs rhythmically from birth (think of kicking) but they lack the balance necessary to walk until the end of the first year (Thelen, Bradshaw, & Ward, 1981). The key to embodied learning is to highlight the appropriate body parts and how they feel, and then let the neurodevelopmental process of self-awareness and self-discovery take root.

Examples like these from human development are endless. When children are given help in identifying and monitoring their own movements and expressions, they can learn very quickly (Moore, Mealiea, Garon, & Povinelli, 2007). Partly this is because young children spend a great deal of time focused on exploring their own body, its movements and sensations, and comparing it to other bodies. Infants as young as 5 months will look longer at pictures of other people's faces compared to their own and will listen more attentively to other people's voices compared to hearing their own recorded voice, and will show more curiosity toward mirror or video images of parts of their bodies that have been distorted (Legerstee, Anderson, & Schaffer, 1998; Rochat & Morgan, 1995). Children who are developing normally do this spontaneously and in many types of embodied self-awareness, children actually perform better than adults. Children aged 9 to 11, for example, swayed less in a complex balance task than adults (Schaefer, Krampe, Lindenberger, & Baltes, 2008).

It turns out that the **somatotopic** representations of body parts in the central nervous system are not entirely separate. The locations of the brain representations of each finger of the hand, for example, overlap somewhat with each other, a kind of within-person mirror neuron system in which neural representations of different parts of the body are reflected in each other. *This means that in situations of carefully directed touch in movement training or bodywork touch therapy for self-awareness disorders, the individual can discover the links* *between the part that is touched and links to other related parts of the body that are not touched* (Schieber, 2001). It also means, unfortunately, that in unguided learning or situations of threat, adjacent body areas may be coactivated into patterns of armoring and energy draining postures (Feldenkrais, 1985).

Touching with the goal of gently moving tense or restricted parts of the body—mirroring the feeling of these movements back to the client to enhance embodied self-awareness—occurs in the Alexander Technique, the work of Ida Rolf, and the Body-Mind Centering techniques of Bonnie Bainbridge Cohen (see Johnson, 1995, for a more detailed description), Biodynamic Massage, and in various types of body psychotherapies based on the work of Gerda Boyesen, Wilhelm Reich, Fritz Perls (Gestalt therapy), Alexander Lowen, and Trygve Braatoy (Braatoy, 1952; Johnson, 1995; Lowen, 1958; Westland, 1996). Other similar methods are reviewed in Johnson (1995).

Much like **dance movement psychotherapy** (Case Report 3.1) done on land, a **Watsu** practitioner can kinesthetically mirror the client's patterns of movement and holding in an aquatic environment. In both cases, coregulated movements enhance embodied self-awareness (see Case Report 3.1; Brodie & Lobel, 2004; Dull, 1997). Moshe Feldenkais (see Box 1.1) developed a method of movement self-awareness, in which the student's movement is guided by the touch and movement of the practitioner.

> **Functional integration** turns to the oldest elements of our sensory system—touch, the feelings of pull and pressure; the warmth of the hand, its caressing stroke. The person becomes absorbed in sensing the diminishing muscular tonus, the deepening and regularity of breathing, abdominal ease, and improved circulation in the expanding skin. The person senses his most primitive, consciously forgotten patterns and recalls the well-being of a growing young child. (Feldenkrais, 1981, p. 121)

Functional integration has been shown in research studies to improve ease of movements, reduce pain and disability in a variety of different populations (cf., Lundblad, Elert, & Gerdle, 1999). An example of a functional integration lesson is given in Case Report 6.2.

Case Report 6.2[1]
Working with the Symptoms of Multiple Sclerosis
Roger Russell

The art of giving Functional Integration lessons is one of timing, of watching and waiting, and then of moving with a person as a new self-awareness unfolds in his or her own private time and experience. Rather than directing, the practitioner becomes a participant observer in the movement and sensory life of another person.

Several years ago I worked in a neurological rehabilitation clinic as a guest intern for three weeks. It was in this clinic that I met Thomas. When I walked into Thomas's room the first time, my reaction was that the situation was anything but promising. Thomas sat hunched over in a wheelchair—*collapsed* would be a more defining word. His balance was poor, and he could barely keep himself sitting without support. His speech was slurred. When he reached out to shake my hand, he pulled his right side together such that his shoulder pressed into his ribcage. It was an attempt to suppress his ataxic arm, which shook every time he wanted to use his dominant hand. These difficulties had crippled him, his business, and his marriage. Yet, his eyes told a different story. Thomas was curious and attentive as he looked up at me. I felt the surprising sensation of connecting with a lively spirit: an awake human being.

Thomas told me about his life before MS had caught him: he was a successful business executive—traveling, attending meetings, and selling. He had been an avid marathon runner in his free time until he started stumbling nine years ago. At first, he berated himself for his technique. "Got to work on that swing of the left leg," he would say to himself. But then came numbness, stiffness, and his refusal to see a doctor for fear of the answers. Eventually, the difficulties could no longer be ignored. Life as he had known it came tumbling down around him when Thomas heard the diagnosis of *Multiple Sclerosis*.

Thomas and I worked together every day for about an hour for those three weeks, building a working partnership that included frustration and uncertainty for both of us. We explored, prodded, moved, and waited. We sensed, talked, and waited some more. We worked with balance and the breath because we use most of the same muscles for breathing as we use for balance. We explored how to guide reaching movements with the eyes, one of the first activities a baby learns to coordinate. My assumption was that, if we could find that old experience in Thomas's brain, it would help us find new ways to control his wobbly hand now. We also searched for ways to make rolling on the floor easier, again to improve balance. Rolling is one of the first ways a baby discovers balance and the integrity of the body schema.

I continued to touch Thomas, sense his motion, and carefully pace myself to perfectly match the timing, direction, and forces of his movements. I wanted to find my way into Thomas's world: his experience in his body, his breathing, his uneven voice, and the vanishing sensation in his spastic legs, tight as iron. This is what Moshe Feldenkrais called "dancing together." I observed his rhythms of moving. Although seemingly chaotic, they had a stable pattern: the ataxia, the patterns of breathing and speaking, the pulling of the right side together more than the left.

Despite the impairment of normal movement function, I saw order in the symptoms. I was counting on finding more order, now hidden by habits of compensation that he had learned while fighting his slow, creeping descent into neurological hell. In addition, I was wondering: What does self-awareness mean for Thomas? What do the medical explanations and terminology about damage to the nervous system, the pathology, the sensory deficits, and so forth tell him about himself? Who is he now, nine years later? What does *sense of self* mean for him? How does he experience the statement, "I am able to..."? What is his experience of self-agency and self-coherence?

> **Self-agency** "is the sense of authorship of one's own actions. It involves a sense of volition that precedes an action" as well as "...the proprioceptive feedback that does or does not occur during the act."
> **Self-coherence** "is the sense of being a nonfragmented, physical whole, with boundaries and a locus of integrated action. (Stern 1985, pp. 71–76)

I worked with an understanding that Thomas would benefit from my ability to quiet myself, to attend and listen, to sense and respectfully guide him to an experience of order that he so needed and couldn't find on his own. When we did find a way to connect, it was on a hunch. It wasn't even a thought, just a funny feeling that we should look for a way to take his shaking right hand behind his back. I would say that I was able to quiet myself, my thoughts, my doubts, my concerns, and my hurry until Thomas was able to guide me by the most subtle of cues to take his hand where he needed it to be. Suddenly his hand was quiet—it stopped shaking. We both had the presence of mind to wait and sense the importance of this astounding experience.

With his hand behind his back, Thomas's eyes caught mine. "I can quiet it down...my arm..." were his only words. Yet, his eyes held the realization, even as it unfolded in that slowed-down sense of time of such moments of discovery, that he could learn something new within his seemingly scrambled nervous system. There was a possibility for self-awareness that could be sensed and attended. He could become curious about, explore, and trust that life could go on.

Once Thomas sensed that he could quiet his hand, we brought it out from behind his back. He was able to move it with less shaking than before. In addition, he was able to lift his hand above his head, something he had not been able to do for many months.

When I asked him how he was doing the next day, Thomas proudly lifted his right hand. Although still somewhat wobbly, it was remarkably different. For this to have happened, Thomas needed only to discover that he could sense *in embodied self-awareness* his potential to reorganize his movement. This embodied self-awareness contrasted with his conceptual self-awareness that he had a pathological condition and was stuck with it.

I lost track of Thomas after I left the clinic. I don't know how things continued for him. I do know that I would have enjoyed continuing working with this lively man. My impression is that many of those who have MS acquire some of their symptomatic behavior as they attempt to compensate for the effects of their illness. Their own slumbering abilities to patiently attend, sense, explore, and discover become buried in the stress of finding a path through an increasingly difficult jungle of confusing experiences. The careful touch of another person can help them find their way through this labyrinth of uncertainty. It requires following, pacing, and guiding as both participants move together and wait for the creative moment that unfolds in the awareness process under the protective hand of human connection.

---

[1] The material in Case Report 6.2 is used with the author's permission. Roger Russell, MA, PT is a senior Feldenkrais practitioner and internationally accredited senior Feldenkrais trainer who works in Heidelberg, Germany.

Moving and Touching

This case can be understood from the perspective of the therapeutic guidelines listed in Table 1.1.

- *Resources* in this situation came from the therapeutic encounter but more importantly from Thomas himself. Unlike many individuals who have suffered a trauma that impairs their ability to find their own resources, Thomas had a long history of curiosity, willingness to engage, and ability to enjoy.
- The ability to *slow down* and be in the subjective emotional present occurred throughout these sessions, even in the midst of uncertainty and frustration.
- *Coregulation* also happened throughout and in fact was the central feature of these sessions. It was only through attentive coregulation that the practitioner and Thomas discovered a new way to hold his arm behind his back.
- *Verbalization* seemed less important in this case report than in others in this book. Nevertheless, it seemed emotionally important for Thomas to say, "I can quiet it down…my arm."
- *Linkages and boundaries* came in throughout the work described here, as each person opened up to exploring the possibilities of connection and at the same time calibrating that connection against their own body schema self-awareness.
- *Self-regulation* was the wonderful discovery at the end, which led to a newfound ability to control his arm movements.
- *Reengagement* also occurred throughout, since Thomas was clearly fully engaged from the beginning.
- *Letting go* does not happen in this case. Given the severity of the disease, Thomas may be occupied for the remainder of his life in a more or less constant battle with an unforgiving adversary, a battle to wrest self-coherence and self-agency out of the ongoing chaos of his scrambled neuromotor network.

The practitioner in this case chose to help guide Thomas into relatively simple infantlike movements such as reaching, rolling over, and balance. Parental touch and movement of an infant's body can enhance body schema self-awareness and assist in the development of specific motor patterns. In

Psychophysiology of Self-Awareness

some African cultures, mothers move and massage their babies' bodies in ways that would be surprising in Western cultures (see Figure 6.4). Studies that have compared the babies of women in these cultures who use these dramatic infant gymnastics with women from the same cultures who do not, have shown that the babies thus moved developed postural skills such as head control, sitting upright and standing alone earlier than the babies who did not receive this treatment (Bril & Sabatier, 1986; Hopkins & Westra, 1988).

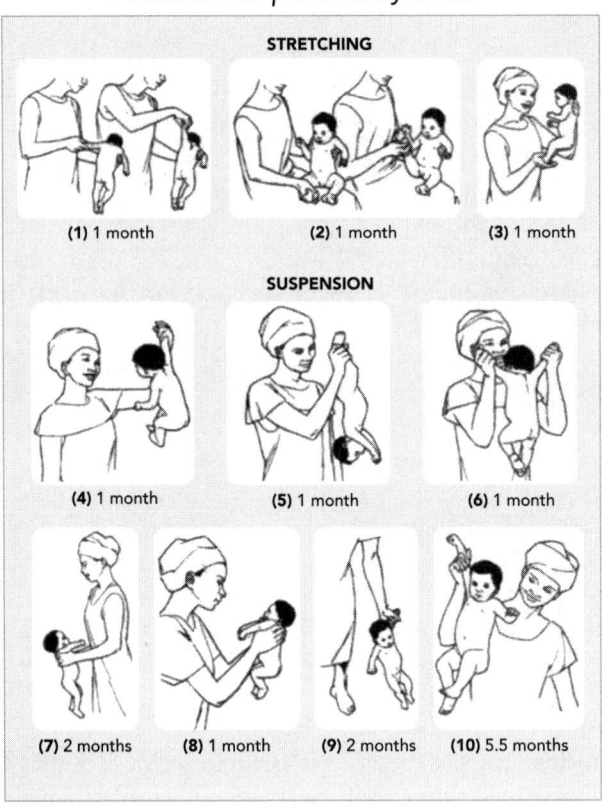

Figure 6.4
Postural manipulation by adults

Taken from Fogel, A. (2009). *Infancy: Infant, family, and society*, 5th Edition. Cornwall-on-Hudson, NY: Sloan Publishing.

Both Moshe Feldenkrais and Marion Rosen were aware of the inseparable links between movement and touch. Rosen developed a method of movement based on physical therapy and modern dance approaches to increasing embodied self-awareness through movement. A Rosen Movement class lasts one hour and involves a series of gentle movements done to music (see Case Report 8.2). Some of the movements and postures are done with people standing in a circle, either with or without holding onto their neighbors. Other movements are done sitting or lying, or walking across the floor, sometimes with and sometimes without partners. Other exercises allow a person to move their arms up and down, for example, while a partner gently touches their shoulder blades, enhancing the awareness of how the shoulder blade moves in relation to the arm. Rosen movement increases flexibility, opens the posture for coregulated engagement with others, emphasizes awareness and the joy of movement, and teaches about finding comfort and enjoyment in touching and moving with other people (Rosen & Brenner, 1992).

> In Rosen movement, healing manifests itself as a reclaiming of movements. The body begins to move again as a whole with the freedom of early childhood. Places long held frozen and unconscious are released. These stuck places are experienced as moving merely because they are no longer held. (Rosen & Brenner, 1992, p. 5)

Another approach to educating self-awareness with movement is **neuromuscular integrative action (NIA)**, a form of group cardiovascular movement awareness done barefoot to music. NIA uses elements of Tai Chi, Aikido, modern dance, Feldenkrais, and Yoga, among other methods. Using the sounds and silences of music, students experience feeling the embodied sense of joy in movement in a way that encourages an embodied self-awareness of agility, mobility, stability, flexibility, and strength. NIA teachers encourage students to actively listen, feel, and observe their bodies in motion (Rosas & Rosas, 2005).

Yoga itself is an ancient movement practice that has enjoyed remarkably widespread popularity in recent years. Although there are many different types of yoga, they all focus on embodied self-awareness of movement, breathing, and posture. There is a growing body of research showing its efficacy in improving neuromotor and psychophysiological function in cardiovascular, respiratory, movement, and psychiatric disorders (Khalsa, 2004a, 2004b).

Rehabilitation work with patients following limb loss or injury, or with stroke victims, uses a variety of techniques to enhance the client's embodied self-awareness with the goal of restoring normal function including comovement, guided exercise, education, and psychotherapy (Lucas & Fleming, 2005). Clients using these comovement methods to enhance self-awareness have shown reorganization in both motor function and in the neural networks related to interoceptive and body schema self-awareness (Liepert et al., 2000; Nelles, 2004). Technology has entered the picture with robotic braces that when placed on a paralyzed limb, can move the limb in response to efferent (from the brain) motor neuron commands that are ineffective in moving the muscles themselves. After training with such devices, the afferent feedback from the passively moved muscles joins with the efferent pathways to improve voluntary movement without the brace (Stein, Narendran, et al., 2007).

These findings about how attending, touching, and moving can activate embodied self-awareness and lead to positive change follow the basic principles of treatment (Table 1.1). The basic *resource* is the help of a knowledgeable trainer, teacher, or therapist. Via *coregulation* with that person, the individual can *slow down* to stay with body sensations in the subjective emotional present. *Verbalization* helps to isolate, locate, and feel tension in the body and its relationship to current and past stressors. This leads to enhancing an awareness of *boundaries* of self and other, *self-regulation* to take the initiative to change the environment and find new resources, and *reengagement* and higher levels of endeavor with self and others.

Interpersonal Touch

In some cases, simply touching another person can contribute to enhancing his or her embodied self-awareness, leading to a reduction of muscle tension and armoring, and an increase in parasympathetic relaxation. How does this happen? Touch stimulates receptors in the skin for pressure, pain, temperature, and movement and receptors in the muscles and tendons for stretch, fatigue, and pain. These receptors are linked directly into the neural networks for interoception and body schema self-awareness.

Moving and Touching

Touch to different parts of the body increases self-awareness of that body part by stimulating the experience dependent growth of neural connections in the **somatotopically** linked areas of the sensory and motor cortices, cerebellum, and brain stem. This is the case for short-term experimental studies as well as long-term effects of rehabilitation exercises for people with pain and sensorimotor loss of function (Behrman, Bowden, & Nair, 2006; Hamdy, Rothwell, Aziz, Singh, & Thompson, 1998; Jenkins, Merzenich, Ochs, Allard, & Guíc-Robles, 1990; Kerr, Wasserman, & Moore, 2007; Luft, Manto, & Ben Taib, 2005; Rosenkranz & Rothwell, 2006; Steihaug, Ahlsen, & Malterud, 2001; Wang, Merzenich, Sameshima, & Jenkins, 1995; Wolpaw & Tennissen, 2001). Touch, in other words, can create the growth of linked cellular pathways along the neuraxis to encode and enhance embodied self-awareness.

The interoceptive neural network, when combined with the emotion network including the prefrontal areas (Figure 3.1), is capable of also sensing the emotional qualities of different types of touch via the nonmyelinated, slow Aδ and C nerve fibers in the dorsal horn of the spinal cord (Hua et al., 2008; McGlone, Vallbo, Olausson, Loken, & Wessberg, 2007; Olausson et al., 2008; Wessberg, Olausson, Fernström, & Vallbo, 2003). In one experiment, people were given emotion words via headphones and asked to communicate those words only by touching the forearm of another person hidden behind a curtain. The person on the other side of the curtain was asked to decide which emotion was being communicated. People successfully decoded anger (hitting, squeezing), fear (trembling), love (stroking, rubbing), sympathy (patting), and disgust (pushing, tapping) (Hertenstein, Keltner, App, Bulleit, & Jaskolka, 2006).

Loving touch and hugs from romantic partners activates the parasympathetic nervous system, lowers blood pressure and heart rate, and induces the secretion of oxytocin (Light, Grewen, & Amico, 2005). Massage therapy has been shown to reduce anxiety and depression with benefits of similar magnitude to those found in traditional psychotherapy. Massage also increases parasympathetic activity and oxytocin secretion (Cottingham, Porges, & Richmond, 1988; Weerapong, Hume, & Kolt, 2005).

While these studies did not measure self-awareness, one can presume that almost any kind of caring touch brings sensitivity and awareness to the areas of the body that are contacted and to the person's relationship with others. It

Psychophysiology of Self-Awareness

is also likely that the people who are doing the touching are becoming aware of their partner's physical and mental state through the touch. **Rosen Method Bodywork** emphasizes specifically the importance of the practitioner using a **listening touch** to touch another person with soft hands that are tactilely attentive to the physical and emotional condition of the receiver.

When used in this way, the hand can be incredibly sensitive. Trained practitioners can feel both the skin and muscles as well as internal organs without necessarily increasing pressure on the skin. Rosen Method practitioners learn to use their own interoceptive self-awareness as a tool to enhance their ability to listen to the client through touch, vision, and sound (see Case Report 6.1; Rosen, 2003).

> As practitioners, when we touch somebody they also touch us. They touch us at a place that is open and undefended, our soft hands . . . It is a growing experience for practitioners as well as patients. Practitioners are replenished at the same time they are giving. (Rosen, 2003, p. 20)

In collaboration with Rosen Method Bodywork senior teacher Sandra Wooten, I helped to design a touch intervention for married couples based on Rosen Method's listening touch. The guidelines for this intervention are given in Box 6.1. Couples were randomly assigned to an experimental group receiving the listening touch intervention or to a control group where the couples kept a diary about their mood and physical affection. The couples were trained and then allowed to do this for 4 weeks. After those 4 weeks, compared to the control group couples, both members of the couples who received the intervention had higher levels of oxytocin and lower levels of stress homones. In addition, the males in the listening touch intervention group had significantly lower blood pressure (Holt-Lunstad, Birmingham, & Light, 2008).

Box 6.1
Rosen Method Listening Touch Intervention for Couples

Alan Fogel and Sandra Wooten[1]

One at a Time
In this exercise, each person gets to practice listening touch while the other person receives that touch. Discussion after the exercise should always begin with a sharing of what each person felt for themselves. Then they can mention what might have made it better for them.

Hands-on-Shoulders
One person sits in a chair while the other stands behind, touching the neck and shoulders; learning to listen through touch, and about different qualities of listening touch; observing breath and relaxation; then roles are changed silently. The touch is nondemanding, no words are used, the person being touched has an opportunity to feel into themselves for whatever is there while the person doing the touching is a witness and "container" (10–15 minutes, followed by a 5-minute dyadic discussion).

Together
This exercise helps the couple move toward more typical romantic types of intimate contact. It focuses on reciprocal listening without judgment or dominance. The discussion proceeds in the same manner as above.

Holding Hands
The couple sits side-by-side holding hands guided by noticing how it is to make contact in a nondemanding and listening way, feeling the quality of such elements as connection, and temperature, and learning to relax and breathe while holding hands by practicing listening touch (5 minutes).

[1] Sandra Wooten is a Rosen Method Body Work senior teacher and practitioner.

Psychophysiology of Self-Awareness

Maternal touch can enhance attention in newborns and young infants to the environment, to their bodies, and to their emotions establishing a very early link between touch and embodied self-awareness (Arditi, Feldman, & Eidelman, 2006; Hertenstein, 2002; Stack & Muir, 1990). Intrusive and unpleasant touch can also impair infants' self-awareness (see Case Report 5.2; Feldman, Keren, Gross-Rozval, & Tyano,2004).

Touch can improve the health and long-term outcomes for premature infants. A lot of touch is detrimental to infants under 1,500 grams because of the fragility of the skin and muscles. Still, very light touch can help them focus attention (Eckerman, Oehler, Medvin, & Hannon, 1994). For infants between 1,500 and 2,000 grams, neck, back, arm, and leg massage for 15 minutes a day allows them to gain more weight than nonmassaged infants and decreases the secretion of cortisol while stimulating the secretion of oxytocin (for relaxation), and growth hormones from the pituitary (Dieter, Field, Hernandez-Reif, Emory, & Redzepi, 2003; Field, 2001; Schanberg, Bartoleme, & Kuhn, 1987).

"Kangaroo care" is an intervention for premies that places the infant, wearing only a diaper, on the bare chest of an adult with the infant's head turned to one side. This allows both tactile contact and the ability to hear the adult's heartbeat, similar to what the fetus would have heard. Kangaroo care babies were better able to gain weight, breathed easier, slept longer, and they cried less than babies who were not treated this way. Kangaroo care and massage of premies and older babies have both been shown to lower stress hormones and activate the parasympathetic nervous system in the parents of the infants, giving them more confidence that they can be there for the baby. Finally, if parents take baths with their babies of any age for relaxation and massage, the parents report higher levels of marital satisfaction and lower levels of depression (Feldman, Weller, Sirota, & Eidelman 2002; Field, 1998; Gitau et al., 2002; Stack, 2000; Tallandini & Scalembra, 2006).

Watsu is a form of touch therapy that is done in a pool of body-temperature water. As in kangaroo care and parent–infant cobathing, the practitioner can cradle, mold, and move the client's body, relatively weightless in the water, in order to replicate prenatal and infantile experiences that may have been lacking in the client's own life (Dull, 1997). In Watsu, in addition to feeling the listening touch from the practitioner, the client also experiences the "touch" and support of the water. Watsu, because of the warm water and the cradling touch, is very much centered on providing **resources** that nurture **restoration** (see Table 1.1). Although I know of no research on Watsu per se, studies on flotation in warm water have shown increased sleep quality, optimism, and oxytocin levels, and decreased pain, stress, anxiety, and depression (Bood et al., 2006).

> Not only does the water allow trauma patterns to unwind, but it is also an excellent medium for the repatterning of a healthy sense of self. In this gravity-free environment, the subtlest neuromuscular impulse can be supported, followed, and sequenced through the body. (Sawyer, 1999, p. 1)

The key to all of these touch interventions is the type of touch. Some touch is unwanted and intrusive, activating the threat response system. Touch that is gentle, listening, safe, and loving, however, has the potential to enhance embodied self-awareness by activating the biobehavioral response of **engagement**, both with others and with self. The parasympathetic nervous system that is coactivated with embodied self-awareness through touch can also lead to opportunities for the reduction of pain and **restoration**.

"Light" touch with a "soft hand," rather than deep touch or massaging movements, to an area of the body that is painful or tense, coupled with verbal guidance to help clients monitor the interoceptive and body schema self-awareness in that area, appears to be the most effective way to relieve pain and evoke muscle relaxation in a variety of conditions (Kerr et al., 2007; Rosen, 2003; Shatan, 1963; Ventegodt & Merrick, 2005; Westland, 1996).

Touching with a soft hand and talking with a soft voice about the observed state of the client's body activates the mirror neuron system, the practitioner's touch and voice serving as a kind of interpersonal mirror for the client's embodied self-awareness. This process is further enhanced if clients can talk about the emotions and memories that may arise as muscles begin to release.

> With touch, there is an awareness in the cells of the body that bypasses intellectual knowing. . . . Touch seems like a sword cutting through red tape, finding the core of the barrier, of the suffering, of the holding. (Rosen, 2003, pp. 20)

Intersubjectivity Through Movement, Emotion, and Communication

In this chapter we have seen that all movement and touch is done in relation to other people and the environment. We also saw that emotion expresses itself via body movements, facial expressions, and postural attitudes, that the muscles are the expressive organs of the body. And we noted that people can understand and perceive the movements of other people by activating the mirror neurons in the same parts of their brains as if they were doing the movement themselves. It follows, then, that we should be able to perceive the emotions of others spontaneously by means of a similar mirror activation of our own neuromotor system.

Indeed, studies have shown that when watching another's emotional body movements, similar areas are activated in the brains of the perceiver that would be activated if they were doing those movements: including the amygdala, orbitofrontal cortex (OFC, hedonic evaluation), anterior cingulate cortex (ACC, motivation leading to movement activation), anterior insula (sensation of emotional body feelings), brain stem homeostatic centers (regulatory aspects of emotion), and the somatosensory (SS) cortices (leading to movement expression).

Of interest is that not only the interoceptive areas (the felt emotional state) but also the motivational-action areas are activated. Research shows that observing someone's whole body in motion, and not just their face, is more likely to activate the entire neural network for interoception, body schema, and emotion in the perceiver (see Figure 3.1; de Gelder, 2006; de Gelder, Snyder, Greve, Gerard, & Hadjikhani, 2004). Perceiving emotion from the body may be more important for the biobehavioral responses than observing facial expressions when others are at a distance, such as to decide whether a stranger is friendly or dangerous (van den Stock, Righart, & de Gelder, 2007). Body movements are better at communicating emotional intensity and level of arousal compared to the face alone (jumping for joy, pounding one's fists, wound up) (Ekman, 1965; Wallbott, 1998).

Much of emotional perception is not part of embodied self-awareness simply because the brain is continually picking up this information via the mirror neuron system in the emotional and movement centers. An individual may not be aware that the emotion they are feeling can be attributed to the situation or the present company. In order to enter self-awareness, the emotional

Moving and Touching

experience must be rerepresented via the network that involves the insula, ACC, OFC, SS, and motor areas. This leads to the possibility of becoming aware of the linkages and boundaries that may indicate the emotion "belongs" to someone else. In this case, the individual can assess the nature and source of the emotion, and make appropriate decisions about how to respond.

The sense of agency, of having a purpose to notice or empathize with the other, and the perception of the other as an independent agent, is related to the inferior parietal lobe while feelings of self-agency arise in the anterior insula. Because the anterior parietal is related to feelings of body ownership (i.e., identifying the other's body as not mine), it contributes to the network responsible for differentiating self and other emotions.

On the opposite side are situations in which the interoceptive and body schema boundary networks are not activated when viewing another's emotional expressions. Autistic individuals have difficulty imitating and also understanding the emotions and gestures of others. They also have difficulties appreciating their own or another's sense of agency or purpose, suggesting that the insula is not being engaged to create a self-representation in awareness. Most likely, these individuals fail to appreciate the link between the body's movements and sensations, and the emotions (Hobson & Meyer, 2005; Muratori & Maestro, 2007).

In normal development, by 12 months infants can begin to perceive the intentions of others merely by watching their actions. Twelve-month-olds will look longer at adults who are looking at the infants compared to adults who are looking away from the infants, suggesting that infants are becoming aware of the adult's intention to communicate or not to communicate (Stenberg, Campos, & Emde, 1983; Striano & Rochat, 1999). They will look more at adults whose actions are appropriately directed toward an object compared to adults whose actions are unrelated to that object (Carpenter, Call, & Tomasello, 2005; Johnson, Ok, & Luo, 2007). By 18 months, infants are more likely to imitate intentional compared to random movements (Meltzoff, 1995).

Any type of coregulated activity with another person is a way of establishing a felt connection between the self and the other through movement, touch, and talk (Bråten, 2003; Fogel, 1993; Meltzoff & Moore, 1994). The nonverbal sense of "being with" another person—a direct result of the interpersonal resonance that occurs during coregulation of movements and sensations and emotions—is called **intersubjectivity** (Trevarthen & Aitken, 2001). Because infants soon after birth have active mirror neurons and can coregulate with others, they can experience intersubjectivity.

Intersubjective states can have either a positive or negative tone, depending upon the circumstances. In either case, in **intersubjectivity** one's awareness is expanded beyond the boundaries of the body to include the shared emotional states of others, a dyadically expanded state of consciousness (Tronick, 2007). Comparable to the concept of **neural integration** in secure attachment, people can develop coherently matching physiological states in which both individuals share either sympathetic or parasympathetic dominance or a balance between the two (Ham & Tronick, in press).

Intersubjectivity allows practitioners of embodied self-awareness methods to "tune into" their students and clients. With **listening touch**, there is a resonance that develops between the practitioner's hand and the client's body. This resonance creates an intersubjective awareness that goes both ways: the client can feel more deeply into herself and the practitioner can open to the possibility of feeling both her own and her client's experiences.

The teacher or practitioner must herself embody a certain quality of openness and curiosity toward her own embodied self-awareness and to the discoveries made by the students. Training programs for many of the self-awareness disciplines require 3 to 6 years of inquiry into the trainee's own embodied self-awareness, uncovering her or his own traumas and tensions, and learning to remain self-aware while working with other people. We have all been in situations in which intersubjectivity is not possible.

> You may have experienced at least a few frustrations in being part of a group trying to organize itself for action toward a single goal. . . . You may notice, even come to expect, that some people will lapse readily into familiar postures, straining to be right, pushing to convince, or gesticulating to win an argument. Instead of being able to respond to each other and the overall needs of the group, people react in mechanical ways, bouncing off each other and creating distance and hostility. Healing these social fractures is not just a mental but a somatic accomplishment. It requires sensory awakening. (Johnson, 1992, pp. 178–179)

All practitioners of embodied awareness practices must learn the ways in which their own postures may impede openness to their students and clients. Practitioners must learn, through their own intensive ventures into the pleasures and pains of embodied self-awareness, to remain in the subjective emotional present and access their own resources while working with someone else.

During the early part of my training as a Rosen practitioner, when I was doing practice bodywork sessions in the company of a supervisor, it was very easy for me to lose track of my own body awareness. A client's shoulder and neck tension may not be responsive to the practitioner's touch. The client is lost is conceptual self-awareness and suppressing their embodied self-awareness. Or, they may be absorbed in a dissociative or ruminative state.

When this happened with one of my clients, I "wanted" the client to relax and that wanting was related to my insecurity about my ability to help them, which transformed into a fear of failure. I also discovered, receiving Rosen Bodywork treatments from skilled practitioners, that this fear was related to an early childhood need to please my parents, the fear of not being sufficiently worthy, the fear of the physical beatings I might (and did) receive. I took on the "job" of pleasing others at an early age until it became an unwitting habit, one that led to postures of trying and wanting, straining my neck forward to anticipate someone's needs, and holding my breath until I could make sure that I had not offended anyone. As I think back on this now, I can feel in my body how exhausting this posture was for me and I'm amazed at the suppressive subversions of my nervous system that kept me unaware of that exhaustion for more than half a century!

This posture of excessive trying did not fully enter my awareness until I was doing the internship portion of my training, after some 4 or 5 years of receiving Rosen bodywork as a client and attending classes on technique. I am exceedingly grateful to the supervisors of my internship who helped me to see how this effort was impairing my ability to be fully in the subjective emotional present with my clients. The client's reasons for their own postural tension were different from mine but until I could relax into my own body and finally begin to *let go* of the need to please, I could not help the clients to discover in their own embodied self-awareness what lay behind their movement and emotional limitations.

I said, "begin to *let go*," because it is an ongoing process for me. I'm now better able to catch myself getting caught up with the old pattern, better able to self-regulate, but I still need help from time to time. As my awareness of the client–practitioner relationship grew, I could more easily relax and wait for an opening to occur. I was no longer threatened if the client could not relax in that moment. Eventually, with patience and presence, I learned to trust that the client's breakthrough moment would occur in its own way, without my wanting or trying to make it happen.

All humans have a social body whose movements and postures are acquired through the experiences of living in a particular family, in a particular education system, in a particular work environment, in a particular culture. These postures of relating or distancing can be learned and unlearned once we become aware of how our bodies enter the social psychological discourse. The resonant intersubjective comovement in emotionally close relationships leads to experience dependent pathways that create and maintain the patterns of emotional, interoceptive, and body schema self-awareness and distortions of self-awareness that have been described throughout this book (Young, 2002).

All the forms of self-awareness and self-suppression described earlier can be traced to experiences in social encounters, experiences that create lasting impressions not only in mental imagery and autobiographical memory and narrative, but more fundamentally in the flesh. Being moved and being touched, moving and touching, in the listening ways described in this chapter, are the very human connections that engender the growth of embodied self-awareness.

7

Catching Our Breath, Finding Our Voice

You cannot finally hold on to anything, just as you cannot inhale and hold your breath indefinitely. The breath teaches you about the process of life, of gathering in and giving out, of giving up the old in order to make space for the new, just as the stale air is expelled to allow a tide of fresh air and energy to flow in.
(Vessantara, 2005, p. 120)

If we observe the carriage of people in the street, we find that one person walks as if he had no right to breathe the air without securing someone's permission; and in fact he does hold his breath most of the time. He has to justify his existence by being good; he has to earn his right to breathe.
(Feldenkrais, 1985, pp. 55–56)

These two quotes appear to be in contradiction with each other. The first one talks about the impossibility of holding onto anything, just as one cannot hold onto one's breath, at least not for very long. The second quote, however, imagines a person who is doing just that, holding his breath habitually. Yet both of these observations are accurate.

It is certainly true that if we stopped breathing by literally holding our breath, we would die. Breathing must go on and each breath brings something new into our bodies. It is also true, however, that we can hold tension in the muscles used for breathing—muscles in the chest and abdominal walls, in the shoulders and neck, and the diaphragm. If these muscles are tense, it limits the full range of breathing in and breathing out.

All chronic muscle tension is related to a past or a current sense of threat. No less is true for restrictions of the breath. Why does the man in the second quote feel that he does not have the right to breathe, that he has to be "good" to justify his taking even the smallest breath? One can imagine any number of personal histories—a cruel and demanding parent, racial or religious or political persecution, a domineering spouse—all of which can be traced to development of experience dependent neuromotor pathways that entrench biobehavioral responses to threat in the neuromotor system.

Respiratory Anatomy and Physiology

There is no other body function like breathing because it is partly automatic and partly voluntary. Its muscles are the most active in the body, working at all times even when other muscles are at rest. Respiratory muscles are also similar to all other muscles of the body: respiration is quickly altered according to our emotions and to our state of threat and safety.

The muscles involved in respiration are shown in Figure 7.1. These include the thoracic diaphragm, and some of the abdominal, chest, neck, and shoulder muscles. The primary muscles of inspiration are the dorsal (back) intercostal muscles (which increase or decrease the spaces between the ribs), and the active downward expansion of the diaphragm. The diaphragm is always the first muscle to contract, followed by the intercostals, and later by accessory muscles. During normal breathing, expiration is primarily passive, the relaxation of the principal inspiratory muscles (J. E. Butler, 2007; Saboisky, Gorman, DeTroyer, Gandevia, & Butler, 2007).

The **thoracic diaphragm** behaves much like a skeletal muscle although it has some characteristics of smooth muscle. It is attached to bones although it does not move any joints: to the lowest ribs around the circumference of the body, to the bottom of the sternum (breast bone) in front and to the upper lumbar vertebrae in back (see Figure 7.1). It can move voluntarily like skeletal muscle but it also moves involuntarily to maintain breathing at all times. In this sense, it functions like the skeletal muscle that controls voluntary and involuntary eye blinks. Like skeletal muscle, the diaphragm is divided into **motor units** (see Figure 6.1). This means that only parts of the diaphragm may contract at any time. It also means that low-threshold motor units can maintain chronic tension in the diaphragm even during the expiration phase of normal breathing (J. E. Butler, 2007; Hammond, Gordon, Fisher, & Richmon, 1989; Sieck & Fournier, 1989).

Catching Our Breath, Finding Our Voice

This is important clinically because many people hold unnecessary tension in the diaphragm and other breathing muscles, which leads to compromised breathing and ultimately impacts health and well-being. The quote at the beginning of the chapter by Feldenkrais is a good example of how threat, past or present, can restrict breathing.

Figure 7.1
Muscles of respiration

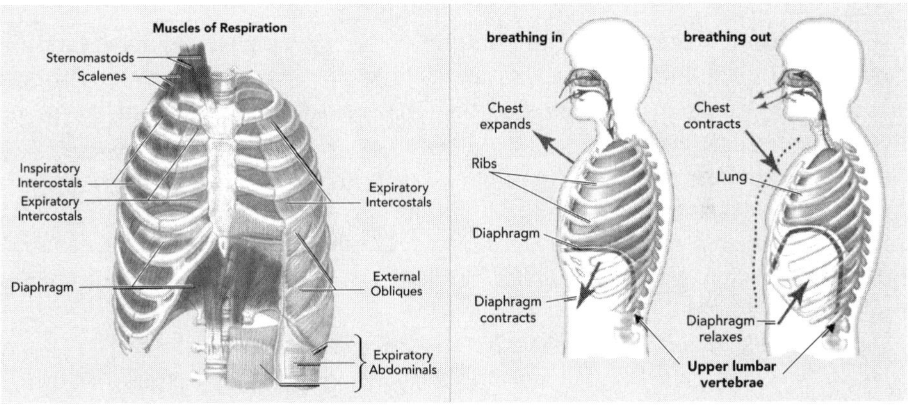

Breathing musles. Inspiration is controlled principally by the dorsal (back) intercostal muscles (between the ribs) and the active downward expansion of the diaphragm. In forced inspiration due to heavy exercise or stress, inspiration is aided by accessory muscles including scalenes and sternomastoids that attach in the neck, and pectoralis minor muscles that attach to the inside of the shoulder blade and lift the ribs. Expiration is primarily passive, the relaxation of the principle inspiratory muscles. In exercise or stress, expiration can be assisted by the lateral intercostals and the abdominal wall muscles.

The diaphragm is one of the largest muscles in the body. The diaphragm moves downward to expand the lung capacity during inspiration and relaxes upward to decrease lung capacity and expel the air. Depending upon the type of breathing and the individual, the center of the diaphragm can move between 7 mm (2.7 in) and 19 mm (7.5 in) from its highest to its lowest point (Scott, Fuld, Carter, McEntegart, & MacFarlane, 2006).

During normal respiration, we breathe about 12 to 15 times per minute. During forced inspiration due to heavy exercise or stress, breathing rate increases to as much as 40 times per minute and forced inspiration is aided by accessory muscles including the scalenes (upper attachment to the sides of the upper neck [cervical] vertebrae; lower attachment to the upper two ribs) and sternomastoids (upper attachment to the mastoid process of the lower skull; lower attachment to the sternum and clavicles), and the pectoralis minor muscles (upper attachment to the inside of the shoulder blade and lower attachment to the front surface of ribs 3, 4, and 5). In exercise or stress, expiration, which is normally a passive process, can be assisted by the lateral intercostals and the abdominal wall muscles (Figure 7.1).

There are two branches of the phrenic nerve that provides efferent motor control to the left and right sides of the diaphragm. The phrenic nerve also has afferent sensory branches that send information to the brain from the inner lining of the chest wall and the outer covering of the lungs. The phrenic nerve originates from the spinal cord in the neck (cervical) region along with nerves for the intracostal muscles. These motor nerves are connected to homeostatic and autonomic nervous system areas in the middle (pons) and lower (medulla) brain stem (see Figure 5.2) which provide the regulation of the automatic function of breathing.

Breathing can also be controlled voluntarily. This involves direct links from the motor cortex, via the thalamus and limbic system, to the respiratory spinal motor neurons, bypassing the automatic breathing control centers in the brain stem. Voluntary control of the breath is required for many different activities such as speaking, singing, holding the breath, whistling, swallowing, sipping and drinking, coughing, or effortful activity of other skeletal muscles like during lifting of heavy weights, vomiting, or defecation (Butler, 2007). The diaphragm can also be used for controlling postural stability (see Case Report 6.2). Experiments in which people are thrown off balance show that the thoracic diaphragm as well as another diaphragm that spans the pelvic floor will contract to maintain postural stability, probably by increasing abdominal wall pressure to stabilize the lower spine (Butler, 2007; Gandevia, Butler, Hodges, & Taylor, 2002).

The ability to become aware of the distinction between voluntary effortful breathing and normal and relaxed automatic breathing is the basis of many approaches to meditation. Box 7.1 gives a simple meditation exercise to help enhance embodied self-awareness of the breath.

> **BOX 7.1**
> **Simple Breathing Meditation**
>
> 1. Sit in a comfortable position, either on a cushion on the floor, or in a chair. Make sure your back is relatively erect and the room is free of distractions. You can also do this in a quiet outdoor location.
> 2. Focus your awareness on the sensation of the breath as it moves across the skin just below the nostrils and above the upper lip. Don't change how you breathe. Just observe your natural breath, where it seems free and relaxed and where it feels false or constrained.
> 3. If your attention drifts, thank yourself for noticing and bring yourself back to the breath and how it feels on your skin. Notice which parts of your body move as you breathe. Can you feel the breath move your belly? Your chest? Your shoulders?
> 4. You can also imagine and feel the air moving in and out of your body and notice how that connects you with other organisms that also breathe.

An added benefit of breath meditation is that sometimes it leads us into noneffortful breathing, in which the body enters a state of parasympathetic relaxation where not only the breathing but the skeletal muscles can let go of tension, allowing for the restorative effects of such meditation practice (see Chapter 8).

Stress and Respiration

Social demands and other threats lead to chronic muscle tension which is always associated with tension in the diaphragm (Feldenkrais, 1985; Rosen, 2003). This unfortunate link actually has adaptive origins. The diaphragm contracts to inhale when there is sympathetic activation in the ANS, preparing the body to respond to a stressor.

How does the ANS—which innervates smooth muscles but not skeletal muscles or the diaphragm—increase tension in the diaphragm and other breathing muscles when the body is under stress? In Chapter 6, we saw that there are two causes of sympathetic-induced skeletal muscle tension. The first is that stress hormones in the blood can induce the **α–MN**s in the diaphragm and skeletal breathing muscles to contract by activating the stretch reflex in the muscle spindles. The second is the dilation of the vascular smooth muscles in those skeletal muscles, causing pain and secondarily tension to suppress the pain. It also happens the other way: increased respiration rate increases blood flow and vasodilation (Dempsey, Sheel, St. Croix, & Morgan, 2002).

In breathing, however, there are *four additional sources* of ANS-related respiratory muscle tension. Third, as blood pressure increases from sympathetic activation of the heart, there is the need for more oxygen in the blood. Chemoreceptors in the arteries will signal the brain stem respiratory (phrenic and intercostal) motorneurons to discharge when they sense an increase in CO_2 in the blood (Butler, 2007).

Fourth, the areas of the **periaqueductal grey** (PAG) in the upper brain stem that organize the body's actions in the biobehavioral response modes of fight, flight, and freeze are activated by the sympathetic ANS centers in the middle brain stem and by the threat and safety neural network including the hypothalamus, amygdala, insula, ACC, and prefrontal areas. The PAG has direct links to the respiratory (phrenic and intercostal) motor neurons in the lower brain stem (Gaytán, Pásaro, Coulon, Bevengut, & Hilaire, 2002; Li, 2004; Macefield, Gandevia, & Henderson, 2005; Zhang, Hayward, & Davenport, 2005). Pain, also processed in the threat and safety neural network and the upper and lower brain stem centers, impacts breathing by increasing respiration rate (Jiang, Alheid, Calandriello, & McCrimmon, 2004)

Fifth, baroreceptors (for pressure) in the larynx and in the chest cavity send information about air flow and pressure to the ANS and respiratory centers in the brain stem. If the volume of air taken in is too low, this will activate the sympathetic ANS which will activate the respiratory motorneurons in the brain stem (Fokkema, 1999).

Finally, the ANS influences breathing via the heart rate itself, not related to increases in blood pressure, CO_2 levels, or vasodilation. The parasympathetic vagus nerve that can speed up (vagal inhibition) or slow down (vagal activation) heart rate interacts in the brain stem with the respiratory motorneurons of the phrenic and skeletal muscle nerves.

The threat-safety neural network neurochemicals including CRH, and ACTH (threat) and oxytocin (safety) activate the vagal motorneurons that regulate heart rate (Kc, Karibi-Ikiriko, Rust, Jayham-Trouth, & Haxhiu, 2006). In fact, there is an ongoing coregulation between vagal and phrenic nerves to produce **respiratory sinus arrhythmia (RSA)**. The phrenic nerve is activated during inhalation, which signals sympathetic nerve activation that increases blood pressure (BP) and vagal inhibition which increases heart rate (HR). Exhalation is the inhibition of the phrenic nerve and the relaxation of the diaphragm and intercostals, accompanied by parasympathetic (vagus) nerve activation that slows HR and sympathetic inhibition that reduces BP (see Figure 7.2; Berntson, Cacioppo, & Quigley 1993; Leiter & St.-John, 2004). The word *sinus* is one of the anatomical terms for the heart.

Figure 7.2
Respiratory sinus arrhythmia (RSA)

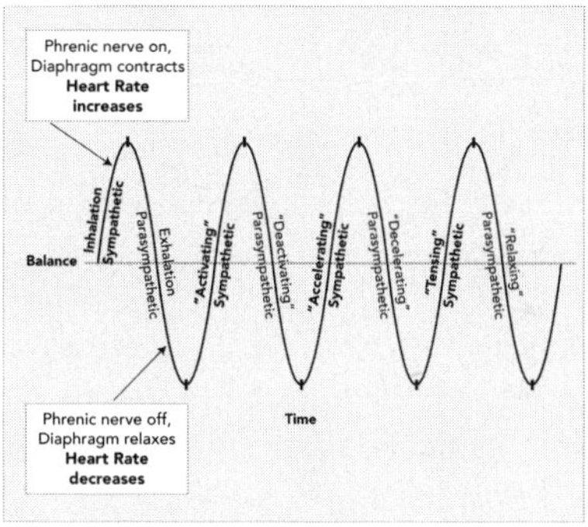

In normal breathing, inhalation is controlled by the phrenic motor nerve to the diaphragm and the intercostals. It is accompanied by sympathetic nerve activation that increases heart rate (HR) and blood pressure (BP). Exhalation is the inhibition of the phrenic nerve and the relaxation of the diaphragm and intercostals, accompanied by parasympathetic (vagus) nerve activation that slows HR and BP. RSA is the normal variability in HR between inspiration and expiration. If there is a sense of threat or high metabolic demands from exercise, the sympathetic activation continues through the expiration phase leading to increased tension of breathing muscles, increased heart rate and blood pressure, and a decrease in RSA (the HR does not slow during expiration). Low RSA is an indicator of both physiological and psychological stress.

Psychophysiology of Self-Awareness

RSA is the variability in HR between inspiration and expiration. If there is a sense of threat or high metabolic demands from exercise, the sympathetic activation and parasympathetic inhibition continues through the expiration phase leading to increased tension in breathing muscles, increased heart rate and blood pressure, and a decrease in RSA (the HR does not slow during expiration). Low RSA is an easily measured indicator of both physiological and psychological stress.

Figure 7.3
Sympathetic activation of respiratory muscle contraction and tension

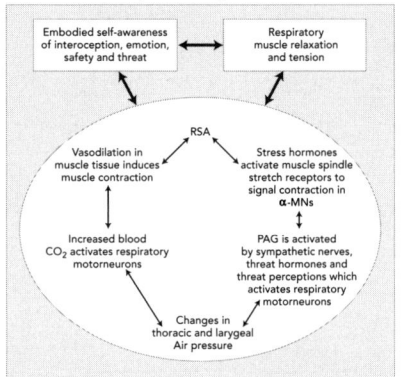

ANS=autonomic nervous system; RSA=respiratory sinus arrhythmia; MN=moror neuron; PAG=periaqueductal grey.

The five sources of ANS regulation of breathing are summarized in Figure 7.3 which is included here to emphasize that *breathing is exquisitely sensitive to the condition of safety and threat and it is neurophysiologically linked to the biobehavioral response modes*. An ongoing sense of threat, as in situations of trauma or persistent environmental stress, because it involves chronic sympathetic activation, will cause chronic tension in the diaphragm and perhaps other respiratory muscles in both inspiration and expiration.

It is not a coincidence, therefore, that many body-based clinicians have observed breathing abnormalities in patients suffering from prior physical and mental trauma. *An effortful breath, therefore, is a diagnostic indicator of the emotions and sensations that have been suppressed by current and past situations of threat, as well as emotions that may be suppressed in the moment but not yet part of embodied self-awareness* (Braatoy, 1952; Rosen, 2003; Shatan, 1963).

Relaxed breathing occurs when there is relatively little muscle tension in the body, when inspiration and expiration are relatively rhythmical, and when there is a detectable expiratory pause. An **expiratory pause** is the cessation of movement in the breathing muscles at the end of an expiration. A longer expiratory pause indicates greater relaxation while a short or nonexistent expiratory pause indicates a sense of threat (Cook, 1996). **Effortful breathing** occurs in states of threat when there is contraction of breathing muscles through both the inspiration and expiration (sympathetic arousal), and generally higher levels of muscle tension in the body (see Table 7.1; Bloch, Lemeignan, & Aguilera, 1991).

Table 7.1
Respiratory patterns associated with emotions

Emotion	Respiration	Muscle tension
Tenderness/joy	Regularly spaced, slow breaths with longer expiration than inspiration and long **expiratory pause**	*Relaxed*
Erotic love	Deep, fast breaths sequenced with slower and shorter breaths (high variability depending on level of engagement), which may or may not have an **expiratory pause**	*Relaxed* and *effortful* alternation
Laughter	Deep and abrupt inspiration with short expiratory bursts and short **expiratory pause**	*Relaxed*
Sadness/cry	Longer inspiration with short bursts and tremors, and sighs during expiration. May or may not have an **expiratory pause**	Mostly *relaxed* but there may be some tension in the chest in inspiration
Anger	Extremely deep and fast breathing with little variability and **no expiratory pause**	*Effortful*
Fear/anxiety	Very fast, highly variable, shallow breaths with incomplete exhalations and no **expiratory pause**	*Effortful*

Sources: Bloch et al. (1991), Philippot et al. (2002), Takase and Haruki (2001)

Psychophysiology of Self-Awareness

Different emotions are associated with effortful vs. relaxed breathing, as well as with different variations of depth, duration, and rate of breathing (Bloch et al., 1991; Philippot, Chapelle, & Blairy, 2002). In general, as shown in Table 7.1, anger and fear are associated with effortful breathing patterns accompanied by tension in the abdomen and chest. Chronic and unresolved anger, aggression and hostility in childhood and adulthood is associated with breathing disorders such as asthma and shortness of breath, as well as cardiovascular disease (Jackson, Kubzansky, Cohen, Jacobs, & Wright, 2007; Lehrer, Isenberg, & Hochron, 1993).

Other emotions, such as joy, tenderness, and sadness, induce a state of relaxation and are accompanied by a more relaxed breath. This is especially true if the sadness is in the form of a "good" cry rather than a suppressed cry (see Box 4.1; Takase & Haruki, 2001; Umezawa, 2001). The link between breathing and emotion, and their clinical significance, is illustrated in Case Report 7.1.

Case Report 7.1
Somatic Psychotherapy Leads to More Relaxed Breathing

Dolores is a 58-year-old successful engineer with an advanced degree. She is the sole survivor of her nuclear family, with the deaths of her parents and sisters beginning when she was nineteen. Her early life had been full of neglect along with physical, emotional, and sexual abuse by men inside and outside her family. Like my client Joan, Dolores survived via dissociation. She had been in traditional psychotherapy for several years before being referred to somatic psychotherapy for help with her body-based symptoms. The following is an account of one of these sessions. The therapist uses the resonance of her own body with that of the client to help inform her interventions.

"My sister Rebecca and I shared a bedroom. I would lie in my bed and with my fingers I would scratch and peel the paint on the wall. The patch of peeled paint on the wall was big; my sister would be so upset. I didn't want to feel so upset."

I see Dolores across from me. To me she looks wide-eyed and frozen in terror. I feel a panicky trembling in my belly which I did not have before. "I wonder if you were really scared," I say gently and with concern.

"Yes. My sister would bang her head on the wall to get to sleep." She added, "I don't know how she could. I could never do that so I would peel the paint."

The trembling in my belly and the panic lessen somewhat. "What was that like for you peeling and peeling?" I ask.

"I don't know, I guess when I was peeling with my hands like that I wouldn't think or feel, and it would help me to go to sleep."

"What's you inner experience as you talk to me?"

"Yeah, I guess I'm holding my breath. I don't feel so good."

"Holding your breath and feeling a little scared. No wonder, given what you've experienced in the past. I wonder if you feel uncertain as to how I may respond to you."

"No, you're always very gentle."

"Mm. What's it like inside holding your breath?"

"I feel tight in my chest, trapped."

"Mm...it must have been so frightening for you to feel so alone with your fear and hurt, confused and uncertain about what was happening."

"My sister and I were there for each other but sometimes she was so upset. I didn't want to upset her more."

"Of course you wouldn't want to upset her more and see her in pain. It sounds like you were very upset and scared also."

"Yeah, I was scared. It was scary."

"I wonder who was there for you?" I ask.

"No one," she says quietly.

"I can really understand how important it was for you to try not to be upset when your sister was, and it seems sad to me that at times you were so alone and overwhelmed with scary feelings."

"Yeah," she says, tears welling in her eye, breathing a little deeper.

I breathe deeper both in a mirroring response and in response to my own inner ease as she is able to integrate some of the powerful affect laden in the account.

We sit quietly with her sadness. In time she says, "I feel better, my chest isn't so tight."

"You're feeling a little easier, your chest not so tight...and your breath?"

"Yes, breathing a little more, just experiencing that feeling of breathing a little easier."

In some small but significant way I feel I have been let into her room, the room she describes as having been so isolated and trapped in. She recounts to me that she and Rebecca together would push the heavy chest of drawers against the door to keep out the terror, the unpredictable. Then Dolores would lie in her bed listening for and not wanting to hear the creaking wood stairs, footfalls, often her father's, which could only mean the pain of being yelled at or being the target of some heavy object heaved in anger or the hinted-at but hard-to-hold possibility of sexual assault.

And so we worked slowly like this. By attending to my own felt sensation, inquiring into it, I feel on a visceral level some sense of what Dolores might have experienced. Through this embodied attunement I can more fully hold an empathic container for her terror. Initially, I thought of my somatic experiences with Dolores as part of a projective identification sequence. As I learned more about our intersubjective field, I came to think of my feelings, like these, as a kind of somatic attunement or resonance. I was experiencing with her what she could not name, experiences about which she was mute.

The material in Case Report 7.1 (Holifield, 1998, pp. 66–68), is used with permission of Don Hanlon Johnson and Ian Grand.

- *Resources* are found in the trust developed between client and practitioner, which took many sessions prior to this one.
- *Slowing down* occurred during this session in the client's willingness to take the time to attend to her body sensations.
- *Coregulation* was based upon the therapist's ability to resonate with the client in her own embodied self-awareness.
- *Verbalization* was essential in this session, as the client became able to name and feel her fear and loneliness as they related to the interoceptive sensations of effortful breathing.
- *Linkages and boundaries* came up primarily for the therapist: sensing that she had been finally "let into" the client's room to discover what had happened there and, importantly, that her own embodied sensations

were allowed to enter the process rather than being suppressed by a conceptual judgement about projection.
- *Self-regulation* occurred in a small but significant way, with the sense that Dolores could, in fact, breathe a little easier.
- *Reengagement* was only beginning in this session, with the ability to tolerate the feelings of what had happened in her bedroom as a child.
- *Letting go* does not happen in this session but it did emerge gradually later in the treatment.

As Figure 7.3 and Case Report 7.1 show, there is a complex feedback system between all the components of autonomic control over breathing and the embodied self-awareness of the sense of safety or threat. Individuals with panic disorder, for example, are more sensitive to experimental increases in CO_2 levels inhaled, showing more increases in rapid breathing, hyperventilation, and skeletal muscle tension than nonanxious subjects. Further, the onset of hyperventilation and gasping can lead to increased activation of the threat response neural network to amplify the feeling of panic due to air hunger (Beck & Scott, 1988; Han, Stegen, Schepers, Van den Berg, & Van de Woestijne, 1998; Lum, 1987; Macefield & Burke, 1991; Papp et al., 1997).

Hyperventilation involves breathing in excess of metabolic needs and results in an abnormal reduction of blood CO_2 levels and an abnormal increase of blood pH, becoming more alkaline. Both these conditions create risk factors for all the muscles in the body, including the heart, and for the brain. Anxious individuals in general experience a higher incidence of hyperventilation, muscle tension, and fatigue. Extreme hyperventilation can cause muscle spasms in the chest respiratory muscles, chest pains, heart palpitations, reductions in blood flow to the cardiac muscles, and gastrointestinal distress, and is thus a serious threat to health (Gardner, 1996; B. L. Lewis, 1957; Magarian & Hickam, 1986; Robertson, Pagel, & Johnson, 1977; Schleifer, Ley & Spalding, 2002).

The Art of Breathing: Sound, Resonance, Connection

In 5th century China, Xie He developed six principles of painting. The first principle, *qiyun shengdong* (literally, "breath-resonance, life-motion"), has since been widely applied in all the Chinese arts, including the performing arts.

Psychophysiology of Self-Awareness

This principle requires the artist to bring the subject (or score or script) to life by means of a deep sense of connection. That connection is linked to relaxed breathing.

> The most important consideration in the technique of performance, then, is not the question of finger dexterity or any other technical aspect, but the question of how *qi* is manipulated. *Qi* in musical performance entails breathing, and breathing is essential in shaping the line . . . *Qi* is the creative force that begins, sustains and completes a work of art, without which there is no life. (Ho, 1997, p. 38)

Chinese and other ancient Asian cultures have cultivated the "art" of breathing as a way of focusing the mind and calming the body. This is typically done by focusing one's attention on the breath (see Box 7.1), prolonging the exhalation compared to the inhalation, slowing the breathing, and using primarily abdominal breathing. This type of breathing practice is found in yoga, tai chi, meditation, and other Asian methods.

The Asian ideas about the link between breathing and well-being were incorporated into body-oriented treatment approaches beginning in late-19th-century Europe, leading to the work of Elsa Gindler (1885–1961). Gindler influenced a wide range of 20th-century practitioners who went on to establish their own treatment practices. These include the touch and movement therapies of Marion Rosen, Moshe Feldenkrais, M. F. Alexander, Gerda Alexander, Ilse Middendorf, Bonnie Bainbridge Cohen, and the diverse field of body psychotherapy (Aposhyan, 2004; Boadella, 1994). Gindler's original work was spread beyond Europe by Charlotte Selver, Emmi Pickler, Magda Proskauer, and others where it became known as *sensory awareness* (Buchholz, 1994).

Psychophysiological research has shown that breath awareness and control training has the effect of activating the parasympathetic nervous system, replacing effortful with relaxed breathing, reducing pain, anxiety, and depression, and enhancing both **normal absorption** and **engagement** in everyday and occupational activities (Han, Stegen, De Valck, Clément, & Van de Woestijlne, 1996; Haruki & Takase, 1991; Lum, 1987; MacDougall & Münsterberg, 1896; Mehling, Hamel, Acree, Byl, & Hecht, 2005; Sawada, 2001; Tweeddale, Rowbottom, & McHardy, 1994). Breathing meditation has been shown to have a positive impact on a variety of conditions including anxiety, depression, PTSD, mood disorders, addictions, and stress tolerance (R. P. Brown & Gerbarg, 2005). Breath control has also been shown to reduce pain and require less medical intervention in childbirth (Copstick, Taylor, Hayes, & Morrison, 1986; Hodnett & Osborn, 1989).

Hyperventilation, paradoxically, is used in some types of religious rituals. The increased CO_2 levels and decreased oxygen to the brain likely create ecstatic trance states and the sense of a deeper communion with another being. In many languages of ancient origin, the word for *breath* and the word for *spirit* are identical. In Greek it is *pneuma*, in Latin *spiritus*, in Hebrew *neshama*, and in English (from the Latin) *inspiration* (Lyon, 1999). A similar function of hyperventilation is used in the technique of Holotropic Breathwork which, as an adjunct to psychotherapy, may help some individuals shift awareness into more embodied and less conceptual modes (S. Proskauer, 2007; Rhinewine & Williams, 2007).

Short bursts of hyperventilation are an accompaniment to **normal absorption** into the intensely pleasurable state of sexual intercourse and climax (Passie, Hartmann, Schneider, & Emrich, 2004). Assuming that there is a feeling of safety in the lovemaking, the increased muscle tension, shortness of breath, and heart palpitations—typically accompanied by gasping and moaning—actually serve to intensify the pleasure and feelings of intersubjective resonant communion. Hyperventilation-type rapid respiration—also with gasps and moans—can also occur with forceful muscle exertion (Eldridge, 1975). This could occur in fighting, lifting heavy objects, and in intense athletic exertion.

*The breath, therefore, can serve as a vehicle for entering into powerful states of **engagement** and **normal absorption**. It can be a passageway into deep and **restorative** realms of relaxation. Or it can signal **mobilization**, **immobilization**, and **vigilance**. In all these ways, an awareness of our breathing is a direct link to embodied self-awareness, a way of tuning into, localizing, and identifying our current **biobehavioral** response mode.*

Breath and Voice

The link between respiration and vocalization is illustrated by another somatic psychotherapy case.

> As Marilyn attended to her abdomen with the question of how this part of her body wanted to move, breathe, and sound, she con-

tracted her belly even further. As she did this, her face, and particularly her mouth, drew into a tight grimace. I encouraged this. "Good. Give those feelings lots of permission. How do you want to breathe from this place?" She made a forced aspirated exhalation. I acknowledged, "That sounds almost like a growl. Keep going. Are there sounds? Are there words?" Her fist begins to clench. "Yes, let your hands get involved and every other part of you that wants to get involved." At this point she popped quickly out of her focused state and said, "Wow, I had no idea I was so angry at my mother. This is so weird." (Aposhyan, 2004, p. 125)

This example of suppressed anger is similar to Case Report 2.1 of my client, Doug. The case of Marilyn shows, in addition, how breathing is related not only to suppressed emotions and tense muscles, but also to speech and other vocal sounds.

Vocalization is the breath made audible. Vocal sounds are created as the exhaled breath passes through the larynx, mouth, and nose. The larynx contains the vocal cords, two folds of muscle that can leave a larger opening between them for lower pitches or a smaller opening for higher pitches.

The quality of the sound depends upon the size of the mouth opening and the size of the internal mouth cavity which is altered by raising or lowering the soft palate at the back of the roof of the mouth. Sound quality also depends upon whether the air passes through the nostrils, the shape and tension in the tongue, and on whether the sound is allowed to resonate in the sinuses and facial bones. The tongue and teeth are responsible for articulation, the creation of particular syllabic (consonant and vowel combinations) sounds (see Figure 7.4; Ohala, 1980).

Sound quality also depends on the breath. In normal breathing, inspiration and expiration are roughly equal in duration and there is a sinusoidal pattern of continuous ebb and flow in the movement of the breathing muscles. The resulting air pressure through the mouth also has this sinusoidal pattern (see Figure 7.2). During speech, however, expirations are much longer and with a relatively constant air pressure, while inspirations are very brief. This allows people to talk or vocalize more or less continuously without long interruptions for inspiration (Langlois, Baken, & Wilder, 1980). Sometimes this is true metaphorically as well as physiologically!

Catching Our Breath, Finding Our Voice

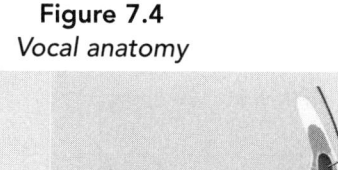

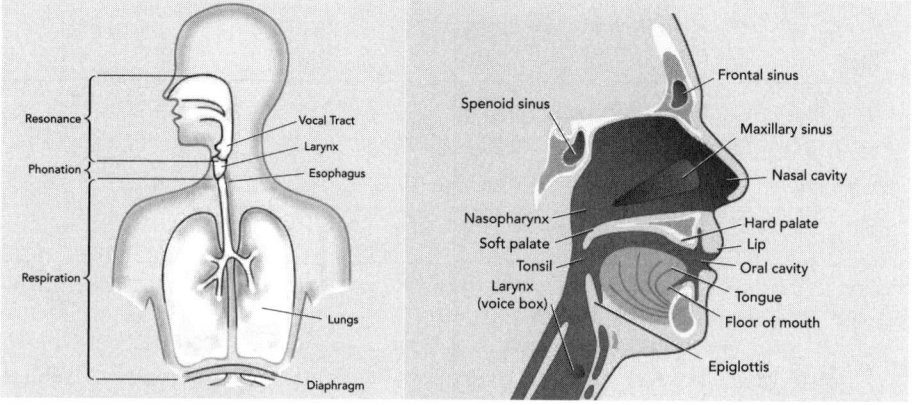

Figure 7.4
Vocal anatomy

Sound is created as breath moves through the larynx (voice box) which creates different pitches. The quality of the sound depends on the size and shape of the opening in the mouth, nose, and sinuses. Loudness depends upon the amount of air pressure created by the intensity of contraction in the breathing muscles.

While speaking, we are typically aware of our thoughts as we attempt to put them into words. We may also be aware of emotions that we are trying to express or suppress and how our speech may affect our relationships with others. We are not typically aware that the sounds of speech (or any other vocal sounds) are created by breath, muscle, skin, and bone. There are several ways in which you may have occasion to be aware of the embodied aspects of voice: if you are an infant or young child, if you have ever had voice or speech lessons, or if you learned to play a wind instrument.

At birth, infant cries use the breath to alter patterns of sound and emotional meaning. Researchers have distinguished four phases of the newborn cry: expiration (the actual creation of the crying sound), an expiratory pause, inspiration, and an inspiratory pause. As shown in Table 7.2, the different types of infant cries can be distinguished according to the length of these phases.

Psychophysiology of Self-Awareness

Table 7.2
Properties of neonatal cries (all values are time in seconds)

Cry Phase	Basic Cry	Angry Cry	Pain Cry	Being-Teased Cry
Expiratory	0.62	0.69	3.83	2.67
Rest	0.08	0.20	3.99	0.07
Inspiratory	0.04	0.05	0.18	0.13
Rest	0.20	0.11	0.16	0.13

Source: P. H. Wolff (1966). The causes, controls, and organization of behavior in the neonate. *Psychological Issues*, 5, 202–204.

The neonatal pain cry has an exceptionally long expiratory pause, which gives the listener the feeling that the baby has stopped breathing. The pain cry also has a long expiration phase (Wolff, 1966). In addition, crying involves a pattern of body movement including facial expressions of distress, movement of the arms and legs, changes in muscle tone and skin color, and alterations in breathing patterns (Clarici et al., 2002; Green, Gustafson, Irwin, Kalinowski, & Wood, 1995; Lock, 2000).

Newborns also make nonvoluntary "vegetative" sounds like grunting, hiccupping, burping, sighing, and coughing. By 3 months of age, however, vocalizations become more voluntary. By this age, infants are beginning to deliberately explore how to link self-made sounds with the embodied self-awareness of breath, sensation, and movement. As infants discover "interesting" sounds, they will repeat them endlessly (Ley, 1999). Jean Piaget, one of the founders of the modern science of developmental psychology made detailed observations of his own three children as infants. Here are his descriptions of two of the children. Ages are given as years; months (days).

> ... at 0;2(12) Lucienne, after coughing, recommences several times for fun and smiles. Laurent puffs out his breath, producing an indefinite sound. At 0;2(26) he reproduces the peals of his voice which ordinarily accompany his laughter, but without laughing and out of pure phonetic interest. At 0;2(15) Lucienne uses her voice in similar circumstances. (Piaget, 1952, p. 79)

These infants are playing with the voice and how it feels to make sounds in their bodies. It is around this age that we see the onset of pleasurable sounds such as cooing and laughing (Langlois et al., 1980). Cooing (oooo, ahhhh) is made up primarily of vowel-like sounds but babbling, which emerges a few months later, has syllables with both vowels and consonants (bababa, gagaga). By 6 months, babbling sounds are already related to meaning, although most people would not be able to notice. Computer analysis of different sounds made by infants show that sound quality is differentiated according to whether the baby is exploring an object, eating, or making a request (Blake & Fink, 1987).

This could not happen if infants were unaware of their breath and vocal muscles. First, infants have to adapt to a rapidly changing anatomy. Between birth and 4 months, the infant's tongue fills most of the oral cavity so there's not much room for auditory resonance. Until 4 months, the epiglottis (see Figure 7.4) is in contact with the soft palate at the back of the roof of the mouth to prevent choking and inhaling of food. Beginning at 4 months, the oral cavity and larynx enlarge and the epiglottis moves away from the soft palate. This means the infant can create more air pressure and the epiglottis can be used to help stop the air flow to form consonants (Bosma, 1975; R. D. Kent, 1981).

Second, without any conceptual self-awareness, infants have to discover the links between sound and meaning using their embodied sensations. This becomes especially important in the beginning of the second year of life, as infants first produce recognizable words. The baby learns the felt connection between the exteroceptive sensation (a color, a sound, a tactile impression) of an object to be named, with the interoceptive sense of how it feels to make the sound of that name and hear oneself making it, and the body schema awareness of knowing which parts of the body need to be moved to create the sound and the action related to the object, like grasping or pointing (Gogate, Walker-Andrews, & Bahrick, 2001; Goldring-Zukow, Reilly, & Greenfield, 1982).

Early speech also requires the ability to be aware of all the embodied sensations related to coregulation with adults, who are speaking, pointing, making requests, and engaging the infant in vocal games and songs. Interacting with infants is also a good way for adults to tune into the embodied sensations of their own speech. **Infant-directed speech** (IDS) has a higher pitch and more exaggerated contrasts between high- and low-pitched sounds and is more melodic than speech directed toward adults. IDS occurs even in tonal languages such as Mandarin Chinese in which the pitch of a syllable conveys linguistic meaning (Grieser & Kuhl, 1988). This is because these speech characteristics fit the kinds of listening preferences of infants (Colombo, Frick, Ryther, Coldren, & Mitchell, 1995; Papousek, Bornstein, Nuzzo, Papousek, & Symmes, 1990). Adults can sense their own bodies making the sounds and they can see how the infants respond to the sounds with sounds of their own. This is the beginning of interpersonal vocal **resonance**.

Both IDS and infant vocalization have been compared to poetry and music, having a poetic pattern of rhythm, meter, melody, repetition, phonetic contrasts and similarities, and a music-like structure (Miall & Dissanayake, 2003). Infants are also very good at recognizing different melodies and appear to acquire their own musical tastes. In one study, 6-month-olds could tell the difference between two different passages of the same piece by Schubert (Mélen & Wachsmann, 2001). They can recognize the differences between simple melodies and change their behavior accordingly (Trehub, 2003). Consonant (as opposed to dissonant) music causes them to look toward the sound, become quiet, and listen intently (Zentner & Kagan, 1998). Infants prefer songs that are sung directly to them in a loving tone of voice, compared to prerecorded songs (Trainor, 1996; Trainor, Clane, Huntley, & Adams, 1997) and they direct more attention to their own bodies when being sung lullabies (Rock-A-Bye Baby) and more attention to the singer when being sung play songs (Eensy-Weensy Spider) (Rock, Trainor, & Addison, 1999).

Infants can also make body movements and vocalizations to the beat of music (Phillips-Silver & Trainor, 2007). The body-sense of music continues into adulthood.

> Whatever else music is about, it is inevitably about the body: it is invariably an embodied practice. When we hear a musical performance, we don't just "think," we don't just "hear," we participate with our whole bodies. We enact it. We feel melodies in our muscles as much as we process them in our brains—or perhaps more accurately, our brains process them as melodies only to the extent that our corporeal schemata render that possible. (Bowman, 2000, p. 50)

This quote refers to the proprioceptors and ergoreceptors in the muscles, skin, and sensory organs that partake in the embodied engagement with music. Music produces distinct physiological and movement reactions such as chills, goose bumps, tapping, dancing, and finger snapping, and these are associated with "good" neurochemicals like oxytocin and parasympathetic activation related to the onset of relaxation (Burns, Labbé, Williams, & McCall, 1999; Grewe, Nagel, Kopiez, & Altenmuller, 2007; Panksepp & Bernatzky, 2002) and, as in movie music, music can enhance emotions communicated visually (Baumgartner, Lutz, Schmidt, & Jäncke, 2006).

The emotions conveyed in music fall into three broad categories as judged by listeners from different cultures. The first is *sublimity*, a sense of wonder, transcendence, tenderness, nostalgia, and peacefulness. The second is *vitality*, the feelings of power and joy that makes someone want to get up and dance. The third is *unease*, which is created by a sense of tension or sadness. Some music may provoke more of one type of feeling than another (Zentner, Grandjean, & Klaus, 2008). All these emotions require the listener to be in a state of **engagement** or **normal absorption** with the music.

These three types of musical emotions correspond directly to embodied states of muscle and breath. Sublimity relates to a relaxed breath and relaxed muscles; unease to muscle tension and effortful breathing. Vitality seems to correspond to the exertion of physical exercise but without threat, so that the body can return to a balance of sympathetic and parasympathetic activation characteristic of a relaxed state of engagement.

The main point of this research is that sound making and music making partake of similar neurophysiological pathways in infancy and all through life, the same pathways as for interoception and emotion. The vocal muscles are regulated by the same motor pathways of the interoceptive, emotional, and body schema neural networks: via the motor cortex, supplementary motor area, the ACC, thalamus, insula, amygdala, prefrontal emotional areas, and the middle and lower brain stem centers (Brown, Martinez, & Parsons, 2006; Kent, 1984; Kleber, Birnbaumer, Veit, Trevorrow, & Lotze, 2007). This also means that *the original and primary function of sound making is to express emotion and to share emotion with others* (Panksepp & Bernatzky, 2002).

Evocative Language in the Subjective Emotional Present

Vocal music, poetry, theater, film, and storytelling have all used the spoken word—carried on the breath—for the purpose of communicating the full range of human emotions. *Unlike conceptual self-awareness that is focused on evaluative language,* evocative language can be used to enhance interoceptive and emotional self-awareness.

The best practitioners of the treatments for enhancing embodied self-awareness reviewed in this book use evocative language. In **evocative language**, words are chosen to resonate in felt experience. *If words "reach us," they are felt as "true," "deep," and "powerful." Words—evocatively spoken from the practitioner's own embodied self-awareness—can enhance and amplify feelings.* You can also notice, from the cases presented in this book, that evocative words uttered during a treatment session are often experienced as surprising and unexpected by the practitioner who speaks them. This is because they do not arise from logical thought processes but from the untamed, nonsuppressed flow of embodied self-awareness.

Caution is required: words can easily take a person out of their embodied experience and into their conceptual thoughts and judgments about themselves. Actors, singers, storytellers, and embodied awareness practitioners can only reach people if their voices expose their own emotions that bring them up against their most vulnerable states of being.

The ability to portray sexuality and sensuality on stage or film, for example, requires the performer to literally or figuratively undress and to expose to an audience his or her most personal and private sensibilities, those usually reserved for the intimacy of attachment relationships. No less is true for a peace loving performer or writer to portray a murderer or sadist. Somewhere inside of themselves, suppressed fury and hatred can be encountered in embodied self-awareness, feelings that might otherwise be shameful or dissonant to their self-concept.

Self-awareness practitioners too must be able to identify within themselves the emotions of their clients and students. The student can only be expected to uncover suppressed feelings to the extent that the teacher can do the same. Surely, this ability to reveal without self-consciousness is why we love particular artists and why people seek gifted practitioners of embodied self-awareness.

A practitioner's listening touch with soft hands allows clients to feel more deeply into themselves. *Soft hands also express the undefended vulnerability of the practitioner to be open to receive the client's feeling states and emotions* (Rosen, 2003). In embodied self-awareness practices, *words can be similarly uttered with a tone that expresses the speaker's feelings as they reach out to touch the listener.* "Practitioners use words to touch people, we use our hands to touch people, and we use our words and hands together to touch people" (Rosen, 2003, pp. 20–22).

Each time a practitioner or a performer uses this deeply emotional and evocative way of using the voice, it is like speaking for the very first time. This is the essence of the *Zen* concept of *beginner's mind*, or *Shoshin* in Japanese. Beginner's mind is an attitude of openness, vulnerability, and lack of judgment and evaluative conceptions when connecting with a person or object. "It's best for practitioners to start every session with a beginner's mind because when patients return it is a new beginning and a new experience will come up" (Rosen, 2003, p. 37).

The concept of beginner's mind is based on allowing the adult to be more childlike, more receptive, less judgmental, more innocent and aware. The beginning speakers of language, children between 1½ and 4 years of age, use words in exactly this way. Each time a word is uttered, it is laden with emotion expressed in body motion and vocal tone. It is spoken each time as if it is new (see Table 7.3).

Table 7.3
Use of internal state language by toddlers between 1½ and 4 years

Internal State	Toddler speech
Happy	"I give a hug. Baby be happy." "I not cry now. I happy." "Mommy having a good time."
Sad	"Me fall down. Me cry" "Katie not happy face. Katie sad."
Hurt	"I'm hurting your feelings, 'cause I was mean to you." "I feel bad. Mommy tummy hurts."
Fear	"It's dark. I'm scared." "I scared of the shark. Close my eyes."
Anger	"Grandma mad. I wrote on wall." "Mommy's mad at you." "I'm mad at you Daddy. I'm going away. Goodbye."
Bad	"I bad girl. I wet my pants." "Lisa not nice to me. Lisa bad."
Love	"I love Mommy. I want to hold Mommy."

Source: Bertherton, Fritz, Zahn-Waxler, & Ridgeway (1986).

Psychophysiology of Self-Awareness

During this age period, toddlers learn words for sensations and emotions in embodied self-awareness, words such as for feeling sleepy (*go night-night*), taste (*yum*), pain (*owey*), restoration (*kiss better*), and many other body states. (Dunn, Bretherton, & Munn, 1987; Taumoepeau & Ruffman, 2008). They also learn words for themselves, like *mine*, *me*, and *I* (Levine, 1983; Lewis & Ramsay, 2004). These words are not just symbolic abstractions. They are feelings translated into sound. This can't be replicated in a book, so take the time to listen to a toddler speak. Note the punctuated emphasis of words and syllables, the facial expressions, and the body motions.

In addition to the coupling of the voice with the breath, vocalizations are also linked to body movements and gestures. Beginning at the age of babbling—about 6 months—we begin to see infants moving while making sounds. Repeating syllables in babbling and other vocal play are coordinated with rhythmic movements of the hands, arms, and legs (Iverson & Fagan, 2004). What is even more surprising is that deaf infants babble with their hands—making repeating movements like hand open and closed, or waving like movements—purely for the sake of exploration and not to convey meaning. When researchers studied hearing infants, they found the same pattern of manual babbling (Petitto, Holowka, Sergio, Levy, & Ostry, 2004). Blind adults, even when talking to other blind adults, use gestures to punctuate their speech (Iverson & Goldin-Meadow, 2001).

It is not until 3 to 4 years of age that we begin to see autobiographical narratives in children's speech. Although at this age they need a lot of help from adults, they can talk about themselves in story form and relate events from their past. At this age, however, and probably continuing through adolescence, children's autobiographical narratives are not primarily expressions of conceptual self-awareness. Rather, they are created from a growing conceptual self-awareness (the ability to put oneself into a category like boy or girl, or a religious affiliation) that is usually linked to an embodied self-awareness in the subjective emotional present and in the subjective emotional past.

This ability to express one's embodied self-awareness in the context of conceptual self-awareness and relationships to others is called **voice**, the sense of being the author of the expression of one's **True Self**, the sense that one is speaking of the self with honesty and confidence in a way that is consonant with embodied feelings (Bakhtin, 1981; Day & Tappan, 1996). Too often, we lose our true voice because our feelings are unacceptable and need to be sup-

Catching Our Breath, Finding Our Voice

pressed. *Having a voice, finding one's voice, is the ability to put embodied self-awareness into words that resonate with self and others. Evocative language in embodied self-awareness practices (Table 1.1) aims toward helping the client to develop his or her evocative language to express the truth of the subjective emotional present.*

Remembering and Autobiography

Autobiographical narratives always contain verbal accounts of past events. This raises the issue of how we remember the past and how past embodied experience is translated into language. The period between 1½ and 4 years of age marks the emergence of verbal autobiographical remembering. Given that children of this age live primarily in a world of embodied interoceptive and emotional experience, and that their first words are primarily evocative of embodied states, can they use narrative to capture this experience?

Most people do not have autobiographical memories earlier than 3 or 4 years of age (so-called infantile amnesia), because as adults we come to encode experience linguistically and before that age, we had limited ability to construct linguistic narratives for that experience. What happens to all those preverbal infancy experiences in memory? Can a 4- or 5-year-old child still remember and recount in narrative form something that happened to them when they were a 1-year-old?

These questions also have important implications for working with the suppression of embodied self-awareness in people with prior trauma. There is often an amnesia about the actual events that occured during the trauma, an amnesia that is based partly in the suppression of pain and threat. How do trauma survivors talk about their experience? How can the practitioner's language be used to bring them back into embodied self-awareness in both the present and in the past?

Researchers typically categorize memory into two types: autobiographical and procedural. In **autobiographical memory**, we are able to think about and talk about an event that happened to us in the past. There is a story to tell—first this happened, then that, then this other thing. The story has a location in time and space, and the story is typically kept at an emotional distance. Autobiographical memories (sometimes called declarative, explicit, semantic, or episodic memories) are organized by the **hippocampus** (see Figures 5.2 and 5.3), a horseshoe-shaped or seahorse-shaped structure (hippocampus means "seahorse" in Latin) that encircles the limbic system, which is believed to help in the mental organization of sensory impressions into coherent "events" with a beginning, middle, and ending, and with a remembered spatial location and organization (Eichenbaum & Cohen, 2001; Morris, 2007; Moscovitch et al., 2005).

Many people refer to the limbic system as the "emotional" part of the brain. The location of the hippocampus in the limbic system, and its role in spatial and event cognition, shows that the limbic system is not simply related to emotion. The thalamus, at the center of the limbic system, plays an important role in sensory and motor control, while the hypothalamus regulates many of the autonomic functions of the body like digestion and respiration. The limbic system is thus involved in virtually all brain and body functions, not just emotion. In addition, in order for us to have an embodied self-awareness of emotion, we need the prefrontal cortex and the insula, both part of the neocortex. To express emotion, we need the premotor and motor areas of the neocortex. To perceive the emotions of others, we need the body schema networks in the parietal cortex mirror neurons. A complete understanding of embodied self-awareness requires us to move away from modular thinking and to embrace the ideas of dynamic systems and complex neurophysiological networks that span the whole brain and body.

Procedural memories, in contrast to hippocampally regulated autobiographical memories, are primarily nonverbal. Rather than stories about the self, procedural memories (sometimes called motor, skill, perceptual, or implicit memories) can be described as the memory of "ways of doing and sensing things" (Kolers & Roediger, 1984). Face recognition, the memory of how to ride a bicycle or drive a car, and how to dance or sing, are all examples of procedural memories which underlie our ability to act in the world on the basis of what we have learned in the past, but these memories need not be encoded verbally and typically are not.

From a dynamic systems perspective, both procedural and autobiographical memories are organized across the four parts of the neural networks for self-awareness (see Figure 5.6) and the memory traces in the brain—permanent experience dependent alterations of interneuronal connections—are distributed across those networks and not located in any one place. The hippocampus, which helps to bind experience into "events" with a coherent time-and-space story structure, works in concert with the self-awareness neural networks (Conway et al., 1999; Fink, Markowitsch, & Reinkemeier, 1996; Wheeler, Stuss, & Tulving, 1997). The emotional distance from the past experienced when telling autobiographical stories is related to a relative deactivation of the emotional areas of the brain (Levine et al., 2004). Autobiographical memory, therefore, is a form of **conceptual self-awareness**.

Research supporting the dynamic systems view of the brain has shown that the sensory, premotor, motor, and parietal cortices involved in both interoception and body schema when doing a particular action are also activated when the person is asked to repeat that action at a later time. Procedural memories of sensations—like music, pictures, and touch—activate the relevant areas of the sensory cortices. Procedural memories of coordinated actions activate the premotor, motor, and parietal areas involved in sensing movement and body location (Goldberg, Perfetti, & Schneider, 2006; Nyberg et al., 2001; Wheeler, Peterson & Buckner, 2000). Procedural memories, in other words, are felt in the body parts that are activated by efferent feedback from these sensory and motor brain areas, although they need not be and often are not part of one's embodied self-awareness. Because procedural memories partake of these neural networks, however, with training and practice one can become aware of them and use that awareness to change old procedural habits.

Most autobiographical memory actually has a procedural component. When telling a story about a past event, people often gesture and move their bodies to indicate direction, action, and sensation that had been part of the original experience, showing that interoceptive and body schema networks are involved even when the memory becomes verbalized (Kolers & Roediger, 1984).

The same is true for emotion. Experiencing any emotion will bind that emotion into the memory in addition to binding the sensations, actions, and locations (LeDoux, 2002). This is because emotion is already bound into the interoceptive and body schema networks via the prefrontal cortex (in particular the orbitofrontal cortex [OFC] involved in hedonic evaluation), the anterior cingulate cortex (ACC), cingulate motor area (CMA), and premotor cortex involved in emotionally based plans and urges to act, and the insula involved in the organization and rerepresentation of experience into a recognizable felt emotion (see Chapters 2 and 3).

This binding of embodied experience into emotional packages in the insula is analogous to the binding of space and time information into events in the hippocampus. The implication of the different brain circuits for emotional binding compared to event binding means that *emotional memories are more like procedural memories than like autobiographical memories*: emotional memories are more embodied and event memories are more conceptual (Craig, 2008; Eichenbaum & Cohen, 2001). This helps to explain why people cannot recall, autobiographically, their experiences during infancy.

Once the hippocampus develops the capacity to organize and cohere experiences (around the age of 4 years), and once coherent narratives are produced, the child becomes able to verbally engage with adults about the past. This leads to the further development of narrative skills and the experience dependent development of the hippocampus, which leads to more conversations. The result is that storytelling becomes highly rewarding to both adults and children. Over time, language comes to stand for the world of sensation and emotion, leading to a decline of embodied self-awareness in favor of the more socially rewarded conceptual-linguistic self-awareness (Fivush, Haden, & Adam, 1995; Harley & Reese, 1999; Peterson, Grant, & Boland, 2005; Simcock & Hayne, 2003). That is another way of saying that we become less childlike—less emotional, less spontaneous, more conceptual—as we age.

Memory of Threat and Safety

Autobiographical narratives, however, can be expressed in evocative language. Autobiographical memory and internal state language are related to one's history of threat or safety. It turns out that those children who are more securely attached to their mothers and fathers have more detailed conversations about feeling states with their parents. Securely attached children are more emotionally expressive in their first words, sentences, and body movements, and they have the most sophisticated vocabulary for a wide range of emotions and interoceptive states, (Asendorph, Warkentin, & Baudonniere, 1996; Fivush, 1991; Pasupathi, 2001; Pipp, Easterbrooks, & Brown, 1993; Zahn-Waxler, Radke-Yarrow, Wagner, & Chapman, 1992).

Insecurely attached toddlers are less able to talk about emotions. If they do mention emotions, they are more likely to talk about their own negative, as compared to positive, feelings and they have higher resting cortisol levels than securely attached children (Lemche, Klann-Delius, Koch, & Joraschky, 2004; Lemche, Krepner, Joraschky, & Klann-Delius, 2007). Adolescents with childhood histories of parental spousal violence, or physical or sexual abuse used fewer emotion words when talking about conflict or negative situations compared to non-abused teens. These children describe previous difficult experiences in very general terms with few details (Dagleish et al., 2003; Greenhoot,

Johnson, & McCloskey, 2005). Adults who have few emotion words in their talk about themselves have higher levels of anxiety and depression, and worse physical health (Pennebaker & Beall, 1986).

These findings suggest that suppression of emotions and the words to describe those emotions results when previous events create emotions accompanied by a sense of threat and in the absence of another person with whom the emotions could be shared (Ebeling, Moilanen, & Räsänen, 2001). This effect goes beyond autobiographical memory. Children who reported difficult and noncaring relationships with parents had higher levels of anxiety and stress, and poorer performance on elementary school classroom oral presentations (Sideridis & Kefetsios, 2008). For such children, any situation of perceived threat is likely to constrain their breath and their voice. *It appears that evocative language is an essential part of child and adult health and well-being. Without the ability to talk about our feelings, they remain suppressed and take their increasingly costly toll on our bodies over time.*

In the case of Peter (Case Report 5.2), a lack of coregulated emotional communication with his mother in the first year developed into avoidance and muscle tension. The father's job loss that led to the family stress was resolved when Peter was 18 months. By age 2 years, Peter's mother was more relaxed and gave Peter more room to take initiative and to feel his own emotions. In our observations of Peter when he was 2 and 3 years old, he seemed emotionally expressive with the typical lilting contours of children's evocative speech. He also made emotionally alive sounds like sighs and chirps.

It seems that by this time, Peter and his mother had recovered and were reestablishing a way of emotionally connecting that they had experienced together during Peter's first half year of life. The only indication of their prior difficulties was that Peter, even at age 3, still squinted when he smiled. A full-face joyful smile might be accompanied by the raising of the cheeks and the crinkling of the eye corners, accomplished by the *outer* portion of the circular orbicularis oculi muscles around the eyes. This makes the eyes seem more closed as a result, due to the upward contraction of the cheek muscles. (But the muscle movements of eye squinting involve the *inner* portion of the orbicularis oculi, closing off visual access to the world.) Peter was still apparently suppressing some of his joy.

The spontaneous recovery of Peter and his mother is hopeful and reflects a tendency of attachment relationships to repair themselves when love and safety take precedence over threat (Shorey & Snyder, 2006). The only word that fully describes this possibility is *redemption*. It is important to recognize, however, that *even though redemption can powerfully transcend past hurts, it may take a long time for a complete sense of safety and trust to return in intimate relationships, and for each person to regain their ability to honestly voice all of their feelings with the other.*

Fearful and painful memories, especially if they were traumatically sustained, as well as memories of safety, have a particular quality that sets them apart from procedural and autobiographical remembering. Fear memories can become very much alive in the subjective emotional present even though the events being remembered may have occurred dozens of years earlier. This was the case with Joan's memories of fraternal abuse (see Case Report 5.1) that arose as she began to "come out" of her dissociative state. These memories can seem so real in the present moment that they become, in themselves, sources of fear and threat, suppression and more dissociation. This is why, clinically, they need to be recognized, approached slowly, and with the support of soothing resources.

Why are safety and threat memories different? This is because they are bound together, and remembered, via the safety and threat neural network (Figure 5.4). This means that memories for both safety and threat, although they partake of the interoceptive and body schema pathways used in forming other types of memory, also involve the considerably larger neurochemical network shown in Figure 5.4 (Amorapanth et al., 2000; Frankland, Bontempi, Talton, Kaczmarek, & Silva, 2004; Grove et al., 1997; Kim & Gorman, 2005; Liberzon, Britton, & Luan Phan, 2003; Packard & Cahill, 2001).

Because threat activates not only neural networks but stress hormones, endogenous opiates, and cytokines we can begin to appreciate that memory for threat may be experienced in a very different way from autobiographical and procedural memory. Safety activates parasympathetic and restorative pathways as well as hormones like oxytocin. We have already hinted that the neurochemicals secreted into the blood, lymph, and neural pathways eventually return to the brain and can alter its structure and function. These alterations further account for the differences between safety and threat memories and other types of memory (Dębiec & LeDoux, 2006; van der Kolk, 1996).

Research has shown that the neurochemicals (neurotransmitters, hormones, and opioids) from persistent threat—whether from psychosocial or physical stressors—destroy or impair the normal function of the safety, threat, and self-awareness areas of the brain (McGaugh, Cahill, & Roozendaal, 1996; Pecoraro et al., 2006; Post et al., 1998). The amygdala becomes hypersensitive to the environment, seeing threat even when in the present moment none is there. The entire HPA axis becomes overreactive, leading to hypersensitivity to threat because the amygdala, hippocampus, and prefrontal cortex are especially sensitive to alteration from cortisol. In the long run, the oversecretion of cortisol also exhausts adrenal function so that insufficient cortisol (a condition called **hypocortisolism**) is secreted and the individual does not have the resources to cope with ordinary, everyday tasks. Hypocortisolism also results in stress hypersensitivity, pain, and fatigue (Fries, Hesse, Hellhammer, & Hellhammer, 2005; Ostrander et al., 2006).

The ventromedial prefrontal cortex (VMPFC) is also impaired under continuing threat conditions by the same neurochemicals, leading, as we have seen, to a decreasing ability of the individual to stay in the subjective emotional present of embodied self-awareness and leading, as discussed above, to a predisposition toward suppression and absorption as well as being easily kindled by fearful events (Maroun, 2006; Tucker, 2001).

Finally, the cellular structure of the hippocampus can be impaired in several important ways. One way is damage that leads to the inability of the individual to bind memory into event packages that are easily processed into autobiographical stories. Autobiography, and conceptual self-awareness, is an essential part of what it means to be human. Persistent threat leads to selective amnesias for threatening events and to a lowered ability to concentrate, learn, and remember in general (Bremner, Narayan et al., 1998; Gould, 2007; Izquierdo & Medina, 1997; Nadel & Jacobs, 1998; Sandi, Merino, Cordera, Touyarot, & Venero, 2001).

The hippocampus is unique because it is one of the few sites in the brain, along with the olfactory bulb and some parts of the cortex, where new nerve cells grow during adulthood, a process called **neurogenesis**. Most of our new nerve cells grow during the prenatal months and then begin to decline in number across the life span as an increasing number of interconnections are made between the cells that remain. Adult neurogenesis is believed to contribute to brain repair in the event of physical tissue damage due to injury, stroke, or infection (Kozorovitskiy & Gould, 2003). Stress and threat, in addition to impairing existing hippocampal cells, also blocks the ability of the hippocampus to generate new neurons, thus making brain restoration more difficult in cases of severe trauma (Bremner, 2006; Gould, 2007)

If dissociation occurs during the actual trauma, the individual cannot fully attend to the circumstances of the assault resulting in impaired memory for the trauma and continued rekindling of the trauma via intrusive flashback memories (not organized into event structures because of impaired hippocampal function) typical of PTSD (Diseth, 2005; Holmes et al., 2005; Nijenhuis, Van der Hart, Kruger, & Steele, 2004; Payne et al., 2006; Scaer, 2001). Dissociation during the trauma inhibits the insula and the hippocampus from binding the memories into cohesive packages, whereas attention to the trauma assists in consolidation of memories (Critchley, Mathius, & Dolan, 2002). The unbound trauma memories become "free-floating." They may be come attached to a sensory or motor situation which, when reenacted in the present, allows the memory to lurch into awareness without warning and with no ability to control it.

When trauma prohibits appropriate action, the emotional aspects induce memory formation not only for the emotion (the fear associated with the stimulus), but also for both the realized and the unrealized motor patterns (failure to escape, inability to avoid being hurt) and emotional expressions (terror, anger, screaming). Breuer and Freud (1893–1895), postulated that the symptoms of **somatization** (which they called hysteria) seen in their adult clinical cases resulted from childhood maltreatment in which the child could not effectively respond to the insult, thus allowing the memory to retain its somatic and emotional impact. They also talked about resources as aids to treatment.

> Even if the person who has been insulted neither hits back nor replies with abuse, he can nevertheless reduce the affect attaching to the insult by calling up such contrasting ideas as those of his own worthiness, of his enemy's worthlessness, and so on. (p. 13)

Children, however, have a limited ability to do this. Instead, like my client Joan, they retreat to dissociative states in which they pretend that everything is as it should be. Here is another of Piaget's descriptions, this time of his daughter, Jacqueline, at 2 years, 1 month of age. What Piaget called "liquidating pretend play," occurred when she became afraid in the morning when sitting on a new chair at the table.

In the afternoon, she put her dolls in uncomfortable positions and said to them: *"It doesn't matter. It will be all right,"* repeating what had been said to her. When she was two years and three months, there was a similar scene with some medicine, which she afterward gave to a sheep. (Piaget, 1962, p. 133)

This is similar to what is described in Case Report 5.1, as Joan developed a "little girl" persona who made the world around her "all right."

Memory for trauma, organized by strong emotions and remembered urges and actions, is distributed across the entire **neuraxis** of the body as a systemic network, from the peripheral effectors and receptors, through the spinal cord and brain stem, the limbic system, the emotional and interoceptive areas of the cortex, and the sensory and motor areas of the cortex (Tucker, 2001). *Trauma memory is as much in the sensory receptors, in the skin and in the muscles as it is in the brain.*

Since the memory is not bound into cohesive packages by normal hippocampal and insular function, and therefore accounts for the poor autobiographical narratives of insecurely attached and abused children, memory may instead appear in extremely vivid bursts with disturbing sensory details, flashbacks, feelings of panic, anger, and terror all of which are sudden, intrusive, and frightening because they seem to come from nowhere and can't seem to be regulated in conceptual–autobiographical self-awareness (see Box 5.2; Jacobs & Nadel, 1985, 1999; Porter & Birt, 2001; Schacter, 1999; Schönfeld & Ehlers, 2006; van der Kolk, 1996).

This helps us to understand the persistence of PTSD symptoms like intrusive and vivid memories. The person feels they are back in the original situation with accompanying terror, mobilization (the veteran who tries to attack innocent people or family members) or immobilization (inability to function). *It is as if the traumatic event is "locked inside" because the unrealized urges—the failure to be able to act as one would have expected—which have not been integrated by the hippocampus into an autobiographical memory are in a sense holding the neural network hostage.* The representations for urges to act in the supplementary motor area, cingulate motor area, and premotor areas that would normally be transient as they are passed into action via the motor cortex and cerebellum, remain active and attached to the strong emotions related to the trauma. Urges to express pain or cry out for help, as when a sexually abused child is told to keep quiet and not tell anyone, may also be suppressed.

Psychophysiology of Self-Awareness

In summary, if there is some strong emotion and the body cannot make an appropriate motor response, the memory of the urge to act in relation to the fear or anger (in the example of trauma) is preserved along with any visual or auditory imagery. *These urges, "forgotten" for most trauma victims in autobiographical-conceptual self-awareness, account in part for low-level chronic muscle tension that drains energetic resources. This tension could be, for example, in the arms or legs (the unrealized urges to fight or flee), or in the neck, throat and face (the unrealized urges to speak or scream or cry), or in the chest (the unrealized urges to breathe).*

I call these unregulated and vivid recollections **participatory memory** because when remembering, the person feels as if they are again participating in the past situation.

> **Participatory memories** are lived re-enactments of personally significant experiences that have not yet become organized into a verbal or conceptual narrative. Participatory memories are . . . experienced in the present that are not *about* a past experience, meaning that the past experience is not represented as an image or concept divorced from emotional significance. Rather, participatory memories are emotionally experienced as a *being with* or a *re-living of past* experiences. . . . When experiencing a participatory memory, one is not thinking about the past. One is directly involved in a past experience as if were occurring in the present. (see Box 5.2; Fogel, 2004, pp. 209–210)

Participatory memory is a form of remembering something in the past that is felt (re-lived) in the subjective emotional present of embodied self-awareness (Bråten, 1998; Fogel, 1993; Heshusius, 1994). Participatory memories have also been called body memories, somatosensory memories, state dependent memories (because they reenact the entire physiological state of the organism at the time of the event), and trauma memories (Gaensbauer, 2002; Holmes et al., 2005; Terr, 1988, 1994; van der Kolk, 1996). Examples of both trauma and safety participatory memories are given in Box 7.2.

Box 7.2
Participatory Memory

Participatory memories are alive with sensory impressions. In verbal accounts, they are described in very concrete terms of sensation and movement with little evaluation and judgment. There is often an acceptance of irrationality. Typically, as they are being told or recollected, they involve strong emotions: the same fear or anger or joy of the original situation. If the person had been running or fighting, for example, they may sweat and gesture and breathe hard and shake in the recounting.

Participatory memory for trauma is very well documented in the research and clinical literature. It is impossible to convey the vividness and whole body activation of participatory memory in words in a book. Keeping in mind that the verbal transcriptions presented here are only the words and not the body activation, here are some examples. The first is from an Italian Holocaust survivor.

> I remember everything about the piazza ... the piazza, my dad still holding me like this (demonstrates) ... holding my legs ... and what did my dad do? He got down on his knees, holding me tight ... and he said to the German ... there was only one German ... quite far away from us: "Have pity! Have pity!" And it seemed humiliating to me that my dad got down like that and he asked for pity for this little girl ... I remember the German taking aim ... quite far away from us but not that far ... but he didn't have the courage and I ... I remember seeing the dead ... well, all piled up, the dresses burnt, the jackets burnt, and I said "Whatever for?" (Cappelletto, 2003, p. 251)

This is not an autobiographical narrative, a story told by an adult about her childhood self. Rather, the adult woman *becomes* the child, her

continued

Psychophysiology of Self-Awareness

> **BOX 7.2** (continued)
>
> voice is the voice of that child in that situation. Note that the description is disconnected; not filtered with narrative embellishments typical of a good story. It is filled with sensory details—"far away" and "dresses burnt"—and movements—"down on his knees" and "holding my legs"—and emotions "humiliating" as well as obvious fear and confusion that would be more clear if one was listening to the teller.
>
> Note also how the rational conceptual and autobiographical thinking is noticed but suspended: "Whatever for?" The teller goes on to describe, in similar manner, the detailed sensory and emotional impressions of seeing her dead uncle on the piazza, her lack of comprehension, and many other details of that day.
>
> As noted earlier, most people do not have autobiographical memory for events occurring earlier than 3 or 4 years of age (Rubin, 2000). Participatory memories can be so vivid and so entrenched in the threat and safety neurochemical pathways, however, that they can in fact be memories of infantile experiences (Gaensbauer, 2002; Morris & Baker-Ward, 2007; Peterson & Rideout, 1998; Terr, 1988). Under what conditions can infantile participatory memories be evoked, and more generally, what conditions evoke any kind of participatory memory at any age?
>
> If the person is reasonably secure in her or his attachments and has experienced trauma outside the family, but then is allowed to be comforted and soothed, as in the case of the Italian survivor above, participatory memories can occur in the company of caring individuals who are willing to allow the feelings to emerge. Research on normally developing children exposed to a traumatic tornado reveals that they use more words related to direct perception than nonexposed children when recalling past events. In interviews with a trained psychologist, the exposed children talked about "seeing" and "hearing" and "smelling" the things that happened during the storm (Bauer et al., 2005; Peterson & Whalen, 2001).
>
> *continued*

> **BOX 7.2** (continued)
>
> In another case, a child needed major surgery at the age of 2 years.
>
> > At age five she developed pneumonia, was taken to the hospital by ambulance and was immediately rushed to the intensive care unit on a gurney. Following her discharge, her mother found her in bed crying one night. When her mother asked her why she was crying she said, "The same thing happened this time that happened last time (i.e., when she was two). The nurse took me away on that [gurney] and no one was with me." (Gaensbauer, 2002, p. 267)
>
> Participatory memories can be evoked in ordinary life when the sensory and motor conditions similar to the trauma recur (Fogel, 2004). This is the case for war veterans who superimpose the stress of a traffic jam, or a family argument, on the "forgotten" traumatic event, resulting in unprovoked rage or attack.
>
> In a case of participatory memories from infancy, a 16-month-old fell, severely cutting his forehead. In the emergency room he had to be tightly wrapped in a blanket to keep him from moving during the stitching. The parents and child were interviewed at the time the child was 3 years old. He still had no autobiographical memory of the traumatic events in the hospital, but the parents reported that he refused to be wrapped in a smock when getting his hair cut (Peterson & Rideout, 1998).
>
> In cases of more serious and ongoing trauma, therapeutic re-creation of the sensory, motor, and emotional conditions of the past event—coupled with the provision of resources and all the therapeutic processes listed in Table 1.1—can allow a person to safely reexperience participatory memories in a way that they can be translated into evocative language and perhaps then coherent autobiographical narratives. Trauma treatment, done effectively, can restore emotional well-being and also create experience dependent neural pathways in the hippocampus and insula to begin the process of autobiographical reconstruction.
>
> *continued*

Psychophysiology of Self-Awareness

> **BOX 7.2** (continued)
>
> There are also reported cases of *participatory memories of safety*. Given the highly intense psychological and neurochemical flooding that occurs in romantic and sexual encounters, such memories are common to anyone who has ever been in love. These memories of encounters with the love object can be compelling, irrational, vivid, disturbing, distracting, intrusive, perhaps unwanted, but potentially thrilling.
>
> In my college textbook on infant and child development (Fogel, 2009), there are a series of exercises that allow readers to enter into the sensations, emotions, and movements of a baby or young child. Many of these exercises are about embodied self-awareness, including one that uses a mirror to look into one's face and eyes, in much the same way that a young child might, to discover more about oneself. After doing this exercise, one of my students wrote the following.
>
>> After looking at my face in different ways [during the mirror exercise], the face of my mom all of a sudden came into my mind. I didn't get it then but I do now. I spent three years looking straight into my mother's eyes [when I was a baby] and I noticed over Thanksgiving holiday that her eyes look just like mine! Every time I look at my eyes, I am reminded of her and I feel safe, I feel at home! (p. 523)
>
> Many traumatized children and adults have lasting and troubling participatory memories of their early experience. These trauma memories have been called "ghosts in the nursery" (Fraiberg, Adelson, & Shapiro, 1975). Traumatized children have been helped clinically by being able to remember good things about the past, "angels in the nursery" (Lieberman, Padrón, van Horn, & Harris, 2005).
>
>> My aunt . . . she was just always a very gentle, very loving . . . she'd brush my hair very gently and never pulled my hair,
>
> *continued*

Catching Our Breath, Finding Our Voice

> **BOX 7.2** (continued)
>
> like my mom did. My mom was always in a hurry to get the hair brushed . . . get it over and done with, and my aunt would just take her time, and be so gentle. . . . She was like a warm blanket, she was just wonderful. (Lieberman et al, 2005, p. 509)
>
> Even without being able to hear the telling of these memories, perhaps you can feel their aliveness, their sensory and emotional immediacy. The people here are not talking about the past as if it were a completed autobiography, but rather reliving the past in the present moment. "Angels in the nursery" are participatory memories of safety and because they are participatory, they can be used as resources in treating trauma at any age.

Case Report 7.2
Participatory Memory of a Surgical Trauma

The client, Rebecca, 45 years of age, came to see me about persistent abdominal pain that had lasted for years following a surgery in which some large, nonmalignant uterine fibroids had been removed. At the time of the session described here, we had worked together for 12 prior sessions during which abdominal pain occurred when talking about her pregnancy with her daughter (who was 18 years old at the time of Rebecca's visits to me), during a period in which her (now ex-) husband became alcoholic and abusive.

By the sixth or seventh session, as Rebecca became more familiar with me, she would spend the first 10 or 15 minutes of each session gradually relaxing with audible sighs as I touched her upper back and neck (*resources, slowing down, coregulation*). I found her abdominal, pelvic, and lower back muscles, however, extremely tight and not responsive to my touch.

Psychophysiology of Self-Awareness

Was it something about a trauma related to her childbirth experience, or about Rebecca's likely invasive sexual relationship with the ex-husband that created this protective muscle tension and eventually led to a difficult reaction to the surgery for the fibroids? The relationship trauma, the fibroids, and the surgery had all given Rebecca's belly, back, and pelvis good enough reasons to armor themselves. I had no idea how or if any of this mattered and I had to let go of my thoughts about it. I did not ask her directly, preferring instead to allow her to begin to feel into that area at a pace that she could tolerate. In Rosen work, we are more interested in what the body may reveal than in the autobiographical narrative that has been created in conceptual self-awareness.

By her 13th session, the one described here, Rebecca finally began to allow the lower belly muscles to relax somewhat when she was lying face up. She continued to breathe easily and I could feel the **resonance** between my hand and her body.

After a few minutes, she said, "I feel like there's a division between the right and left side of my belly down there."

In a request to deepen her attention to the interoceptive sensations, I asked, "Does one side of your belly feel different than the other side?"

"I don't know," was the reply.

I found myself holding my breath momentarily as I hoped this question did not throw her into conceptual self-awareness. In fact it led her to be more curious interoceptively but not directly related to my question.

So, I breathed easier when, a few minutes later, she said, "You know that vertical split in my belly . . . (a long pause followed) . . . that's where they made the incision."

Her voice was a bit shaky with this so I could tell there was some emotion behind it. As I waited to see if there was a response in her body, I wondered about this statement. Surely, I thought, she knew the location of the scar. Then I began to feel her uterus itself beginning to soften and her breathing slowing down with a longer expiratory pause.

I must have felt that this was a participatory memory but I was not fully aware of how this affected me and of what this meant for her until I said, decisively and surprising myself, "You've been assaulted here, cut into."

There was more relaxation, more breath, and silent tears began to flow. I can say truthfully that I don't know where statements like this come from. I've learned to trust my body in these moments in the sense that I don't try to analyze and think too much about it. Resonance works its mysterious way into the body tissues and the breath and the words that come when there is no suppression.

Riding the wave of her emotions, I continued in a softer tone, "Your body remembers the surgery even if you were anesthetized, even if you thought you were asleep." As I talked, I was actually thinking of the invasion of her reproductive anatomy and emotions by the ex-husband and the no doubt complicated nature of the early formation of an attachment bond with her only daughter. I imagined that this revelation of the surgical assault—another kind of invasion of her uterus and vulnerably soft belly—was working through her in deep and unknown ways. My hand, fortunately, remained soft and attentive while I was thinking about this so Rebecca could remain in her remembering process.

After a while she said, "I bet they put a wedge into me, to hold me open." Noting the relaxation response and the confidence in her voice when she said this, I replied, "Yes, that's probably what happened."

As the session came to an end, Rebecca reported that she felt warmth and energy flowing through her whole body, and a complete absence of the pain in her abdomen that had been there since the surgery. That energy was infectious. I was tingling and goose bumpy, with a shared experience of gratitude and grace between us that I did not feel compelled to voice.

This case illustrates how surgery can be a hidden form of trauma. It may be that when a physical injury or wound occurs in the same region of the body where some emotional trauma has previously lodged itself, the trauma from the surgical wound becomes linked to the earlier trauma in a way that amplifies the effect. It may be the case that the earlier trauma predisposes one to be more vulnerable to posttraumatic stress in that same region of the body.

The lasting effects of the surgery could also come from the interpersonal context of the surgical procedure. Research has shown that in some cases patients can hear and remember words spoken in the operating room, although they are typically not aware of such memories. If one of the doctors or nurses expresses dismay or shock about the condition, it could have a negative impact. On the other hand, one study found that women who listened to a recording of "positive therapeutic suggestions" while anesthetized for abdominal hysterectomy needed 24% less pain medication even though the patients claimed to not remember anything that was on the tape (Bennett & Disbrow, 1995). If words can be remembered under anesthesia, it is even more likely that the surgical wound and its repair can be remembered in the interoceptive and body schema neural networks.

Rebecca's abdominal pain did not completely disappear following that session. It returned whenever she faced conflicts in her various romantic encounters, none of which led to a long-term relationship. The pain also recurred in relation to her daughter's leaving for college. The session was a breakthrough, however, in that now the link between the pain and her attachment relationships could be named and thus brought into the orbit of self-regulation and reengagement with self and others. Eventually, she came to let go of her worries about the pain, realizing that it was informative and that it didn't last long once she was able to feel it and its linkages to her interpersonal situations.

I have worked with people who have so-called undiagnosed chest pains consequent to open heart surgery or pacemaker implantation. In these few cases, there was also a related attachment trauma, as if the surgical wound has a posttraumatic effect on the emotional wound of a broken heart.

It is not always the case that tension around the heart relates to protection against failed love, or that tension in the pelvis relates to sexual or reproductive trauma. It would be contrary to a beginner's mind to presume that the verbal metaphor of a broken heart explains the physical symptoms of every person with chest tension or pain. Yet the body does have certain muscular modes of expressing itself and protecting itself which can't be ignored.

The bottom line in any embodied practice is whether the words resonate in the subjective emotional present—whether the muscles relax, the tears come, the breath deepens and becomes effortless—or whether the words shift people into conceptual thought at the expense of embodied self-awareness. No less is true for the words in this book. I hope these words make you think. More importantly, however, these words are empty if they do not help you to catch your breath, or to find your own true voice.

8

Coming Home to Ourselves: Restorative Embodied Self-Awareness

> *When the restoration of sensation is complete, when the patient has been fully reawakened, he usually gives utterance to feelings of astonishment and joy. . . . These feelings of well-being make the patient laugh, and give him a general aspect of gaiety and health.*
> (Soller, 1897; as quoted in Ogden et al., 2006, p. 297)

This book documents the importance of embodied self-awareness for health and well-being, and describes everyday practices, educational methods, and clinical treatments that enhance embodied self-awareness. The goal of these practices is to allow individuals free access to a state of restorative self-awareness that is characterized by the self-regulated personal choice to experience their inner sensations, emotions, movements, linkages, and boundaries that are directly felt in the absence of conceptual interpretation. This brings clarity to conceptual self-awareness, the ability to understand ourselves in light of our feelings in the **subjective emotional present** and to make life choices that are supportive of those feelings and thus more in line with the **True Self**.

What does this state of awareness feel like? What are the possibilities for the person acting from this state? Those who have witnessed and assisted people in the process of recovery from a loss of embodied self-awareness have particularly insightful answers to these questions. The restoration of embodied self-awareness out of the suffering of suppression and pathological absorption provides a clear contrast, a way to highlight the characteristics of restorative self-awareness. These characteristics, culled from the work of different types of therapists and educators, are summarized in Table 8.1.

Table 8.1
Characteristics of restorative embodied self-awareness

Openness to embodied self-awareness	The discovery of "all the richness that exists within" (Rogers, 1961, p. 112). The ability to take in, feel, and experience what is in the self without suppression. The ability to tolerate pain and to stay in the **subjective emotional present**.
Trust in embodied self-awareness	Sensing that one's own experiences are trustworthy, ability to use positive and negative feelings, comforts and pains, as diagnostic of the current situation and as reliable information on which to learn and to make choices. The ability to find pleasure and tolerate positive emotions.
Balancing closeness and distance	Reliance on the self to make choices independent of social expectations, the alignment of **conceptual self-awareness** with **embodied self-awareness**, the clarity of linkages and boundaries, security of attachments and the ability to appropriately use others as resources.
Willingness to be a process	The sense that one is not static but always in a *process of becoming*. The ability to feel safe in states of creative **engagement** and **normal absorption**. The ability to *let go* of pretenses and expectations and the ability to *laugh* at oneself. The growth of spirituality in terms of *acceptance* of one's limitations and strengths and those of others, the ability to *forgive* self and others, *compassion* for and acceptance without suppression of other individuals, and of the state of society, *gratitude* for whatever happens and for whatever one is given.

Sources: Ogden et al. (2006), Rogers (1961), Siegel (2003), van der Hart et al. (2006), Winnicott (1971).

The first aspect is *openness to embodied self-awareness* in the subjective emotional present. This is the opposite of suppression and pathological absorption, a turning toward the self with an increased capacity to feel and tolerate both physical and emotional pain. The second aspect takes this openness a bit further, to include a genuine sense of *trust in embodied self-awareness*. This is a sense that not only can one directly feel what is present, but that indulging in those feelings is safe, worthwhile, and can inform choices about future action.

An example of trust in embodied self-awareness is making friends with pain (Box 5.1), including the events that occur when we feel pain and the possibility for pain to inform us about what needs to be done to recover and restore. This embracing of pain as a source of valuable information was a central part of Case Report 2.1, as my client Doug learned to feel his anger and also began to use that feeling to help him understand why people affected him in frustrating ways.

A tolerance for and an embracing of positive feelings of pleasure is also part of this sense of trust in the body. Positive emotions, similar to negative ones, increase heart rate, respiration, and sympathetic nervous system arousal (Giuliani, McRae, & Gross, 2008). Because of a fear of the intensity of these physiological reactions, people suffering from trauma have difficulty enjoying even simple pleasures like comforting touch, warm baths, and good food. It is as if these pleasures are "too much" for them. Part of the treatment for such individuals may involve the gradual desensitization of pleasure. This occurred in the middle part of the treatment with my client, Joan (Case Report 5.1), where I worked with her on feeling my touch as a comforting resource to which she could return when needed.

The third characteristic of restorative embodied self-awareness mentioned in Table 8.1 is the *balancing of closeness and distance*. This is the ability to feel our own emotions, for example, and distinguish them from those of the people around us. This differentiation of self and other can lead to making choices about keeping a necessary distance from people around whom one feels discomfort. This can be an emotional distance—as in accepting one's feelings about the other but remaining empathic and available—or a physical distancing as in separation from a long-term partner.

Awareness of linkages and boundaries can also lead to the choice to connect more closely to people with whom one feels safe and supported, to seek out secure attachments or to work toward the restoration of security in previously troubled long-term relationships. One can speak about this in terms of the emergence of the ability to *love* both self and other.

> When I accept myself, love is reborn. When nothing will make me abandon myself or hurt myself, love is present—I am loving myself in the same unconditional way that a parent can love a child. If I did not get this unconditional love the first time around, I must discover and re-create it in myself. (Caldwell, 1996, p. 139)

The ability to form loving, secure relationships with self and others requires a sense of safety, the ability to trust one's experience and not run away from it. "In my view love and hate are not opposites. The real polarity is between love and fear. Only when there is no fear, love flourishes" (Ghent, 1990).

Much of this work of loving, however, requires the final characteristic, a *willingness to be a process*. In relationship repair work—with parents, children, spouses, and other family members—one needs the ability to accept what can and cannot change, forgive others for past hurts, empathize with how others grew to become who they are, and let go of expectations for what should or should not happen. These are all aspects of realizing that *we will never have all the answers and that there will always be unsettling and painful feelings in embodied self-awareness*. Carl Rogers, one of the early transpersonal psychotherapists, describes one of his clients in this way.

> One client, at the conclusion of therapy, says in a rather puzzled fashion, "I haven't finished the job of integrating and reorganizing myself, but that's only confusing, but not discouraging, now that I realize this is a continual process . . . . It's exciting, sometimes upsetting, but deeply encouraging to feel yourself in action, apparently knowing where you are going even though you don't always consciously know where that is." Here is a personal description of what it seems like to accept oneself as a stream of becoming, not a finished product. (Rogers, 1961, p. 123)

This statement involves all the characteristics of Table 8.1: openness to and trust in experience, feeling the fuzziness of boundaries, and acceptance of what is, in the moment, always incomplete. How does a person know that, in spite of the uncertainties, it is possible to move into the world on their own as a relatively autonomous and aware being? This client's embodied self-awareness of "excitement" and "encouraging" is more diagnostic of success—because it is part of embodied self-awareness—than conceptual reasons and justifications.

The willingness to be a process cannot occur without letting go. It is important to reemphasize that *the final stage of restorative embodied self-awareness is letting go*. Letting go requires a sense of safety and a history of acquiring the necessary skills and resources to enhance and maintain embodied self-awareness. It is also important to realize that *it is our expectations coming from conceptual self-awareness that require letting go*. Holding on to a particular expectation for our own behavior, a particular pathway of change, a particular desire to have others be and behave in certain ways are all forms of grasping that show up in muscle tension and in the effects of stress on the body.

Again, Doug (Case Report 2.1), had the expectation from his family of needing to please others, a standard to which he held himself accountable. Doug's every interpersonal action was judged and evaluated against this standard in conceptual self-awareness. We have also talked about expectations for performance at work or for appropriate behavior in social situations, all of which lead to a suppression of embodied self-awareness because of the perceived need to meet the expectation at all costs.

One aspect of letting go is the ability to laugh at oneself and to laugh with others about miscommunications and differences of opinion. Research shows that humor is associated with the ability to form close interpersonal relationships and secure attachments, with enhanced empathy for others, and with emotional self-awareness (Hampes, 2001). A sense of humor increases as clients enter the final phases of treatment for PTSD, while people who are more likely to suppress emotions by ruminative worry show less of a sense of humor (Davidson et al., 2005; Kelly, 2002). Case Report 8.1 shows how humor develops in infancy in relation to embodied self-awareness.

Case Report 8.1
The Development of Humor in Relation to Linkages and Boundaries
---

This is report of another mother–infant dyad, Susan and Sheryl, from my longitudinal study of 13 dyads from which I have already reported the case of Peter and his mother (Case Report 5.2). I have published several articles on Susan and her mother (cf. Fogel & DeKoeyer-Laros, 2007) but here I emphasize a different element: the development of a sense of humor in Susan. This occurred around the age of 10 months and coincided with the emergence of increased awareness of self in relation to other along with the ability to signal "no" with a head shake. This example shows how humor is used to soften the formation of boundaries between self and other in the context of prior linkages. In addition to the video material we collected, Sheryl kept a journal of events related to the growth of Susan's communication.

When Susan was 10 months old, Sheryl wrote in her journal, "This has been a good visit for Grandma, she got a lot of firsts. Susan gives her first kiss, claps her hands, and learns how to shake her head 'no.'" This "no" is not the same as the "no" that emerges at the end of the second year. The head shaking of the 1-year-old is not defiant but rather a means to explore the nature of linkages and boundaries, the first steps in differentiating her own embodied self-awareness from that of the people in her life (Fogel, 2009).

In the same journal entry, Sheryl goes on to describe a new game related to "no" and showed how it emerged in the context of play. "Susan likes to play a game shaking her head 'no' when Mommy says 'yes.' She responds with a big smile and starts the game all over again. The beginnings of defiance? It's cute anyway." It is not uncommon for normally developing children of this age to appreciate and engage in games of teasing as a means to safely explore boundaries (Reddy, 2001).

In the videotaped observation reported here, Susan wants to play a game of pounding on the table of her high chair but Sheryl says, "I wanna show off how you can do pat-a-cake." Sheryl starts to sing and clap "pat-a-cake." While staring intently at her mother initiating the pat-a-cake game, Susan begins to pound the table again. Sheryl says, "No, show them how you clap, okay?" while taking Susan's hands and clapping them together. Both are smiling at each other while Sheryl begins singing and clapping once again. This time in response, Susan kicks against the bottom of the high chair in the same rhythm as Sheryl's claps. Sheryl laughs, "Are you doing it with your feet?" Susan drops her jaw in mock surprise, looks at her mother, and continues the kicking while laughing (see Figure 8.1).

It becomes clear to Sheryl that Susan is making a joke out of all of this and she asks, playfully, "You're not going to do it, are ya?" As shown in Figure 8.1, Susan looks at Sheryl, tilts her head to one side raising her eyebrows. She smiles and then shakes her head "no." Smiling at each other, the two begin a new game in which Sheryl playfully repeats the words *yes* and *no*, nodding and shaking her head. Susan shakes her head a few more times. They smile and laugh together.

Figure 8.1
Development of a sense of humor at 10 months of age

Infant Susan looks at Mother Sheryl. Sheryl wants Susan to play pat-a-cake but Susan does not want to join in the game. Susan tilts her head, and raises her eyebrows. She smiles and then shakes her head "no." They smile and laugh together. Mother finally says, with a smile and mock intonation, "You're not going to do it, are ya?"

The teasing pattern is new for this dyad and it reveals a coregulation and enjoyment of the embodied self-awareness of being different from each other. In this normally developing mother–infant pair, the mother can let go of her own expectations and celebrate the real developmental achievement that "no" implies for her daughter.

In the case of Peter and his mother (Case Report 5.2), we never saw Peter express "no" at this age in this conventional way that reveals a shared understanding. Peter expressed "no" by suppression and withdrawal, tensing his whole body and face, turning away, and freezing. He was not able to establish an embodied self-awareness of linkages and boundaries with his mother and he was not able to have the interoceptive awareness of the accomplishment of "no" and the enjoyment of sharing.

We also noticed that beginning in this session, Sheryl uses her voice more matter-of-factly, speaks faster and moves more with her entire body, a more adultlike speech pattern compared to the baby talk of all previous sessions. Other research shows that changes in maternal communication patterns are typically coordinated with changes in the infants' ability to engage in more advanced gestural and verbal discourse (Bruner, 1983; Stern, 1985; Trevarthen, 1998). Sheryl writes in her journal, "She likes to get my attention by wrinkling her nose into a funny face. It's her personality starting to blossom. She really is a happy baby."

Letting go of expectations is to surrender to what is rather than to hold out for what should be. Surrender has some of the following characteristics. It is not voluntary but just happens under facilitative conditions, it occurs in the subjective emotional present and without conceptual self-awareness, it enhances a discovery of one's identity and connection with other beings, there is an absence of domination and control, and it is accompanied by an acceptance of what is (Ghent, 1990). This type of surrender, of letting go, is often classified under the domain of spiritual work. Many religious traditions emphasize acceptance, forgiveness, compassion (or loving-kindness), and gratitude as key ingredients in spiritual growth.

Both gratitude and forgiveness have been linked to health and well-being, including lower sympathetic nervous system activation, lower blood pressure and reduced heart rate, fewer medications, fewer medical symptoms, less fatigue and less somatic complaints. Gratitude and forgiveness are also related to better interpersonal conflict management, lower expressed anger, and lower levels of perceived stress (Emmons & McCullough, 2003; Lawler et al., 2005;

Lawler-Row, Karremans, Scott, Ellis-Matityahou, & Edwards, 2008; Oman, Shapiro, Thoresen, Plante, & Flinders, 2008; Rozanski & Kubzansky, 2005).

A final aspect of the willingness to be a process is play and creativity. This is the ability to be immersed in the moment, to be engaged and to allow oneself to get "lost" in the flow states of normal absorption. Winnicott, who introduced the concept of the **True Self**, suggested the following three conditions for restorative embodied self-awareness:

(a) relaxation in conditions of trust based on experience;
(b) creative, physical, and mental activity manifested in play;
(c) the summation of these experiences forming the basis for a sense of self. (Winnicott, 1971, p. 56)

Another psychoanalyst, Ernst Schachtel, had this to say:

> Only the adult who is able to be completely absorbed, again and again, often for many hours and days, in an object that arouses his interest will be the one who enlarges his, and sometimes man's, scope of perception and of experience. A painter may spend many days, weeks or months, or even years, in looking at the same mountain, as Cézanne did, or at blades of grass or bamboo leaves or branches of a tree, as many of the Chinese and Japanese masters did, without tiring of it and without ceasing to discover something new in it. (Schachtel, 1959, p. 238)

If I may be permitted to translate this into more gender neutral language and in the terms developed in this book, the point being made is that normal absorption not only enlarges a person's own embodied self-awareness but it may also enlarge the embodied self-awareness—the capacity for the fullest possible human experience—in others who come into the contact with that person or with their work.

This is certainly the case of the embodied self-awareness practitioner whose personal explorations of the light and shadow of his or her own experiences make it possible for clients and students to grow into similar realms within themselves. It is also true of artists who illuminate human nature by exposing their own. And it is true of our friends and family whose inner journeys give them the compassion to provide the resources to allow us to find our own way in the darkness. *The ability to become normally absorbed in our own experience—far from being selfish and insular—is an act of love.* Why an act of love? "When I accept my experience, I commit one of the most loving acts possible—I stay out of the way of your experience" (Caldwell, 1996, p. 139).

Selfish absorption is pathological and dissociative. It cuts us off from others and therein lies its suppressive power. To truly love, to genuinely go outside of ourselves to meet another person absolutely requires that we know our True Self, our embodied self, that we have learned not to turn away from it but to love and embrace it for whatever it may be. Love is not about reason or logic, not about standards and judgments. Love is a meeting in the subjective emotional present of embodied beings who lay bare their vulnerabilities.

Table 8.1 describes what it might be like to have developed restorative embodied self-awareness. Regardless of how this ability is acquired—by means of some of the therapeutic interventions discussed in this book or via normal developmental processes—maintenance is necessary. Like any skilled activity, practice is required to keep it going. The remainder of this chapter lists a few of the ways this might be done: being with the natural world, embodied exercise, meditation, and spiritual pursuits. Many other means exist and have been mentioned already, including the arts and music, participation in supportive social activity, being touched literally and metaphorically, and slow food practices, to name only a few.

Perhaps the most important maintenance activity is the practice of coming home to ourselves, many times each day, to check in with our feelings and sensations in the subjective emotional present. Am I getting tired? Do my muscles ache? Do I need to change postures or movements? Am I breathing in a relaxed way? Am I sad, or lonely, or happy, or frustrated? Am I ignoring my pain? Are my boundaries being violated by unreasonable demands? How can I meet the expectations of others while remaining true to my own embodied experiences? And finally, do I have the self-awareness to realize that if—at this moment—I can't do these simple acts of self-care, can I promise myself to seek help sooner rather than later?

Earth as Home: Where It All Started

> *I still feel the crush of the last bed of wild violets in the Aleutian hills where one day I flung myself down in a rapture, knowing who I was, what the wild violets meant. Despite loss and disillusion, I count*

myself rich, fertile, and magical. I tell you now. You can go home
(Mary TallMountain, Kokuyon Athabascan writer,
quoted in Reichel-Dolmatoff, 1978, pp. 21–23).

If, then, we would indeed restore mankind . . . let us first be as simple and well as Nature ourselves, dispel the clouds which hang over our brows, and take up a little life into our pores
(Thoreau, 1910, p. 102).

The first quote is chosen as a resolution to the one in the first chapter, both by American Indian writers. Lame Deer in that earlier excerpt laments how people have forgotten their bodies. TallMountain tells us we can go home. Thoreau, America's well-known 19th-century naturalist, who was very familiar with Indian traditions, reminds us that there is hope for human restoration, respite from our troubles, by paying close attention to the natural world. This embodied wisdom about restoration can be found in all the ancient traditions.

I feel it with my body,
With my blood.
Feeling all those trees,
All this country . . .
When this wind blow you can feel it.
Same for country . . .
You can feel it.
You can look,
But feeling . . .
That make you.
(Big Bill Neidjie, Australian Aboriginal Elder, in McLuhan, 1994, p. 55)

There is an abundance of eloquent writing, using evocative language, about the restorative power of our connection to the natural world, to bring us to our senses, to remember who we are. There is now science to support the effects of the natural environment on embodied self-awareness. A **restorative environment** is one in which a person's energies and effectiveness are enhanced (Kaplan & Kaplan, 1989). Restorative environments depend upon the perceiver. It might be one's bedroom, bathroom, or kitchen. Locations of

Psychophysiology of Self-Awareness

natural beauty, however, are almost always restorative to almost everyone (Berto, 2005).

Restorative environments are places to recover from mental and physical fatigue and the stresses of daily life. They are places where one can "get away from it all," to seek a change, to rest. These are places that fascinate us, draw us into **engagement** and **normal absorption** in ways that allow us to forget our troubles and to find safety and comfort. Restorative environments occupy our attention by the opportunities they provide for play, exploration, curiosity, and rest. They are big enough to contain all of this, big like a mountain or a vast wilderness, but safe enough to allow us to enter them with relative ease (trails, maps, campgrounds, guides).

From the perspective of self-awareness, restorative environments have been shown to bring us more in touch with ourselves and remind us what is important in our lives; and they enhance our sense of connection—a feeling of "oneness"—between ourselves and other people, animals, plants and trees, and the earth itself (Berto, 2005; Kaplan & Kaplan, 1989). Mountains and fir trees reflected in a clear lake, waves breaking over a rocky shore, canyons and gorges cut through stone by rivers, the stillness of a forest floor: these places fill our senses, stir our emotions, and create clarity in the linkages and boundaries that define who we are in relation to all else. Our evolutionary history, millions of years of living in close proximity to nature, helps us to make sense of the simple and powerful effect that nature has on our embodied self-awareness.

> Our sensory organs are meant to perceive the world. The sensory capacities of the human ear were shaped by the sounds of the world, our smell formed through long associations with the delicate chemistries of plants, our touch by the nonlinear, multidimensional surfaces of Earth, our sight by the images that constantly flow into our eyes. Human senses emerged from immersion in the world. They are part of Earth. . . . (Buhner, 2004, p. 139)

Put another way, engagement and normal absorption in the non-human world is the natural state of our senses. Our aches, longings, tensions, and diseases arise partly from a lack of contact with nature, as if by losing that world we lose ourselves.

The rhythms of the earth mirror those of our bodies. Storms, volcanic eruptions, fires, floods, and earthquakes are periods of high activation and high energy compared to periods of calm in which the earth can recover from those events. The relaxed respiratory cycle of inhalation with sympathetic activation followed by an expiratory pause and parasympathetic exhalation is the most basic embodied manifestation of those earth cycles. On a daily basis there are periods of responding to challenges and hopefully times to come back to ourselves and rest. Weekdays contrast with weekends, annual work days with vacation periods. The earth as teacher reminds us about the importance of taking time for restoration.

Nature for Nurture

Restorative natural environments are especially important for children, and most especially for children who suffer from the effects of stress and trauma. With increasing urbanization, increasing use of technologies like Internet and cell phones, increasing demands for test taking performance in schools replacing the arts and physical education, increasing threats of crimes against children such as kidnapping and molestation, the opportunities for children to freely contact the natural world are becoming more limited. This has recently been called "nature deficit disorder" (Louv, 2005) and has led to calls for more outdoor free play.

Access to green areas such as parks and nearby countryside has been shown to enhance cognitive functioning, reduce stress, improve sensory and motor skills, and ameliorate the symptoms of attention deficit hyperactivity disorder in children (Kuo & Taylor, 2008; Nabhan & Trimble, 1994; Wells, 2000; Wells & Evans, 2003). The body is alive and well when children are getting their hands dirty, smelling plants, running through grass, climbing trees, walking in the surf, listening to birds, and watching the clouds roll by or the stars twinkle.

Even if children can't regularly be in a natural environment, one of the most accessible ways for children to contact nature is through animals. Animals have a special appeal to children, who often love pretending to be an animal, imitating animal movements and sounds, playing with and cuddling pets, and going to zoos and farms. Research shows that these encounters enhance self-awareness of linkages and boundaries because the child who pretends to be a bear, for example, knows that she is not a bear (Melson, 2001). Yet, at the same time, the child isn't merely play-acting but rather *becoming* the bear in a fundamentally embodied way. This is illustrated by observations in a classroom of children observing a turtle.

> Dawn crawls forward facing the turtle, crouches down on the rug, and tucks her head down. . . . She raises up suddenly, saying, "I know how to be a turtle in my shell." (Myers, 1998, p. 130)

After some discussion with the teacher about what a turtle can see, another child, Chris, tries to find out. "He is in 'turtle' position, crouched down over his legs, but holding his hands by his face, and pointing his head forward rather awkwardly" (Myers, 1998, p. 130). The children don't try to figure out what it is like to be a turtle by thinking about it. They embody the turtle to find out. Only then can there be a discussion.

> Mr. Lloyd: "How do you think it feels, what does it feel like to be a turtle?" Solly: "Safe . . . *safe*." Mr. Lloyd: "You think it feels safe, why?" Solly: "Because you have a shell." (Myers, 1998, p. 57).

Some scientists of animal and plant behavior have learned more about their chosen subjects by using this childlike strategy of becoming like them. Barbara Smuts, a biological psychologist, reports her experience of joining a wild baboon troop by being with them and acting like them as much as possible.

> The baboons had perfected the art of balancing hunger with the need for shelter. Just when it seemed inevitable to me that we would all get drenched, the troop would rise as one and race for the cliffs, reaching protection as big drops began to fall. For many months, I wanted to run well before they did. Then something shifted, and I knew without thinking when it was time to move. . . . I had gone from thinking about the world analytically to experiencing the world directly and intuitively. It was then that something long slumbering awoke inside me, a yearning to be in the world as my ancestors had done, as all creatures were designed to do by eons of evolution. Lucky me. I was surrounded by experts who could show the way. (Smuts, 2001, p. 299)

Pets also help children to identify and experience their emotions. Children use animal characters to express their own fears and desires, joys and sorrows, thereby enhancing their interoceptive self-awareness. Pets have been shown to serve as willing confidants, "hearing" about angry, sad, happy and secret experiences.

> Animal silence can be taken as assent, body movement and sound as encouragement. The wide-eyed, silent attentiveness of a dog, cat, or rabbit can seem like a deep pool of understanding. . . . Many children and their parents have described to me incidents when their dog, cat, bird, or even Vietnamese pot-bellied pig sensed their emotional distress and nuzzled, licked, or just gazed soulfully at them. (Melson, 2001, p. 48)

These studies point to the conclusion that restoration resulting from engagement with the natural world works in part because such contact enhances embodied self-awareness and that type of conceptual self-awareness which is informed by embodied self-awareness.

Embodied Exercise

A green wilderness or park area cannot be fully appreciated without moving through it, most especially on foot or on a human powered conveyance like a bicycle or skis. Playing with a pet involves movement and often physical exercise, like running or wrestling with a dog. Exercise can enhance our engagement with and absorption in nature as we learn to pay attention to our bodies while hiking a rocky slope, cycling on a dirt path, or walking through the woods.

Randomized clinical trial studies show that exercise enhances cognitive and brain function, improves health, and has protective effects that reduce disease formation and slow the neurodegenerative effects of aging. Sweat, generated by the sympathetic nervous system, has a similar composition as tears (see Box 4.1 and Table 5.3) with high levels of stress hormones that are thus cleared from the body reducing their toxicity to neural tissues. These studies also show, however, that exercise alone is not particularly helpful. Brain function is more likely to be improved when exercise is combined with diets rich in antioxidants, omega-3 fatty acids, and B-vitamins, in people who have regular and supportive social contacts, and—in support of the theme of this book—for people who are aware of their bodies while exercising (Kramer & Erickson, 2007).

Psychophysiology of Self-Awareness

Physiatry, also called physical medicine and rehabilitation, is a field of medicine dedicated to helping people restore optimal function following injuries to the muscles, bones, tissues, and nervous system resulting from illness, accidents, or medical interventions. Exercise, diet, and practices that enhance embodied self-awareness are recommended by physiatrists to help people recover from injuries, cancer, chronic pain, and many other conditions (Silver, 2004).

You cannot effectively play soccer or basketball or even hide-and-seek without noticing in embodied self-awareness how your own activity and muscular exertion interfaces with that of your teammates. Athletic training is about highlighting the athlete's self-awareness of how to move efficiently, but the athlete must cultivate the practice of self-awareness in the real-life situation of stress during competition to maintain and amplify the lessons from the trainer. Runners who scored higher on tests of embodied self-awareness, for example, used less oxygen, ran faster, and with less build-up of muscle tension (Martin, Craib, & Mitchell, 1995). Children who spent more time in structured recreational sports where they were taught to pay attention to their bodies had higher achievement scores in their school work and better social skills (Bar-Haim & Bart, 2006; Hofferth & Sandberg, 2001).

> To learn to swim in not merely a matter of reproducing mechanical patterns of movement. . . . To learn to swim is to grasp principles of buoyancy and propulsion which different strokes utilize in different ways and which competent swimmers can orient to as improvised play. (Crossley, 2007)

The same is not necessarily true for competitive varsity sports where money, winning, and stress take precedence, increasing the likelihood of injuries to both body and self-esteem.

Preschool children who were enrolled in a creative dance movement program as part of their Head Start experience had greater gains in social competence and more reductions in behavior problems than children who were given a program of learning to control attention without the accompanying awareness of movement used in creative dance (Lobo & Winsler, 2006). Similar effects have been observed with dance movement therapy programs for the elderly who would otherwise engage in sedentary activity, for depressed adolescents, and for female survivors of child sexual abuse (Hoban, 2000; Jeong et al., 2005; Mills & Daniluk, 2002). Introducing movement with awareness into the otherwise sedentary classroom has beneficial effects on both social and intellectual development for both normal and developmentally delayed children (DeGangi, Wietlisbach, Goodin, & Scheiner, 1993; Mullen & Cancienne, 2003).

Neuromotor degeneration is a common occurrence in older individuals. Balance difficulties, to take one example, are more frequent in the elderly, a serious health problem because of the risk of falling (Hobeika, 1999). Fear of falling, as one might expect, is related to higher postural sway and lower stability (Binda, Culham, & Brower, 2003; Burker et al., 1995). Impaired balance in the elderly is not, as one might think, only a problem of the vestibuloreceptors of the inner ear. Rather, *it is a gradual decline of sensitivity in the proprioceptors in muscles and tendons that are part of the body schema self-awareness neural network.* As the proprioceptor signals to the brain become attenuated, the body schema network is less able to provide corrective efferent (back to the body) signals to maintain homeostasis for balance (Jan et al., 2005; Shaffer & Harrison, 2007).

Movement training for the elderly that emphasizes embodied self-awareness for agility and movement coordination is more likely to improve balance and reduce the risk of falls than training focused only on building muscle strength (Liu-Ambrose, Khan, Eng, Janssen, et al., 2003; Liu-Ambrose, Khan, Eng, Lord, et al., 2004). Awareness-based training emphasizing the link between proprioception and vision is most helpful, and awareness is enhanced when people are either barefoot or in light athletic shoes with nonskid soles so that they can more completely sense their feet and ankles (Arnadottor & Mercer, 2000; Jan et al., 2005; Lord & Menz, 2000; Robitaille et al., 2005).

One of the best methods for improving balance in the elderly is Tai Chi, most likely because it emphasizes embodied self-awareness of slow, coordinated movements of different body parts in relation to each other and stability of stance in different postures (McGibbon et al., 2004; Taylor-Piliae, Haskell, Stotts, & Froelicher, 2006; Wolf et al., 2003). The Rosen Method of Movement (see Chapter 6) is also likely to be effective in alleviating age-related declines in self-awareness since it focuses on the embodied awareness of gentle movements, coordinated between different parts of the body, alone, with other people, and with music (see Case Report 8.2).

Case Report 8.2
Finding the Right Balance
[1]Jacqueline Fogel

More than a "work-out," a Rosen Movement class is a "work-in." In Rosen Method Movement, people learn to listen to their bodies in new ways as they begin to explore and expand preconceived limitations, reaching and extending their range of motion, stretching toward an inner vision of who they really are from the inside out. When people move from that dimension, so much more is possible. Feeling into their bodies, people remember how joyful it is to move to music.

The class segments are: Warm Up, Stretch, Circle, Across the Floor, and On the Floor. In Warm Up, the diaphragm awakens and moves bringing more air into the lungs—more breath into the body, so muscles can move with greater ease. The muscles of the body are enlivened as limbs begin to open, close, raise, or rotate, stimulating the flow of synovial fluid in the joint capsules. In the Stretch section the individual extends the limbs and torso, reaching to full extension, exploring their range of motion in the joints and extremities—going deeper into their body with slow, guided movement.

In Circle, participants hold hands to support one another in larger, lower body movement that requires balance. More complicated steps and sequences of movement are introduced in Circle, encouraging cross-body coordination (engaging both hemispheres of the brain). In Across the Floor, more energetic dancelike moves and combinations are incorporated as individuals move from one side of the room to the other, either with a partner or by themselves, to many different musical styles. People can now dance and move with ease after completely warming, stretching, and balancing. Finally, in On the Floor, people's spines are fully supported allowing the head, spine, extremities, and pelvis, to move without the fear of falling or hurting oneself. In addition to spinal support, On the Floor work encourages the body to interoceptively integrate all the movement and feelings that had been experienced throughout the previous segments of the class.

Sandy is a tiny woman in her late 70s, trim with bouncy, curly hair, and a contagious sense of humor. When Sandy first joined the Rosen Movement class I teach at a county senior center, she told me she had been in an automobile accident resulting in a crushed left leg. Four years after the accident, the left leg had healed but was somewhat shorter, less mobile, and less flexible than her right leg. During those first classes she attended, I noticed that when she stood, her hips were not level—her left hip was several inches higher than the right. When she walked, the left leg shuffled behind, with weight placed on the ball of the left foot and not on the whole foot. It seemed as though Sandy was counting on her right leg for assistance, not putting much weight on the left leg, and not trusting that leg to hold her.

Although people stand facing one another in a circle for Warm Up and Stretch, we do not hold hands until we come to the Circle segment of class, so that others can help support individuals with balance issues due to weak knees, ankles, hips, or feet. Holding hands in a circle enables all students to execute much larger moves while shifting balance from one leg to another. Body schema self-awareness grows as students learn to trust one another and feel where their body is in relation to itself and to the people next to them. Circle music often has a more upbeat rhythm, inviting dance and joyful engagement by the participants.

Here I describe a class that Sandy attended about 18 months after she began taking classes with me. I selected *The Beat Goes On*, by Sonny and Cher, for the Circle part of this class. Sandy particularly likes this song. With the first note she begins to wag her tail, clap her hands, and move dance-strutting into closer range as we reach for each other's hands. I guided the students to turn their left shoulders into the center of the circle and begin walking around in a forward motion, still holding hands—heel to toe and backwards, toe to heel—attending to the sensations in the feet and ankles. One time when I asked them to reverse directions, JoAnne, one of the tallest women in class, didn't turn with the rest of the group, bumping into her neighbors, walking against the flow.

We all laugh as Carol yells out, "Glad it's you today and not me causing the train wreck!" Carol, a plump, lively woman in her mid-70s, with short spiky white hair, twinkling eyes, and a pixie smile, goes on, "Every time I hear this song, I want to move. It gives me a great feeling of energy and happiness. I feel energetic and younger. I can really feel the beat." In the 2½ years since she first began coming to class, Carol has lost quite a bit of weight, but more importantly has lost inches in her "girth," as she fondly calls it, has become more toned, and is more confident in her moves. She continues, "My family has said I move better, feel better about everything in general, seem to feel happier, and have a better outlook on life since I began coming to movement classes. I feel better about myself." Outside of class, Carol has told me that her husband noted, "She has always been a 'go getter', but now she goes more gracefully."

In the past month, I have noticed that Sandy had become more confident and trusting of her left leg as she moved in class. Today, there was something different about Sandy. She put more weight onto the left leg and more evenly distributed her weight across the entire foot as she raised her right knee up higher opening her right hip as she rotated the leg to the side (a move I've called "The Barn Door"). Katherine said, "Would you look at Sandy, before we know it she's going to be trying out for the Rockettes." Once again everyone broke into peals of laughter as I imagined all of us in feathered and rhinestone costumes kicking up our heels on Broadway. The shared joy, emotion, and sense of community enhance interoception in all the students as they experience themselves doing lifts and kicks they never thought they were capable of executing.

Sandy laughed and said,

Yeah, in the last several weeks my leg feels stronger, I can do more on it and I think it's because of the different moves we do with our legs. The other day I got up onto the ladder to paint— (I gasped!). I needed to stretch a little to get to the spot I wanted to reach. I thought about some of the moves we do in *Stretch* and *Circle* as I climbed the two steps. I remembered the 'Barn Door' and it seemed like just the right thing to do. I shifted my weight, grounded myself on the rung of the ladder, and was able to paint the spot. So today I thought I'd try to see how much I could do while balanced on my left leg.

I was both astonished and pleased at the same time. I wanted my students to gain a sense of confidence in what their bodies could do, but I didn't expect them to translate their ever increasing skills and abilities to balancing on a ladder. I could see, however, that Sandy was becoming more creative with her body, translating information she had gotten in class into everyday activities in her life. She seemed to feel safer in how she moved and less threatened by what she had perceived as a hindrance to her mobility. I said, "It seems like we're all becoming stronger, more capable, and more confident in our ability to move, but please be especially careful on ladders!" We all clapped for Sandy's newly gained sense of mastery and found partners to move with Across the Floor. There was a sense of resonance among the group, as they could all feel their own bodies move in ways they had not expected.

After class JoAnne came up to me. In her late 60s, JoAnne is somewhat younger than many of the other students in the class. She seems to have some right-left dyslexia and sometimes gets confused when we change directions or shift between right and left legs. She began, "After missing a few classes, I was weak in my ankles and a little shaky, but after moving in class today, I feel much better and know I have to continue coming, not only for my balance, but for my well-being." She said that she was aware of changes in her own body and was so excited about what she saw Sandy do today. She continued, "These classes have made my whole life better. I feel it all week, not just when I'm here. I know my balance, like Sandy's has improved immensely. I'm getting better. We all are!"

[1]Case Report 8.2 is used with permission of Jacqueline Fogel, MA, LMT, a Rosen Method Movement Teacher, NIA Instructor, and Watsu Practitioner.

As this case demonstrates, just exercising in a group class increases the chances of continuing to exercise, especially in the elderly, because of the social rewards of affiliation. Group classes also bring a new self-awareness about one's body and abilities reflected in the eyes of classmates (Burdette & Whataker, 2003; Denault & Poulin, 2007; Pellegrini & Smith, 1998; Riediger, 2007).

All of this research on awareness-based movement has important implications for how to structure exercise programs for not only building cardiovascular fitness but also changing one's sense of self. Being a member of a team, or a community of fellow exercisers, adds value to one's own activity. Another benefit of self-focused attention during movement and exercise is the building of new neural pathways across the entire neuraxis related to embodied self-awareness and health. As the student comments in Case Report 8.2 reveal, this can create a sense of a more integrated body, a sense of safety in the body and its movements and sensations, improvements in sensory and motor function, cardiovascular and respiratory function, and immune system function. It can also contribute to the rebuilding of damaged spinal and brain tissue due to injury and stroke, and to partially reverse the otherwise degenerative processes of normal aging (Hoban, 2000; Wolpaw & Tennissen, 2001).

Embodied Meditation

Mindfulness—derived from the practice of meditation—is one of the terms being used currently for one type of embodied self-awareness, the ability to stay focused on the subjective emotional present, to notice one's feelings and sensations whether positive or negative, to remain nonreactive and nonevaluative to those feelings and sensations, and to avoid conceptual judgment. The term *mindfulness* is derived from the meditation practice of sitting quietly and either (1) simply noticing sensations and thoughts without holding onto them, or (2) training oneself to stay focused on particular emotions or body sensations, whether pleasant or unpleasant (Epstein, 1998; Goleman, 1977; Hayward, 1987; Stern, 2004; Wallace, 2000). Mindfulness can also occur in standing and movement meditations derived from ancient Eastern practices such as Tai Chi, Yoga, and the martial arts.

A number of scientific self-report measures have been developed to assess an individual's degree of mindfulness. Typical items from these instruments are given in Table 8.2. As might be expected from the association between embodied self-awareness, self-regulatory homeostasis, and health, people who score higher on mindfulness scales are less anxious, less ruminative, and less likely to suffer from pathological absorption. They are also less likely to be affected by life stress and they are less depressed (Brown & Ryan, 2003). These effects of meditation are mediated by the activation of parasympathetic relaxation responses including reduced heart rate, blood pressure, and metabolism, accompanied by enhanced immune and digestive function (Benson, Greenwood, & Klemchuk, 1975).

Table 8.2
Items on mindfulness measurement scales

Positive items	Reversed items
I accept myself as I am.	I could be experiencing some emotion and not be aware of it until sometime later.
I am able to smile when I see how sometimes I make my life difficult.	I find it difficult to stay focused on what's happening in the present.
In difficult situations, I can pause without immediately reacting.	I tend not to notice feelings of physical tension or discomfort until they really grab my attention.
I experience moments of inner peace and ease, even when things get hectic and stressful.	I get so focused on the goal I want to achieve that I lose touch with what I'm doing right now to get there.
I remain present with sensations and feelings even when they are unpleasant or painful.	I snack without being aware of what I'm eating.

Sources: Brown & Ryan, (2003), Walach, Buchheld, Buttenmüller, Kleinknect, & Schmidt, (2006).

While the characteristics of mindfulness are common to all the embodied self-awareness disciplines discussed in this book, mindfulness research has focused primarily on the practice of meditation. The ability of experienced meditators to focus attention on emotions and body sensations shows up in neuroimaging studies with activation in the dorsolateral prefrontal cortex (working memory), the ACC and insula (emotion), and parietal cortex (body schema) (Brefczynski-Lewis, Lutz, Schaefer, Levinson, & Davidson, 2007; Lazar et al., 2000; Lutz, Brefczynski-Lewis, Johnstone, & Davidson, 2008). Meditators were less distractible on attention focusing tasks and their ability to focus was correlated with the amount they meditated each day (Chan & Woollacott, 2007).

Psychophysiology of Self-Awareness

In studies comparing expert (having had more than 10,000 hours of meditation practice) vs. novice meditators who were asked to meditate on compassion and loving-kindness, experts had higher activation in the insula and ACC, which was correlated with self-reported intensity of the meditative state. Experts were also more sensitive to distress sounds during meditation, showing that these areas of the brain increase sensitivity and compassion to the distress of others (Lutz et al., 2008). Long-term meditators were also more able to discriminate subtle emotional feelings and expressions (Nielsen & Kaszniak, 2006).

When guided meditations are oriented specifically to increasing embodied self-awareness without the goal of changing anything, this proves to be the most helpful in ultimately inducing the ability to stay in the subjective emotional present with feelings and sensations, increased relaxation, reduction of pain, and a return of well-being. Meditation has also been shown to increase positive interpersonal qualities such as empathy, gratitude, and forgiveness. Mindfulness meditation has produced these effects in treatments for sleep disorders, obsessive compulsive disorder, cancer, headache, dystonia, and stress reduction. It is also useful in helping people prepare for and recover from medical interventions. Relaxation in meditation, in particular, is accompanied by parasympathetic activation and a reduction of muscle tension (Andrasik & Holroyd, 1980; Borkovec, Kaloupek, & Slama, 1975; Deepak & Behari, 1999; Esch, Fricchione, & Stephano, 2003; Gevirtz, Hubbard, & Harpin, 1996; Hutcherson, Seppala, & Gross, 2008; Kabat-Zinn, 1994; Lutz et al., 2008; Mandle, Jacobs, Arcari, & Domar, 1996; Rausch, Gramling, & Auerbach, 2006; Shannahoff-Khalsa, 2004; Sime & DeGood, 1977; Tacón, Caldera, & Ronaghan, 2004; Wallace & Shapiro, 2006).

Various forms of "relaxation" therapies have been devised for treating similar problems as those to which mindfulness treatments have been applied (Benson, 1975). Relaxation can be done by guided meditation and self-monitoring of different body areas, starting from the head (scalp, face, eyes, and tongue) and moving down the body, so-called **progressive relaxation methods**. They can also be done using **biofeedback**, in which people are given access to physiological indicators of sympathetic nervous system activation and asked to alter body state to reduce arousal. These methods have similar effects on relaxation and well-being as those found for mindfulness meditation (Deckro et al., 2002; Engel, Jensen, & Schwartz, 2004; Lundgren, Carlsson, & Berggren 2006).

Many of the ancient practices of embodied self-awareness are framed in the context of art and beauty. In expert practitioners, the meditative movements of Tai Chi, for example, have a grace all their own. The same could be said for the artistic aspects of athletics, dance and music, and literature. In all these cases, practitioners blend heightened embodied self-awareness with creative expression and an aesthetic sensibility. All the arts have the possibility to heighten embodied self-awareness and our connections with others and with the spiritual dimensions of being human.

Embodied Spirituality

The body is the harp of your soul,
And it is yours to bring forth sweet music from it or confused sounds.
—(Gibran, 1997, p. 44)

In all the world's religions, the human body is the vehicle through which spiritual transformation may take place. Catholic saints suffer countless wounds, pain, and death, sometimes self-inflicted. Buddhists sit in unmoving postures for extended periods, enduring deprivation and discomfort. Ecstatic worship—as in Hasidism, Sufism, and Pentacostalism—may involve singing, chanting, dancing, whirling, rocking, speaking in tongues, and the laying on of hands, all meant to induce trance and meditative states. Orthodox Jews bind their foreheads and forearms with leather straps, cover their heads with a shawl, and rock while they pray. Yogis ritualize and regulate their breathing and Tantrics their sexual and other body functions. Catholic priests, some yogis, nuns, Shakers, and Buddhist monks abstain from sex. Ordinary Muslim, Christian, and Jewish worship requires sitting and standing, kneeling and bowing, prostration, chanting and praying, all in a community of others. From baptism to Bar Mitzvah, from birth to the beyond, the body is enlivened in awareness and its joys and pains tolerated, celebrated, and regulated by ritual (Levin, 1985).

What is taken into the body is prescribed for some spiritual seekers. Fasting occurs at Ramadam, Yom Kippur, and Lent. Wine, holy water, peyote, tobacco, wafers, and other substances may be ingested in the context of sacred ceremonies, each representing or calling forth an embodied sentiment, movement, or posture. And much is not to be eaten or drunk, or is prohibited as not kosher.

Spiritual quests call people to move from their habitual locales to other less familiar ones. Some make a pilgrimage to Mecca amidst multitudes, some crawl up rocky slopes on hands and knees past the stations of the cross, some venture into the desert for days and nights without food or water seeking a vision. Some are called to face the doubt, deprivation, and disease of missionary work. Ritual guides people into the mind and body transformations of coming of age, the consecration of sexual unions, and dying. Many of these practices have been received from prior generations, from ancient rituals passed down. These practices, invoking both the pain and pleasure of the flesh, hold a place of reverence for followers and have been repeated ceremoniously, religiously, daily, weekly, or yearly over millennia.

Religion has found a need to enshrine sensing, moving, and feeling within ritual practice as a pathway to the spiritual growth of believers. The ancients discerned, and those who followed verified, that particular embodied practices led to renewed closeness to a sense of God and to all living things, a cleansing purification of the body and soul, or a lifting of the weight of hopelessness and despair. Like restorative environments, these practices teach us that embodied self-awareness can contribute profoundly to mental and physical health, to the growth of the mind, and to the expansion of what it means to be human.

The epic tenacity of ritualized embodied practice is one source of evidence about the importance of paying attention to the body for a human life of engagement, normal absorption, and restoration. Ritual institutionalizes embodied self-awareness and provides a legitimate reason for believers to come back home to the body, again and again. One could say that *practicing embodied self-awareness on a regular basis is a spiritual quest, or that practicing embodied self-awareness leads to greater awareness of things deemed spiritual: feelings of connection, compassion, love and gratitude, forgiveness, surrender, and acceptance.*

An increasing number of research studies on health and well-being are taking spiritual and religious practices into account, particularly with regard to the role of these practices in recovery from stress and trauma. People who survive war, genocide, fires, and sinking ships, for example, often mention religion or spirituality as the most important factor in helping them endure. Veterans Affairs Medical Centers in the United States have found that incorporating religious rituals into treatment facilitates therapeutic outcomes for PTSD. For people in general, religious openness, readiness to face questions related to the meaning of one's life, and religious participation are also associated with enhanced recovery from PTSD (Weaver, Flannelly, Garbarino, Figley, & Flannelly, 2003).

It may be that both religious practices and the social benefits of affiliation in a religious community become **resources** for helping in recovery (Shaw, Joseph, & Linley, 2005; Taylor, 2001). Other research shows that the direct participation of the body in religious ritual and practice helps individuals to remember and finally feel suppressed emotions from loss and trauma, which enhances embodied self-awareness, which in turn promotes healing of physical and emotional wounds (Kovach, 2002; Norris, 2005). The ability of religious practice to evoke participatory memories of emotion has been linked specifically to the interoceptive neural networks that are known to be activated during meditation (Blakeslee, 2008; Norris, 2005)

The research on the importance of religion and spirituality has turned up another important finding: recovery from traumatic life events leads to a greater involvement in spiritual or religious life pursuits *regardless of whether or not spiritual practices were used in the treatment of trauma*. Research shows, for example, that religious converts report a greater number of traumatic events during childhood than nonconverts and a majority of people who suffered trauma reported that religion and spirituality became more important to them as they reached a state of recovery (Shaw et al., 2005). This appears to occur because recovery from trauma leads people to question their assumptions about what is important in life. The therapeutic, family, and religious resources that help in trauma recovery are like restorative environments: they lead to questions about the meaning of one's life that are at the core of embodied and conceptual self-awareness. On the other hand, some people respond to trauma with greater cynicism and a loss of religious beliefs due to feeling abandoned by God, typically associated with unresolved traumatic emotions or grief (Shaw et al., 2005).

For many but not for all, *experiencing and resolving the effects of trauma can be a pathway to developing a more encompassing sense of self*. Depending upon the person, this could mean any of the things listed in Table 8.1: acceptance, forgiveness, humor, compassion, gratitude. In trauma recovery, we come to realize that the events surrounding the trauma and the body's protective

Psychophysiology of Self-Awareness

response to the threat of those events are beyond our control. The "I" of our conceptual self-awareness—who we think we are, what we think we can do—has to be revised to more accurately reflect what we actually did and felt and lost in that fateful assault by a chunk of the universe much bigger than that "I." Recovery and restoration occurs at the point when the "I" feels and accepts and forgives the human frailties arising in embodied self-awareness, when the "I" becomes the True Self.

Reprise: The Body as a Dynamic System

The neural networks for embodied self-awareness, for threat and safety, and for immune function all link together as a complex and highly dynamic system into the capacity for self-regulation and homeostasis. The different cases presented in this book show how particular linkages across this whole-body network may produce individually unique sensitivities for embodied self-awareness, individually unique symptomologies, and individually unique pathways for recovery.

Because of my personal relationship to the effects of visual experience on embodied self-awareness and well-being (see Case Report 8.3), I will focus in this section on the eyes as the entry point in one final example of the holistic nature of our embodied self-awareness and its links across the entire system of body function. Our eyes, it turns out, are in multiple ways connected to many different types of neural networks. One navigates in space via vision and the path of movement changes the direction of the gaze. Our visual system is capable of registering a wide perceptual array of shape, size, depth and distance, color, texture, and movement.

The eyes are related to emotion, as are the other sense organs, each in their own way. Research has revealed, for example, that when presented with both happy and angry faces, people who are more anxious tend to avert their gaze from the angry faces. This shows that gaze direction is related to the threat and safety neural network, and also that a history of threat leads to a diminished ability to see the world for what it is, to really see, accept, and empathize with different types of emotions displayed by other people (Rohner, 2004). In another study, research participants who were given oxytocin showed greater visual attention to all types of emotional faces and especially to the eyes, suggesting that a sense of safety enhances interpersonal visual connection and empathy (Guastella, Mitchell, & Dadds, 2008).

Aside from the visual sensations of the eyes, their movements are linked into the threat and safety neural network. Eye movements during REM sleep have been shown to activate the HPA axis in a restorative way that helps to consolidate emotional memories, by stimulating the amygdala's cortisol receptors (Wagner & Born, 2008). Repeated and compulsive eye and head turning, on the other hand, are characteristics of threat **vigilance.**

During **Eye Movement Desensitization and Reprocessing (EMDR)** therapy, patients are asked to imagine traumatic or difficult situations while at the same time being asked to visually attend to an external stimulus that alternates from one side to another. Typically, patients follow alternating flashing lights, one on the left and one on the right, or the therapist's finger movements, with their eyes. The treatment can also be done with listening to sounds alternating to the left and right of the head, or by touching in left-right alternation. Although controversial, the treatment appears to be successful for some cases of PTSD, first by increasing arousal and participatory memory with body sensations, then decreasing it, followed by the ability to integrate the autobiographical memory into conceptual self-awareness (Welch & Beere, 2002).

When it works, EMDR heightens embodied self awareness, allowing the individual to stay in the subjective emotional present with previously suppressed memories and emotions. One explanation for its effect is that the demand to continue switching attention to alternating sides while experiencing embodied self-awareness helps the person to integrate the left and right cerebral hemispheres, the right presumed to be more related to unfelt emotions and fears, the left more to attention and conceptual processing (Schore, 2003; Siegel, 2003; Welch & Beere, 2002). Another possible explanation, which seems more plausible in light of the neurophysiology of embodied self-awareness, is that the alternating attention to the external stimulus, coupled with attention to embodied feelings, allows for attention in the prefrontal cortex to be decoupled from previous patterns of avoidance and suppression (Welch & Beere, 2002).

Psychophysiology of Self-Awareness

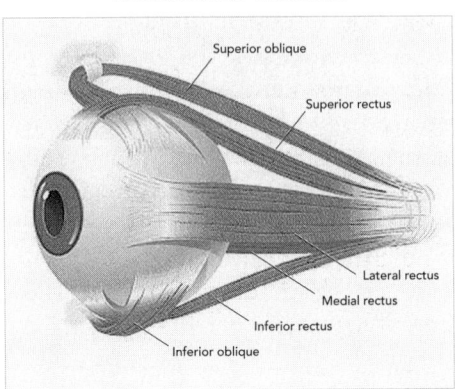

Figure 8.2
Extraocular muscles

This is similar, then, to the flexible patterns of eye movements in conditions of safety and of REM sleep compared to the more impulsive gaze alternations of **vigilance**. Although any muscle in the body can become tense in threat conditions, the extraocular muscles behind the eyes become tense in a way that restricts the free pursuit of the gaze and that consequently causes facial muscle tension and eye strain (see Figure 8.2). These extraocular muscles differ from the ciliary muscle inside the eye that changes the shape of the lens to focus images on the retina, and the iris which is a muscle that changes the size of the pupil. The ciliary muscle may also develop undue tension when visual acuity is poor.

There are many types of Feldenkrais Awareness Through Movement lessons that involve eye movements. By slowly moving the eyes left-right, up-down, or rotating them, one can begin to feel how these movements, and the patterns of holding in the extraocular muscles, are linked to patterns of muscle tension in the head, face, tongue, mouth, neck, chest, abdomen, and pelvis. One way this linkage between tension in the eyes muscles corresponds to tension elsewhere is because head turning, linked to visual search, involves muscles in the neck including the scalenes and sternomastoids, which are linked, across their attachment bones of the upper ribs, sternum, and clavicle, to the breathing muscles. And, these muscles are linked via respiratory function with its multiple ties to the autonomic nervous system, to the diaphragm and to muscles in the abdomen and pelvis. These respiratory muscles attach to other bones in the rib cage, spine, and pelvis, bones to which other pelvic and leg muscles are attached. Eye movement, then, can evoke referred pain, tension, and relaxation in muscles throughout the body.

Another link in this complex system of relationships between the eyes and other nearby muscles is due in part to how these muscles are innervated. There are a number of different cranial nerves that serve the movements and secretions of the eye. The oculomotor nerve (3rd cranial nerve) provides efferent signals to regulate the movement of the extraocular, ciliary, and iris muscles. The trochlear nerve (4th cranial nerve) controls eye rotation. The link between the eyes and the rest of the face and head, however, is via the trigeminal nerve (5th cranial nerve) which has three (tri) branches: ophthalmic, maxillary, and mandibular.

The ophthalmic branch innervates the lachrymal glands, upper eyelid, cornea, nasal mucosa, the skin on the tip of the nose, and the skin on the upper eyelid, forehead and scalp above the eyes. The maxillary branch innervates the upper teeth and gums, the nasal cavity, soft and hard palates, upper lip, side of the nose, lower eyelid, the skin on the cheek and side of the head behind the eye, and many of the sinuses. Finally, the mandibular branch serves the temporomandibular joint, skin over part of the ear, the skin above the ears, oral mucosa, the front 2/3 of the tongue, the floor of the mouth, lower teeth and gums, lower lips (including the muscles that control the lip retraction when smiling), the muscles of the neck responsible for chewing and swallowing, and a muscle in the ear that helps to damp loud noises. It is remarkable that the same nerve plays a role in sadness and happiness, dental pain in the teeth and bones, sinus congestion, tongue sensations and movements (but not taste), chewing and swallowing as well as some of the movements involved in vocalizations like speech, laughter, and crying.

When some of the muscles innervated by the trigeminal nerve contract, they inspire contractions in adjacent muscles linked to other nerves. Strong contractions of the zygomatic muscle of the trigeminal nerve that pulls the lips upward for smiling and laughter, for example, activates contractions of the orbicularis oculi muscle that surrounds each of the eyes. Innervated by the facial nerve (7th cranial nerve), the orbicularis oculi muscles has an outside portion that lifts the cheeks upward in both intense crying and intense smiling (crow's feet behind the eyes), and an inner portion that makes the eyes squint. Recall that squinting was characteristic of the tense facial expressions displayed by the infant Peter in Case Report 5.2.

Psychophysiology of Self-Awareness

This same facial nerve supplies parasympathetic innervation to the lachrymal glands. Emotional tears from the lachrymal glands are stimulated by the parasympathetic outflow. Emotional tears are related to different types of emotions (tears of joy or sorrow), to help cleanse the body of toxic stress hormones, and to increase parasympatheticly induced relaxation (see Box 4.1 and Table 5.3).The facial nerve also provides motor control over the stapedius muscle of the inner ear that helps to dampen sounds from the environment to regulate the effects of auditory stimulation on the body (responsive to safety and threat), taste sensations to the front of the tongue, and the movements of many of the muscles of facial expression.

Isolating and exploring the movements of any of the facial and eye muscles via embodied self-awareness exercises and treatments will result, typically, in the activation of sensations and changes in muscle tension across the face, neck, and jaw, and possibly in other parts of the body. Further exploration of these same movements can lead to an identification of the emotional suppression that may be held within the face, which may possibly be related to whole body patterns of muscle tension, all in some way linked to the eyes. Case report 8.3 gives an example of these eye-related patterns in a particular individual.

Case Report 8.3
The Eyes Have It: A Personal History

Conceptual thinking is not necessarily directed toward conceptual self-awareness. The former refers to the principles of logic and the relationships between the concepts of a particular field of inquiry, such as neuroscience or psychology. The latter is the network of concepts about the self. These concepts may or may not be resonant with embodied self-awareness. In writing this book, I was challenged in several ways. The first was to integrate conceptual and scientific thinking into a book that is essentially about non-conceptual embodied self-awareness. The second was to link these conceptual principles of embodied self-awareness to my own embodied self-awareness and conceptual self-awareness of my history of personal experiences. And the third was to use my embodied self-awareness to find a reasonably comfortable balance between the physical act of writing on a computer and the regulation of muscle strain and tension.

As I wrote in earlier chapters about the stress and tension generated in computer office work, it exaggerated awareness of my own body doing these things: how I used my head, neck, and eyes for screen-reading, how I held my upper torso and placed my arms and hands at the keyboard, how I was breathing. I often adjusted my posture, the position of my chair, and my distance to the keyboard and screen. Just as often, however, I lost track of my body, caught up in and not wanting to let go of my expectation to reach a certain (arbitrary, conceptually arrived at) goal at the end of each writing session, or becoming totally absorbed in the emotional rush of the act of creation.

Inevitably, invariably, and inexorably the writer's "high" and the self-imposed deadlines took a toll. When I "woke up" from these binges, my neck and shoulders would be achy, my face tense, and my eyes tired. I would also be grouchy and discouraged. I did, fortunately, follow these excesses with exercise, meditation, music, or just enjoying life. In these phases of relief and restoration, I would vow to myself, "Never again." The next day, however, often brought the same sad story.

Over the time period that I was actively writing this book, it took me at least 4 months to break into this cycle and to write at a pace that was more kind to my body. Having gotten enough of the manuscript drafted by then to feel as if I could eventually complete it was no small contributor to my ability to relax and let go of all those expectations. Also, knowing that I had successfully worked through other pains and stresses in my life made me hopeful about this challenge. I'm not unhappy with this process—in hindsight, when I'm not aching—because it allowed me to remember and integrate the relationship between my eyes and both my embodied and conceptual self-awareness.

Eye strain comes from tense extraocular, orbicularis oculi, and ciliary muscles. Research available on eye strain shows it to be related to stress in the workplace, especially around computer work in high pressure environments (Seppälä, 2001). Eye strain occurs in individuals who are highly sensitive to environmental stress and is often compounded with muscle tension in the face, jaw, upper back and shoulders, most likely because of links across the trigeminal nerve and the muscular demands of holding the head upright and stationary for long periods (Hollis, Allen, Fleischmann, & Aulak, 2007; Treaster, Marras, Burr, Sheedy, & Hart, 2006).

Psychophysiology of Self-Awareness

A condition that results in temporarily compromised visual acuity (central serous chorioretinopathy) has been linked to a combination of stressful life events and suppression of emotions related to those events (Conrad et al., 2007; Middleton, Sinason, & Davids, 2008). Because the body is a complex system and because each of us grows our physiological linkages in a different way, each person has their own version of an Achilles heel, particular parts of the body that "act up" with pain or strain when the person is under stress.

Myopia (nearsightedness) arises from an inability of the lens to focus images clearly on the retina because of an elongated eyeball. In compensation, the ciliary and inner orbicularis oculi muscles strain to push the focal length back farther and to compress the eyeball from the front while the extraocular muscles strain to compress the eyeball from the back. Depending upon the person, these efforts to see more clearly may be accompanied by craning the head and neck forward resulting in additional neck and upper body strain.

I am extremely myopic and have been so since birth. This was not diagnosed and corrected, however, until I was in the third grade. That means I lived for over 9 years with limited visual abilities. Perhaps this explains in part why as a child, I was easily frightened, wary of social contacts, and extremely shy. I remember having difficulty looking people in the eye, avoiding their gaze, and suppressing my emotions. If I could not clearly see the other person, then I could not know how they might react to my feelings. It was better to hide and I learned to do that in order to avoid encounters with particular people. As I got older, I began to acquire the emotional, sensory, and physical strength to feel safer in the world but the childhood experiences left a lasting imprint on my physiology with muscle tension in the eyes, face, and elsewhere across my body along with continued wariness, especially in some types of social situations.

As a child I was hypersensitive to other sensory experiences: easily irritated by woolen clothing, the texture of certain foods (like peach skins), bright lights, and loud sounds. Perhaps it was an excessive focus on the near environment, including my own body, that helped to develop my acute interoceptive self-awareness? I thought for a long time that these hypersensitivities were a kind of curse. Only recently have I come to realize that I was gifted with a precocious talent for interoception.

Fortunately, there is now a growing recognition that some proportion of young children have sensory sensitivities similar to mine. **Sensory integration dysfunction** is believed to be a neurologically based hypo- or hyper-sensitivity of some or all of the basic five senses. It is often seen together with other neurological disorders such as autism and ADHD but it may occur on its own. Treatments tend to focus on developing in the child a tolerance for exposure to more intense sensations, self-awareness of the effects of this exposure, and self-regulation in handling it (Rogers & Ozonoff, 2005; Schaaf & Miller, 2005).

Because of the closeness of my childhood visual world, I spent many joyful hours investigating what I could see up close, leaves and stones and insects. I loved physical activities like running, climbing, and biking. When I began school in the first grade I was unable to see the teacher or read the blackboard, although no one, especially me, was aware of that limitation. I would carve and color my desk, poke the person sitting in front of me, and chase the girls so I could hug them. For these transgressions and annoyances I was punished with extra homework and by being forced to stay after school. My mother could not comprehend how her "good" little boy had so quickly become a problem child. I am forever grateful to Mrs. Grissom, my third grade teacher, wherever she may be now, for discovering my visual limitations, recommending an eye exam from the school nurse, and thus—in that simple act of noticing something about me—changing the course of my educational career and indeed, my whole life.

There is a correlation between visual impairment in children and introversion as well as behavior problems (Preisler, 1997). In adults, some studies find a correlation between severe myopia and introversion while others do not (Lauriola, 1997; van de Berg, Dirani, Chen, Haslam, & Baird, 2008). This may be due to differences in methodologies, to the alteration of personality with age as new resources for self-regulation are acquired, and to corrected vision. Even these supports, however, do not completely wipe clean the slate of early experience and the already grown cellular networks that supported those experiences.

> In my own case of early childhood visual impairment, in spite of most of a lifetime of corrected vision, I have never escaped the feeling that touch and sound are more real, more sensual expe-

riences than vision. I often have the feeling of *not believing my eyes*. When I look at a mountain landscape, I cannot psychologically connect with it until I have the opportunity to walk in those mountains and touch the earth. I feel the most *myself* during athletic activities, listening to music, and when I speak or write. (Fogel, 1997, p. 93)

Although I currently thrive in close and safe interpersonal relationships and enjoy secure attachments with my family and close friends, I remain subject to involuntary feelings of anxiety and avoidance when thrust into social situations that are busy and noisy, especially when I do not already know the people who inhabit those places and when I am without the companionship of people I know well.

Ann Truitt (1982), a sculptor, also ascribes her choice of medium and her "interiority" to the fact that her myopia was not discovered until she was in the fifth grade. On a visit to Florence, Italy in 1997, just wandering through the city, I happened to discover an exhibit of sculpture intended for the blind. The curators had collected some original works in stone and bronze, and also human body size reproductions of some of the famous works, such as Michelangelo's David, found in that Renaissance capitol and set them up under the porticos of a 14th century monastery courtyard. Visitors were invited to explore these objects with their hands. I felt suddenly like a child, thinking: "You mean I can actually . . . touch this?"

I took off my glasses, closed my eyes, and became totally absorbed for hours. I arrived at a new grasp of these works, many of which I have only seen before, and of sculpture in general, a way of knowing that I never could have gained by looking alone. The detailed indentations and protrusions that represented muscle and bone under skin, rendered into stone or bronze, felt as if I were touching a living person, evoking a feeling of voyeuristic shame that eventually passed into unrestrained curiosity and waves of tactile pleasure. Touching the male nudes was equally inspiring as touching the females. Now that I think of it, this chance event may have opened a gateway to the possibility—three years later—of beginning my training as a touch therapist.

The elongation of my eyeball as a result of myopia has led in recent years to a detached retina, frightening, but thankfully laser-repaired without further incident. Yet with advancing age the quality of my corrected vision has declined. I had to stop wearing glasses because even the best lenses led to distortions at the edges, vertigo, and visual disorientation. Contact lenses were a great improvement but I don't like to be corrected to 20/20 because it gives me headaches. So, I've learned to enjoy a world with softer edges while still feeling that I can see safely enough to navigate the environment.

Coming back to the role of vision in writing, it was difficult to find an optimal distance between my head and the computer screen. With reading glasses, I have to sit closer to the screen but sometimes I find myself craning my neck forward. Without reading glasses, I'd have to sit too far away to type comfortably. It helps to enlarge the size of the print on the screen, and I also decided to acquire a 23" wide monitor late in the writing process for this book. With these accommodations it all can work, but only when I pay close attention. The strains that result when absorption gets out of control are from my myopic desire for more clarity of vision than the mechanical refractory devices covering my own lenses can provide, as if that optical clarity might translate into a clarity of mind.

What I discovered in the writing of this book is the possibility that the clarity of mind and the flow of the words can be achieved without the clarity of the physical vision and without the strain on my body. I knew this in some way before I began the book but here was another opportunity to re-tune my embodied self-awareness, another chance to shed an additional layer of old habits, another chance for this man to find and remember the real person, the True Self, within the enclosed and protected psyche of that little boy.

In my personal experience and also in my work as a Rosen Method Bodywork practitioner, I continue to be surprised at the way in which relationships within systemic networks manifest themselves. Problems in interpersonal relationships translate into particular patterns of relationships within the person's body, as in the case of my client Rebecca (Case Report 7.2) with complex and not completely understood connections between uterine fibroids and the surgery to remove them, sexual abuse from the ex-husband, the complex emotions of a giving birth to the child of her own flesh mixed with that of the despised ex, all carried downstream aggregating with it who knows what other fragments from the past.

Psychophysiology of Self-Awareness

I have the strong impression that each of these factors holds the others in place, giving each a certain type of meaning in relation to the others, as if the process of living requires a periodic binding of things together, a binding for the sake of binding, a way of making meaning out of chaos. Start anywhere in the body—the eyes, the uterus, the hip, anywhere—and discover in embodied self-awareness to what else that part had become lashed in the intensity of surviving the storms of life.

Sometimes the binding is tight and seemingly immobile and one has to find a way in, a place where at least one knot can be worked free and a little feeling, a tiny sensation, can find its way into embodied self-awareness. Sometimes that binding is loose, soft, open to creative alterations and happy discoveries of self-acceptance and self-understanding. The former is the opening gambit in the developmental journey toward wholeness and the latter is the highest humanely attainable level of being, the acceptance of being a process. Either way, it is all bound together by circumstance, happy or unhappy.

There is no escape from the pressures of the world. Even in the best of times we must tie off a part of ourselves to please others, to make the grade, to survive and we bind up that part as best we can at that moment. I know of no coming of age story, from Homer's Odyssey all the way up to any of hundreds of contemporary films, in which the hero or heroine does not have to withstand many trials and deprivations before finding redemption and love. We have no home other than the unique warp and weft of our own body tissues. Following the strands of that twisted garment, all else may be revealed. When there is no end to curiosity about our living tapestry—knotted and torn, pulsing with desire—we can finally and completely embrace life in all its possibilities.

Glossary

Absorption: A way to exaggerate and amplify attention, the effect of which is the sense of getting "lost in" and "fully engaged with" experience so that the periphery is eliminated.

Addiction: Unrestrained and self-injurious compulsion.

Adrenocorticotropic hormone (ACTH): One of the hormones from the pituitary that stimulates the adrenals to secrete cortosol; part of the HPA axis.

Afferent nervous system: All neural information that flows from the body toward the brain.

Alexithymia: (*a*=non, not, *lexi*=words, *thymia*=without) Difficulty experiencing and naming emotional states.

α - motor neurons (α–MN): Neurons from the ventral (toward the front of the body) horn of the spinal cord that activate motor units. They are large, myelinated neurons with fast conduction speeds.

Amygdala: Part of the limbic system, located on either side of the hypothalamus and just at the end of the horseshoe shaped structure called the hippocampus, by which threat is detected quickly by the brain without the need for conscious awareness, but it also plays a role in fear memories, learned responses to fearful situations, and thus anticipatory anxiety and panic.

Anosognosia: (*a*=not, none, *nosos*=disease, *gnosis*=knowledge) Having severe motor deficits, paralysis, or even blindness from a stroke but without an awareness of the existence of the condition.

Anterior cingulate cortex (ACC): Lies just dorsal to (above) the thalamus, and adjacent to the insula; plays a role in the feelings of motivation that accompany an emotion.

Armoring: The experience dependent development of a protective shell of muscle tension grown over time in response to a history of threat, anxiety, and trauma.

Psychophysiology of Self-Awareness

Asomatognosia (*somato*=body): When parts the body are reported as missing or have disappeared from awareness and a lack of feeling that a part of the body belongs to the self.

Attachment: The long-term emotional tie between two individuals based on the urge to find safety with each other, the need for coregulatory communication of movement and touch for close proximity, and the resulting resonant states of emotion for and with the other person.

Attractors: Stable patterns that emerge in dynamic systems.

Autobiographical memory: Memories for which we are able to think about and talk about an event that happened to us in the past. There is a story to tell, the story has a location in time and space, and the story is typically kept at an emotional distance.

Autonomic nervous system (ANS): Neural pathways responsible for the homeostatic regulation of all the important internal organs of the body including heart, lungs, and gut; includes both the sympathetic and parasympathetic nervous systems.

Awareness through Movement: Verbally guided group classes that allow people to slow down and enter a state of embodied self-awareness of their movements and how one part of the body is linked to other parts. Part of the Feldenkrais method.

Beginner's mind: An attitude of openness, vulnerability, and lack of judgment and evaluative conceptions when connecting with a person or object.

Binge eating: Eating food in quantities that surpasses the body's capacity to process it.

Biobehavioral response patterns: Six semiautomatic responses to threat and safety that are regulated, often unconsciously, by our nervous system: vigilance, threat mobilization, threat immobilization, restoration, engagement, and normal absorption.

Biofeedback: A method of self-awareness and relaxation in which people are given access to physiological indicators of sympathetic nervous system activation and asked to alter body state to reduce arousal.

Body schema: The part of embodied self-awareness that can sense that our body belongs to us and to no one else, our sense of movement and balance, our ability to locate particular parts of ourselves, to sense our body size and shape, and the awareness that our body has boundaries that separate us from other objects and bodies.

Glossary

Caudal: Toward the tail, or spinal cord.

Cerebrospinal fluid (CSF): A clear fluid that serves as a cushion for the brain, protecting it from injury inside the skill and also affording some immunological protection for the brain.

Chaos: Variability within stability, a recognizable pattern but one that never precisely and exactly repeats itself in the same way.

Cingulate motor area (CMA): A part of the cingulate cortex, adjacent to the anterior cingulate cortex (ACC), which when coupled with activation in the supplementary motor area (SMA) represents the preparation to act.

Compartmentalization: A state of consciousness that "incorporates dissociative amnesia and the 'unexplained' nuerological symptoms characteristic of the conversion disorders, such as conversion paralysis, sensory loss, seizures, gait disturbance, and pseudo-hallucinations" (Holmes et al., 2005, p. 7).

Conceptual self-awareness: What I *think* about myself in the realm of concepts that obey the rules of grammar, reason, and logic. It may not be directly connected to feelings from the body.

Conversion disorder: The contemporary name for what Freud called "hysteria," the substitution of a painful traumatic memory for a somatic symptom, basically, a psychosomatic disorder having no physical cause or diagnosis.

Coregulation: The movement process by which two or more individuals dynamically coordinate actions in a joint activity.

Corticotrophin releasing factor (CRF): A hormone from the hypothalamus that stimulates activation of the pituitary; part of the HPA axis.

Cortisol: Part of the HPA axis, secreted from the adrenal glands to increase blood pressure and blood glucose.

Critical period: A relatively circumscribed period of the life course in which particular forms of environmental input are required to sustain psychobiological development.

Dance movement psychotherapy: A creative arts therapy that uses movement and dance as a communication tool, as a diagnostic tool, and as a therapeutic intervention.

Defense mechanisms: Forms of suppression having the goal of avoiding what is unpleasant or threatening to the self: denial, repression, intellectualization, and projection.

Denial: A defense mechanism involving the suppression of self-awareness of the possibly difficult and painful outcomes of one's embodied experience, an experience of which one is aware.
Depersonalization syndrome: A feeling of living outside one's body and outside the world.
Detachment: An "altered state of consciousness characterized by a sense of separation (or 'detachment') from certain aspects of everyday experience, be it their body (as in out-of-body experiences), their sense of self (as in depersonalization), or the external world (as in derealization)" (Holmes et al., 2005, p. 5).
Developmental trauma: The result of exposure to threat over a long period of time such as to warfare, child abuse, or work stress.
Disorganized-disoriented attachment: Connected with the biobehavioral response mode of immobilization and dissociation and occurs when the infant suffers from extreme and consistent threat from the attachment figure such as from physical or sexual abuse, maltreatment, parental psychopathology, and parental substance abuse.
Dopamine: A neurotransmitter related to the activation of feelings of pleasure, enjoyment, and the motivation to perform activities that contribute to those feelings.
Dopaminergic receptors: Receptors in nerve cells that activate that cell when dopamine is present.
Dorsal: Toward the back, superior and posterior.
Dorsolateral prefrontal cortex (DLPFC): Serves to take sensory impressions from both interoceptive and exteroceptive networks and to "hold" them temporarily in awareness; working memory.
Dorsomedial prefrontal cortex (DMPFC): Works with other regions of the brain to create conceptual self-awareness.
Dynamic system: A complex entity in which the parts are linked by interdependence and coregulation. Dynamic systems are living processes rather than fixed structures.
Dysmorphophobia: (*dys*=disturbance, *morph*=form, *phobia*=fear) Obsession with real or imagined physical flaws like the size or shape of the nose, breast, or penis.
Dystonia: A movement disorder characterized by sustained contractions of the muscles, sometimes located in particular regions of the body.
Efferent nervous system: Pathways from the brain to the rest of the body.

Glossary

Effortful breathing: Occurs in states of threat when there is contraction of breathing muscles through both the inspiration and expiration (sympathetic arousal), and generally higher levels of muscle tension in the body.

Embodied self-awareness: The ability to pay attention to ourselves, to feel our sensations, emotions, and movements on-line, in the present moment, without the mediating influence of judgmental thoughts. It is composed of sensations like warm, tingly, soft, nauseated, dizzy; emotions such as happy, sad, threatened; and body senses like feeling the coordination (or lack of coordination) between the arms and legs while swimming, or sensing our shape and size (fat or thin), and sensing our location relative to objects and other people.

Emergence: A property of a dynamic system in which a pattern of activity is spontaneously created across all the elements of the system and is not contained in any single element.

Emotion: An embodied experience reflecting how good or bad something feels to us (called its hedonic value) accompanied by a motivation or urge to act in a particular manner in relation to that sensation, thing, or being that seems to be causing the emotion.

Engagement: Activity during periods of perceived safety, including all forms of embodied self-awareness, conceptual self-awareness coupled with embodied self-awareness, normal forms of absorption (focused attention and flow), and social engagement with others in the subjective emotional present.

Enteric nervous system (ENS): Embedded in the lining of the tissues of the gastrointestinal system. In addition to acting on information from the ANS, the ENS can act independently to control contraction and relaxation of the gut muscles, and to secrete digestive enzymes, in response to enteric mechanoreceptors and chemoreceptors in the interior of the gut.

Epinephrine (also known as adrenaline): Secreted from the adrenal medulla as a result of SNS arousal, epinephrine has similar arousing affects on the body as cortisol to raise blood glucose and increase heart function.

Ergoreceptors: Receptors designed to convert different forms of physical stimulation into neural signals for transmission to the brain, including mechano-, chemo-, baro-, metabo-, thermo-receptors, and nociceptors about the internal state of the body.

Evocative language: A form of speech in which words are chosen to resonate in felt experience. If words "reach us," they are felt as "true," "deep," and "powerful." Words in evocative language—spoken from the practitioner's own embodied self-awareness—can enhance and amplify feelings.

Experience dependent brain development: The growth of neural pathways through practice and repeated experience.

Expiratory pause: The cessation of movement in the breathing muscles at the end of an expiration. A longer expiratory pause indicates greater relaxation while a short or non-existent expiratory pause indicate a sense of threat.

Exteroceptors: The sense organs in the visual, auditory, olfactory, gustatory, and tactile systems of the body.

Eye Movement Desensitization and Reprocessing (EMDR): A form of embodied self-awareness treatment in which patients are asked to imagine traumatic or difficult situations while at the same time being asked to attend to an external stimulus that alternates from one side to another.

False Self: Conceptual self-awareness in the condition that it becomes divorced from embodied self-awareness.

Feeling: Any interceptive sensation that is experienced as coming from our own bodies. Feelings can be tingly, warm, calm, jumpy, "butterflies," etc.

Fibromyalgia: Musculoskeletal pain across different regions of the body, highly tender regions, fatigue, problems with sleep, and negative mood.

Flow: A state that occurs when one's skills perfectly match the task, when there is a sense of pleasure or "high," when your attention is totally focused on your activity, a loss of self-consciousness (but not necessarily self-awareness), and an expansion of the felt sense of time.

Functional integration: A method of hands-on movement education, in which the student's movement is guided by the practitioner. This is part of the Feldenkrais Method.

γ – motor neurons (γ – MN): Myelinated neurons that terminate in muscle spindles but have a lower conduction speed than the α - motor neuron fibers. They do not contract the extrafusal muscle fibers in the motor units. Rather, they stretch the muscle spindle slightly from the ends to make it more receptive.

Golgi tendon organs: Proprioceptors for tendon stretch.

Glossary

Hippocampus: A horseshoe-shaped or seahorse-shaped structure (hippocampus means seahorse in Latin) that encircles the limbic system, which is believed to help in the mental organization of sensory impressions into coherent "events" with a beginning, middle, and ending, and with a remembered spatial location and organization.

Homeostasis (*homeo*=equal, *stasis*=to stand or stay): The autonomic regulation of all the functional systems of the body.

HPA axis: The vertical arrangement and linkages between the hypothalamus, pituitary gland (located in the base of the brain just below the hypothalamus) and adrenal glands (located above the kidneys).

Hyperventilation: Breathing in excess of metabolic needs that results in an abnormal reduction of blood CO_2 levels and an abnormal increase of blood pH, becoming more alkaline. Both these conditions create risk factors for all the muscles in the body, including the heart, and for the brain.

Hypocortisolism: Long-term oversecretion of cortisol that exhausts adrenal function so that insufficient cortisol is produced. Results in stress sensitivity, pain, fatigue, and a lowered ability to cope with daily tasks.

Hypothalamus (*hypo*=under): Part of the limbic system that links to the autonomic nervous system and also to the production of regulatory hormones.

Immobilization: A response to inescapable threat that takes the form of *freezing or fainting*, types of dissociative detachment.

Infant-directed speech: Speech that has a higher pitch and more exaggerated contrasts between high- and low-pitched sounds and is more melodic than speech directed toward adults.

Insecure avoidant-dismissive attachment: Occurs when infants do not outwardly shown signs of distress under threat. These infants will actively resist attempts to pick them up or comfort them, by turning away or squirming to get down. Typically occurs when parents are intolerant of the child's feelings of distress, threat, and anger, or when parents become angry at the child in response to the child's distress.

Insecure anxious-resistant attachment: A type of relationship characterized by vigilance. The threatened child will seem ambivalent, sometimes approaching the parent and sometimes hesitant. They have a difficult time calming, are watchful of the environment and of the parent, and do not readily return to states of engagement. Infants with this type of attachment are either temperamentally susceptible to stress or have parents who are inconsistently emotionally available in times of stress.

Psychophysiology of Self-Awareness

Insula: A region located in the interior of the temporal lobe, adjacent to the thalamus and other limbic structures such as the amygdalae, involved in interoception.
Intellectualization: A defense mechanism involving a judgment or reinterpretation in conceptual self-awareness as a way of suppressing embodied self-awareness.
Interoception: The ability to feel one's own internal body states such as heat/cold, pain, respiration.
Intersubjectivity: The nonverbal sense of "being with" another person, a direct result of the interpersonal resonance that occurs during coregulation of movements, sensations, and emotions.
Lateral: Toward the outside, left or right.
Limbic system: Located at the center of the brain, it includes the amygdala, hypothalamus, hippocampus, and cingulate cortex.
Listening touch: Touching another person with soft hands that are tactilely attentive to the physical and emotional condition of the receiver.
Lobes: The basic regions of the cerebral cortex.
Locus ceruleus: A part of the upper brain stem located next to the PAG, secretes norepinephrine (NE), considered both hormone and a neurotransmitter.
Medial: Toward the center.
Mindfulness: A form of meditative embodied self-awareness characterized by being in the subjective emotional present, noticing feelings, and avoiding coceptual thought and judgement.
Misoplegia (*miso*=hatred, *plegia*=paralysis): Hatred of body parts.
Mobilization: A response to escapable threat in the form of active defensive strategies, in particular, *fight and flight*.
Modularity: The assumption that particular areas of the brain are "responsible" for causing and therefore explaining the particular behaviors to which they have been associated.
Motor unit: Bundles of muscle cells (also called muscle fibers) regulated by a single α - motor neuron that contracts all the cells in that unit at the same time.
Muscle spindles are located in the muscle belly and are fatter in the middle and narrower at the ends. They contain the proprioceptors that sense the extent and speed of muscle stretch (mechanorecpetors) and contraction, and they are regulated by γ – motor neurons.

Myalgia (*myo*=muscle, *algia*=pain): Symptomatic muscle weakness or pain.
Myelin: A protective coating around nerve cell fibers that speeds transmission.
Myoclonic twitches (*myo*=muscle, *clonus*=contraction): Spontaneous and involuntary muscle contractions.
Neoplastic disease: The growth of nonmalignant and malignant tumors.
Neural integration: The balanced functioning of the neural networks associated with attachment, health, and self-awareness.
Neural network: Separate brain regions are coactivated and communicate with each other producing a unified and systemic state of neural activity.
Neuraxis: The vertical line from the peripheral receptors to the cerebral cortex.
Neuroception: The ability of our nervous system to assess safety and threat and make appropriate adjustments to prepare our bodies to survive. This can occur without awareness.
Neurogenesis: The generation of new neurons within the brain, occurring primarily in the hippocampus, olfactory bulb, and parts of the cortex.
NIA: Neuromuscular Integrative Action, is a form of group cardiovascular movement exercise and awareness done barefoot to music. NIA uses elements of Tai Chi, Aikido, and other martial arts, dance, Feldenkrais, and Yoga, among other methods.
Nociceptors: Ergoreceptors for pain that send signals to the brain when the mechanoreceptors, thermoreceptors and other ergoreceptors sense a *threat* to the body tissues.
Nonlinear transition: The sudden shifting of a dynamic system from one into an entirely different attractor state.
Norepinephrine (NE): A stress hormone that activates the brain stem sympathetic nerve centers and also feeds back to the hypothalamus to increase the secretion of CRF.
Normal absorption: The experience of being lost in an activity, including pleasure, creativity, and deep states of concentration.
Orbitofrontal cortex (OFC): Part of the prefrontal cortex that helps in the appraisal of body states as positive or negative. It works together with the ACC to regulate whether to take approach or withdrawal action in relation to an interoceptive feeling.
Out of body experience (OBE): One experiences the self as if from a distant location.

Psychophysiology of Self-Awareness

Oxytocin: A hormone and a neurotransmitter, stimulates maternal behavior and female reproductive function. It also plays a role in affiliation, attachment, and the reduction of anxiety in both males and females.

Parasympathetic nervous system: Part of the autonomic nervous system that creates states of relaxation, recovery, and restoration.

Participatory memory: Lived reenactments of personally significant experiences that have not yet become organized into a verbal or conceptual narrative; conscious experiences in the present that are not *about* a past experience, but rather emotionally experienced as a *being with* or a *reliving* of past experiences.

Pathological dissociation: A disconnection between self and body having two basic forms: detachment and compartmentalization.

Periaqueductal grey (PAG): A structure located at the very top of the brain stem (most rostral portion), just behind (dorsal to) the hypothalamus, which helps to locate, regulate, and modulate pain signals.

Physiatry: Also called physical medicine and rehabilitation, is a field of medicine dedicated to helping people restore optimal function following injuries to the muscles, bones, tissues, and nervous system resulting from illness, accidents, or medical interventions.

Plasticity: The ability of the brain to develop new experience dependent pathways as a result of learning or repair.

Posttraumatic stress disorder: A condition precipitated by an extremely threatening event that is characterized by persistently high arousal, flashbacks, memory loss, lack of ability to concentrate, and impairment of social functioning.

Posture: Describes the use of the entire self in achieving and maintaining this or that change of configuration and position. Posture is therefore describing action, and is a dynamic term.

Procedural memories: Rather than stories about the self (see autobiographical memory), procedural memories (sometimes called motor, skill, perceptual, or implicit memories) are nonverbal memories of "ways of doing and sensing things."

Progressive relaxation method: Relaxation done by guided meditation and self-monitoring of different body areas, typically starting from the head (scalp, face, eyes, and tongue) and moving down the body.

Proinflammatory cytokines: The immune cells that initiate the inflammatory response in response to tissue injury and psychosocial stressors.
Projection: A defense mechanism in which one imputes a feeling or emotion as a problem caused by someone else.
Proprioception: The felt sense of the location and relative position of different parts of the body in relation to objects and to other individuals.
Proprioceptors: Receptors at the periphery of the body for position and movement: the sense of touch, the sense of muscle stretch, and the sense of balance in the middle ear.
Psychoperistalsis: Involuntary noises of relaxation from the gut—gurgles, tummy rumbles—that are not related to digestion, a sign of possible parasympathetic activation.
Relaxed breathing: Occurs when there is relatively little muscle tension in the body, when inspiration and expiration are relatively rhythmical, and when there is a detectable expiratory pause.
Representation: A specific neural pattern of activation in the brain that corresponds to the original activity at the peripheral receptor site.
Repression: A defense mechanism that involves the covering up of the feeling itself so that it does not enter embodied self-awareness.
Rerepresentation: The ability of the brain—in particular the neural network that includes the anterior insula—to form an image of the original sensations and to keep that image "alive" and in awareness.
Resonance: The amplification of shared emotion in coregulated encounters.
Resources: A constant and reliable presence in your body or your surroundings that feels safe, stable, and supportive: used for treating pain and trauma.
Respiratory sinus arrhythmia (RSA): The variability in heart rate between inspiration and expiration in relaxed breathing.
Restoration: A quiescent state following threat or stress that has characteristics similar to "sickness" behavior—feelings of muscle weakness, fatigue, and perhaps inflammation—that leads the individual to tend to wounds, rest, sleep, and recover. In humans, restoration can take the form of meditation, relaxation, normal absorption, and positive engagement in the subjective emotional present.

Psychophysiology of Self-Awareness

Restorative environments: These are environments in which a person's effectiveness is enhanced, which facilitate recovery from mental and physical health problems, bring us more in touch with ourselves, remind us what is important in our lives, and enhance our sense of connection with others and with nature.

Rosen Method Bodywork: A form of touch and talk therapy that emphasizes enhancing embodied self-awareness. Rosen Method uses a "listening" form of touch that simultaneously helps the client and the practitioner become more aware of the client's embodied experience.

Rosen Method of Movement: A group class using gentle movements done to music that increases flexibility, opens the posture for engagement with others, emphasizes awareness and the joy of movement, and teaches about finding comfort and enjoyment in touching and moving with other people.

Rostral: Toward the head, or forehead.

Rumination: "The tendency to repetitively focus on symptoms of distress and possible causes and consequences of those symptoms without engaging in active problem solving" (Nolen-Hoeksema et al., 2007, p. 198).

Secure attachment: A type of attachment relationship in which the infant who feels threatened will seek proximity and comfort from the parent, be easily calmed, and then be able to return to normal patterns of engagement.

Self-agency: The sense of authorship of one's own actions. It involves a sense of volition that precedes an action as well as the proprioceptive feedback that occurs during the act.

Self-coherence: The sense of being a nonfragmented, physical whole, with boundaries and a locus of integrated action.

Sensory integration dysfunction: A neurologically based impairment of the basic five senses including both hypo- and hypersensitivity.

Shock trauma: The effect of a relatively brief and sudden event like an assault or a drug overdose.

Skeletal muscles: These muscles control the physical movements of the body by attaching to bone and contracting to move the joints.

Smooth muscles: These muscles are found in most of the internal organs including the gut, respiratory tract, arteries and veins, bladder, reproductive tracts, and uterus.

Glossary

Somatic experiencing: A method of treating trauma developed by Peter Levine (1997) that focuses on awareness of embodied sensations and titrating the traumatic memories with an ongoing sense of safety to help the person find a way out of the "trauma vortex."

Somatic psychotherapy: Focuses on enhancing embodied self-awareness. Therapists call attention to their client's postures and gestures, patterns of muscle holding and tensions, movement patterns and movement limitations, the breath and other body rhythms, and forms of suppression of emotion and sensation.

Somatization: Dwelling on and amplifying inner experience to the point of exaggerating its importance or interpreting it as illness.

Somatoparaphrenia (*para*=beside, *phrenia*=mental disorder): Denial of ownership of a body part, as if it belonged to someone else or that someone else left it behind.

Somatosensory (SS) cortex: Where all sensory information is interpreted, with particular cells in the SS responding somatotopically to particular parts of the body and particular receptors.

Somatotopic organization: Brain organization in which specific cells are linked to specific groups of peripheral muscles and receptors; representational maps in the brain that directly link to and correspond to specific regions in the body.

Stress: The condition that results when the body is unable to achieve homeostatic balance.

Subjective emotional present: The time during which neural rerepresentations remain activated across the entire neural network; a state of embodied self-awareness in which the individual is fully immersed, fully present to the self, fully alive.

Supplementary motor area (SMA): Part of the motor cortex related to the preparation for action, i.e., urges. In works in connection with the cingulate motor area (CMA).

Suppression: A lack of embodied self-awareness that occurs whenever there is a sense of threat that prevents us from finding resources, slowing down, and/or coregulating with an empathic other.

Psychophysiology of Self-Awareness

Sympathetic nervous system: Part of the autonomic nervous system that arouses the body for action and defense.

Thalamus: Part of the limbic system that is a relay station where inputs from different parts of the body, spinal cord, and brain stem get sorted out and sent to regions of the cortex for further processing.

Therapeutic dissociation: A shared awareness, coregulated between the client and the practitioner by which the client can come to better understand the dissociated part, where it came from, and what it needs from the adult.

Therapeutic massage: "The manipulation of the soft tissue structures of the body to prevent and alleviate pain, discomfort, muscle spasm, and stress; and, to promote health and wellness" (http://www.holisticonline.com/massage/mas_def.htm).

Thoracic diaphragm: A skeletal muscle to assist breathing. It is attached to bones although it does not move any joints: to the lowest ribs around the circumference of the body, to the bottom of the sternum (breast bone) in front and to the upper lumbar vertebrae in back. It can move voluntarily like skeletal muscle but it also moves involuntarily to maintain breathing at all times.

Threat: The felt sense of fear that one or one's property or one's significant others are under attack and in danger of physical or psychological harm.

Trauma: The condition that results from prolonged exhaustion of resources, a condition in which the person becomes unable to integrate the resulting interoceptive experiences, emotions, changes in body schema, and thoughts thus creating another level of stress on the system.

True Self: Embodied self-awareness, the ability to stay comfortably in the chaos of the subjective emotional present, and to use that to inform, verify, and update conceptual self-awareness.

Vagus nerve: A cranial parasympathetic nerve, originating in the brain stem autonomic area and traveling directly to all the internal organ systems without passing through the spinal cord. Restoration is regulated by the ventral (toward the front of the neck) portion of the vagus nerve while immobilization is regulated by the dorsal (toward the back of the neck) portion of the vagus nerve.

Ventral: Toward the front; anterior and inferior.

Glossary

Ventromedial prefrontal cortex (VMPFC): Anatomically adjacent to the DMPFC, the VMPFC helps with on-line decision making that occurs when one is in the subjective emotional present.

Vigilance: A slowing or cessation of movement and increased attention to the environment in response to threat.

Voice: The sense of being the author of the expression of one's **true self**, the sense that one is speaking of the self with honesty and confidence in a way that is consonant with embodied feelings.

Watsu: An aquatic form of touch therapy in which the client's body, floating in body-temperature water, is moved and massaged by the practitioner.

References

Aalten, A. (2007). Listening to the dancer's body. *Sociological Review, 55*(Suppl 1), 109–125.

Abram, D. (1997). *The spell of the sensuous.* New York: Vintage Books.

Adolph, K. E., Vereijken, B., & Denny, M. A. (1998). Learning to crawl. *Child Development, 69*(5), 1299–1312.

Alexander, T. (2003). Narcissism and the experience of crying. *British Journal of Psychotherapy, 20*(1), 27–37.

Amat, J., Baratta, M. V., Paul, E., Bland, S. T., Watkins, L. R., & Maier, S. F. (2005). Medial prefrontal cortex determines how stressor controllability affects behavior and dorsal raphe nucleus. *Nature Neuroscience, 8*(3), 365–371.

American Psychiatric Association (1994). *Diagnostic and statistical manual of mental disorders* (4th ed.). Washington, DC: Author.

Amorapanth, P., LeDoux, J. E., & Nader, K. (2000). Different lateral amygdala outputs mediate reactions and actions elicited by a fear-arousing stimulus. *Nature Neuroscience, 3*(1), 74–79.

Anda, R. F., Felitti, V. J., Bremner, J. D., Walker, J. D., Whitfield, C., Perry, B. D., et al. (2006). The enduring effects of abuse and related adverse experiences in childhood. A convergence of evidence from neurobiology and epidemiology. *European Archives of Psychiatry and Clinical Neuroscience, 256*(3), 174–186.

Andrasik, F., & Holroyd, K. A. (1980). A test of specific and nonspecific effects in the biofeedback treatment of tension headache. *Journal of Consulting and Clinical Psychology, 48*(5), 575–586.

Anton, P. M., Gay, J., Mykoniatis, A., Pan, A., O'Brien, M., Brown, D. et al. (2004). Corticotropin-releasing hormone (CRH) requirement in Clostridium difficile toxin A-mediated intestinal inflammation. *Proceedings of the National Academy of Sciences, 101*(22), 8503–8508.

Antoniazzi, A., Zivian, M. T., & Hynie, M. (2005). Women with and without eating disorders: Their values and eating attitudes. *Journal of Social & Clinical Psychology, 24*(4), 449–470.

Aposhyan, S. (2004). *Body-mind psychotherapy.* New York: Norton.

Arditi, H., Feldman, R., & Eidelman, A. I. (2006). Effects of human contact and vagal regulation on pain reactivity and visual attention in newborns. *Developmental Psychobiology, 48*(7), 561–573.

Argiolas, A., & Melis, M. R. (1998). The neuropharmacology of yawning. *European Journal of Pharmacology, 343*(1), 1–16.

Arnadottir, S. A., & Mercer, V. S. (2000). Effects of footwear on measurements of balance and gait in women between the ages of 65 and 93 years. *Physical Therapy, 80*(1), 17–27.

Arndt, J., & Goldenberg, J. L. (2004). From self-awareness to shame-proneness: Evidence of causal sequence among women. *Self and Identity, 3*(1), 27–37.

Aron, A., Fisher, H., Mashek, D. J., Strong, G., Li, H., & Brown, L. L. (2005). Reward, motivation, and emotion systems associated with early-stage intense romantic love. *Journal of Neurophysiology, 94*(1), 327–337.

Arzy, S., Overney, L., Landis, T., Blanke, O. (2006). Neural mechanisms of embodiment: Asomatognosia due to premotor cortex damage. *Archives of Neurology, 63,* 1022–1025.

Asendorpf, J. B., Warkentin, V., & Baudonniere, P. (1996). Self-awareness and other-awareness II: Mirror self-recognition, social contingency awareness, and synchronic imitation. *Developmental Psychology, 32*(2), 313–321.

Ashina, S., Babenko, L., Jensen, R., Ashina, M., Magerl, W., & Bendtsen, L. (2005). Increased muscular and cutaneous pain sensitivity in cephalic region in patients with chronic tension-type headache. *European Journal of Neurology, 12*(7), 543–549.

Askenasy, J. J. (1989). Is yawning an arousal defense reflex? *Journal of Psychology: Interdisciplinary and Applied, 123*(6), 609–621.

Askenasy, J. J., & Askenasy, N. (1996). Inhibition of muscle sympathetic nerve activity during yawning. *Clinical Autonomic Research, 6*(4), 237–239.

Azevedo, T. M., Volchan, E., Imbiriba, L. A., Rodrigues, E. C., Oliveira, J. M., Oliveira, L. F. et al. (2005). A freezing-like posture to pictures of mutilation. *Psychophysiology, 42*(3), 255–260.

Baenninger, R., Binkley, S., & Baenninger, M. (1996). Field observations of yawning and activity in humans. *Physiology & Behavior, 59*(3), 421–425.

Baier, B. & Karnath, H. (2008). Tight link between our sense of limb ownership and self-awareness of actions. *Stroke, 39,* 486–488.

Bakal, D. (1999). *Minding the body: Clinical uses of somatic awareness.* New York: Guilford Press.

References

Bathktin, M. M. (1981). *The dialogical imagination: Four essays by M. M. Bahktin.* University of Texas Press: Austin.

Bandler, R., & Keay, K. A. (1996). Columnar organization in the midbrain periaqueductal gray and the integration of emotional expression. *Progress in Brain Research, 107*, 285–300.

Bandler, R., Keay, K. A., Floyd, N., & Price, J. (2000). Central circuits mediating patterned autonomic activity during active vs. passive emotional coping. *Brain Research Bulletin, 53*(1), 95–104.

Banfield, J. F., Wyland, C. L., MacRae, C. N., Münte, T. R., & Heatherton, T. F. (2007) The cognitive neuroscience of self-regulation. In R. F. Baumeister & K. D. Vohs (Eds.), *Handbook of self-regulation: Research, theory, and applications* (pp. 62–83). New York: Guilford Press.

Barch, D. M., Braver, T. S., Nystrom, L. S., Forman, S. D., Noll, D. C., & Cohen, J. D. (1997). *Neuropsycologia, 35*, 1373–1380.

Bar-Haim, Y., & Bart, O. (2006). Motor function and social participation in kindergarten children. *Social Development, 15*(2), 296–310.

Barker, E. T., Williams, R. L., & Galambos, N. L. (2006). Daily spillover to and from binge eating in first-year university females. *Eating Disorders, 14*(3), 229–242.

Bar-On, R., Tranel, D., Denburg, N. L., & Bechara, A. (2003). Exploring the neurological substrate of emotional and social intelligence. *Brain, 126*(Pt 8), 1790–1800.

Barrett, J., Pike, G. B., & Paus, T. (2004). The role of the anterior cingulate cortex in pitch variation during sad affect. *European Journal of Neuroscience, 19*(2), 458–464.

Bass, G. (2007). Sweet are the uses of adversity. In F. Anderson (Ed.), *Bodies in treatment: The unspoken dimension.* Boca Raton, FL: CRC Press.

Bates, J. E., Maslin, C. A., & Frankel, K. A. (1985). Attachment security, mother-child interaction, and temperament as predictors of behavior-problem ratings at age three years. *Monographs of the Society for Research in Child Development, 50* (Serial No. 209), 167–193.

Bauer, P. J., Stark, E. N., Lukowski, A. F., Rademacher, J., Van Abbema, D. L., & Ackil, J. K. (2005). Working together to make sense of the past: Mothers' and children's use of internal state language in conversations about traumatic and non-traumatic events. *Journal of Cognition and Development, 6*(4), 463–488.

Baumgartner, T., Lutz, K., Schmidt, C. F., & Jäncke, L. (2006). The emotional power of music: How music enhances the feeling of affective pictures. *Brain Research, 1075*(1), 151–164.

Bazhenova, O. V., Plonskaia, O., & Porges, S. W. (2001). Vagal reactivity and affective adjustment in infants during interaction challenges. *Child Development, 72*(5), 1314–1326.

Beales, D. L., & Dolton, R. (2000). Eating disordered patients: personality, alexithymia, and implications for primary care. *The British Journal of General Practice, 50*(450), 21–26.

Beauregard, M., Lévesque, J. Bourgouin, P. (2001). Neural correlates of conscious self-regulation of emotion. *Journal of Neuroscience, 21*, 165.

Bechara, A., Damasio, H., & Damasio, A. R. (2000). Emotion, decision making and the orbitofrontal cortex. *Cerebral Cortex, 10*(3), 295–307.

Beck, J. G., & Scott, S. K. (1988). Physiological and symptom responses to hyperventilation: A comparison of frequent and infrequent panickers. *Journal of Psychopathology and Behavioral Assessment, 10*(2), 117–127.

Beebe, B., & Lachmann, F. M. (2002). *Infant research and adult treatment: Co-constructing interactions.* Hillsdale, NJ: Analytic Press.

Behrman, A. L., Bowden, M. G., & Nair, P. M. (2006). Neuroplasticity after spinal cord injury and training: An emerging paradigm shift in rehabilitation and walking recovery. *Physical Therapy, 86*(10), 1406–1425.

Belsky, J. (2008). War, trauma and children's development: Observations from a modern evolutionary perspective. *International Journal of Behavioral Development, 32*(4), 260–271.

Bennett, H. & Disbrow, E. (1995). Preparing for surgery and medical procedures. In D. Goleman & J. Gurin (Eds.), *Mind, Body Medicine: How to Use Your Mind for Better Health* (pp. 401–404). New York: Choice Books.

Benson, C. (1993). *The absorbed self: Pragmatism, psychology and aesthetic experience.* New York: Harvester Wheatsheaf.

Benson, H. (1975). *The relaxation response.* New York: Morrow.

Benson, H., Greenwood, M.M., Klemchuk, H. (1975). The relaxation response: Psychophysiologic aspects and clinical applications. *Psychiatry Medicine, 6*, 87–98.

Berger, A. A. (1981). Too much television. In S. J. Mule (Ed.), *Behavior in excess* (pp 282–296). New York: Free Press.

Berger, D. (1997). Rosen Method Bodywork. In C. M. Davis (Ed.), *Complementary therapies in rehabilitation: Holistic approaches for prevention and wellness.* (pp. 49–65). Thorofare, NJ: SLACK.

Berlin, L. J., Cassidy, J., & Belsky, J. (1995). Loneliness in young children and infant-mother attachment: A longitudinal study. *Merrill-Palmer Quarterly, 41*, 91–103.

References

Berlucchi, G., & Aglioti, S. (1997). The body in the brain: neural bases of corporeal awareness. *Trends in Neuroscience, 20*(12), 560–564.

Berntson, G. G., Cacioppo, J. T., & Quigley, K. S. (1993). Respiratory sinus arrhythmia: Autonomic origins, physiological mechanisms, and psychophysiological implications. *Psychophysiology, 30*(2), 183–196.

Berto, R. (2005). Exposure to restorative environments helps restore attentional capacity. *Journal of Environmental Psychology, 25*(3), 249–259.

Bialas, I., & Craig, T. K. J. (2007). 'Needs expressed' and 'offers of care': An observational study of mothers with somatisation disorder and their children. *Journal of Child Psychology and Psychiatry, 48*(1), 97–104.

Biedermann, H. J. & Forrest, W. J. (1991). Excessive muscle fatigue response: The culprit in fibromyalgia. In P. A. Anderson, D. J. Hobart, & J. V. Danoff (Eds.), *Electromyographical Kinesiology: Proceedings of the 8th Congress of the International Society of Electrophysiological Kinesiology* (pp. 79–82). Bridgewater, NJ: Excerpta Medica.

Bifulco, A., Moran, P. M., Baines, R., Bunn, A., & Stanford, K. (2002). Exploring psychological abuse in childhood: II. Association with other abuse and adult clinical depression. *Bulletin of the Menninger Clinic, 66*(3), 241–258.

Binda, S. M., Culham, E. G., & Brouwer, B. (2003). Balance, muscle strength, and fear of falling in older adults. *Experimental Aging Research, 29*(2), 205–219.

Binder, M. C., Bawa, P., Ruenzel, P., & Henneman, E. (1983). Does orderly recruitment of motoneurons depend on the existence of different types of motor units? *Neuroscience Letters, 36*(1), 55–58.

Blackburn, S., Johnston, L., Blampied, N., Popp, D., & Kallen, R. (2006). An application of escape theory to binge eating. *European Eating Disorders Review, 14*, 23–31.

Blake, J. & Fink, R. (1987). Sound-meaning correspondences in babbling. *Child Language, 14*, 229–253.

Blakeslee, S. (2008). Flesh made soul: A new theory in the neuroscience of spiritual experience. *Science and Spirit, 19*(2), 26–31.

Blanke, O., Mohr, C., Michel, C. M., Pascual-Leone, A., Brugger, P., Seeck, M. et al. (2005). Linking out-of-body experience and self processing to mental own-body imagery at the temporoparietal junction. *Journal of Neuroscience, 25*(3), 550–557.

Bloch, S., Lemeignan, M., & Aguilera, N. (1991). Specific respiratory patterns distinguish among human basic emotions. *International Journal of Psychophysiology, 11*(2), 141–154.

Blumberg, M. S., & Lucas, D. E. (1996). A developmental and component analysis of active sleep. *Developmental Psychobiology, 29*(1), 1–22.

Boadella, D. (1987). *Lifestreams: An introduction to biosynthesis.* London: Routledge & Kegan Paul.

Boadella, D. (1994). Styles of breathing in Reichian therapy. In B. H. Timmons & R. Ley (Eds.), *Behavioral and psychological approaches to breathing disorders* (pp. 233–242). New York: Plenum Press.

Bongers, P. M., de Winter, C. R., Kompier, M. A., & Hildebrandt, V. H. (1993). Psychosocial factors at work and musculoskeletal disease. *Scandinavian Journal of Work Environmental Health, 19*(5), 297–312.

Bood, S. Å., Sundequist, U., Kjellgren, A., Norlander, T., Nordström, L., Nordenström, K., et al. (2006). Eliciting the relaxation response with the help of flotation-REST (restricted environmental stimulation technique) in patients with stress-related ailments. *International Journal of Stress Management, 13*(2), 154–175.

Borkovec, T. D., Kaloupek, D. G., & Slama, K. M. (1975). The facilitative effect of muscle tension-release in the relaxation treatment of sleep disturbance. *Behavior Therapy, 6*(3), 301–309.

Bosma, J. F. (1975). Anatomic and physiologic development of the speech apparatus. In D. B. Tower (Ed.), *The nervous system: Vol 3. Human communication and its disorders* (pp. 469–481). New York: Raven Press.

Bosnak, R. (2003). Embodied imagination. *Contemporary Psychoanalysis, 39*, 683–695.

Bowman, W. (2000). A somatic, "Here and Now" semantic: Music, body, and self. *Bulletin of the Council for Research in Music Education, 144*, 45–60.

Braatoy, T. (1952). Psychology vs. anatomy in the treatment of "arm neuroses" with physiotherapy. *Journal of Nervous and Mental Disorders, 115*(3), 215–245.

Bradley, M. M., Sabatinelli, D., Lang, P. J., Fitzsimmons, J. R., King, W., & Desai, P. (2003). Activation of the visual cortex in motivated attention. *Behavioral Neuroscience, 117*(2), 369–380.

Bråten, S. (1998). Infant learning by altercentric participation: The reverse of egocentric observation in autism. In S. Bråten (Ed.), *Intersubjective communication and emotion in early ontogeny. Studies in emotion and social interaction, 2nd series* (pp. 105–124). New York: Cambridge University Press.

Bråten, S. (2003). Participant perception of others' acts: Virtual otherness in infants and adults. *Culture & Psychology, 9*(3), 261–276.

References

Brefczynski-Lewis, J. A., Lutz, A., Schaefer, H. S., Levinson, D. B., & Davidson, R. J. (2007). Neural correlates of attentional expertise in long-term meditation practitioners. *Proceedings of the National Academy of Sciences, 104*(27), 11483–11488.

Bremner, J. D. (2006). Stress and brain atrophy. *CNS & Neurological Disorders - Drug Targets, 5*(5), 503–512.

Bremner, J. D., Narayan, M., Staib, L. H., Southwick, S. M., McGlashan, T., & Charney, D. S. (1999). Neural correlates of memories of childhood sexual abuse in women with and without posttraumatic stress disorder. *The American Journal of Psychiatry, 156*(11), 1787–1795.

Bremner, J. D., Staib, L. H., Kaloupek, D., Southwick, S. M., Soufer, R., & Charney, D. S. (1999). Neural correlates of exposure to traumatic pictures and sound in Vietnam combat veterans with and without posttraumatic stress disorder: a positron emission tomography study. *Biological Psychiatry, 45*(7), 806–816.

Bretherton, I., Fritz, J., Zahn-Waxler, C., & Ridgeway, D. (1986). Learning to talk about emotions: A functionalist perspective. *Child Development, 57,* 529–548.

Breuer, J. & Freud, S. (1893, January). Studies on hysteria. In J. Strachey (Trans. & Ed.), *The standard edition of the Complete psychological works of Sigmund Freud* (Vol. 2, pp. 1–19). London: Hogarth. (Original work published 1893–1895).

Bril, B., & Sabatier, C. (1986). The cultural context of motor development: Postural manipulations in the daily life of Bambara babies (Mali). *International Journal of Behavioral Development, 9,* 439–453.

Brodie, J. & Lobel, E. (2004). Integrating fundamental principles underlying somatic practices into the dance technique class. *Journal of Dance Education, 4*(3), 80–87.

Brosschot, J. F., Pieper, S., & Thayer, J. F. (2005). Expanding stress theory: prolonged activation and perseverative cognition. *Psychoneuroendocrinology, 30*(10), 1043–1049.

Brown, K. W., & Ryan, R. M. (2003). The benefits of being present: Mindfulness and its role in psychological well-being. *Journal of Personality and Social Psychology, 84*(4), 822–848.

Brown, R. J. (2004). Psychological mechanisms of medically unexplained symptoms: An integrative conceptual model. *Psychological Bulletin, 130*(5), 793–812.

Brown, R. P., & Gerbarg, P. L. (2005). Sudarshan Kriya Yogic breathing in the treatment of stress, anxiety, and depression: Part II—clinical applications and guidelines. *Journal of Alternative and Complementary Medicine, 11*(4), 711–717.

Brown, S., Martinez, M. J., & Parsons, L. M. (2006). Music and language side by side in the brain: A PET study of the generation of melodies and sentences. *European Journal of Neuroscience, 23*(10), 2791–2803.

Bru, E., Mykletun, R. J., & Svebak, S. (1993). Neuroticism, extraversion, anxiety and Type A behaviour as mediators of neck, shoulder and lower back pain in female hospital staff. *Personality and Individual Differences, 15*(5), 485–492.

Bruner, J. (1983). *Child's talk: Learning to use language.* New York: Norton.

Buchholz, I. (1994). Breathing, voice, and movement therapy: Applications to breathing disorders. *Biofeedback and Self-Regulation, 19*(2), 141–153.

Bugental, D. B., Martorell, G. A., & Barraza, V. (2003). The hormonal costs of subtle forms of infant maltreatment. *Hormones and Behavior, 43*(1), 237–244.

Buhner, S. H. (2004). *The secret teachings of plants: The intelligence of the heart in the direct perception of nature.* Rochester, VT: Bear.

Burdette, H. L., & Whitaker, R. C. (2005). Resurrecting free play in young children: Looking beyond fitness and fatness to attention, affiliation, and affect. *Archives of Pediatric Adolescent Medicine, 159*(1), 46–50.

Burker, E. J., Wong, H., Sloane, P. D., Mattingly, D., Preisser, J., & Mitchell, C. M. (1995). Predictors of fear of falling in dizzy and nondizzy elderly. *Psychology and Aging, 10*(1), 104–110.

Burns, J., Labbé, E., Williams, K., & McCall, J. (1999). Perceived and physiological indicators of relaxation: As different as Mozart and Alice in chains. *Applied Psychophysiology and Biofeedback, 24*(3), 197–202.

Burns, J. W. (2006a). Arousal of negative emotions and symptom-specific reactivity in chronic low back pain patients. *Emotion, 6*(2), 309–319.

Burns, J. W. (2006b). The role of attentional strategies in moderating links between acute pain induction and subsequent psychological stress: Evidence for symptom-specific reactivity among patients with chronic pain versus healthy nonpatients. *Emotion, 6*(2), 180–192.

Butler, E. A., Egloff, B., Wlhelm, F. H., Smith, N. C., Erickson, E. A., & Gross, J. J. (2003). The social consequences of expressive suppression. *Emotion, 3*(1), 48–67.

Butler, E. A., Lee, T. L., & Gross, J. J. (2007). Emotion regulation and culture: Are the social consequences of emotion suppression culture-specific? *Emotion, 7*(1), 30–48.

Butler, J. E. (2007). Drive to the human respiratory muscles. *Respiratory Physiology & Neurobiology, 159*(2), 115–126.

Butler, L. D. (2006). Normative dissociation. *Psychiatric Clinics of North America, 29*(1), 45–62.

Cacioppo, J. T., Priester, J. R., & Berntson, G. G. (1993). Rudimentary determinants of attitudes: II. Arm flexion and extension have differential effects on attitudes. *Journal of Personality and Social Psychology, 65*(1), 5–17.

Caldwell, C. (1996). *Getting our bodies back: Recovery, healing, and transformation through body-centered psychotherapy.* Boston, MA: Shambhala.

Campbell-Sills, L., Barlow, D. H., Brown, T. A., & Hofmann, S. G. (2006). Acceptability and suppression of negative emotion in anxiety and mood disorders. *Emotion, 6*(4), 587–595.

Cappelletto, F. (2003). Long-term memory of extreme events: From autobiography to history. *Journal of the Royal Anthropological Institute, 9,* 239–257.

Carlsson, K., Petersson, K. M., Lundqvist, D., Karlsson, A., Ingvar, M., & Ohman, A. (2004). Fear and the amygdala: Manipulation of awareness generates differential cerebral responses to phobic and fear-relevant (but nonfeared) stimuli. *Emotion, 4*(4), 340–353.

Carpenter, M., Call, J., & Tomasello, M. (2005). Twelve- and 18-month-olds copy actions in terms of goals. *Developmental Science, 8*(1), F13–F20.

Carter, C. S., MacDonald, A. W., 3rd, Ross, L. L., & Stenger, V. A. (2001). Anterior cingulate cortex activity and impaired self-monitoring of performance in patients with schizophrenia: An event-related fMRI study. *American Journal of Psychiatry, 158*(9), 1423–1428.

Cartwright, M., Wardle, J., Steggles, N., Simon, A. E., Croker, H., & Jarvis, M. J. (2003). Stress and dietary practices in adolescents. *Health Psychology, 22*(4), 362–369.

Cassidy, J. (1994). Emotion regulation: Influences of attachment relationships. *Monographs of the Society for Research in Child Development, 59,* 228–249.

Cassidy, J., & Berlin, L. J. (1994). The insecure/ambivalent pattern of attachment: Theory and research. *Child Development, 65,* 971–991.

Centonze, D., Palmieri, M. G., Boffa, L., Pierantozzi, M., Stanzione, P., Brusa, L. et al. (2005). Cortical hyperexcitability in post-traumatic stress disorder secondary to minor accidental head trauma: A neurophysiologic study. *Journal of Psychiatry and Neuroscience, 30*(2), 127–132.

Chan, D., & Woollacott, M. (2007). Effects of level of meditation experience on attentional focus: Is the efficiency of executive or orientation networks improved? *Journal of Alternative and Complementary Medicine, 13*(6), 651–657.

Chapman, C. R. & Nakamura, Y. (1999). Pain and consciousness: A constructivist approach. *Pain Forum, 8*(3), 113–123.

Chemtob, C. M., Nomura, Y., & Abramovitz, R. A. (2008). Impact of conjoined exposure to the World Trade Center attacks and to other traumatic events on the behavioral problems of preschool children. *Archives of Pediatric Adolescent Medicine, 162*(2), 126–133.

Chen, S. (1985). Infant cry: Does crying have a tension releasing function? *Research & Clinical Center for Child Development Annual Report, 7,* 49–56.

Cicchetti, D. (2002). The impact of social experience on neurobiological systems: Illustration from a constructivist view of child maltreatment. *Cognitive Development, 17*(3–4), 1407–1428.

Ciesla, J. A., & Roberts, J. E. (2007). Rumination, negative cognition, and their interactive effects on depressed mood. *Emotion, 7*(3), 555–565.

Cioffi, D., & Holloway, J. (1993). Delayed costs of suppressed pain. *Journal of Personality and Social Psychology, 64*(2), 274–282.

Clarici, A., Clarici, A., Travan, L., Accardo, A., De Vonderweid, U., & Bava, A. (2002). Crying of a newborn child: Alarm signal or protocommunication? *Perceptual and Motor Skills, 95*(3, Pt 1), 752–754.

Clark, L., & Tiggemann, M. (2006). Appearance culture in nine- to 12-year-old girls: Media and peer influences on body dissatisfaction. *Social Development, 15*(4), 628–643.

Cohen, B. M., & Carlezon, W. A., Jr. (2007). Can't get enough of that dopamine. *American Journal of Psychiatry, 164*(4), 543–546.

Cohen, F., & Lazarus, R. S. (1973). Active coping processes, coping dispositions, and recovery from surgery. *Psychosomatic Medicine, 35*(5), 375–389.

Cohen, R. A., Kaplan, R. F., Zuffante, P., Moser, D. J., Jenkins, M. A., Salloway, S., et al. (1999). Alteration of intention and self-initiated action associated with bilateral anterior cingulotomy. *Journal of Neuropsychiatry Clinical Neuroscience, 11*(4), 444–453.

Cole, J. & Paillard, J. (1998). Living without touch and peripheral information about body position and movement: Studies with deafferented subjects. In J. Bermudez, A. Marcel, N. Eilan (Eds.), *The body and the self* (pp. 245–266). Cambridge, MA: MIT Press.

Colman, R. A., & Widom, C. S. (2004). Childhood abuse and neglect and adult intimate relationships: A prospective study. *Child Abuse and Neglect, 28*(11), 1133–1151.

Colombo, J., Frick, J. E., Ryther, J. S., Coldren, J. T., & Mitchell, D. W. (1995). Infant's detection of analogs of "motherese" in noise. *Merrill-Palmer Quarterly, 41,* 104–113.

References

Conrad, R., Weber, N. F., Lehnert, M., Holz, F. G., Liedtke, R., & Eter, N. (2007). Alexithymia and emotional distress in patients with central serous chorioretinopathy. *Psychosomatics, 48*(6), 489–495.

Conway, M. A., Turk, D. J., Miller, S. L., Logan, J., Nebes, R. D., Meltzer, C. C. et al. (1999). A positron emission tomography (PET) study of autobiographical memory retrieval. *Memory, 7*(5–6), 679–702.

Cook, L. B. (1996). The importance of the expiratory pause. Comparison of the Mapleson A, C and D breathing systems using a lung model. *Anaesthesia, 51*(5), 453–460.

Coombes, S. A., Cauraugh, J. H., & Janelle, C. M. (2007). Emotional state and initiating cue alter central and peripheral motor processes. *Emotion, 7*(2), 275–284.

Coombes, S. A., Janelle, C. M., & Duley, A. R. (2005). Emotion and motor control: Movement attributes following affective picture processing. *Journal of Motivational Behavior, 37*(6), 425–436.

Copstick, S., Taylor, K., Hayes, R., & Morris, N. (1986). The relation of time of day to childbirth. *Journal of Reproductive and Infant Psychology, 4*(1–2), 13–22.

Corstorphine, E. (2006). Cognitive-emotional-behavioural therapy for the eating disorders: Working with beliefs about emotions. *European Eating Disorders Review, 14*, 448–461.

Cottingham, J. T., Porges, S. W., & Richmond, K. (1988). Shifts in pelvic inclination angle and parasympathetic tone produced by Rolfing soft tissue manipulation. *Physical Therapy, 68*(9), 1364–1370.

Craig, A. D. (2002). How do you feel? Interoception: the sense of the physiological condition of the body. *Nature Reviews Neuroscience, 3*(8), 655–666.

Craig, A. D. (2008). Interoception and emotion. In M. Lewis, J. M. Haviland-Jones, & L. F. Barrett (Eds.), *Handbook of emotions* (3rd ed., pp. 272–288). New York, NY: Guilford Press.

Critchley, H. D., Mathias, C. J., & Dolan, R. J. (2001). Neuroanatomical basis for first- and second-order representations of bodily states. *Nature Neuroscience, 4*(2), 207–212.

Critchley, H. D., Mathias, C. J., & Dolan, R. J. (2002). Fear conditioning in humans: The influence of awareness and autonomic arousal on functional neuroanatomy. *Neuron, 33*(4), 653–663.

Critchley, H. D., Wiens, S., Rotshtein, P., Ohman, A., & Dolan, R. J. (2004). Neural systems supporting interoceptive awareness. *Nature Neuroscience, 7*(2), 189–195.

Crombez, G., Van Damme, S., & Eccleston, C. (2005). Hypervigilance to pain: an experimental and clinical analysis. *Pain, 116*(1–2), 4–7.

Crossley, N. (2007). Researching embodiment by way of 'body techniques'. *Sociological Review, 55*(Suppl. 1), 80–94.

Csikszentmihalyi, M. (1990). *Flow: The psychology of optimal experience.* New York: Harper Perennial.

Cunnington, R., Windischberger, C., & Moser, E. (2005). Premovement activity of the pre-supplementary motor area and the readiness for action: Studies of time-resolved event-related functional MRI. *Human Movement Science, 24*(5–6), 644–656.

Dalgleish, T., Tchanturia, K., Serpell, L., Hems, S., Yiend, J., de Silva, P. et al. (2003). Self-reported parental abuse relates to autobiographical memory style in patients with eating disorders. *Emotion, 3*(3), 211–222.

Damasio, A. R. (1999). How the brain creates the mind. *Scientific American, 281*(6), 112–117.

Damasio, A. R. (1996). The somatic marker hypothesis and the possible functions of the prefrontal cortex. *Philosophical Transactions: Royal Society of London B Biological Sciences, 351*(1346), 1413–1420.

Damasio, A. R., Grabowski, T. J., Bechara, A., Damasio, H., Ponto, L. L. B., Parvizi, J., et al. (2000). Subcortical and cortical brain activity during the feeling of self-generated emotions. *Nature Neuroscience, 3*(10), 1049–1056.

Dantzer, R. (2005). Somatization: A psychoneuroimmune perspective. *Psychoneuroendocrinology, 30*(10), 947–952.

Daubenmier, J. J. (2005). The relationship of yoga, body awareness, and body responsiveness to self-objectification and disordered eating. *Psychology of Women Quarterly, 29*(2), 207–219.

Davidson, J. R., Payne, V. M., Connor, K. M., Foa, E. B., Rothbaum, B. O., Hertzberg, M. A. et al. (2005). Trauma, resilience and saliostasis: Effects of treatment in post-traumatic stress disorder. *International Clinical Psychopharmacology, 20*(1), 43–48.

Davies, J. M. (1996). Linking the "pre-analytic" with the postclassical. *Contemporary Psychoanalysis, 32,* 553–576.

Davison, K. K., & Birch, L. L. (2002). Processes linking weight status and self-concept among girls from ages 5 to 7 years. *Developmental Psychology, 38*(5), 735–748.

Day, J. M., & Tappan, M. B. (1996). The narrative approach to moral development: From the epistemic subject to dialogical selves. *Human Development, 39,* (2), 67–82.

References

De Berardis, D., Campanella, D., Gambi, F., La Rovere, R., Sepede, G., Core, L. et al. (2007). Alexithymia, fear of bodily sensations, and somatosensory amplification in young outpatients with panic disorder. *Psychosomatics: Journal of Consultation Liaison Psychiatry, 48*(3), 239–246.

Dębiec, J., & LeDoux, J. E. (2006). Noradrenergic signaling in the amygdala contributes to the reconsolidation of fear memory: Treatment implications for PTSD. *Annals of the New York Academy of Sciences, 1071*, 521–524.

Decety, J., & Chaminade, T. (2003). When the self represents the other: A new cognitive neuroscience view on psychological identification. *Consciousness and Cognition: An International Journal, 12*(4), 577–596.

Deckro, G. R., Ballinger, K. M., Hoyt, M., Wilcher, M., Dusek, J., Myers, P., et al. (2002). The evaluation of a mind/body intervention to reduce psychological distress and perceived stress in college students. *Journal of American College Health, 50*(6), 281–287.

Deepak, K. K., & Behari, M. (1999). Specific muscle EMG biofeedback for hand dystonia. *Applied Psychophysiology and Biofeedback, 24*(4), 267–280.

DeGangi, G. A., Wietlisbach, S., Goodin, M., & Scheiner, N. (1993). A comparison of structured sensorimotor therapy and child-centered activity in the treatment of preschool children with sensorimotor problems. *The American Journal of Occupational Therapy, 47*(9), 777–786.

de Gelder, B. (2006). Towards the neurobiology of emotional body language. *Nature Reviews Neuroscience, 7*(3), 242–249.

de Gelder, B., Snyder, J., Greve, D., Gerard, G., & Hadjikhani, N. (2004). Fear fosters flight: a mechanism for fear contagion when perceiving emotion expressed by a whole body. *Proceedings of the Natioal Academy of Sciences, 101*(47), 16701–16706.

Dehaene, S., & Naccache, L. (2001). Towards a cognitive neuroscience of consciousness: Basic evidence and a workspace framework. *Cognition, 79*(1–2), 1–37.

Delinsky, S. S., & Wilson, G. T. (2006). Mirror exposure for the treatment of body image disturbance. *International Journal of Eating Disorders, 39*(2), 108–116.

Dempsey, J. A., Sheel, A. W., St Croix, C. M., & Morgan, B. J. (2002). Respiratory influences on sympathetic vasomotor outflow in humans. *Respiratory Physiology & Neurobiology, 130*(1), 3–20.

Denault, A.-S., & Poulin, F. (2007, November). Sports as peer socialization contexts. *International Journal of Behavioral Development, 31*(6, Suppl. 2 Serial No. 52), 5–7.

Deutsch, F. (1952). Analytic posturology. *Psychoanalytic Society Quarterly, 21,* 196–214.

Devinsky, O., Morrell, M. J., & Vogt, B. A. (1995). Contributions of anterior cingulate cortex to behaviour. *Brain, 118* (Pt 1), 279–306.

Dewey, J. (1934). *Art as experience.* New York: Minton, Balch & Company.

Diamond, L. M. (2001). Contributions of psychophysiology to research on adult attachment: Review and recommendations. *Personality and Social Psychology Review, 5*(4), 276–295.

Dickerson, S. S., Gruenewald, T. L., & Kemeny, M. E. (2004). When the social self is threatened: Shame, physiology, and health. *Journal of Personality, 72*(6), 1191–1216.

Dieter, J. N. I., Field, T., Hernandez-Reif, M., Emory, E. K., & Redzepi, M. (2003). Stable preterm infants gain more weight and sleep less after five days of massage therapy. *Journal of Pediatric Psychology, 28*(6), 403–411.

Ding, C., Walcott, B., & Keyser, K. T. (2003). Sympathetic neural control of the mouse lacrimal gland. *Investigative Ophthalmology & Visual Science, 44*(4), 1513–1520.

DiPalma, E. (1996). *Dance movement psychotherapy.* http://www.dmtgroup.com.

DiPietro, J. A., Hilton, S. C., Hawkins, M., Costigan, K. A., & Pressman, E. K. (2002). Maternal stress and affect influence fetal neurobehavioral development. *Developmental Psychology, 38*(5), 659–668.

Diseth, T. H. (2005). Dissociation in children and adolescents as reaction to trauma—An overview of conceptual issues and neurobiological factors. *Nordic Journal of Psychiatry, 59*(2), 79–91.

Dittmar, H., Halliwell, E., & Ive, S. (2006). Does Barbie make girls want to be thin? The effect of experimental exposure to images of dolls on the body image of 5- to 8-year-old girls. *Developmental Psychology, 42*(2), 283–292.

Dobbs, C. M., Vasquez, M., Glaser, R., & Sheridan, J. F. (1993). Mechanisms of stress-induced modulation of viral pathogenesis and immunity. *Journal of Neuroimmunology, 48*(2), 151–160.

Dodt, C., Wallin, G., Fehm, H. L., & Elam, M. (1998). The stress hormone adrenocorticotropin enhances sympathetic outflow to the muscle vascular bed in humans. *Journal of Hypertension, 16*(2), 195–201.

Dohnt, H., & Tiggemann, M. (2006). The contribution of peer and media influences to the development of body satisfaction and self-esteem in young girls: A prospective study. *Developmental Psychology, 42*(5), 929–936.

References

Drolet, G., Dumont, E. C., Gosselin, I., Kinkead, R., Laforest, S., & Trottier, J. F. (2001). Role of endogenous opioid system in the regulation of the stress response. *Prog Neuropsychopharmacology Biology Psychiatry, 25*(4), 729–741.

Duan, Y. F., Winters, R., McCabe, P. M., Green, E. J., Huang, Y., & Schneiderman, N. (1996). Behavioral characteristics of defense and vigilance reactions elicited by electrical stimulation of the hypothalamus in rabbits. *Behavioural Brain Research, 81*(1–2), 33–41.

Dull, H. (1997). *Watsu: Freeing the body in water* (2nd ed). Harbin, CA: Harbin Springs.

Dunn, A. J., Swiergiel, A. H., & Palamarchouk, V. (2004). Brain circuits involved in corticotropin-releasing factor-norepinephrine interactions during stress. *Annals of the New York Academy of Sciences, 1018*, 25–34.

Dunn, J., Bretherton, I., & Munn, P. (1987). Conversations about feeling states between mothers and their young children. *Developmental Psychology, 23*(1), 132–139.

Dybdahl, R. (2001). Children and mothers in war: An outcome study of a psychosocial intervention program. *Child Development, 72*(4), 1214–1230.

Ebeling, H., Moilanen, I., Linna, S. L., & Räsänen, E. (2001). Somatically expressed psychological distress and alexithymia in adolescence—Reflecting unbearable emotions? *Nordic Journal of Psychiatry, 55*(6), 387–393.

Eckerman, C. O., Oehler, J. M., Medvin, M. B., & Hannan, T. E. (1994). Premature newborns as social partners before term age. *Infant Behavior and Development, 17*, 55–70.

Edelstein, R. S. (2006). Attachment and emotional memory: Investigating the source and extent of avoidant memory impairments. *Emotion, 6*(2), 340–345.

Egger, H. L., Costello, E. J., Erkanli, A., & Angold, A. (1999). Somatic complaints and psychopathology in children and adolescents: Stomachaches, musculoskeletal pains, and headaches. *Journal of the American Academy of Child and Adolescent Psychiatry, 38*(7), 852–860.

Ehrsson, H. H., Holmes, N. P., & Passingham, R. E. (2005). Touching a rubber hand: Feeling of body ownership is associated with activity in multisensory brain areas. *Journal of Neuroscience, 25*(45), 10564–10573.

Ehrsson, H. H., Kito, T., Sadato, N., Passingham, R. E., & Naito, E. (2005). Neural substrate of body size: Illusory feeling of shrinking of the waist. *PLoS Biology, 3*(12), e412.

Ehrsson, H. H., Spence, C., & Passingham, R. E. (2004). That's my hand! Activity in premotor cortex reflects feeling of ownership of a limb. *Science, 305*(5685), 875–877.

Ehrsson, H. H., Wiech, K., Weiskopf, N., Dolan, R. J., & Passingham, R. E. (2007). Threatening a rubber hand that you feel is yours elicits a cortical anxiety response. *Proceedings of the National Academy of Sciences USA, 104*(23), 9828–9833.

Eichenbaum, H., & Cohen, N. J. (2001). *From conditioning to conscious recollection.* New York: Oxford University Press

Eisen, M. L., Goodman, G. S., Qin, J., Davis, S., & Crayton, J. (2007). Maltreated children's memory: Accuracy, suggestibility, and psychopathology. *Developmental Psychology, 43*(6), 1275–1294.

Eisenberg, N., Cumberland, A., Spinrad, T. L., Fabes, R. A., Shepard, S. A., Reiser, M. et al. (2001). The relations of regulation and emotionality to children's externalizing and internalizing problem behavior. *Child Development, 72*(4), 1112–1134.

Eisler, R. (1987). *The chalice and the blade: Our history, our future.* San Francisco: HarperCollins.

Ekman, P. & Friesen, W. V. (1982). Felt, false, and miserable smiles. *Journal of Nonverbal Behavior, 6,* 238–252.

Ekman, P. (1965). Differential communication of affect by head and body cues. *Journal of Personality and Social Psychology, 2*(5), 726–735.

Eldridge, R. L. (1975). Relationship between respiratory nerve and muscle activity and muscle force output. *Journal of Applied Physiology, 39*(4), 567–574.

Emmons, R. A., & McCullough, M. E. (2003). Counting blessings versus burdens: An experimental investigation of gratitude and subjective well-being in daily life. *Journal of Personality and Social Psychology, 84*(2), 377–389.

Engel, J. M., Jensen, M. P., & Schwartz, L. (2004). Outcome of biofeedback-assisted relaxation for pain in adults with cerebral palsy: Preliminary findings. *Applied Psychophysiology and Biofeedback, 29*(2), 135–140.

Epstein, M. (1998). *Going to pieces without falling apart: A buddhist perspective on wholeness.* New York: Broadway Books.

Erickson, M. F., Sroufe, L. A., & Egeland, B. (1985). Relationship between quality of attachment and behavior problems in preschool in a high-risk sample. In I. Bretherton & E. Waters (Eds.), Growing points of attachment theory and research. *Monographs of the Society for Research in Child Development, 50* (Serial No. 209), 147–166.

Erikson, E. (1950). *Childhood and society.* New York: Norton.

Esch, T., & Stefano, G. B. (2005). The neurobiology of love. *Neuroendocrinology Letters, 26*(3), 175–192.

References

Esch, T., Fricchione, G. L., & Stefano, G. B. (2003). The therapeutic use of the relaxation response in stress-related diseases. *Medical Science Monitor: International Medical Journal of Experimental and Clinical Research, 9*(2), RA23–RA34.

Éthier, L. S., Lemelin, J.-P., & Lacharité, C. (2004). A longitudinal study of the effects of chronic maltreatment on children's behavioral and emotional problems. *Child Abuse & Neglect, 28*(12), 1265–1278.

Fagot, B. I. (1997). Attachment, parenting, and peer interactions of toddler children. *Developmental Psychology, 33*(3), 489–499.

Farrell, M. J., Laird, A. R., & Egan, G. F. (2005). Brain activity associated with painfully hot stimuli applied to the upper limb: A meta-analysis. *Human Brain Mapping, 25*(1), 129–139.

Farrer, C., & Frith, C. D. (2002). Experiencing oneself vs another person as being the cause of an action: The neural correlates of the experience of agency. *Neuroimage, 15*(3), 596–603.

Feldenkrais, M. (1981). *The elusive obvious or basic Feldenkrais.* Capitola, CA: Meta.

Feldenkrais, M. (1985). *The potent self: A study of spontaneity and compulsion.* Berkeley, CA: Frog & Somatic Resources.

Feldman, R. (2006). From biological rhythms to social rhythms: Physiological precursors of mother-infant synchrony. *Developmental Psychology, 42*(1), 175–188.

Feldman, R., Keren, M., Gross-Rozval, O., & Tyano, S. (2004). Mother-child touch patterns in infant feeding disorders: Relation to maternal, child, and environmental factors. *Journal of the American Academy of Child and Adolescent Psychiatry, 43*(9), 1089–1097.

Feldman, R., Weller, A., Sirota, L., & Eidelman, A. I. (2002). Skin-to-skin contact (kangaroo care) promotes self-regulation in premature infants: Sleep-wake cyclicity, arousal modulation, and sustained exploration. *Developmental Psychology, 38*(2), 194–207.

Feldman, R., Weller, A., Zagoory-Sharon, O., & Levine, A. (2007). Evidence for a neuroendocrinological foundation of human affiliation: Plasma oxytocin levels across pregnancy and the postpartum period predict mother–infant bonding. *Psychological Science, 18*(11), 965–970.

Fellous, J. (1999). The neuromodulatory basis of emotion. *The Neuroscientist, 5,* 283–294.

Fenz, W. D., & Epstein, S. (1967). Gradients of physiological arousal in parachutists as a function of an approaching jump. *Psychosomatic Medicine, 29*(1), 33–51.

Ferrari, P. F., Gallese, V., Rizzolatti, G., & Fogassi, L. (2003). Mirror neurons responding to the observation of ingestive and communicative mouth actions in the monkey ventral premotor cortex. *European Journal of Neuroscience, 17*(8), 1703–1714.

Field, T. (1998). Touch therapy effects on development. *International Journal of Behavioral Development, 22*(4), 779–797.

Field, T. (2001). Massage therapy facilitates weight gain in preterm infants. *Current Directions in Psychological Science, 10*(2), 51–54.

Fields, H. (2004). State-dependent opioid control of pain. *Nature Reviews Neuroscience, 5*(7), 565–575.

Fiese, B. H. & Schwartz, M. (2008). Reclaiming the family table: Mealtimes and child health and wellbeing. *Social Policy Report, SRCD, 22*(4), 3–18.

Fink, G. R., Markowitsch, H. J., & Reinkemeier, M. (1996). Cerebral representation of one's own past: Neural networks involved in autobiographical memory. *Journal of Neuroscience, 16*(13), 4275–4282.

Fischer, A. H., & Jansz, J. (1995). Reconciling emotions with Western personhood. *Journal for the Theory of Social Behaviour, 25*(1), 59–80.

Fivush, R. (1991). The social construction of personal narratives. *Merrill-Palmer Quarterly, 37*(1), 59–81.

Fivush, R., Haden, C., & Adam, S. (1995). Structure and coherence of preschoolers' personal narratives over time: Implications for childhood amnesia. *Journal of Experimental Child Psychology, 60*(1), 32–56.

Flodmark, B. T., & Aase, G. (1992). Musculoskeletal symptoms and type A behaviour in blue collar workers. *British Journal of Industrial Medicine, 49*(10), 683–687.

Flor, H., & Turk, D. C. (1989). Psychophysiology of chronic pain: Do chronic pain patients exhibit symptom-specific psychophysiological responses? *Psychological Bulletin, 105*(2), 215–259.

Flor, H., Birbaumer, N., Schugens, M. M., & Lutzenberger, W. (1992). Symptom-specific psychophysiological responses in chronic pain patients. *Psychophysiology, 29*(4), 452–460.

Flor, H., Turk, D. C., & Birbaumer, N. (1985). Assessment of stress-related psychophysiological reactions in chronic back pain patients. *Journal of Consulting and Clinical Psychology, 53*(3), 354–364.

Fogel, A. (1993). *Developing through relationships: Origins of communication, self and culture.* Chicago: University of Chicago Press.

Fogel, A. (1997). Seeing and being seen. In V. Lewis & G. M. Collis (Eds.), *Blindness and psychological development in young children.* (pp. 86–98). Leicester, England: The British Psychological Society.

Fogel, A. (2004). Remembering infancy: Accessing our earliest experiences. In G. Bremner & A. Slater (Eds.), *Theories of infant development.* Blackwell Publishers.

Fogel, A. (2009). *Infancy: Infant, family, and society, 5th Edition.* Cornwall-on-Hudson, NY: Sloan.

Fogel, A., & DeKoeyer-Laros, I. (2007). The development transition to secondary intersubjectivity in the 2nd half year: A microgenetic case study. *Journal of Developmental Processes, 2,* 63–90.

Fogel, A., Garvey, A., Hsu, H., & West-Stroming, D. (2006). *Change processes in relationships: A relational—historical research approach.* Cambridge, UK: Cambridge University Press.

Fokkema, D. S. (1999). The psychobiology of strained breathing and its cardiovascular implications: A functional system review. *Psychophysiology, 36*(2), 164–175.

Forbes, L. M., Evans, E. M., Moran, G., & Pederson, D. R. (2007). Change in atypical maternal behavior predicts change in attachment disorganization from 12 to 24 months in a high-risk sample. *Child Development, 78*(3), 955–971.

Fox, N. A. (2004). Temperament and early experience form social behavior. *Annals of the New York Academy of Sciences, 1038,* 171–178.

Fraiberg, S., Adelson, E., & Shapiro, V. (1975). Ghosts in the nursery: A psychoanalytic approach to the problem of impaired mother-infant relationships. *Journal of the American Academy of Child Psychiatry, 14,* 387–421.

Francati, V., Vermetten, E., & Bremner, J. D. (2007). Functional neuroimaging studies in posttraumatic stress disorder: Review of current methods and findings. *Depression and Anxiety, 24*(3), 202–218.

Frankland, P. W., Bontempi, B., Talton, L. E., Kaczmarek, L., & Silva, A. J. (2004). The involvement of the anterior cingulate cortex in remote contextual fear memory. *Science, 304*(5672), 881–883.

Freeman, G. L., & Katzoff, E. T. (1932). Minor studies from the psychological laboratory of Northwestern University. I. Muscular tension and irritability. *American Journal of Psychology, 44,* 789–792.

Freud, S. (1903/1953). Three essays on the theory of sexuality. In J. Strachey (Ed. & Trans.), *The standard edition of the complete works of Sigmund Freud, (Vol. 7),* (pp. 1550–1669). London: Hogarth Press. (Original work published 1903)

Frewen, P. A., & Lanius, R. A. (2006). Toward a psychobiology of posttraumatic self-dysregulation: Reexperiencing, hyperarousal, dissociation, and emotional numbing. *Annals of the New York Academy of Sciences, 1071*, 110–124.

Frewen, P. A., Lanius, R. A., Dozois, D. J. A., Neufeld, R. W. J., Pain, C., Hopper, J. W. et al. (2008). Clinical and neural correlates of alexithymia in posttraumatic stress disorder. *Journal of Abnormal Psychology, 117*(1), 171–181.

Fridlund, A. J., Hatfield, M. E., Cottam, G. L., & Fowler, S. C. (1986). Anxiety and striate-muscle activation: Evidence from electromyographic pattern analysis. *Journal of Abnormal Psychology, 95*(3), 228–236.

Fries, A. B., Ziegler, T. E., Kurian, J. R., Jacoris, S., & Pollak, S. D. (2005). Early experience in humans is associated with changes in neuropeptides critical for regulating social behavior. *Proceedings of the National Academy of Sciences, 102*(47), 17237–17240.

Fries, E., Hesse, J., Hellhammer, J., & Hellhammer, D. H. (2005). A new view on hypocortisolism. *Psychoneuroendocrinology, 30*(10), 1010–1016.

Frijda, N. H. (1986). *The emotions.* New York: Cambridge University Press.

Fuchs, T. (2005). Corporealized and disembodied minds: A phenomenological view of the body in melancholia and schizophrenia. *Philosophy, Psychology & Psychiatry, 12*(2), 95–107.

Gaensbauer, T. J. (2002). Representations of trauma in infancy: Clinical and theoretical implications for the understanding of early memory. *Infant Mental Health Journal, 23*(3), 259–277.

Gallese, V. (2000). The brain and the self: Reviewing the neuroscientific evidence. Psychology, 11, http://www.logsci.ecs.soton.ac.uk/cgi/psyc/newpsy?11.034.

Gallese, V., Fadiga, L., Fogassi, L., & Rizzolatti, G. (1996). Action recognition in the premotor cortex. *Brain, 119 (Pt 2)*, 593–609.

Gandevia, S. C., Butler, J. E., Hodges, P. W., & Taylor, J. L. (2002). Balancing acts: Respiratory sensations, motor control and human posture. *Clinical and Experimental Pharmacology and Physiology, 29*(1–2), 118–121.

Gardner, W. N. (1996). The pathophysiology of hyperventilation disorders. *Chest, 109*(2), 516–534.

Garner, D. M. & Garfinkel, P. E. (1981–1982). Body image in anorexia nervosa: Measurement, theory and clinical implications. *International Journal of Psychiatry in Medicine, 11*(3), 263–284.

Gaytán, S. P., Pásaro, R., Coulon, P., Bevengut, M., & Hilaire, G. (2002). Identification of central nervous system neurons innervating the respiratory muscles of the mouse: A transneuronal tracing study. *Brain Research Bulletin, 57*(3–4), 335–339.

Gendlin, E. T. (1962). *Experiencing and the creation of meaning.* New York: The Free Press of Glencoe.

Gendolla, G. H. E., Abele, A. E., Andrei, A., Spurk, D., & Richter, M. (2005). Negative mood, self-focused attention, and the experience of physical symptoms: The joint impact hypothesis. *Emotion, 5*(2), 131–144.

George, M. (2005). Making sense of muscle: The body experiences of collegiate women athletes. *Sociological Inquiry, 75*(3), 317–345.

Gerardi, M., Rothbaum, B. O., Ressler, K., Heekin, M., & Rizzo, A. (2008). Virtual reality exposure therapy using a virtual Iraq: Case report. *Journal of Traumatic Stress, 21*(2), 209–213.

Gershoff, E. T. (2002). Corporal punishment by parents and associated child behaviors and experiences: A meta-analytic and theoretical review. *Psychological Bulletin, 128*(4), 539–579.

Gevirtz, R. N., Hubbard, D. R., & Harpin, R. E. (1996). Psychophysiologic treatment of chronic lower back pain. *Professional Psychology: Research and Practice, 27*(6), 561–566.

Ghent, E. (1990). Masochism, submission, surrender: Masochism as a perversion of surrender. *Contemporary Psychoanalysis, 26*(1), 108–136.

Gianino, A. & Tronick, E. Z. (1988). The mutual regulation model: The infant's self and interactive regulation and coping and defensive capacities. In T. M. Field, P. M. McCabe, & N. Schneiderman (Eds.), *Stress and coping across development* (pp. 47–68). Hillsdale, NJ: Erlbaum.

Gibran, K. (1997). *The prophet.* New York: Knopf.

Gilbert, N., & Meyer, C. (2005). Fear of negative evaluation and the development of eating psychopathology: A longitudinal study among nonclinical women. *International Journal of Eating Disorders, 37*(4), 307–312.

Gilio, F., Curra, A., Inghilleri, M., Lorenzano, C., Suppa, A., Manfredi, M. et al. (2003). Abnormalities of motor cortex excitability preceding movement in patients with dystonia. *Brain, 126*(Pt 8), 1745–1754.

Gillath, O., Bunge, S. A., Shaver, P. R., Wendelken, C., & Mikulincer, M. (2005). Attachment-style differences in the ability to suppress negative thoughts: Exploring the neural correlates. *Neuroimage, 28*(4), 835–847.

Ginsburg, C. (1999). Body-image, movement and consciousness: Examples from a somatic practice in the Feldenkrais Method. *Journal of Consciousness Studies, 6*(2–3), 79–91.

Gitau, R., Modi, N., Gianakoulopoulos, X., Bond, C., Glover, V., & Stevenson, J. (2002). Acute effects of maternal skin-to-skin contact and massage on saliva cortisol in preterm babies. *Journal of Reproductive and Infant Psychology, 20*(2), 83–88.

Giuliani, N. R., McRae, K., & Gross, J. J. (2008). The up- and down-regulation of amusement: Experiential, behavioral, and autonomic consequences. *Emotion, 8*(5), 714–719.

Goel, N., & Bale, T. L. (2007). Identifying early behavioral and molecular markers of future stress sensitivity. *Endocrinology, 148*(10), 4585–4591.

Gogate, L. J., Walker-Andrews, A. S., & Bahrick, L. E. (2001). The intersensory origins of word comprehension: An ecological–dynamic systems view. *Developmental Science, 4*(1), 1–18.

Goldberg, R. F., Perfetti, C. A., & Schneider, W. (2006). Perceptual knowledge retrieval activates sensory brain regions. *The Journal of Neuroscience, 26*(18), 4917–4921.

Goleman, D. (1977). *The varieties of the meditative experience.* New York: E. P. Dutton.

Gonge, H., Jensen, L. D., & Bonde, J. P. (2002). Are psychosocial factors associated with low-back pain among nursing personnel? *Work & Stress, 16*(1), 79–87.

Goodsitt, A. (1983). Self-regulatory disturbances in eating disorders. *International Journal of Eating Disorders, 2*(3), 51–60.

Goodwin, R. D., Fergusson, D. M., & Horwood, L. J. (2005). Childhood abuse and familial violence and the risk of panic attacks and panic disorder in young adulthood. *Psychological Medicine, 35*(6), 881–890.

Goodyer, I. M., Park, R. J., Netherton, C. M., & Herbert, J. (2001). Possible role of cortisol and dehydroepiandrosterone in human development and psychopathology. *British Journal of Psychiatry, 179*, 243–249.

Gormally, S., Barr, R. G., Wertheim, L., Alkawaf, R., Calinoiu, N., & Young, S. N. (2001). Contact and nutrient caregiving effects on newborn infant pain responses. *Developmental Medicine & Child Neurology, 43*(1), 28–38.

Gottman, J. M., & Levenson, R. W. (1992). Marital processes predictive of later dissolution: Behavior, physiology, and health. *Journal of Personality and Social Psychology, 63*(2), 221–233.

Gould, E. (2007). Structural plasticity. In P. Andersen, R. Morris, D. Amaral, T. Bliss, & J. O'Keefe (Eds.), *The hippocampus book* (pp. 321–341). NY: Oxford University Press.

References

Grassi, C., Deriu, F., Roatta, S., Santarelli, R., Azzena, G. B., & Passatore, M. (1996). Sympathetic control of skeletal muscle function: possible co-operation between noradrenaline and neuropeptide Y in rabbit jaw muscles. *Neuroscience Letters, 212*(3), 204–208.

Grazianom, M. (1999). Where is my arm? The relative role of vision and proprioception in the neuronal representation of limb position. *Proceedings of the National Academy of Sciences, 96,* 10418–10421.

Green, J. A., Gustafson, G. E., Irwin, J. R., Kalinowski, L. L., & Wood, R. M. (1995). Infant crying: Acoustics, perception, and communication. *Early Development and Parenting, 4*(4), 161–175.

Greenhoot, A. F., Johnson, R., & McCloskey, L. A. (2005). Internal state language in the childhood recollections of adolescents with and without abuse histories. *Journal of Cognition and Development, 6*(4), 547–570.

Grewe, O., Nagel, F., Kopiez, R., & Altenmuller, E. (2007). Emotions over time: Synchronicity and development of subjective, physiological, and facial affective reactions to music. *Emotion, 7*(4), 774–788.

Grieser, D. L., & Kuhl, P. K. (1988). Maternal speech to infants in a tonal language: Support for universal prosodic features in motherese. *Developmental Psychology, 24*(1), 14–20.

Gross, J. J., & Levenson, R. W. (1993). Emotional suppression: Physiology, self-report, and expressive behavior. *Journal of Personality and Social Psychology, 64*(6), 970–986.

Gross, J. J., Frederickson, B. L., & Levenson, R. W. (1994). The psychophysiology of crying. *Psychophysiology, 31*(5), 460–468.

Gross, K. J., & Pothoulakis, C. (2007). Role of neuropeptides in inflammatory bowel disease. *Inflammatory Bowel Disease, 13*(7), 918–932.

Grove, G., Coplan, J. D., & Hollander, E. (1997). The neuroanatomy of 5-HT dysregulation and panic disorder. *Journal of Neuropsychiatry & Clinical Neurosciences, 9*(2), 198–207.

Guastella, A. J., Mitchell, P. B., & Dadds, M. R. (2008). Oxytocin increases gaze to the eye region of human faces. *Biological Psychiatry, 63*(1), 3–5.

Guggisberg, A. G., Mathis, J., Herrmann, U. S., & Hess, C. W. (2007). The functional relationship between yawning and vigilance. *Behavioural Brain Research, 179*(1), 159–166.

Gunnar, M. R., & Cheatham, C. L. (2003). Brain and behavior interfaces: Stress and the developing brain. *Infant Mental Health Journal, 24*(3), 195–211.

Gunnar, M. R., & Donzella, B. (2002). Social regulation of the cortisol levels in early human development. *Psychoneuroendocrinology, 27*(1–2), 199–220.

Gusnard, D. A., Akbudak, E., Shulman, G. L., & Raichle, M. E. (2001). Medial prefrontal cortex and self-referential mental activity: Relation to a default mode of brain function. *Proceedings of the National Academy of Sciences USA, 98*(7), 4259–4264.

Hägg, G. M. (1991). Static work loads and occupational myalgia: A new explanation model. In P. A. Anderson, D. J. Hobart, & J. V. Danoff (Eds.), *Electromyographical kinesiology: Proceedings of the 8th Congress of the International Society of Electrophysiological Kinesiology* (pp.141–143). Bridgewater, NJ: Excerpta Medica.

Hajcak, G., Molnar, C., George, M. S., Bolger, K., Koola, J., & Nahas, Z. (2007). Emotion facilitates action: A transcranial magnetic stimulation study of motor cortex excitability during picture viewing. *Psychophysiology, 44*, 91–97.

Haley, D. W., & Stansbury, K. (2003). Infant stress and parent responsiveness: Regulation of physiology and behavior during still-face and reunion. *Child Development, 74*(5), 1534–1546.

Ham, J. & Tronick, E. (in press). Relationship psychophysiology: Physiologic substrates of dyadically expanded states of consciousness: Lessons from mother-infant relational physiology. *Journal of Psychotherapy Research.*

Hamdy, S., Rothwell, J. C., Aziz, Q., Singh, K. D., & Thompson, D. G. (1998). Long-term reorganization of human motor cortex driven by short-term sensory stimulation. *Nature Neuroscience, 1*(1), 64–68.

Hammond, C. G., Gordon, D. C., Fisher, J. T., & Richmond, F. J. (1989). Motor unit territories supplied by primary branches of the phrenic nerve. *Journal of Applied Physiology, 66*(1), 61–71.

Hampes, W. P. (2001). Relation between humor and empathic concern. *Psychological Reports, 88*(1), 241–244.

Han, J. N., Stegen, K., De Valck, C., Clément, J., & Van de Woestijne, K. P. (1996). Influence of breathing therapy on complaints, anxiety and breathing pattern in patients with hyperventilation syndrome and anxiety disorders. *Journal of Psychosomatic Research, 41*(5), 481–493.

Han, J. N., Stegen, K., Schepers, R., Van den Bergh, O., & Van de Woestijne, K. P. (1998). Subjective symptoms and breathing pattern at rest and following hyperventilation in anxiety and somatoform disorders. *Journal of Psychosomatic Research, 45*(6), 519–532.

Hanson, E. K. S., Schellekens, J. M. H., Veldman, J. B. P., & Mulder, L. J. M. (1993). Psychomotor and cardiovascular consequences of mental effort and noise. *Human Movement Science, 12*(6), 607–626.

References

Hariri, A. R., Mattay, V. S., Tessitore, A., Fera, F., & Weinberger, D. R. (2003). Neocortical modulation of the amygdala response to fearful stimuli. *Biological Psychiatry, 53*(6), 494–501.

Harley, K., & Reese, E. (1999). Origins of autobiographical memory. *Developmental Psychology, 35*(5), 1338–1348.

Harré, R. (1991). *Physical being.* Oxford: Blackwell.

Harrington, E. F., Crowther, J. H., Payne Henrickson, H. C., & Mickelson, K. D. (2006). The relationships among trauma, stress, ethnicity, and binge eating. *Cultural Diversity and Ethnic Minority Psychology, 12*(2), 212–229.

Hart, K., & Kenny, M. E. (1997). Adherence to the Super Woman ideal and eating disorder symptoms among college women. *Sex Roles, 36*(7–8), 461–478.

Harter, S., Waters, P. L., & Whitesell, N. R. (1997). Lack of voice as a manifestation of false self-behavior among adolescents: The school setting as a stage upon which the drama of authenticity is enacted. *Educational Psychologist, 32*(3), 153–173.

Haruki, Y. & Takase, H. (2001). Effects of the Eastern art of breathing. In Y. Haruki, I. Homma, A. Umezawa, & Y. Masaoka (Eds.), *Respiration and emotion* (pp. 101–111). New York: Springer-Verlag.

Hastings, P. D., Sullivan, C., McShane, K. E., Coplan, R. J., Utendale, W. T., & Vyncke, J. D. (2008). Parental socialization, vagal regulation, and preschoolers' anxious difficulties: Direct mothers and moderated fathers. *Child Development, 79*(1), 45–64.

Haugstad, G. K., Haugstad, T. S., Kirste, U. M., Leganger, S., Wojniusz, S., Klemmetsen, I. et al. (2006). Posture, movement patterns, and body awareness in women with chronic pelvic pain. *Journal of Psychosomatic Research, 61*(5), 637–644.

Hayward, J. W. (1987). *Shifting worlds, changing minds: Where sciences and Buddhism meet.* Boston, MA: Shambhala.

Heatherton, T. F., & Baumeister, R. F. (1991). Binge eating as escape from self-awareness. *Psychological Bulletin, 110*(1), 86–108.

Hefferline, R. F. (1958). The role of proprioception in the control of behavior. *Transactions of the New York Academy of Sciences, 20*(8), 739–764.

Heim, C., & Nemeroff, C. B. (2001). The role of childhood trauma in the neurobiology of mood and anxiety disorders: Preclinical and clinical studies. *Biological Psychiatry, 49*(12), 1023–1039.

Helminen, E., & Punamäki, R.-L. (2008). Contextualized emotional images in children's dreams: Psychological adjustment in conditions of military trauma. *International Journal of Behavioral Development, 32*(3), 177–187.

Hendriks, M. C. P., Rottenberg, J., & Vingerhoets, A. J. J. M. (2007). Can the distress-signal and arousal-reduction views of crying be reconciled? Evidence from the cardiovascular system. *Emotion, 7*(2), 458–463.

Henneman, E., Somjen, G., & Carpenter, D. O. (1965). Functional significance of cell size in spinal motoneurons. *Journal of Neurophysiology, 28*, 560–580.

Hennig, R., & Lømo, T. (1985). Firing patterns of motor units in normal rats. *Nature, 314*(6007), 164–166.

Herskowitz, M. (1997). *Emotional armoring: An introduction to psychiatric orgone therapy.* New Brunswick, NJ: Transaction.

Hertenstein, M. J. (2002). Touch: Its communicative functions in infancy. *Human Development, 45*(2), 70–94.

Hertenstein, M. J., Keltner, D., App, B., Bulleit, B. A., & Jaskolka, A. R. (2006). Touch communicates distinct emotions. *Emotion, 6*(3), 528–533.

Heshusius, L. (1994). Freeing ourselves from objectivity: Managing subjectivity or turning toward a participatory mode of consciousness? *Educational Researcher, 23*(3), 15–22.

Hinz, A., Seibt, R., & Scheuch, K. (2001). Covariation and temporal stability of peripheral and brachial blood pressure responses to mental and static stress. *Journal of Psychophysiology, 15*(3), 198–207.

Hjortskov, N., Skotte, J., Hye-Knudsen, C., & Fallentin, N. (2005). Sympathetic outflow enhances the stretch reflex response in the relaxed soleus muscle in humans. *Journal of Applied Physiology, 98*(4), 1366–1370.

Ho, E. (1997). Aesthetic considerations in understanding Chinese literati musical behavior. *British Journal of Ethnomusicology, 6*, 35–49.

Hoban, S. (2000). Motion and emotion: The dance/movement therapy experience. *Nursing Homes Magazine*, 33–34.

Hobeika, C. P. (1999). Equilibrium and balance in the elderly. *Ear, Nose & Throat Journal, 78*(8), 558–562, 565–556.

Hobson, R. P., & Meyer, J. A. (2005). Foundations for self and other: A study in autism. *Developmental Science, 8*(6), 481–491.

Hodnett, E. D., & Osborn, R. W. (1989). Effects of continuous intrapartum professional support on childbirth outcomes. *Research in Nursing and Health, 12*(5), 289–297.

Hoehn-Saric, R., & McLeod, D. R. (2000). Anxiety and arousal: Physiological changes and their perception. *Journal of Affective Disorders, 61*(3), 217–224.

Hofferth, S. L., & Sandberg, J. F. (2001). How American children spend their time. *Journal of Marriage and Family, 63*, 295–308.

Holifield, B. (1998). Against the wall / her beating heart: Working with the somatic aspects of transference, countertransference, and dissociation. In D. H. Johnson & I. J. Grand (Eds.), *The body in psychotherapy: Inquiries in somatic psychology* (pp. 59–84). Berkeley, CA: North Atlantic Books.

Hollis, J., Allen, P. M., Fleischmann, D., & Aulak, R. (2007). Personality dimensions of people who suffer from visual stress. *Ophthalmic & Physiological Optics, 27*(6), 603–610.

Holmes, E. A., Brown, R. J., Mansell, W., Fearon, R. P., Hunter, E. C. M., Frasquilho, F., et al. (2005). Are there two qualitatively distinct forms of dissociation? A review and some clinical implications. *Clinical Psychology Review, 25*(1), 1–23.

Holodynski, M. (2004). The miniaturization of expression in the development of emotional self-regulation. *Developmental Psychology, 40*(1), 16–28.

Holt-Lunstad, J., Birmingham, W. A., & Light, K. C. (2008). The influence of a "warm touch" support enhancement intervention among married couples on ambulatory blood pressure, oxytocin, alpha amylase and cortisol. *Psychosomatic Medicine, 70*, 976–985.

Hopkins, B. & Westra, T. (1988). Maternal handling and motor development: An intercultural study. *Genetic, Social and General Psychology Monographs, 114*(3), 377–408.

Hua, Q. P., Zeng, X. Z., Liu, J. Y., Wang, J. Y., Guo, J. Y., & Luo, F. (2008). Dynamic changes in brain activations and functional connectivity during affectively different tactile stimuli. *Cell and Molecular Neurobiology, 28*(1), 57–70.

Huizinga, J. (1998). *The waning of the middle ages.* New York: Courier Dover.

Hunt, C., Keogh, E., & French, C. C. (2006). Anxiety sensitivity: The role of conscious awareness and selective attentional bias to physical threat. *Emotion, 6*(3), 418–428.

Hurwitz, T. A. (2004). Somatization and conversion disorder. *Canadian Journal of Psychiatry, 49*(3), 172–178.

Hutcherson, C. A., Seppala, E. M., & Gross, J. J. (2008). Loving-kindness meditation increases social connectedness. *Emotion, 8*(5), 720–724.

Idhe, D. (2002). *Bodies in technology.* Minneapolis: University of Minnesota Press.

Iverson, J. M., & Fagan, M. K. (2004). Infant vocal-motor cooordination: Precursor to the gesture-speech system? *Child Development, 75*(4), 1053–1066.

Iverson, J. M., & Goldin-Meadow, S. (2001). The resilience of gesture in talk: Gesture in blind speakers and listeners. *Developmental Science, 4*(4), 416–422.

Izquierdo, I., & Medina, J. H. (1997). The biochemistry of memory formation and its regulation by hormones and neuromodulators. *Psychobiology, 25*(1), 1–9.

Jabusch, H. C., Müller, S. V., & Altenmüller, E. (2004). Anxiety in musicians with focal dystonia and those with chronic pain. *Movement Disorders, 19*(10), 1169–1175.

Jackson, B., Kubzansky, L. D., Cohen, S., Jacobs, D. R., & Wright, R. J. (2007). Does harboring hostility hurt? Associations between hostility and pulmonary function in the Coronary Artery Risk Development in (Young) Adults (CARDIA) Study. *Health Psychology, 26*(3), 333–340.

Jacobs, W. J., & Nadel, L. (1985). Stress-induced recovery of fears and phobias. *Psychological Review, 92*(4), 512–531.

Jacobs, W. J., & Nadel, L. (1999). The first panic attack: A neurobiological theory. *Canadian Journal of Experimental Psychology/Revue canadienne de psychologie experimentale, 53*(1), 92–107.

James, W. (1976). *Essays in radical empiricism*. Cambridge, MA: Harvard University Press. (Original work published 1912)

Jamner, L. D., Schwartz, G. E., & Leigh, H. (1988). The relationship between repressive and defensive coping styles and monocyte, eosinophile, and serum glucose levels: Support for the opioid peptide hypothesis of repression. *Psychosomatic Medicine, 50*(6), 567–575.

Jan, M. H., Chai, H. M., Lin, Y. F., Lin, J. C., Tsai, L. Y., Ou, Y. C. et al. (2005). Effects of age and sex on the results of an ankle plantar-flexor manual muscle test. *Physical Therapy, 85*(10), 1078–1084.

Jenkins, W. M., Merzenich, M. M., Ochs, M. T., Allard, T., & Guíc-Robles, E. (1990). Functional reorganization of primary somatosensory cortex in adult owl monkeys after behaviorally controlled tactile stimulation. *Journal of Neurophysiology, 63*(1), 82–104.

Jeong, Y. J., Hong, S. C., Lee, M. S., Park, M. C., Kim, Y. K., & Suh, C. M. (2005). Dance movement therapy improves emotional responses and modulates neurohormones in adolescents with mild depression. *International Journal of Neuroscience, 115*(12), 1711–1720.

Jiang, M., Alheid, G. F., Calandriello, T., & McCrimmon, D. R. (2004). Parabrachial-lateral pontine neurons link nociception and breathing. *Respiratory Physiology & Neurobiology, 143*(2–3), 215–233.

Johansson, B. (1962). Circulatory response to stimulation of somatic afferents. *Acta Physiologica Scandinavica, 62*(Suppl. 198), 1–91.

Johnson, D. H. (1992). *Body: Recovering our sensual wisdom*. Berkeley, CA: North Atlantic Books.

Johnson, D. H. (1995). *Bone, breath, & gesture: Practices of embodiment*. Berkeley, CA: North Atlantic.

References

Johnson, M. K., Raye, C. L., Mitchell, K. J., Touryan, S. R., Greene, E. J., & Nolen-Hoeksema, S. (2006). Dissociating medial frontal and posterior cingulate activity during self-reflection. *SCAN, 1*, 56–64.

Johnson, S. C., Baxter, L. C., Wilder, L. S., Pipe, J. G., Heiserman, J. E., & Prigatano, G. P. (2002). Neural correlates of self-reflection. *Brain, 125*(Pt 8), 1808–1814.

Johnson, S. C., Ok, S. J., & Luo, Y. (2007). The attribution of attention: 9-month-olds' interpretation of gaze as goal-directed action. *Developmental Science, 10*(5), 530–537.

Joireman, J. A., Parrott, L., III, & Hammersla, J. (2002). Empathy and the self-absorption paradox: Support for the distinction between self-rumination and self-reflection. *Self and Identity, 1*(1), 53–65.

Jones, J. F. (2008). An extended concept of altered self: chronic fatigue and post-infection syndromes. *Psychoneuroendocrinology, 33*(2), 119–129.

Juberg, D. R., Alfano, K., Coughlin, R. J., & Thompson, K. M. (2001). An observational study of object mouthing behavior by young children. *Pediatrics, 107*(1), 135–142.

Junker, J., Oberwittler, C., Jackson, D., & Berger, K. (2004). Utilization and perceived effectiveness of complementary and alternative medicine in patients with dystonia. *Movement Disorders, 19*(2), 158–161.

Kabat-Zinn, J. (1994). *Wherever you go, there you are: Mindfulness meditation in everyday life*. New York: Hyperion.

Kaelin-Lang, A., Luft, A. R., Sawaki, L., Burstein, A. H., Sohn, Y. H., & Cohen, L. G. (2002). Modulation of human corticomotor excitability by somatosensory input. *Journal of Physiology, 540*(Pt 2), 623–633.

Kamarck, T. W., & Jennings, J. R. (1991). Biobehavioral factors in sudden cardiac death. *Psychological Bulletin, 109*(1), 42–75.

Kanbara, K., Mitani, Y., Fukunaga, M., Ishino, S., Takebayashi, N., & Nakai, Y. (2004). Paradoxical results of psychophysiological stress profile in functional somatic syndrome: Correlation between subjective tension score and objective stress response. *Applied Psychophysiology and Biofeedback, 29*(4), 255–268.

Kaplan, R. & Kaplan, S. (1989). *The experience of nature: A psychological perspective*. Cambridge, UK: Cambridge University Press.

Karnath, H. O., Baier, B., & Nagele, T. (2005). Awareness of the functioning of one's own limbs mediated by the insular cortex? *Journal of Neuroscience, 25*(31), 7134–7138.

Kasuya, Y., Murakami, T., Oshima, T., & Dohi, S. (2005). Does yawning represent a transient arousal-shift during intravenous induction of general anesthesia? *Anesthesia & Analgesia, 101,* 382–384.

Kc, P., Karibi-Ikiriko, A., Rust, C. F., Jayam-Trouth, A., & Haxhiu, M. A. (2006). Phenotypic traits of the hypothalamic PVN cells innervating airway-related vagal preganglionic neurons. *Respiratory Physiology and Neurobiology, 154*(3), 319–330.

Kelley, W. M., Macrae, C. N., Wyland, C. L., Caglar, S., Inati, S., & Heatherton, T. F. (2002). Finding the self?: An event-related fMRI study. *Journal of Cognitive Neuroscience, 14*(5), 785–794.

Kelly, W. E. (2002). An investigation of worry and sense of humor. *Journal of Psychology: Interdisciplinary and Applied, 136*(6), 657–666.

Kennedy-Moore, E. & Watson, J. C. (2001). How and when does emotional expression help? *Review of General Psychology, 5*(3), 187–212.

Kent, R. (1984). Brain mechanisms of speech and language with special reference to emotional interactions. In A. L. Holland (Ed.) *Language science: Recent advances* (pp. 281–384). Oxford, UK: Taylor & Francis.

Kent, R. D. (1981). Articulatory-acoustic perspectives on speech development. In R. Stark (Ed.), *Language development in infancy and early childhood* (pp. 105–106). New York: Elsevier.

Kerr, C. E., Wasserman, R. H., & Moore, C. I. (2007). Cortical dynamics as a therapeutic mechanism for touch healing. *The Journal of Alternative and Complementary Medicine, 13*(1), 59–66.

Kessler, H., Schwarze, M., Filipic, S., Traue, H. C., & von Wietersheim, J. (2006). Alexithymia and facial emotion recognition in patients with eating disorders. *International Journal of Eating Disorders, 39*(3), 245–251.

Khalsa, S. B. (2004a). Treatment of chronic insomnia with yoga: A preliminary study with sleep-wake diaries. *Applied Psychophysiology and Biofeedback, 29*(4), 269–278.

Khalsa, S. B. (2004b). Yoga as a therapeutic intervention: A bibliometric analysis of published research studies. *Indian Journal of Physiological Pharmacology, 48*(3), 269–285.

Khashan, A. S., Abel, K. M., McNamee, R., Pedersen, M. G., Webb, R. T., Baker, P. N. et al. (2008). Higher risk of offspring schizophrenia following antenatal maternal exposure to severe adverse life events. *Archives of General Psychiatry, 65*(2), 146–152.

References

Khazipov, R., Sirota, A., Leinekugel, X., Holmes, G. L., Ben-Ari, Y., & Buzsaki, G. (2004). Early motor activity drives spindle bursts in the developing somatosensory cortex. *Nature, 432*(7018), 758–761.

Kim, J., & Gorman, J. (2005). The psychobiology of anxiety. *Clinical Neuroscience Research, 4,* 335–347.

King, A. C., Taylor, C. B., Albright, C. A., & Haskell, W. L. (1990). The relationship between repressive and defensive coping styles and blood pressure responses in healthy, middle-aged men and women. *Journal of Psychosomatic Research, 34*(4), 461–471.

Kirmayer, L. J., Robbins, J. M., & Paris, J. (1994). Somatoform disorders: Personality and the social matrix of somatic distress. *Journal of Abnormal Psychology, 103*(1), 125–136.

Kleber, B., Birbaumer, N., Veit, R., Trevorrow, T., & Lotze, M. (2007). Overt and imagined singing of an Italian aria. *Neuroimage, 36*(3), 889–900.

Knardahl, S. (2002). Psychophysiological mechanisms of pain in computer work: The blood vessel-nociceptor interaction hypothesis. *Work & Stress, 16*(2), 179–189.

Kneier, A. W., & Temoshok, L. (1984). Repressive coping reactions in patients with malignant melanoma as compared to cardiovascular disease patients. *Journal of Psychosomatic Research, 28*(2), 145–155.

Knost, B., Flor, H., Birbaumer, N., & Schugens, M. M. (1999). Learned maintenance of pain: Muscle tension reduces central nervous system processing of painful stimulation in chronic and subchronic pain patients. *Psychophysiology, 36*(6), 755–764.

Koff, E., & Benavage, A. (1998). Breast size perception and satisfaction, body image, and psychological functioning in Caucasian and Asian American college women. *Sex Roles, 38*(7–8), 655–673.

Kohyama, J., & Iwakawa, Y. (1991). Interrelationships between rapid eye and body movements during sleep: Polysomnographic examinations of infants including premature neonates. *Electroencephalography and Clinical Neurophysiology, 79*(4), 277–280.

Kolassa, I. T., Wienbruch, C., Neuner, F., Schauer, M., Ruf, M., Odenwald, M., et al. (2007). Altered oscillatory brain dynamics after repeated traumatic stress. *BMC Psychiatry, 7,* 56.

Kolers, P. A., & Roediger, H. L. (1984). Procedures of mind. *Journal of Verbal Learning & Verbal Behavior, 23*(4), 425–449.

Konner, M. (1982). *The tangled wing: Biological constraints on the human spirit.* New York: Holt, Rinehart, & Winston.

Kovach, J. (2002). The body as the ground of religion, science, and self. *Zygon, 37*(4), 941–961.

Koyama, T., McHaffie, J. G., Laurienti, P. J., & Coghill, R. C. (2005). The subjective experience of pain: where expectations become reality. *Proceedings of the National Academy of Sciences USA, 102*(36), 12950–12955.

Kozlowska, K. (2005). Healing the disembodied mind: Contemporary models of conversion disorder. *Harvard Review of Psychiatry, 13*(1), 1–13.

Kozorovitskiy, Y., & Gould, E. (2003). Adult neurogenesis: A mechanism for brain repair? *Journal of Clinical and Experimental Neuropsychology, 25*(5), 721–732.

Kramer, A. F., & Erickson, K. I. (2007). Capitalizing on cortical plasticity: Influence of physical activity on cognition and brain function. *Trends in Cognitive Sciences, 11*(8), 342–348.

Kramer, K. M., Choe, C., Carter, C. S., & Cushing, B. S. (2006). Developmental effects of oxytocin on neural activation and neuropeptide release in response to social stimuli. *Hormones and Behavior, 49*(2), 206–214.

Krantz, G., Forsman, M., & Lundberg, U. (2004). Consistency in physiological stress responses and electromyographic activity during induced stress exposure in women and men. *Integrative Physiological & Behavioral Science, 39*(2), 105–118.

Krueger, D. W. (1989). *Body self and psychological self: A developmental and clinical integration of disorders of the self.* New York: Brunner/Mazel.

Kübler-Ross, E. (2005). *On grief and grieving: Finding the meaning of grief through the five stages of loss.* New York: Simon & Schuster.

Kuhtz-Buschbeck, J. P., van der Horst, C., Wolff, S., Fillippow, N., Nabavi, A., Jansen, O., & Braun, P. M. (2006). Activation of the supplementary motor area (SMA) during voluntary pelvic floor muscle contractions: An fMRI study. *NeuroImage, 35*(2), 449–457.

Kuiken, T. A., Miller, L. A., Lipschutz, R. D., Lock, B. A., Stubblefield, K., Marasco, P. D., et al. (2007). Targeted reinnervation for enhanced prosthetic arm function in a woman with a proximal amputation: A case study. *Lancet, 369*(9559), 371–380.

Kulkarni, B., Bentley, D. E., Elliott, R., Youell, P., Watson, A., Derbyshire, S. W. G. et al. (2005). Attention to pain localization and unpleasantness discriminates the functions of the medial and lateral pain systems. *European Journal of Neuroscience, 21*(11), 3133–3142.

Kuo, F. E., & Taylor, A. F. (2004). A potential natural treatment for attention-deficit/hyperactivity disorder: Evidence from a national study. *American Journal of Public Health, 94*(9), 1580–1586.

References

Kurosaki, M., Shirao, N., Yamashita, H., Okamoto, Y., & Yamawaki, S. (2006). Distorted images of one's own body activates the prefrontal cortex and limbic/paralimbic system in young women: a functional magnetic resonance imaging study. *Biological Psychiatry, 59*(4), 380–386.

Kwan, C. L., Crawley, A. P., Mikulis, D. J., & Davis, K. D. (2000). An fMRI study of the anterior cingulate cortex and surrounding medial wall activations evoked by noxious cutaneous heat and cold stimuli. *Pain, 85*(3), 359–374.

Lambie, G. W. (2005). Child abuse and neglect: A practical guide for professional school counselors. *Professional School Counseling, 8*(3), 249–258.

Lambie, J. A., & Marcel, A. J. (2002). Consciousness and the varieties of emotion experience: A theoretical framework. *Psychological Review, 109*(2), 219–259.

Lame Deer & Erdoes, R. (1972), *Lame Deer: Seeker of visions.* New York: Simon & Schuster.

Langlois, A., Baken, R. J., & Wilder, C. N. (1980). Pre-speech respiratory behavior during the first year of life. In T. Murray & J. Murray (Eds.), *Infant communication: Cry and early speech* (pp. 56–84). Houston, TX: College Hill Press.

Laplante, D. P., Zelazo, P. R., Brunet, A., & King, S. (2007). Functional play at 2 years of age: Effects of prenatal maternal stress. *Infancy, 12*(1), 69–93.

Larson, S. J., & Dunn, A. J. (2001). Behavioral effects of cytokines. *Brain, Behavior, and Immunity, 15*(4), 371–387.

Lauriola, M. (1997). Psychological correlates of eye refractive errors. *Personality and Individual Differences, 23*(5), 917–920.

Lawler, K. A., Younger, J. W., Piferi, R. L., Jobe, R. L., Edmondson, K. A.; & Jones, W. H. (2005). The unique effects of forgiveness on health: An exploration of pathways. *Journal of Behavioral Medicine, 28*(2), 157–167.

Lawler-Row, K. A., Karremans, J. C., Scott, C., Edlis-Matityahou, M., & Edwards, L. (2008). Forgiveness, physiological reactivity and health: The role of anger. *International Journal of Psychophysiology, 68*(1), 51–58.

Lazar, S. W., Bush, G., Gollub, R. L., Fricchione, G. L., Khalsa, G., & Benson, H. (2000). Functional brain mapping of the relaxation response and meditation. *Neuroreport, 11*(7), 1581–1585.

Ledebt, A. (2000). Changes in arm posture during the early acquisition of walking. *Infant Behavior & Development, 23*(1), 79–89.

LeDoux, J. E. (1989). Cognitive-emotional interactions in the brain. *Cognition & Emotion, 3*(4), 267–289.

LeDoux, J. E. (2002). Emotion, memory and the brain. *Scientific American, Special Edition, 12*(1), 62–71.

Lee, W. W. (2007). An overview of pediatric obesity. *Pediatric Diabetes, 8* (Suppl. 9), 76–87.

Legerstee, M. (1997). Contingency effects of people and objects on subsequent cognitive functioning in three-month-old infants. *Social Development, 6*(3), 307–321.

Legerstee, M., Anderson, D., & Schaffer, A. (1998). Five- and eight-month-old infants recognize their faces and voices as familiar and social stimuli. *Child Development, 69*(1), 37–50.

Lehrer, P. M., Isenberg, S., & Hochron, S. M. (1993). Asthma and emotion: A review. *Journal of Asthma, 30*(1), 5–21.

Leiter, J. C., & St.-John, W. M. (2004). Phrenic, vagal and hypoglossal activities in rat: Pre-inspiratory, inspiratory, expiratory components. *Respiratory Physiology & Neurobiology, 142*(2–3), 115–126.

Lemche, E., Klann-Delius, G., Koch, R., & Joraschky, P. (2004). Mentalizing language development in a longitudinal attachment sample: implications for alexithymia. *Psychotherapy and Psychosomatics, 73*(6), 366–374.

Lemche, E., Kreppner, J. M., Joraschky, P., & Klann-Delius, G. (2007). Attachment organization and the early development of internal state language: A longitudinal perspective. *International Journal of Behavioral Development, 31*(3), 252–262.

Levenson, M. (2001–2009). *Life is problems. Stress relief in a stressed-out society.* Portland, OR: Feldenkrais Educational Foundation of North America. www.feldenkrais.com/method/article_category/C99/.

Leventhal, E. A., Leventhal, H., Shacham, S., & Easterling, D. V. (1989). Active coping reduces reports of pain from childbirth. *Journal of Consulting and Clinical Psychology, 57*(3), 365–371.

Levin, D. M. (1985). *The body's recollection of being: Phenomenological psychology and the deconstruction of nihilism.* Boston, MA: Routledge & Kegan Paul

Levine, B., Turner, G. R., Tisserand, D., Hevenor, S. J., Graham, S. J., & McIntosh, A. R. (2004). The functional neuroanatomy of episodic and semantic autobiographical remembering: A prospective functional MRI study. *Journal of Cognitive Neuroscience, 16*(9), 1633–1646.

Levine, L. E. (1983). Mine: Self-definition in 2-year-old boys. *Developmental Psychology, 19*(4), 544–549.

Levine, P. A. (1997). *Waking the tiger: Healing trauma.* Berkeley, CA: North Atlantic.

Levine, S. (2005). Developmental determinants of sensitivity and resistance to stress. *Psychoneuroendocrinology, 30*(10), 939–946.

Levitt, H., Butler, M., & Hill, T. (2006). What clients find helpful in psychotherapy: Developing principles for facilitating moment-to-moment change. *Journal of Counseling Psychology, 53*(3), 314–324.

Lewis, B. I. (1957). Hyperventilation syndromes; clinical and physiologic observations. *Postgraduate Medicine, 21*(3), 259–271.

Lewis, M. D. (2005). Self-organizing individual differences in brain development. *Developmental Review, 25*(3–4), 252–277.

Lewis, M. D. (2008). Emotional habits of brain and behavior: A window on personality development. In A. Fogel, B. J. King, & S. Shanker (Eds.), *Human development in the 21st century: Visionary policy ideas from systems scientists* (pp. 72–80). Cambridge, UK: Cambridge University Press.

Lewis, M., & Carmody, D. P. (2008). Self-representation and brain development. *Developmental Psychology, 44*(5), 1329–1334.

Lewis, M., & Ramsay, D. (2004). Development of self-recognition, personal pronoun use, and pretend play during the 2nd year. *Child Development, 75*(6), 1821–1831.

Lewis, T., Amini, F., & Lannon, R. (2000). *A general theory of love.* New York: Vintage.

Ley, R. (1999). The modification of breathing behavior: Pavlovian and operant control in emotion and cognition. *Behavior Modification, 23*(3), 441–479.

Li, J. (2004). Central integration of muscle reflex and arterial baroreflex in midbrain periaqueductal gray: Roles of GABA and NO. *Americian Journal of Physiology: Heart and Circulatory Physiology, 287*(3), H1312–H1318.

Li, J., & Mitchell, J. H. (2000). c-Fos expression in the midbrain periaqueductal gray during static muscle contraction. *Americian Journal of Physiology: Heart and Circulatory Physiology, 279*(6), H2986–H2993.

Liberzon, I., Britton, J. C., & Luan Phan, K. (2003). Neural correlates of traumatic recall in posttraumatic stress disorder. *Stress: The International Journal on the Biology of Stress, 6*(3), 151–156.

Lieberman, A. F., Padron, E., van Horn, P., & Harris, W. W. (2005). Angels in the nursery: The intergenerational transmission of benevolent parental influence. *Infant Mental Health Journal, 26*, 504–520.

Liepert, J., Bauder, H., Wolfgang, H. R., Miltner, W. H., Taub, E., & Weiller, C. (2000). Treatment-induced cortical reorganization after stroke in humans. *Stroke, 31*(6), 1210–1216.

Light, K. C., Grewen, K. M., & Amico, J. A. (2005). More frequent partner hugs and higher oxytocin levels are linked to lower blood pressure and heart rate in premenopausal women. *Biological Psychology, 69*, 5–21.

Light, K. C., Smith, T. E., Johns, J. M., Brownley, K. A., Hofheimer, J. A., & Amico, J. A. (2000). Oxytocin responsivity in mothers of infants: A preliminary study of relationships with blood pressure during laboratory stress and normal ambulatory activity. *Health Psychology, 19*(6), 560–567.

Lipp, O. V., & Waters, A. M. (2007). When danger lurks in the background: Attentional capture by animal fear-relevant distractors is specific and selectively enhanced. *Emotion, 7*(1), 192–200.

Lischetzke, T., & Eid, M. (2003). Is attention to feelings beneficial or detrimental to affective well-being? Mood regulation as a moderator variable. *Emotion, 3*(4), 361–377.

Liu-Ambrose, T., Khan, K. M., Eng, J. J., Janssen, P. A., Lord, S. R., & McKay, H. A. (2004). Resistance and agility training reduce fall risk in women aged 75 to 85 with low bone mass: A 6-month randomized, controlled trial. *Journal of the American Geriatric Society, 52*(5), 657–665.

Liu-Ambrose, T., Khan, K. M., Eng, J. J., Lord, S. R., & McKay, H. A. (2004). Balance confidence improves with resistance or agility training. Increase is not correlated with objective changes in fall risk and physical abilities. *Gerontology, 50*(6), 373–382.

Lloyd, D., Morrison, I., & Roberts, N. (2006). Role for human posterior parietal cortex in visual processing of aversive objects in peripersonal space. *Journal of Neurophysiology, 95*(1), 205–214.

Lobo, Y. B., & Winsler, A. (2006). The effects of a creative dance and movement program on the social competence of head start preschoolers. *Social Development, 15*(3), 501–519.

Lock, A. (2000). Preverbal communication. In J. G. Bremner & A. Fogel (Eds.), *Handbook of infant development* (pp. 504–521). Oxford, UK: Blackwell.

Longhurst, J. C., & Mitchell, J. H. (1979). Reflex control of the circulation by afferents from skeletal muscle. *International Review of Physiology, 18*, 125–148.

Lord, S. R., & Menz, H. B. (2000). Visual contributions to postural stability in older adults. *Gerontology, 46*(6), 306–310.

Louv, R. (2005). *Last child in the woods: Saving our children from nature-deficit disorder.* New York: Algonquin Books.

Lowen, A. (1958). *The language of the body.* New York: Macmillan.

Lucas, S. E., & Fleming, J. M. (2005). Interventions for improving self-awareness following acquired brain injury. *Australian Occupational Therapy Journal, 52*(2), 160–170.

References

Luft, A. R., Manto, M. U., & Ben Taib, N. O. (2005). Modulation of motor cortex excitability by sustained peripheral stimulation: The interaction between the motor cortex and the cerebellum. *Cerebellum, 4*(2), 90–96.

Lum, L. C. (1987). Hyperventilation syndromes in medicine and psychiatry: A review. *Journal of the Royal Society of Medicine, 80*(4), 229–231.

Lund, J. P., Donga, R., Widmer, C. G., & Stohler, C. S. (1991). The pain-adaptation model: A discussion of the relationship between chronic musculoskeletal pain and motor activity. *Canadian Journal of Physiology and Pharmacology, 69*(5), 683–694.

Lundberg, U., Dohns, I. E., Melin, B., Sandsjo, L., Palmerud, G., Kadefors, R. et al. (1999). Psychophysiological stress responses, muscle tension, and neck and shoulder pain among supermarket cashiers. *Journal of Occupational Health Psychology, 4*(3), 245–255.

Lundberg, U., Forsman, M., Zachau, G., Eklöf, M., Palmerud, G., Melin, B., et al. (2002). Effects of experimentally induced mental and physical stress on motor unit recruitment in the trapezius muscle. *Work & Stress, 16*(2), 166–178.

Lundblad, I., Elert, J., & Gerdle, B. (1999). Randomized controlled trial of physiotherapy and Feldenkrais interventions in female workers with neck-shoulder complaints. *Journal of Occupational Rehabilitation, 9*(3), 179–194.

Lundgren, J., Carlsson, S. G., & Berggren, U. (2006). Relaxation versus cognitive therapies for dental fear—A psychophysiological approach. *Health Psychology, 25*(3), 267–273.

Lutz, A., Brefczynski-Lewis, J., Johnstone, T., & Davidson, R. J. (2008). Regulation of the neural circuitry of emotion by compassion meditation: Effects of meditative expertise. *PLoS ONE, 3*(3), e1897.

Lyon, M. L. (1999). Emotion and embodiment: The respiratory mediation of somatic and social processes. In A. L. Hinton (Ed.), *Biocultural approaches to the emotions* (pp. 182–212). New York: Cambridge University Press.

Lyons-Ruth, K. (2000). "I sense that you sense that I sense . . .": Sander's recognition process and the specificity of relational moves in the psychotherapeutic setting. *Infant Mental Health Journal, 21*(1–2), 85–98.

Lyons-Ruth, K., Dutra, L., Schuder, M. R., & Bianchi, I. (2006). From infant attachment disorganization to adult dissociation: Relational adaptations or traumatic experiences? *Psychiatric Clinics of North America, 29*(1), 63–86.

MacDougall, R., & Münsterberg, H. (1896). Studies from the Harvard Psychological Laboratory (IV): The physical characteristics of attention. *Psychological Review, 3*(2), 158–180.

Macefield, G., & Burke, D. (1991). Paraesthesiae and tetany induced by voluntary hyperventilation. Increased excitability of human cutaneous and motor axons. *Brain, 114 (Pt 1B)*, 527–540.

Macefield, V. G., Gandevia, S. C., & Henderson, L. A. (2006). Neural sites involved in the sustained increase in muscle sympathetic nerve activity induced by inspiratory capacity apnea: A fMRI study. *Journal of Applied Physiology, 100*(1), 266–273.

MacLeod, C., Mathews, A., & Tata, P. (1986). Attentional bias in emotional disorders. *Journal of Abnormal Psychology, 95*(1), 15–20.

MacNaughton, I. (2004). *Body, breath & consciousness: A somatics anthology.* Berkeley, CA: North Atlantic.

Madigan, S., Moran, G., & Pederson, D. R. (2006). Unresolved states of mind, disorganized attachment relationships, and disrupted interactions of adolescent mothers and their infants. *Developmental Psychology, 42*(2), 293–304.

Magarian, G. J., & Hickam, D. H. (1986). Noncardiac causes of angina-like chest pain. *Progress in Cardiovascular Diseases, 29*(1), 65–80.

Main, M. (1999). Attachment theory: Eighteen points with suggestions for future studies. In J. Cassidy & P. Shaver (Eds.), *Handbook of attachment: Theory, research, and clinical applications* (pp. 865–887). New York: Guilford.

Main, M., & Cassidy, J. (1988). Categories of response to reunion with the parent at age 6: Predictable from infant attachment classifications and stable over a 1-month period. *Developmental Psychology, 24*, 415–426.

Malmo, R. B., & Shagass, C. (1949). Physiologic study of symptom mechanisms in psychiatric patients under stress. *Psychosomatic Medicine, 11*(1), 25–29.

Mandle, C. L., Jacobs, S. C., Arcari, P. M., & Domar, A. D. (1996). The efficacy of relaxation response interventions with adult patients: A review of the literature. *Journal of Cardiovascular Nursing, 10*(3), 4–26.

Mangan, G. L., Murphy, G., & Farmer, R. G. (1980). The role of muscle tension in "repression." *Pavlov Journal of Biological Science, 15*(4), 172–176.

Mann, T., & Ward, A. (2004). To eat or not to eat: Implications of the attentional myopia model for restrained eaters. *Journal of Abnormal Psychology, 113*(1), 90–98.

Manning, E. (2007). *Politics of touch: Sense, movement, sovereignty.* University of Minnesota Press.

Maroun, M. (2006). Stress reverses plasticity in the pathway projecting from the ventromedial prefrontal cortex to the basolateral amygdala. *European Journal of Neuroscience, 24*(10), 2917–2922.

References

Martin, J. J., Craib, M., & Mitchell, V. (1995). The relationships of anxiety and self-attention to running economy in competitive male distance runners. *Journal of Sports Sciences, 13*(5), 371–376.

Martin-Ginis, K. A., Jung, M. E., & Gauvin, L. (2003). To see or not to see: Effects of exercising in mirrored environments on sedentary women's feeling states and self-efficacy. *Health Psychology, 22*(4), 354–361.

Maxwell, J. S., & Davidson, R. J. (2007). Emotion as motion: Asymmetries in approach and avoidant actions. *Psychological Science, 18*(12), 1113–1119.

Mayer, E. A., Naliboff, B. D., & Craig, A. D. (2006). Neuroimaging of the brain-gut axis: from basic understanding to treatment of functional GI disorders. *Gastroenterology, 131*(6), 1925–1942.

McClelland, J., Dahlberg, K., & Plihal, J. (2002). Learning in the ivory tower: Students' embodied experience. *College Teaching, 50*(1), 4–8.

McGaugh, J. L., Cahill, L., & Roozendaal, B. (1996). Involvement of the amygdala in memory storage: Interaction with other brain systems. *Proceedings of the National Academy of Sciences, 93*(24), 13508–13514.

McGibbon, C. A., Krebs, D. E., Wolf, S. L., Wayne, P. M., Scarborough, D. M., & Parker, S. W. (2004). Tai Chi and vestibular rehabilitation effects on gaze and whole-body stability. *Journal of Vestibular Research, 14*(6), 467–478.

McGlone, F., Vallbo, A. B., Olausson, H., Loken, L., & Wessberg, J. (2007). Discriminative touch and emotional touch. *Canadian Journal of Experimental Psychology/Revue canadienne de psychologie experimentale, 61*(3), 173–183.

McKinley, N. M. (1999). Women and objectified body consciousness: Mothers' and daughters' body experience in cultural, developmental, and familial context. *Developmental Psychology, 35*(3), 760–769.

McLuhan, T. C. (1994). *The way of the earth: Encounters with nature in ancient and contemporary thought.* New York: Simon & Schuster.

Mehling, W. E., Hamel, K. A., Acree, M., Byl, N., & Hecht, F. M. (2005). Randomized, controlled trial of breath therapy for patients with chronic low-back pain. *Alternative Therapies in Health and Medicine, 11*(4), 44–52.

Mélen, M., & Wachsmann, J. (2001). Categorization of musical motifs in infancy. *Music Perception, 18*(3), 325–346.

Melson, G. F. (2001). *Why the wild things are: Animals in the lives of children.* Cambridge, MA: Harvard University Press.

Meltzoff, A. N. (1995). Understanding the intentions of others: Re-enactment of intended acts by 18-month-old children. *Developmental Psychology, 31*(5), 838–850.

Meltzoff, A. N. (2007). "Like me": A foundation for social cognition. *Developmental Science, 10*(1), 126–134.

Meltzoff, A. N., & Moore, M. K. (1994). Imitation, memory, and the representation of persons. *Infant Behavior & Development, 17*(1), 83–99.

Meltzoff, A., & Moore, M. K. (1997). Explaining facial imitation: A theoretical model. *Early Development and Parenting, 6*(1), 179–192.

Mendolia, M. (2002). An index of self-regulation of emotion and the study of repression in social contexts that threaten or do not threaten self-concept. *Emotion, 2*(3), 215–232.

Miall, D. S., & Dissanayake, E. (2003). The poetics of babytalk. *Human Nature, 14*(4), 337–364.

Michetti, P. M., Rossi, R., Bonanno, D., De Dominicis, C., Iori, F., & Simonelli, C. (2007). Dysregulation of emotions and premature ejaculation (PE): Alexithymia in 100 outpatients. *Journal of Sex Medicine, 4*(5), 1462–1467.

Middleton, E. M., Sinason, M. D. A., & Davids, Z. (2008). Blurred vision due to psychosocial difficulties: A case series. *Eye, 22*, 316–317.

Mikulincer, M., & Orbach, I. (1995). Attachment styles and repressive defensiveness: The accessibility and architecture of affective memories. *Journal of Personality and Social Psychology, 68*(5), 917–925.

Milad, M. R., Quinn, B. T., Pitman, R. K., Orr, S. P., Fischl, B., & Rauch, S. L. (2005). Thickness of ventromedial prefrontal cortex in humans is correlated with extinction memory. *Proceedings of the National Academy of Sciences, 102*(30), 10706–10711.

Mills, C. K., & Wooster, A. D. (1987). Crying in the counselling situation. *British Journal of Guidance & Counselling, 15*(2), 125–130.

Mills, L. J., & Daniluk, J. C. (2002). Her body speaks: The experience of dance therapy for women survivors of child sexual abuse. *Journal of Counseling & Development, 80*(1), 77–85.

Miltner, W. H. R., Krieschel, S., Hecht, H., Trippe, R., & Weiss, T. (2004). Eye movements and behavioral responses to threatening and nonthreatening stimuli during visual search in phobic and nonphobic subjects. *Emotion, 4*(4), 323–339.

Mittal, V. A., Tessner, K. D., Trottman, H. D., Esterberg, M., Dhruv, S. H., Simeonova, D. I. et al. (2007). Movement abnormalities and the progression of prodromal symptomatology in adolescents at risk for psychotic disorders. *Journal of Abnormal Psychology, 116*(2), 260–267.

Montagna, M., Cerri, G., Borroni, P., & Baldissera, F. (2005). Excitability changes in human corticospinal projections to muscles moving hand and fingers while viewing a reaching and grasping action. *European Journal of Neuroscience, 22*(6), 1513–1520.

Moore, C., Mealiea, J., Garon, N., & Povinelli, D. J. (2007). The development of body self-awareness. *Infancy, 11*(2), 157–174.

Moore, G. A., & Calkins, S. D. (2004). Infants' vagal regulation in the still-face paradigm is related to dyadic coordination of mother-infant interaction. *Developmental Psychology, 40*(6), 1068–1080.

Moran, J. M., Macrae, C. N., Heatherton, T. F., Wyland, C. L., & Kelley, W. M. (2006). Neuroanatomical evidence for distinct cognitive and affective components of self. *Journal of Cognitive Neuroscience, 18*(9), 1586–1594.

Morgan, R., & Rochat, P. (1997). Intermodal calibration of the body in early infancy. *Ecological Psychology, 9*(1), 1–23.

Morris, G., & Baker-Ward, L. (2007). Fragile but real: Children's capacity to use newly acquired words to convey preverbal memories. *Child Development, 78*(2), 448–458.

Morris, R. (2007). Theories of hippocampal function. In P. Andersen, R. Morris, D. Amaral, T. Bliss, & J. O'Keefe (Eds.), *The hippocampus book* (pp. 581–713). New York: Oxford University Press.

Moscovitch, M., Rosenbaum, R. S., Gilboa, A., Addis, D. R., Westmacott, R., Grady, C., et al. (2005). Functional neuroanatomy of remote episodic, semantic and spatial memory: a unified account based on multiple trace theory. *Journal of Anatomy, 207*(1), 35–66.

Moynihan, J. A. (2003). Mechanisms of stress-induced modulation of immunity. *Brain, Behavior, and Immunity, 17* (Suppl. 1), S11–16.

Mullen, C. A., & Cancienne, M. (2003). Résumé in motion: Sensory self-awareness through movement. *Sex Education, 3*(2), 157–170.

Muratori, F., & Maestro, S. (2007). Autism as a downstream effect of primary difficulties in intersubjectivity interacting with abnormal development of brain connectivity. *International Journal for Dialogical Science, 2*(1), 93–118.

Muraven, M. (2005). Self-focused attention and the self-regulation of attention: Implications for personality and pathology. *Journal of Social & Clinical Psychology, 24*(3), 382–400.

Muris, P. (2006). The pathogenesis of childhood anxiety disorders: Considerations from a developmental psychopathology perspective. *International Journal of Behavioral Development, 30*(1), 5–11.

Murphy, R. F. (1990). *The body silent*. New York: Norton.

Myers, G. (1998). *Children and animals: Social development and our connections to other species.* Boulder, CO: Westview Press.

Myowa-Yamakoshi, M., & Takeshita, H. (2006). Do human fetuses anticipate self-oriented actions? A study by four-dimensional (4D) ultrasonography. *Infancy. 10*(3), 289–301.

Nabhan, G. P., & Trimble, S. (1994). *The geography of childhood: Why children need wild places.* Boston: Beacon Press.

Nadel, L., & Jacobs, W. J. (1998). Traumatic memory is special. *Current Directions in Psychological Science, 7*(5), 154–157.

Nagai, M., Kishi, K., & Kato, S. (2007). Insular cortex and neuropsychiatric disorders: A review of recent literature. *European Psychiatry, 22*(6), 387–394.

Naqvi, N. H., Rudrauf, D., Damasio, H., & Bechara, A. (2007). Damage to the insula disrupts addiction to cigarette smoking. *Science, 315*(5811), 531–534.

Näring, G., & Nijenhuis, E. R. S. (2005). Relationships between self-reported potentially traumatizing events, psychoform and somatoform dissociation, and absorption, in two non-clinical populations. *Australian and New Zealand Journal of Psychiatry, 39*(11–12), 982–988.

Nederhand, M. J., Hermens, H. J., Ijzerman, M. J., Groothuis, K. G., & Turk, D. C. (2006). The effect of fear of movement on muscle activation in posttraumatic neck pain disability. *The Clinical Journal of Pain, 22*(6), 519–525.

Nelles, G. (2004). Cortical reorganization—effects of intensive therapy. *Restorative Neurology and Neuroscience, 22*(3–5), 239–244.

Nelson, J. K. (2000). Clinical assessment of crying and crying inhibition based on attachment theory. *Bulletin of the Menninger Clinic, 64*(4), 509–529.

Nelson, J. K. (2005). *Seeing through tears: Crying and attachment.* New York: Routledge.

Nezlek, J. B. (1999). Body image and day-to-day social interaction. *Journal of Personality, 67*(5), 793–817.

NICHD Early Childhood Research Network. (2004). Affect dysregulation in the mother-child relationship in the toddler years: antecedents and consequences. *Development and Psychopathology, 16*(1), 43–68.

Nielsen, L., & Kaszniak, A. W. (2006). Awareness of subtle emotional feelings: A comparison of long-term meditators and nonmeditators. *Emotion, 6*(3), 392–405.

Nijenhuis, E. R., Vanderlinden, J., & Spinhoven, P. (1998). Animal defensive reactions as a model for trauma-induced dissociative reactions. *Journal of Traumatic Stress, 11*(2), 243–260.

Nijenhuis, E. R., van der Hart, O., Kruger, K., & Steele, K. (2004). Somatoform dissociation, reported abuse and animal defence-like reactions. *Australian and New Zealand Journal of Psychiatry, 38*(9), 678–686.

Nishizawa, Y., Kida, K., Nishizawa, K., Hashiba, S., Saito, K., & Mita, R. (2003). Perception of self-physique and eating behavior of high school students in Japan. *Psychiatry and Clinical Neurosciences, 57*(2), 189–196.

Nolen-Hoeksema, S., Stice, E., Wade, E., & Bohon, C. (2007). Reciprocal relations between rumination and bulimic, substance abuse, and depressive symptoms in female adolescents. *Journal of Abnormal Psychology, 116*(1), 198–207.

Noriuchi, M., Kikuchi, Y., & Senoo, A. (2008). The functional neuroanatomy of maternal love: Mother's response to infant's attachment behaviors. *Biological Psychiatry, 63*(4), 415–423.

Norris, R. S. (2005). Examining the structure and role of emotion: Contributions of neurobiology to the study of embodied religious experience. *Zygon, 40*(1), 181–199.

Northoff, G., & Bermpohl, F. (2004). Cortical midline structures and the self. *Trends in Cognitive Sciences, 8*(3), 102–107.

Nussbaum, M. (2003, October 23). Winnicott: Life and work. *The New Republic Online.* Retrieved from http://www.newrepublic.com. June, 2008

Nyberg, L., Petersson, K. M., Nilsson, L. G., Sandblom, J., Aberg, C., & Ingvar, M. (2001). Reactivation of motor brain areas during explicit memory for actions. *Neuroimage, 14*(2), 521–528.

Ogden, P., Minton, K., & Pain, C. (2006). *Trauma and the body: A sensorimotor approach to psychotherapy.* New York: Norton.

Ohala, J. J. (1980). The origin of sound patterns in vocal tract constraints. In P. F. MacNeilage (Ed.), *The production of speech* (pp. 189–216). New York: Springer-Verlag.

Olausson, H. W., Cole, J., Vallbo, A., McGlone, F., Elam, M., Krämer, H. H. et al. (2008). Unmyelinated tactile afferents have opposite effects on insular and somatosensory cortical processing. *Neuroscience Letters, 436*(2), 128–132.

O'Leary, A. (1990). Stress, emotion, and human immune function. *Psychological Bulletin, 108*(3), 363–382.

Oman, D., Shapiro, S. L., Thoresen, C. E., Plante, T. G., & Flinders, T. (2008). Meditation lowers stress and supports forgiveness among college students: A randomized controlled trial. *Journal of American College Health, 56*(5), 569–578.

Osborne, D., & Swenson, W. M. (1978). Muscle tension and personality. *Journal of Clinical Psychology, 34*(2), 391–392.

Osofsky, J. D. (1999). The impact of violence on children. *The Future of Children, 9*(3), 33–49.

Ostrander, M. M., Ulrich-Lai, Y. M., Choi, D. C., Richtand, N. M., & Herman, J. P. (2006). Hypoactivity of the hypothalamo-pituitary-adrenocortical axis during recovery from chronic variable stress. *Endocrinology, 147*(4), 2008–2017.

Özekmekçi, S., Apaydin, H., Ekinci, B., & Yalçinkaya, C. (2003). Psychogenic movement disorders in two children. *Movement Disorders, 18*(11), 1395–1397.

Packard, M. G., & Cahill, L. (2001). Affective modulation of multiple memory systems. *Current Opinion in Neurobiology, 11*(6), 752–756.

Panksepp, J. (1998). *Affective neuroscience: The foundations of human and animal emotions.* New York: Oxford University Press.

Panksepp, J. (2001). The long-term psychobiological consequences of infant emotions: Prescriptions for the twenty-first century. *Infant Mental Health Journal, 22*, (1–2), 132–173.

Panksepp, J., & Bernatzky, G. (2002). Emotional sounds and the brain: The neuro-affective foundations of musical appreciation. *Behavioural Processes, 60*(2), 133–155.

Panksepp, J., Knutson, B., & Burgdorf, J. (2002). The role of brain emotional systems in addictions: A neuro-evolutionary perspective and new 'self-report' animal model. *Addiction, 97*(4), 459–469.

Papousek, M., Bornstein, M. H., Nuzzo, C., Papousek, H., & Symmes, D. (1990). Infant responses to prototypical melodic contours in parental speech. *Infant Behavior and Development, 13*, 539–545.

Papp, L. A., Martinez, J. M., Klein, D. F., Coplan, J. D., Norman, R. G., Cole, R. et al. (1997). Respiratory psychophysiology of panic disorder: Three respiratory challenges in 98 subjects. *American Journal of Psychiatry, 154*(11), 1557–1565.

Parmelee, A. H., Jr., Schulz, H. R., & Disbrow, M. W. (1961). Sleep patterns of the newborn. *Journal of Pediatrics, 58*, 241–250.

Passie, T., Hartmann, U., Schneider, U., & Emrich, H. M. (2004). Acute hyperventilation syndromes induced by sexual intercourse: Evidence of a psychophysical mechanism to intensify sexual experience? *Archives of Sexual Behavior, 33*(6), 525–526.

Pasupathi, M. (2001). The social construction of the personal past and its implications for adult development. *Psychological Bulletin, 127*(5), 651–672.

Paus, T. (2001). Primate anterior cingulate cortex: Where motor control, drive and cognition interface. *National Review of Neuroscience, 2*(6), 417–424.

References

Payne, J. D., Jackson, E. D., Ryan, L., Hoscheidt, S., Jacobs, W. J., & Nadel, L. (2006). The impact of stress on neutral and emotional aspects of episodic memory. *Memory, 14*(1), 1–16.

Pearce, J. M. (2007). Misoplegia. *European Neurology, 57,* 62–64.

Pecoraro, N., Dallman, M. F., Warne, J. P., Ginsberg, A. B., Laugero, K. D., la Fleur, S. E., et al. (2006). From Malthus to motive: How the HPA axis engineers the phenotype, yoking needs to wants. *Progress in Neurobiology, 79*(5–6), 247–340.

Pellegrini, A. D., & Smith, P. K. (1998). Physical activity play: The nature and function of a neglected aspect of play. *Child Development, 69*(3), 577–598.

Pendry, P., & Adam, E. K. (2007). Associations between parents' marital functioning, maternal parenting quality, maternal emotion and child cortisol levels. *International Journal of Behavioral Development, 31*(3), 218–231.

Pennebaker, J. W., Barger, S. D., & Tiebout, J. (1989). Disclosure of traumas and health among Holocaust survivors. *Psychosomatic Medicine, 51*(5), 577–589.

Pennebaker, J. W., & Beall, S. K. (1986). Confronting a traumatic event: Toward an understanding of inhibition and disease. *Journal of Abnormal Psychology, 95*(3), 274–281.

Peterson, C., Grant, V. V., & Boland, L. D. (2005). Childhood amnesia in children and adolescents: Their earliest memories. *Memory, 13*(6), 622–637.

Peterson, C., & Rideout, R. (1998). Memory for medical emergencies experienced by 1- and 2-year-olds. *Developmental Psychology, 34*(5), 1059–1072.

Peterson, C., & Whalen, N. (2001). Five years later: Children's memory for medical emergencies. *Applied Cognitive Psychology, 15*(7), S7–S24.

Petersson, P., Waldenstrom, A., Fahraeus, C., & Schouenborg, J. (2003). Spontaneous muscle twitches during sleep guide spinal self-organization. *Nature, 424*(6944), 72–75.

Petitto, L. A., Holowka, S., Sergio, L. E., Levy, B., & Ostry, D. J. (2004). Baby hands that move to the rhythm of language: Hearing babies acquiring sign languages babble silently on the hands. *Cognition, 93*(1), 43–73.

Philippot, P., Chapelle, G., & Blairy, S. (2002). Respiratory feedback in the generation of emotion. *Cognition & Emotion, 16*(5), 605–627.

Phillips, D. I. (2007). Programming of the stress response: A fundamental mechanism underlying the long-term effects of the fetal environment? *Journal of Internal Medicine, 261*(5), 453–460.

Phillips-Silver, J. & Trainor, L. J. (2007). Hearing what the body feels: Auditory encoding of rhythmic movement. *Cognition, 105,* 533–546.

Piaget, J. (1952). *The origins of intelligence in children.* New York: International Universities Press.

Pillay, S. S., Gruber, S. A., Rogowska, J., Simpson, N., & Yurgelun-Todd, D. A. (2006). fMRI of fearful facial affect recognition in panic disorder: The cingulate gyrus-amygdala connection. *Journal of Affective Disorders, 94*(1–3), 173–181.

Pipp, S., Easterbrooks, M. A., & Brown, S. R. (1993). Attachment status and complexity of infants' self- and other-knowledge when tested with mother and father. *Social Development, 2,* 4–12.

Plews-Ogan, M., Owens, J. E., Goodman, M., Wolfe, P., & Schorling, J. (2005). A pilot study evaluating mindfulness-based stress reduction and massage for the management of chronic pain. *Journal of General Internal Medicine, 20*(12), 1136–1138.

Polivy, J. (1998). The effects of behavioral inhibition: Integrating internal cues, cognition, behavior, and affect. *Psychological Inquiry, 9*(3), 181–204.

Pollak, S. D., Vardi, S., Bechner, A. M. P., & Curtin, J. J. (2005). Physically abused children's regulation of attention in response to hostility. *Child Development, 76*(5), 968–977.

Pollan, M. (2008). *In defense of food: An eater's manifesto.* Harmondsworth, UK: Penguin Books.

Pollatos, O., & Schandry, R. (2008). Emotional processing and emotional memory are modulated by interoceptive awareness. *Cognition & Emotion, 22*(2), 272–287.

Porges, S. W. (2001). The polyvagal theory: Phylogenetic substrates of a social nervous system. *International Journal of Psychophysiology, 42*(2), 123–146.

Porges, S. W. (2004). Neuroception: A subconscious system for detecting threats and safety. *Zero to Three, 24*(5), 19–24.

Porter, S., & Birt, A. R. (2001). Is traumatic memory special? A comparison of traumatic memory characteristics with memory for other emotional life experiences. *Applied Cognitive Psychology, 15*(7), S101-S117.

Posner, M. I., & Rothbart, M. K. (1998). Attention, self-regulation and consciousness. *Philosophical Transactions of the Royal Society London B Biological Sciences, 353*(1377), 1915–1927.

Post, R. M., Weiss, S. R. B., Li, H., Smith, M. A., Zhang, L. X., Xing, G. et al. (1998). Neural plasticity and emotional memory. *Development and Psychopathology, 10*(4), 829–855.

Preisler, G. (1997). Social and emotional development of blind children: A longitudinal study. In V. Lewis & G. M. Collis (Eds.), *Blindness and psychological development in young children* (pp. 69–85). Leicester, UK: BPS.

Price, C. (2005). Body-oriented therapy in recovery from child sexual abuse: An efficacy study. *Alternative Therapies: Health Medicine, 11*(5), 46–57.

References

Proskauer, S. (2007). *Karmic therapy: Healing the split psyche.* Salt Lake City, UT: Salt City.

Punamäki, R.-L., Qouta, S., El Sarraj, E., & Montgomery, E. (2006). Psychological distress and resources among siblings and parents exposed to traumatic events. *International Journal of Behavioral Development, 30*(5), 385–397.

Putman, P., Hermans, E. J., Koppeschaar, H., van Schijndel, A., & van Honk, J. (2007). A single administration of cortisol acutely reduces preconscious attention for fear in anxious young men. *Psychoneuroendocrinology, 32*(7), 793–802.

Pyszczynski, T., & Greenberg, J. (1987). Self-regulatory perseveration and the depressive self-focusing style: A self-awareness theory of reactive depression. *Psychological Bulletin, 102*(1), 122–138.

Qouta, S., Punamäki, R.-L., & El Sarraj, E. (2008). Child development and family mental health in war and military violence: The Palestinian experience. *International Journal of Behavioral Development, 32*(4), 310–321.

Quirk, G. J., & Gehlert, D. R. (2003). Inhibition of the amygdala: Key to pathological states? *Annals of the New York Academy of Sciences, 985,* 263–272.

Ramachandran, V. S., & Blakeslee, S. (1999). *Phantoms in the brain: Probing the mysteries of the human mind.* New York: Harper Perennial

Ramnani, N. (2006). The primate cortico-cerebellar system: Anatomy and function. *Nature Reviews Neuroscience, 7*(7), 511–522.

Rausch, S. M., Gramling, S. E., & Auerbach, S. M. (2006). Effects of a single session of large-group meditation and progressive muscle relaxation training on stress reduction, reactivity, and recovery. *International Journal of Stress Management, 13*(3), 273–290.

Reddy, V. (2001). Mind knowledge in the first year: Understanding attention and intention. In G. Bremner & A. Fogel (Eds.), *Blackwell handbook of infant development* (pp. 241–264). Oxford: Blackwell.

Reich, W. (1972). *Character analysis* (V. R. Garfagno, Trans.). New York: Simon & Schuster. (Original work published 1933)

Reichel-Dolmatoff, G. (1978). The loom of life: A Kogi principle of integration. *Journal of Latin-American Lore, 4,* 5–27.

Rhinewine, J. P., & Williams, O. J. (2007). Holotropic breathwork: The potential role of a prolonged, voluntary hyperventilation procedure as an adjunct to psychotherapy. *The Journal of Alternative and Complementary Medicine, 13,* 771–776.

Richards, J. C., Cooper, A. J., & Winkelman, J. H. (2003). Interoceptive accuracy in nonclinical panic. *Cognitive Therapy and Research, 27*(4), 447–461.

Richards, J. M., & Gross, J. J. (1999). Composure at any cost? The cognitive consequences of emotion suppression. *Personality and Social Psychology Bulletin, 25*(8), 1033–1044.

Rick, C. (2001). Movement and meaning. *Psychoanalytic Inquiry, 21*(3), 368–377.

Riediger, M. (2007, November). Intergoal relations in the context of starting to exercise: A case of positive development from younger to older adulthood. *International Journal of Behavioral Development, 31*(6, Suppl. 2 Serial No. 52), 8–11.

Rief, W., & Barsky, A. J. (2005). Psychobiological perspectives on somatoform disorders. *Psychoneuroendocrinology, 30*(10), 996–1002.

Riskind, J. H., & Gotay, C. C. (1982). Physical posture: Could it have regulatory or feedback effects on motivation and emotion? *Motivation and Emotion, 6*(3), 273–298.

Rizzo, A., Pair, J., McNerney, P. J., Eastlund, E., Manson, B., Gratch, J. et al. (2005). Development of a VR therapy application for Iraq war military personnel with PTSD. *Studies in Health Technological Information, 111*, 407–413.

Rizzolatti, G., Fadiga, L., Gallese, V., & Fogassi, L. (1996). Premotor cortex and the recognition of motor actions. *Cognitive Brain Research, 3*(2), 131–141.

Robertson, C. H., Jr., Pagel, M. A., & Johnson, R. L., Jr. (1977). The distribution of blood flow, oxygen consumption, and work output among the respiratory muscles during unobstructed hyperventilation. *The Journal of Clinical Investigation, 59*(1), 43–50.

Robitaille, Y., Laforest, S., Fournier, M., Gauvin, L., Parisien, M., Corriveau, H. et al. (2005). Moving forward in fall prevention: An intervention to improve balance among older adults in real-world settings. *American Journal of Public Health, 95*(11), 2049–2056.

Rochat, P., & Hespos, S. J. (1997). Differential rooting response by neonates: Evidence for an early sense of self. *Early Development & Parenting, 6*(3–4), 105–112.

Rochat, P., & Morgan, R. (1995). Spatial determinants in the perception of self-produced leg movements by 3- to 5-month-old infants. *Developmental Psychology, 31*, 626–636.

Rochat, P., Goubet, N., & Senders, S. J. (1999). To reach or not to be reach? Perception of body effectivities by young infants. *Infant and Child Development, 8*(3), 129–148.

Rock, A. M. L., Trainor, L. J., & Addison, T. L. (1999). Distinctive messages in infant-directed lullabies and play songs. *Developmental Psychology, 35*(2), 527–534.

References

Rogers, C. R. (1961). *On becoming a person: A therapist's view of psychotherapy.* Boston, MA: Houghton Mifflin.

Rogers, D. (1992). *Motor disorder in psychiatry: Towards a neurological psychiatry.* New York: Wiley.

Rogers, S. J., & Ozonoff, S. (2005). Annotation: What do we know about sensory dysfunction in autism? A critical review of the empirical evidence. *Journal of Child Psychology and Psychiatry, 46,* 1255–68.

Rohner, J.-C. (2004). Memory-based attentional biases: Anxiety is linked to threat avoidance. *Cognition & Emotion, 18*(8), 1027–1054.

Roisman, G. I., Tsai, J. L., & Chiang, K.-H. S. (2004). The emotional integration: Physiological, facial expressive, and self-reported emotional response during the adult attachment interview. *Developmental Psychology, 40*(5), 776–789.

Roozendaal, B., Koolhaas, J. M., & Bohus, B. (1997). The role of the central amygdala in stress and adaption. *Acta Physiologica Scandinavian Supplement, 640,* 51–54.

Rosas, D. & Rosas, C. (2005). *The NIA technique.* New York: Random House.

Rosen, M., & Brenner, S. (2003). *Rosen method bodywork: Accessing the unconscious through touch.* Berkeley, CA: North Atlantic Books.

Rosenbaum, M. (2007). Epidemiology of pediatric obesity. *Pediatric Annals, 36*(2), 89–95.

Rosenkranz, K., & Rothwell, J. C. (2006). Spatial attention affects sensorimotor reorganisation in human motor cortex. *Experimental Brain Research, 170*(1), 97–108.

Rottenberg, J., Wilhelm, F. H., Gross, J. J., & Gotlib, I. H. (2003). Vagal rebound during resolution of tearful crying among depressed and nondepressed individuals. *Psychophysiology, 40*(1), 1–6.

Rozanski, A., & Kubzansky, L. D. (2005). Psychologic functioning and physical health: A paradigm of flexibility. *Psychosomatic Medicine, 67* (Suppl. 1), S47–S53.

Rubin, D. C. (2000). The distribution of early childhood memories. *Memory, 8*(4), 265–269.

Rydé, K., Friedrichsen, M., & Strang, P. (2007). Crying: A force to balance emotions among cancer patients in palliative home care. *Palliative and Supportive Care, 5*(1), 51–59.

Saboisky, J. P., Gorman, R. B., De Troyer, A., Gandevia, S. C., & Butler, J. E. (2007). Differential activation among five human inspiratory motoneuron pools during tidal breathing. *Journal of Applied Physiology, 102*(2), 772–780.

Sacks, O. (1990) *A leg to stand on.* New York: Harper Perennial.

Sainsbury, P., & Gibson, J. G. (1954). Symptoms of anxiety and tension and the accompanying physiological changes in the muscular system. *Journal of Neurology and Neurosurgical Psychiatry, 17*(3), 216–224.

Sander, L. W. (1965). *Interactions of recognition and the developmental processes of the second eighteen months of life.* Paper presented at Tufts University medical School, Boston, MA.

Sander, L. W. (1962). Issues in early mother-child interaction. *Journal of the American Academy of Child Psychiatry, 1,* 141–166.

Sandi, C., Merino, J. J., Cordero, M. I., Touyarot, K., & Venero, C. (2001). Effects of chronic stress on contextual fear conditioning and the hippocampal expression of the neural cell adhesion molecule, its polysialylation, and L1. *Neuroscience, 102*(2), 329–339.

Savelsbergh, G. J., & van der Kamp, J. (1994). The effect of body orientation to gravity on early infant reaching. *Journal of Experimental Child Psychology, 58*(3), 510–528.

Sawada, Y. (2001). Stress reduction intervention: A theoretical reconsideration with an emphasis on breathing training. In Y. Haruki, I. Homma, A. Umezawa, & Y. Masaoka (Eds.), *Respiration and emotion* (pp. 161–169). New York: Springer-Verlag.

Sawyer, D. (1999). *Birthing the self: Water based methods for healing prenatal and birth trauma.* Boulder, CO: Author. (Brochure).

Scaer, R. C. (2000). *Somatic expressions of traumatic stress: The body bears the burden.* Haworth Press.

Scaer, R. C. (2001). The neurophysiology of dissociation and chronic disease. *Applied Psychophysiology and Biofeedback, 26*(1), 73–91.

Schaaf, R. C. & Miller, L. J. (2005). Occupational therapy using a sensory integrative approach for children with developmental disabilities. *Mental Retardation and Developmental Disabilities Research Review, 11,* 143–8.

Schachtel, E. G. (1959). *Metamorphosis.* New York: Basic Books.

Schacter, D. L. (1999). The seven sins of memory: Insights from psychology and cognitive neuroscience. *American Psychologist, 54*(3), 182–203.

Schaefer, A., Collette, F., Philippot, P., van der Linden, M., Laureys, S., Delfiore, G. et al. (2003). Neural correlates of "hot" and "cold" emotional processing: A multilevel approach to the functional anatomy of emotion. *Neuroimage, 18*(4), 938–949.

Schaefer, S., Krampe, R. T., Lindenberger, U., & Baltes, P. B. (2008). Age differences between children and young adults in the dynamics of dual-task prioritization: Body (balance) versus mind (memory). *Developmental Psychology, 44*(3), 747–757.

References

Schanberg, S., Bartolome, J., & Kuhn, C. (1987, January). *Touching and the brain*. Paper presented at the American College of Neuropsychopharmacology, San Juan, Puerto Rico.

Schieber, M. H. (2001). Constraints on somatotopic organization in the primary motor cortex. *Journal of Neurophysiology, 86*(5), 2125–2143.

Schleifer, L. M., Ley, R., & Spalding, T. W. (2002). A hyperventilation theory of job stress and musculoskeletal disorders. *American Journal of Industrial Medicine, 41*(5), 420–432.

Schneider, M. L., Moore, C. F., Gajewski, L. L., Larson, J. A., Roberts, A. D., Converse, A. K. et al. (2008). Sensory processing disorder in a primate model: Evidence from a longitudinal study of prenatal alcohol and prenatal stress effects. *Child Development, 79*(1), 100–113.

Schofield, L. J., & Abbuhl, S. (1975). The stimulation of insight and self-awareness through body-movement exercise. *Journal of Clinical Psychology, 31*(4), 745–746.

Schönfeld, S., & Ehlers, A. (2006). Overgeneral memory extends to pictorial retrieval cues and correlates with cognitive features in posttraumatic stress disorder. *Emotion, 6*(4), 611–621.

Schooler, J. W. (2002). Re-representing consciousness: Dissociations between experience and meta-consciousness. *Trends in Cognitive Sciences, 6*(8), 339–344.

Schore, A. N. (1997). Early organization of the nonlinear right brain and development of a predisposition to psychiatric disorders. *Development and Psychopathology, 9*(4), 595–631.

Schore, A. N. (2000). Attachment and the regulation of the right brain. *Attachment & Human Development, 2*(1), 23–47.

Schore, A. N. (2002). Dysregulation of the right brain: A fundamental mechanism of traumatic attachment and the psychopathogenesis of posttraumatic stress disorder. *Australian and New Zealand Journal of Psychiatry, 36*(1), 9–30.

Schore, A. N. (2003). *Affect dysregulation and disorders of the self*. New York: Norton.

Schupp, H. T., Junghofer, M., Weike, A. I., & Hamm, A. O. (2003). Emotional facilitation of sensory processing in the visual cortex. *Psychological Science, 14*(1), 7–13.

Schwellnus, M. P., Derman, E. W., & Noakes, T. D. (1997). Aetiology of skeletal muscle "cramps" during exercise: A novel hypothesis. *Journal of Sports Sciences, 15*(3), 277–285.

Scott, S., Fuld, J. P., Carter, R., McEntegart, M., & MacFarlane, N. G. (2006). Diaphragm ultrasonography as an alternative to whole-body plethysmography in pulmonary function testing. *Journal of Ultrasound in Medicine, 25*(2), 225–232.

Seal, B. N., & Meston, C. M. (2007). The impact of body awareness on sexual arousal in women with sexual dysfunction. *Journal of Sex Medicine, 4*(4 Pt 1), 990–1000.

Sella, Y. (2003). Soul without skin, bones with no flesh: Bodily aspects of the self in the treatment of women patients with restrictive anorexic eating patterns. *International Journal of Psychotherapy, 8*(1), 37–51.

Selye, H. (1950). Diseases of adaptation. *Wisconsin Medical Journal, 49,* 515–6.

Seppälä, P. (2001). Experience of stress, musculoskeletal discomfort, and eyestrain in computer-based office work: A study in municipal workplaces. *International Journal of Human-Computer Interaction, 13*(3), 279–304.

Shaffer, S. W., & Harrison, A. L. (2007). Aging of the somatosensory system: A translational perspective. *Physical Therapy, 87*(2), 193–207.

Shagass, C., & Malmo, R. B. (1954). Psychodynamic themes and localized muscular tension during psychotherapy. *Psychosomatic Medicine, 16*(4), 295–313.

Shannahoff-Khalsa, D. S. (2004). An introduction to Kundalini yoga meditation techniques that are specific for the treatment of psychiatric disorders. *Journal of Alternative and Complementary Medicine, 10*(1), 91–101.

Shatan, C. (1963). Unconscious motor behavior, kinesthetic awareness and psychotherapy. *American Journal of Psychotherapy, 17,* 17–30.

Shaver, P. R., & Mikulincer, M. (2002). Attachment-related psychodynamics. *Attachment & Human Development, 4*(2), 133–161.

Shaw, A., Joseph, S., & Linley, P. A. (2005). Religion, spirituality, and posttraumatic growth: A systematic review. *Mental Health, Religion & Culture, 8*(1), 1–11.

Shea, A., Walsh, C., MacMillan, H., & Steiner, M. (2005). Child maltreatment and HPA axis dysregulation to major depressive disorder and post traumatic stress disorder in females. *Psychoneuroendocrinology, 30*(2), 162–178.

Shepard, P. (1998). *Coming home to the Pleistocene.* Covelo, CA: Island Press.

Shorey, H., & Snyder, C. (2006). The role of adult attachment styles in psychopathology and psychotherapy outcomes. *Review of General Psychology, 10*(1), 1–20.

Shostak, M. (1983). *Nisa: The life and words of a Kung woman.* New York: Vintage.

Sideridis, G. D., & Kafetsios, K. (2008). Perceived parental bonding, fear of failure and stress during class presentations. *International Journal of Behavioral Development, 32*(2), 119–130.

References

Sieck, G. C., & Fournier, M. (1989). Diaphragm motor unit recruitment during ventilatory and nonventilatory behaviors. *Journal of Applied Physiology, 66*(6), 2539–2545.

Siegel, D. J. (2001). Toward an interpersonal neurobiology of the developing mind: Attachment relationships, "mindsight," and neural integration. *Infant Mental Health Journal, 22*(1–2), 67–94.

Siegel, D. J. (2003). An interpersonal neurobiology of psychotherapy: The developing mind and the resolution of trauma. In M. F. Solomon & D. J. Siegel (Eds.), *Healing trauma: Attachment, mind, body, and brain* (pp. 1–56). New York: Norton.

Sifneos, P. E. (1973). The prevalence of "alexithymic" characteristics in psychosomatic patients. *Psychotherapy and Psychosomatics, 22*(2), 255–262.

Silver, J. K. (2004). *Chronic pain and the family: A new guide.* Cambridge, MA: Harvard University Press.

Simcock, G., & Hayne, H. (2003). Age-related changes in verbal and nonverbal memory during early childhood. *Developmental Psychology, 39*(5), 805–814.

Sime, W. E., & DeGood, D. E. (1977). Effect of EMG biofeedback and progressive muscle relaxation training on awareness of frontalis muscle tension. *Psychophysiology, 14*(6), 522–530.

Simone, D. A., Marchettini, P., Caputi, G., & Ochoa, J. L. (1994). Identification of muscle afferents subserving sensation of deep pain in humans. *Journal of Neurophysiology, 72*(2), 883–889.

Simpson, J. R., Jr., Drevets, W. C., Snyder, A. Z., Gusnard, D. A., & Raichle, M. E. (2001). Emotion-induced changes in human medial prefrontal cortex: II. During anticipatory anxiety. *Proceedings of the National Academy of Sciences, 98*(2), 688–693.

Sjøgaard, G., & Søgaard, K. (1998). Muscle injury in repetitive motion disorders. *Clinical Orthopaedics and Related Research, 351,* 21–31.

Smuts, B. (2001). Encounters with animal minds. *Journal of Consciousness Studies, 8*(5–7), 293–309.

Solomon, M. F. & Siegel, D. J. (Eds.), (2003). *Healing trauma: Attachment, mind, body, and brain.* New York: Norton.

Sorenson, E. R. (1979). Early tactile communication and the patterning of human organization: A New Guinea case study. In M. Bullowa (Ed.), *Before speech* (pp 289–305). New York: Cambridge University Press.

Spangler, G., & Grossmann, K. E. (1993). Biobehavioral organization in securely and insecurely attached infants. *Child Development, 64,* 1439–1450.

Spencer, J. P. & Thelen, E. (2000). Spatially specific changes in infants' muscle coactivity as they learn to reach. *Infancy, 1*(3), 275–302.

Spoor, S. T., Bekker, M. H., Van Heck, G. L., Croon, M. A., & Van Strien, T. (2005). Inner body and outward appearance: The relationships between appearance orientation, eating disorder symptoms, and internal body awareness. *Eating Disorders, 13*(5), 479–490.

St. James-Roberts, I., & Plewis, I. (1996). Individual differences, daily fluctuations, and developmental changes in amounts of infant waking, fussing, crying, feeding, and sleeping. *Child Development, 67*(5), 2527–2540.

Stack, D. M. (2000). The salience of touch and physical contact during infancy: Unraveling some of the mysteries of the somaesthetic sense. In J. G. Bremner & A. Fogel (Eds.), *Handbook of infant development* (pp. 268–292). Oxford, England: Blackwell.

Stack, D. M., & Muir, D. W. (1990). Tactile stimulation as a component of social interchange: New interpretations for the still-face effect. *British Journal of Developmental Psychology, 8*(2), 131–145.

Steele, H., Steele, M., Croft, C., & Fonagy, P. (1999). Infant-mother attachment at one year predicts children's understanding of mixed emotions at six years. *Social Development, 8*(2), 161–178.

Steihaug, S., Ahlsen, B., & Malterud, K. (2001). From exercise and education to movement and interaction: Treatment groups in primary care for women with chronic muscular pain. *Scandanavian Journal of Primary Health Care*, 19(4), 249–254.

Stein, J., Narendran, K., McBean, J., Krebs, K., & Hughes, R. (2007). Electromyography-controlled exoskeletal upper-limb-powered orthosis for exercise training after stroke. *American Journal of Physical Medicine & Rehabilitation, 86*(4), 255–261.

Stein, M. B., Simmons, A. N., Feinstein, J. S., & Paulus, M. P. (2007). Increased amygdala and insula activation during emotion processing in anxiety-prone subjects. *American Journal of Psychiatry, 164*(2), 318–327.

Stenberg, C., Campos, J. J., & Emde, R. N. (1983). The facial expression of anger in seven-month-old infants. *Child Development, 54,* 178–184.

Sterling, M., Jull, G., & Kenardy, J. (2006). Physical and psychological factors maintain long-term predictive capacity post-whiplash injury. *Pain, 122*(1–2), 102–108.

Stern, D. N. (1985). *The interpersonal world of the infant.* New York: Basic Books.

Stern, D. N. (2004). *The present moment in psychotherapy and everyday life.* New York: Norton.

References

Stice, E. (2008). Relation between obesity and blunted striatal response to food is moderated by TaqIA A1 Allele. *Science, 322,* 449–452.

Stice, E., & Bearman, S. K. (2001). Body-image and eating disturbances prospectively predict increases in depressive symptoms in adolescent girls: A growth curve analysis. *Developmental Psychology, 37*(5), 597–607.

Stice, E., & Whitenton, K. (2002). Risk factors for body dissatisfaction in adolescent girls: A longitudinal investigation. *Developmental Psychology, 38*(5), 669–678.

Stovall-McClough, K. C., & Cloitre, M. (2006). Unresolved attachment, PTSD, and dissociation in women with childhood abuse histories. *Journal of Consulting and Clinical Psychology, 74*(2), 219–228.

Striano, T., & Rochat, P. (1999). Developmental link between dyadic and triadic social competence in infancy. *British Journal of Developmental Psychology, 17,* 1–12.

Sullivan, D. A., Block, L., & Pena, J. D. (1996). Influence of androgens and pituitary hormones on the structural profile and secretory activity of the lacrimal gland. *Acta Ophthalmologica Scandinavica, 74*(5), 421–435.

Taché, Y., & Bonaz, B. (2007). Corticotropin-releasing factor receptors and stress-related alterations of gut motor function. *Journal of Clinical Investigation, 117*(1), 33–40.

Tacón, A. M., Caldera, Y. M., & Ronaghan, C. (2004). Mindfulness-based stress reduction in women with breast cancer. *Families, Systems, & Health, 22*(2), 193–203.

Tallandini, M. A., & Scalembra, C. (2006). Kangaroo mother care and mother-premature infant dyadic interaction. *Infant Mental Health Journal, 27*(3), 251–275.

Talleyrand, R. M. (2006). Potential stressors contributing to eating disorder symptoms in African American women: Implications for mental health counselors. *Journal of Mental Health Counseling, 28*(4), 338–352.

Taumoepeau, M., & Ruffman, T. (2008). Stepping stones to others' minds: Maternal talk relates to child mental state language and emotion understanding at 15, 24, and 33 months. *Child Development, 79*(2), 284–302.

Taylor, A. J. W. (2001). Spirituality and personal values: Neglected components of trauma treatment. *Traumatology, 7*(3), 111–119.

Taylor, S. E. (2006). Tend and befriend: Biobehavioral bases of affiliation under stress. *Current Directions in Psychological Science, 15*(6), 273–277.

Taylor-Piliac, R. E., Haskell, W. L., Stotts, N. A., & Froelicher, E. S. (2006). Improvement in balance, strength, and flexibility after 12 weeks of Tai Chi exercise in ethnic Chinese adults with cardiovascular disease risk factors. *Alternative Theories in Health Medicine, 12*(2), 50–58.

Terr, L. (1994). *Unchained memories*. New York: Basic Books.

Terr, L. (1988). What happens to early memories of trauma? A study of twenty children under age five at the time of documented traumatic events. *Journal of the American Academy of Child and Adolescent Psychiatry, 27*(1), 96–104.

Thayer, J. F., & Brosschot, J. F. (2005). Psychosomatics and psychopathology: looking up and down from the brain. *Psychoneuroendocrinology, 30*(10), 1050–1058.

Thelen, E., Bradshaw, G., & Ward, J. A. (1981). Spontaneous kicking in month-old infants: Manifestation of a human central locomotor program. *Behavioral and Neural Biology, 32*, 45–53.

Thomas, M., & Jankovic, J. (2004). Psychogenic movement disorders: Diagnosis and management. *CNS Drugs, 18*(7), 437–452.

Thompson, E., & Varela, F. J. (2001). Radical embodiment: Neural dynamics and consciousness. *Trends in Cognitive Sciences, 5*(10), 418–425.

Thoreau, H. (1910). *Walden*. New York: Crowell.

Tinazzi, M., Rosso, T., Fiaschi, A., Gambina, G., Farina, S., Fiorio, S. M. et al. (2002). The role of somatosensory feedback in dystonia: A psychophysical [correction of psycophysical] evaluation. *Neurological Science, 23* (Suppl. 2), S113–S114.

Tkachuk, G. A., & Martin, G. L. (1999). Exercise therapy for patients with psychiatric disorders: Research and clinical implications. *Professional Psychology: Research and Practice, 30*(3), 275–282.

Tortora, S. (2006). *The dancing dialogue: Using the communicative power of movement with young children*. Baltimore, MD: Brookes.

Trainor, L. J. (1996). Infant preferences for infant-directed versus noninfant-directed playsongs and lullabies. *Infant Behavior and Development, 19*, 83–92.

Trainor, L. J., Clark, E. D., Huntley, A., & Adams, B. A. (1997). The acoustic basis of preferences for infant-directed singing. *Infant Behavior and Development, 20*(3), 383–396.

Treaster, D., Marras, W. S., Burr, D., Sheedy, J. E., & Hart, D. (2006). Myofascial trigger point development from visual and postural stressors during computer work. *Journal of Electromyography & Kinesiology, 16*(2), 115–124.

Trehub, S. E. (2003). The developmental origins of musicality. *Nature Neuroscience, 6*(7), 669–673.

Trevarthen, C. (1998). The concept and foundations of infant intersubjectivity. In S. Bråten (Ed.), *Intersubjective communication and emotion in early ontogeny*, (pp. 15–46). Cambridge, UK: Cambridge University Press.

Trevarthen, C., & Aitken, K. J. (2001). Infant intersubjectivity: Research, theory, and clinical applications. *Journal of Child Psychology and Psychiatry, 42*(1), 3–48.

Tronick, E. (2007). *The neurobehavioral and social-emotional development of infants and children.* New York: Norton.

Truitt, A. (1982). *Daybook: The journal of an artist.* New York: Pantheon Books.

Tucker, D. M. (2001). Motivated anatomy: A core-and-shell model of corticolimbic architecture. In F. Boller & J. Grafman (Series Eds.), & G. Gainotti (Vol. Ed.), *Handbook of neuropsychology: Vol. 5 Emotional behavior and its disorders* (2nd ed., pp. 125–160). Amsterdam, The Netherlands: Elsevier Science.

Tucker, D. M., Luu, P., Desmond, R. E., Jr., Hartry-Speiser, A., Davey, C., & Flaisch, T. (2003). Corticolimbic mechanisms in emotional decisions. *Emotion, 3*(2), 127–149.

Turner, B. (1996). *The body and society.* London: Sage.

Turton, A. McCabe, C., Harris, N. Filipovic, S. (2007). Sensorimotor integration in complex regional pain syndrome: A transcranial magnetic stimulation study. *Pain, 127,* 270–275.

Tweeddale, P. M., Rowbottom, I., & McHardy, G. J. (1994). Breathing retraining: Effect on anxiety and depression scores in behavioural breathlessness. *Journal of Psychosomatic Research, 38*(1), 11–21.

Umezawa, A. (2001). Facilitation and inhibition of breathing during changes in emotion. In Y. Haruki, I. Homma, A. Umezawa, & Y. Masaoka (Eds.), *Respiration and emotion* (pp. 139–148). New York: Springer-Verlag.

Urry, H. L., van Reekum, C. M., Johnstone, T., Kalin, N. H., Thurow, M. E., Schaefer, H. S. et al. (2006). Amygdala and ventromedial prefrontal cortex are inversely coupled during regulation of negative affect and predict the diurnal pattern of cortisol secretion among older adults. *The Journal of Neuroscience, 26*(16), 4415–4425.

Uvnäs-Moberg, K. (2003). *The ocytocin factor: Tapping the hormone of calm, love, and healing.* Cambridge, MA: Da Capo Press.

van Boxtel, A., Damen, E. J., & Brunia, C. H. (1996). Anticipatory EMG responses of pericranial muscles in relation to heart rate during a warned simple reaction time task. *Psychophysiology, 33*(5), 576–583.

Van Damme, S., Crombez, G., & Eccleston, C. (2004). Disengagement from pain: The role of catastrophic thinking about pain. *Pain, 107,* 70–76

van de Berg, R., Dirani, M., Chen, C. Y., Haslam, N., & Baird, P. N. (2008). Myopia and personality: The genes in myopia (GEM) personality study. *Investigative Ophthalmology & Visual Science, 49*(3), 882–886.

van den Bergh, B. R. H, Mulder, E. J. H., Mennew, M., & Glover, V. (2004). Antenatal maternal anxiety and stress and the neurobehavioural development of the fetus and child: Links and possible mechanisms. A review. *Neuroscience and Biobehavioral Reviews, 20*, 1–22.

van den Stock, J., Righart, R., & de Gelder, B. (2007). Body expressions influence recognition of emotions in the face and voice. *Emotion, 7*(3), 487–494.

van der Hart, O., Nijenhuis, E. R. S., & Steele, K. (2006). *The haunted self: Structural dissociation and the treatment of chronic traumatization*. New York: Norton.

van der Hart, O., Nijenhuis, E., Steele, K., & Brown, D. (2004). Trauma-related dissociation: Conceptual clarity lost and found. *Australian and New Zealand Journal of Psychiatry, 38*(11–12), 906–914.

van der Kolk, B. A. (1996). The body keeps the score: Approaches to the psychobiology of traumatic stress disorder. In B. A. van der Kolk, A. C. McFarlane, & L. Weisaeth (Eds.), *Traumatic stress: The effects of overwhelming experience on mind, body, and society* (pp. 214–241). New York: Guilford Press.

van der Kolk, B. A., Roth, S., Pelcovitz, D., Sunday, S., & Spinazzola, J. (2005). Disorders of extreme stress: The empirical foundation of a complex adaptation to trauma. *Journal of Traumatic Stress, 18*(5), 389–399.

van Dieën, J. H., Selen, L. P., & Cholewicki, J. (2003). Trunk muscle activation in low-back pain patients, an analysis of the literature. *Journal of Electromyography and Kinesiology, 13*(4), 333–351.

van Middendorp, H., Lumley, M. A., Jacobs, J. W., van Doornen, L. J., Bijlsma, J. W., & Geenen, R. (2008). Emotions and emotional approach and avoidance strategies in fibromyalgia. *Journal of Psychosomatic Research, 64*(2), 159–167.

Varela, F. J., Thompson, E., & Rosch, E. (1991). *The embodied mind: Cognitive science and human experience*. Cambridge, MA: MIT Press.

Ventegodt, S., & Merrick, J. (2005). Clinical holistic medicine: Chronic pain in the locomotor system. *The Scientific World Journal, 5*, 165–172.

Verdejo-García, A., Pérez-García, M., & Bechara, A. (2006). Emotion, decision-making and substance dependence: A somatic-marker model of addiction. *Current Neuropharmacology, 4*, 17–31.

Vessantara, V. (2005). *The art of meditation, the breath*. Cambridge, UK: Windhorse.

Vigil, J. M., Geary, D. C., & Byrd-Craven, J. (2005). A life history assessment of early childhood sexual abuse in women. *Developmental Psychology, 41*(3), 553–561.

References

Vlaeyen, J. W., & Crombez, G. (1999). Fear of movement/(re)injury, avoidance and pain disability in chronic low back pain patients. *Manual Therapy, 4*(4), 187–195.

Wærsted, M., & Westgaard, R. H. (1996). Attention-related muscle activity in different body regions during VDU work with minimal physical activity. *Ergonomics, 39*(4), 661–676.

Waersted, M., Eken, T., & Westgaard, R. H. (1996). Activity of single motor units in attention-demanding tasks: Firing pattern in the human trapezius muscle. *European Journal of Applied Physiology and Occupational Physiology, 72*(4), 323–329.

Wagner, U., & Born, J. (2008). Memory consolidation during sleep: Interactive effects of sleep stages and HPA regulation. *Stress, 11*(1), 28–41.

Walach, H., Buchheld, N., Buttenmüller, V., Kleinknecht, N., & Schmidt, S. (2006). Measuring mindfulness—The Freiburg Mindfulness Inventory (FMI). *Personality and Individual Differences, 40*(8), 1543–1555.

Wallace, B. A. (2000). *The taboo of subjectivity: Toward a new science of consciousness.* New York: Oxford University Press.

Wallace, B. A., & Shapiro, S. L. (2006). Mental balance and well-being: Building bridges between Buddhism and Western psychology. *American Psychologist, 61*(7), 690–701.

Wallbott, H. G. (1998). Bodily expression of emotion. *European Journal of Social Psychology,* 28(6), 879–896.

Waller, G., Babbs, M., Wright, F., Potterton, C., Meyer, C., & Leung, N. (2003). Somatoform dissociation in eating-disordered patients. *Behaviour Research and Therapy, 41*(5), 619–627.

Walter, C. (2006). Why do we cry? *Scientific American Mind, 17*(6), 44–51.

Walusinski, O. (2006). Yawning: Unsuspected avenue for a better understanding of arousal and interoception. *Medical Hypotheses, 67*(1), 6–14.

Wang, X., Merzenich, M. M., Sameshima, K., & Jenkins, W. M. (1995). Remodelling of hand representation in adult cortex determined by timing of tactile stimulation. *Nature, 378*(6552), 71–75.

Ward, L. M. (2003). Synchronous neural oscillations and cognitive processes. *Trends in Cognitive Sciences, 7*(12), 553–559.

Waters, E., Merrick, S., Treboux, D., Crowell, J., & Albersheim, L. (2000). Attachment security in infancy and early adulthood: A twenty-year longitudinal study. *Child Development, 71*(3), 684–689.

Watkins, E. (2004). Adaptive and maladaptive ruminative self-focus during emotional processing. *Behaviour Research and Therapy, 42*(9), 1037–1052.

Watkins, E., & Moulds, M. (2005). Distinct modes of ruminative self-focus: Impact of abstract versus concrete rumination on problem solving in depression. *Emotion, 5*(3), 319–328.

Weaver, A. J., Flannelly, L. T., Garbarino, J., Figley, C. R., & Flannelly, K. J. (2003). A systematic review of research on religion and spirituality in the Journal of Traumatic Stress: 1990–1999. *Mental Health, Religion & Culture, 6*(3), 215–228.

Webb, S. J., Monk, C. S., & Nelson, C. A. (2001). Mechanisms of postnatal neurobiological development: Implications for human development. *Developmental Neuropsychology, 19*(2), 147–171.

Webster, J. I., Tonelli, L., & Sternberg, E. M. (2002). Neuroendocrine regulation of immunity. *Annual Review of Immunology, 20,* 125–163.

Weerapong, P., Hume, P. A., & Kolt, G. S. (2005). The mechanisms of massage and effects on performance, muscle recovery and injury prevention. *Sports Medicine, 35*(3), 235–256.

Weimer, J. (1994). *Back talk*. New York: Random House.

Weinberger, D. A., Schwartz, G. E., & Davidson, R. J. (1979). Low-anxious, high-anxious, and repressive coping styles: Psychometric patterns and behavioral and physiological responses to stress. *Journal of Abnormal Psychology, 88*(4), 369–380.

Welch, K. L. & Beere, D. B. (2002). Eye movement desensitization and reprocessing: A treatment efficacy model. *Clinical Psychology and Psychotherapy, 9,* 165–176.

Wells, N. M. (2000). At home with nature: Effects of 'greenness' on children's cognitive functioning. *Environment and Behavior, 32*(6), 775–795.

Wells, N. M., & Evans, G. W. (2003). Nearby nature: A buffer of life stress among rural children. *Environment and Behavior, 35*(3), 311–330.

Wenke, R.J. (1990). *Patterns in prehistory: Humankind's first three million years*. New York: Oxford University Press.

Wessberg, J., Olausson, H., Fernström, K. W., & Vallbo, A. B. (2003). Receptive field properties of unmyelinated tactile afferents in the human skin. *Journal of Neurophysiology, 89*(3), 1567–1575.

Westland, G. (1996). Biodynamic massage. *Complementary Therapies in Nursing and Midwifery, 2*(2), 47–51.

Whalen, P. J., & Kleck, R. E. (2008). The shape of faces (to come). *Nature Neuroscience, 11*(7), 739–740.

Wheeler, K., Greiner, P., & Boulton, M. (2005). Exploring alexithymia, depression, and binge eating in self-reported eating disorders in women. *Perspectives in Psychiatric Care, 41*(3), 114–123.

Wheeler, M. A., Stuss, D. T., & Tulving, E. (1997). Toward a theory of episodic memory: The frontal lobes and autonoetic consciousness. *Psychological Bulletin, 121*(3), 331–354.

Wheeler, M. E., Petersen, S. E., & Buckner, R. L. (2000). Memory's echo: Vivid remembering reactivates sensory-specific cortex. *Proceedings of the National Academy of Sciences, 97*(20), 11125–11129.

Wiederman, M. W. (2000). Women's body image self-consciousness during physical intimacy with a partner. *Journal of Sex Research, 37*(1), 60–68.

Wilhelmsen, I. (2005). Biological sensitization and psychological amplification: Gateways to subjective health complaints and somatoform disorders. *Psychoneuroendocrinology, 30*(10), 990–995.

Wilson, E. A. (2004). *Psychosomatic: Feminism and the neurological body.* Chapel Hll, N.C.: Duke University Press.

Winnicott, D. W. (1960). *The maturational processes and the facilitating environment.* New York: International Universities Press.

Winnicott, D. W. (1971). *Playing and reality.* New York: Basic Books.

Wolf, S. L., Barnhart, H. X., Kutner, N. G., McNeely, E., Coogler, C., & Xu, T. (2003). Selected as the best paper in the 1990s: Reducing frailty and falls in older persons: An investigation of tai chi and computerized balance training. *Journal of the American Geriatrics Society, 51*(12), 1794–1803.

Wolff, P. H. (1966). The causes, controls, and organization of behavior in the neonate. *Psychological Issues, 5*, (Monograph No. 17).

Wolpaw, J. R., & Tennissen, A. M. (2001). Activity-dependent spinal cord plasticity in health and disease. *Annual Review of Neuroscience,* 24, 807–843.

Wooten, S. (1994). Rosen method bodywork. *Journal of Alternative and Complementary Medicine, 12,* 9–13.

Wooten, S. (1995). *Touching the body, reaching the soul: How touch influences the nature of human beings.* Santa Fe, NM: Rosen Method Center Southwest.

Young, K. (2002). The memory of the flesh: The family body in somatic psychology. *Body & Society, 8*(3), 24–47.

Zafar, H., Nordh, E., & Eriksson, P. O. (2000). Temporal coordination between mandibular and head-neck movements during jaw opening-closing tasks in man. *Archives of Oral Biology, 45*(8), 675–682.

Zahn-Waxler, C., Radke-Yarrow, M., Wagner, E., & Chapman, M. (1992). Development of concern for others. *Developmental Psychology, 28*, 126–136.

Zautra, A., Smith, B., Affleck, G., & Tennen, H. (2001). Examinations of chronic pain and affect relationships: Applications of a dynamic model of affect. *Journal of Consulting and Clinical Psychology, 69*(5), 786–795.

Zentner, M. R., & Kagan, J. (1998). Infants' perception of consonance and dissonance in music. *Infant Behavior and Development, 21*(3), 483–492.

Zentner, M. R., Grandjean, D., & Klaus, R. S. (2008). Emotions evoked by the Sound of Music: Characterization, classification, and measurement. *Emotion, 8*(4), 494–521.

Zhang, W., Hayward, L. F., & Davenport, P. W. (2005). Respiratory muscle responses elicited by dorsal periaqueductal gray stimulation in rats. *American Journal of Physiological Regulation and Integrated Comparative Physiology, 289*(5), R1338–R1347.

Zonnevylle-Bender, M. J., van Goozen, S. H., Cohen-Kettenis, P. T., Jansen, L. M., van Elburg, A., & Engeland, H. (2005). Adolescent anorexia nervosa patients have a discrepancy between neurophysiological responses and self-reported emotional arousal to psychosocial stress. *Psychiatry Research, 135*(1), 45–52.

Zukow, P. G., Reilly, J., & Greenfield, P. M. (1982). Making the absent present: Facilitating the transition from sensorimotor to linguistic communication. In K. E. Nelson (Ed.), *Children's language* (pp. 1–90). Hillsdale, NJ: Erlbaum.

Index

Note: *f* denotes figure and *t* denotes table.

!Kung bushmen, 109
4-D ultrasound, 11, 12*f*

abdominal pain case studies, 199–202, 265–67, 268
absorption
 addiction, 129*t*, 138–40, 240–41, 307
 emotional development and, 205*t*
 normal
  biobehavioral responses and, 148*t*, 179, 241
  breathing and, 240–41
  characteristics of, 128*t*, 129–30, 149–50, 277–78
  definition, 307, 315
  environments, restorative, 278–81
  pain due to stress and, 143–44, 145
 pathological dissociation, 128*t*, 130–33, 166, 167, 258, 316
 rumination, 129*t*, 137–38, 166, 205*t*
abuse
 animals, as restorative influence, 281–83
 dissociation and, 167
 memory and, 251, 260–67
 nature, as a restorative environment, 281–83
 suppression of urges during, 108
 temperamental differences in infants and, 183
 see also armoring; memory, of threat and safety; threat
ACTH, *see* adrenocorticotropic hormone (ACTH)
addiction, 129*t*, 138–40, 240–41, 307
Aδ fibers, 45
ADHD, 303
adolescents, and abuse, 254
adolescents, and brain development, 177
adrenaline, 149

adrenal medulla, 149
adrenocorticotropic hormone (ACTH), 111, 148–49, 157, 195, 307
afferent pathways, defined, 42, 307
African culture and infant movement, 213–14, 214*f*
Aikido, 215
Alexander, G., 240
Alexander, M., 240
Alexander Technique, 209
alexithymia, 114, 307
alternative health practices, *see* interventions
α - motor neurons (α - MN), 187–90, 188*f*, 192, 232, 307
amygdala
 definition, 307
 interoception and, 88*f*
 location of, 54*f*
 posttraumatic stress disorder (PTSD), 166
 threat and, 154–56, 257
"angels in the nursery", 264–65
anger, 34–37, 68–69, 110, 192, 235*t*, 236
animals, as restorative influence, 281–83
anorexia nervosa, 122–23
anosognosia, 92, 307
ANS, *see* autonomic nervous system (ANS)
anterior cingulate cortex (ACC)
 definition, 307
 embodied self-awareness and, 88*f*
 interoception and, 56–57
 location of, 54*f*
 posttraumatic stress disorder (PTSD) and, 166
 urge suppression and, 139, 140
 yawning and, 64
antigravity movement, *see* posture
anxiety, 166, 178, 183, 192, 240, 255
armoring, 195–99, 209, 266, 307
Asian culture and breathing, 239–40

Index

asomatognosia, 92, 308
attachment
   definition, 308, 318
   difficulties in children, 76–79, 175, 176
   formation of, 173–77
   secure, 68, 175, 184, 254–55
   see also *Eight Ages of Man*
attractors, defined, 58–59, 308
autism, and intersubjectivity, 223
autism, and sensory integration dysfunction, 303
autobiographical memory, 251–54, 256, 257, 308
autobiographical narratives, 250, 254
   see also True Self
autoimmune disorders, 159–60
autonomic nervous system (ANS), 53, 308
   see also parasympathetic branch of ANS; sympathetic branch of ANS
awareness-based exercise therapy, 198, 285
Awareness through Movement, 24–25, 308

back pain, 5, 7
Bakal, D., 22
balance difficulties, in the elderly, 285
beginner's mind, 249, 308
Benson, C., 130
binge eating, 123, 308
biobehavioral responses
   absorption, normal, 148t, 241, 315
   breathing changes, 232–35, 235t, 311
   definition, 308
   development of, 15
   engagement, 148t, 311
   immobilization
     breathing and, 241
     definition, 313
     disorganized-disoriented attachment and, 175
     effects on body function, 148t, 150–51
     infant self-regulation and, 179
     pathological dissociation and, 167
     periaqueductal grey (PAG) and, 154
   mobilization
     breathing and, 241
     definition, 314
     effects on body function, 148t, 150–51
     infant self-regulation and, 179
     insecure avoidant-dismissive attachment, 175
     periaqueductal grey (PAG) and, 154

neuroception, 152, 315
   neurophysiology of, 147–60, 149t, 153f, 155f, 156f
   posture and, 196
   restoration, 148t, 150, 154, 317
   urge suppression and, 107
   vigilance, 148t, 151, 175, 179, 321
Biodynamic Massage, 209
bioenergetic therapy, 197
biofeedback, 292, 308
body functions, suppression of, 4–5, 7–8
body image, 123–24
   see also dysmorphophobia
Body-Mind Centering, 209
body schema
   attachment difficulties in children and, 76–79
   boundary loss due to abuse, 76
   definition, 11, 26, 71–72, 308
   fetal self-awareness and, 11–12
   impairments in, 82, 91–95
   infant self-awareness and
     conjoined twins example, 18–19
     limb movement, 89
     mirror neurons, 206–7
     nursing, 12–13
     twitching, 85–87
     vocalizations, 244–46
   integration with emotions and interoception, 72, 74, 89–91
   memory and, 252–53
   movement and vocalization, 250
   muscle tension, chronic and, 190–94, 193f
   neurophysiology of, 82–89, 88f, 96f
   object perception and, 88–89
   perception of pain and, 90–91, 95
   phantom limbs, 93–95
   posture, 71–74, 89, 191, 194, 230, 316
     see also armoring
   restoration principles, 23t
   rooting reflex, 89
   somatotopic organizaton, 208–9
   tool use and, 74–75
   twitching and, 85–87
   variations in, 81–82
   virtual reality therapy and, 75
   see also emotions; interoception
body structure, as a dynamic system, 41–43
boundaries, 23t, 271–72, 274–75
   see also body schema; restoration, principles for
Boyesen, G., 209

Index

Braatoy, T., 209
brain, 52*f*, 84–85, 154, 176–77
　see also neurophysiology; specific brain structures
brain stem, *see* interoception, neurophysiology of
breathing
　anatomy and physiology, 228–39, 229*f*, 233*f*, 234*f*, 235*t*
　art and benefits of, 239–41
　relaxed versus effortful, 235, 311, 317
　voice and, 241–47, 243*f*, 244*t*, 321
breath-resonance, life-motion, 239–40
Breuer, J., 258

cathexes, 66
caudal, defined, 51, 52*f*, 309
CEBT, *see* cognitive-emotional-behavior therapy (CEBT)
cerebellum, 83, 88*f*
cerebral aqueduct, 153
cerebral cortex, 52*f*
cerebrospinal fluid (CSF), 153, 309
C fibers, 45
chaos, 65–66, 309
Childhood and Society, 206
children, *see* infant and child
cingulate cortex, see anterior cingulate cortex (ACC)
cingulate motor area (CMA), 107, 253, 309
civilization, *see* hunter-gatherers; technology
CMA, *see* cingulate motor area (CMA)
cognitive-emotional-behavior therapy (CEBT), 125
Cohen, B., 209, 240
compartmentalization, 132, 309
conceptual self-awareness
　anorexia nervosa and, 122–23
　autobiographical narratives and, 250
　defense mechanisms and, 114–15, 116*t*
　definition, 10, 11, 309
　ego and, 115
　embodied self-awareness comparisons, 29–41, 31*t*, 47, 100–101
　neurophysiological links, 43, 95–101, 96*f*, 97–99
　voice and True Self, 250–51, 320, 321
　False Self, 103, 312
　"good cry" and, 112
　language, evaluative versus evocative, 247–48, 312

　memory and, 251–54, 257
　slowing down example, 48–49
　see also dorsomedial prefrontal cortex (DMPFC); engagement; letting go; thought processes
conjoined twins case study, 18–19
conversion disorder, 132, 197, 309
coregulation
　abdominal pain case study, 133–35, 168–71, 199–202
　anger case study, 34–37
　attachment difficulties in children case studies, 77–79, 180–82
　attachment formation, in infants, 173–74, 308, 309
　body schema and, 75–76
　definition, 15–18, 16*f*, 17*f*, 26, 75, 309
　emotions and, 65
　infants and, 161–62, 179
　intersubjectivity, 222–26, 314
　multiple sclerosis case study, 210–12
　neural integration and, 59–61
　resonance, 174, 317
　in Rosen Method Bodywork, 34–37, 133–35, 168–71, 318
　see also restoration, principles for; self-regulation
corticotrophin releasing factor (CRF), 157–58, 195, 309
cortisol
　effects on body function, 148–49, 157, 195, 309
　hypocortisolism, 257, 313
　kangaroo care and, 220
　threat and, 158, 178
cranial nerves, 299–300
craniosacral therapy, 153
critical period, 309
crying, 110–14, 112*t*, 113*t*, 244*t*
CSF, *see* cerebrospinal fluid (CSF)

dance, 33
dance movement psychotherapy, 76–79, 198, 309
dance movement therapy, 284–85
daydreaming, *see* absorption, normal
decision-making, 97–100
defense mechanisms, 114–15, 116*t*, 309
denial, 115, 116*t*, 310
depersonalization syndrome, 82, 131–32, 310

387

Index

depression, 178, 240, 241, 255
detachment, 131, 134, 310
Developing through Relationships, 15
developmental trauma, 310
Dewey, J., 31–32, 130
diaphragm, thoracic, 228–29, 230, 320
disorganized-disoriented attachment, 175, 310
dissociation, *see* pathological dissociation
DLPFC, *see* dorsolateral prefrontal cortex (DLPFC)
DMPFC, *see* dorsomedial prefrontal cortex (DMPFC)
dopamine, 139–40, 310
dopaminergic receptors, 140, 310
dorsal, defined, 51, 52*f*, 310
dorsal horns, 49, 50, 50*f*
dorsolateral prefrontal cortex (DLPFC)
   definition, 310
   embodied self-awareness and, 88*f*, 96*f*
   location of, 57*f*
   working memory and, 59, 69, 105–6
dorsomedial prefrontal cortex (DMPFC)
   conceptual self-awareness and, 53, 95–100, 96*f*
   definition, 310
   location of, 54*f*
   modularity and, 44–45
"double consciousness", 136–37
dynamic systems, 41–42, 296–306, 310
   see also chaos; neural integration; nonlinear transitions
dysmorphophobia, 82, 125, 310
dystonia, 194, 310

eating disorders, 119–20, 122–27
efferent pathways, defined, 42, 310
effortful breathing, 234–35, 311
Eight Ages of Man, 204*t*–5*t*
electromagnetic stimulation, 86
electromyography (EMG), 192
embodied self-awareness
   Asian culture and breathing, 239–40
   balancing of closeness and distance, 270*t*
      see also boundaries
   breathing and, 234–35
   chaos and, 65–66, 103
   conjoined twins case study, 18–19
   decision-making and, 97–100
   defense mechanisms and, 114–15, 116*t*
   definition, 1–2, 10, 311
   exercise and, 283–90
   Eye Movement Desensitization and Reprocessing (EMDR), 297
   growth and decline of, 10–15
   homeostasis, 14, 100, 313
      see also coregulation; self-regulation
   impermanence of, 65–66
   infant vocalizations and, 244–46
   language and, 31–33, 247–51, 249*t*
   loss of, *see* suppression
   memory and, 252–53
   movement, interpersonal and, 207–9, 213–16, 214*t*
      see also muscles
   multiple sclerosis case study, 210–12
   music interoception and, 246–47
   neural integration, 58–61, 160–62, 160*f*
   pain relief and, 162–65
   parent's role in enhancing, 183
      see also movement, interpersonal; touch, interpersonal
   pathologies of, 165–67
   potential for, 27
   relationships and, 15–21, 103
   restorative characteristics of, 270*t*, 271–72, 277
   somatization, 104, 319
   spirituality and, 293–96
   spontaneity of, 61
   suppressed in school and work environments, 8–10
   survival and, 15
   technology's role in decreasing, 4–5
   touch, interpersonal and, 190, 209, 216–21
   True Self, 103–4, 250–51
   trust in, 270*t*, 271
      see also pain, relief through embodied self-awareness
   well-being, as basis of, 103
   Western culture's health system and, 6
   willingness to be a process, 270*t*, 272–73, 277
   yawning example, 63*t*
   see also body schema; conceptual self-awareness; emotions; interoception; interventions; restoration, principles for; subjective emotional present
EMDR, *see* Eye Movement Desensitization and Reprocessing (EMDR)
emergence, 58, 311
EMG, *see* electromyography (EMG)

Index

emotions
  alexithymia, 114
  anger, 34–37, 68–69, 110, 192, 235*t*, 236
  armoring and, 195–99, 209, 266
  attachment, secure, and, 254–55
  attachment difficulties in children case studies, 77–79, 180–82
  breathing patterns and, 235*t*, 236
  chaos in a dynamic system, 65–66
  children's internal state, 249–50, 249*t*
  as a creativity source, 66
  crying, 110–14, 112*t*, 113*t*, 244*t*
  cultural value and, 109–10
  definition, 311
  driving and, 11, 110
  emergence of, 68–69
  eyes and, 296–97
  feelings versus, 39–40
  grief, 91
  hedonic value of, 39, 57
  honoring of, 70, 103
  infant development of, 20
  integration with body schema and interoception, 89–91
  lack of awareness of, 66–67
  learning and, 66
  memory and, 198–202, 252–54, 260–67, 308
  motivation and, 56, 67–68
  music categories and, 247
  neurophysiology of, *see* limbic system
  perception of pain and, 90–91, 95
  phantom limbs and, 93–95
  positive, 271, 276, 278, 292, 294
  posture and, 195–96
  redemption, 256
  rerepresentations, 59–61, 63*t*, 65
  resonance, 174
  self-regulation and homeostasis, 55–56
  sensing through touch, 217
  trauma and, 258–59
  see also body schema; interoception; intersubjectivity; posttraumatic stress disorder (PTSD); suppression
endurance, athletic, 6–7
engagement
  breathing and, 240, 241
  definition, 14, 26–27, 311
  environments, restorative and, 280
  oxytocin and, 159
  relationships and, 19–21
  secure attachment and, 184, 318
  see also biobehavioral responses; restoration, principles for
enteric nervous system (ENS), 195, 311
environments, restorative, 278–81
epinephrine, 149, 311
ergoreceptors, defined, 45, 47, 311
  see also receptors
Erickson, E., 204–5*t*, 206
evocative language, 31–33, 247–51, 249*t*, 255, 312
evolution, hunter-gatherers and, 3–4
exercise, benefits of, 283–90
experience dependent brain development, 61, 100–101, 177, 206–7, 312
  see also phantom limbs; plasticity
expiration, 242–44, 244*t*
expiratory pause, 243, 244, 312
expression, benefits of, 118–19
  see also suppression
exteroception, 46, 46*t*, 49, 155
exteroceptors, 46, 312
extrafusal muscle fibers, 189
eye function, as a dynamic system, 296–305, 298*f*
Eye Movement Desensitization and Reprocessing (EMDR), 297, 312

False Self, 103, 115, 312
"false" smiles, 113
fantasizing, *see* absorption, normal
fatigue, chronic, 5, 194, 257
fear, 6
  see also memory, of threat and safety
feelings, versus emotions, 39–40, 312
Feldenkrais, M., 24–25, 209, 211, 215, 227, 240
Feldenkrais Method, 33, 198, 215, 298–99
fetal self-awareness, 11–12
fibromyalgia, 117, 133, 167, 194, 312
fight or flight, *see* biobehavioral responses
flow, 129–30, 149–50, 312
fMRI, *see* functional magnetic resonance imaging (fMRI)
Fogel, J., 286, 289
forgiveness, 276
Frau Emmy, 202
Freud, S.
  cathexes, 66
  defense mechanisms, 114, 197

389

Index

Frau Emmy, 202
infants and, 13
somatization, 132, 258
unconsious emotions, 67
functional integration, 209–12, 312
functional magnetic resonance imaging (fMRI), 43

Gestalt therapy, 209
"ghosts in the nursery", 264
Gindler, E., 240
γ - MN, see γ - motor neurons (γ - MN)
γ - motor neurons (γ - MN), 189–90, 189f, 312
Golgi tendon organs, 189, 312
"good crying", 110–12, 112t
Grand, I., 238
gratitude, 276
gravity, movement against, see posture
grief, 91
Grissom, Mrs., 303

hallucinations, 92–93
hedonic value, defined, 39
hippocampus, 53, 54f, 251–52, 257, 313
holistic health care, see interventions
Holmes, E., 131
Holotropic Breathwork, 241
homeostasis
　brain stem function in, 50–51, 60t
　crying and, 110–13, 112t, 113t
　definition, 14, 50, 313
　embodied self-awareness and, 100
　medulla oblongata, 153f
　neural integration, 67–69, 147–48, 148t
　neurobiological responses, defined, 22
　restoration principles, 23t
　see also autonomic nervous system (ANS); coregulation
hormones
　adrenocorticotropic hormone (ACTH), 111, 148–49, 157, 195, 307
　corticotrophin releasing factor (CRF), 157–58, 195, 309
　cortisol
　　definition, 309
　　effects on body function, 148–49, 157–58, 178, 195
　　persistent threat and, 257
　　touch and, 220
　epinephrine, 149, 311

hypocortisolism, 257
norepinephrine (NE), 158, 315
oxytocin
　definition, 316
　threat and safety network, 158–59
　touch, interpersonal and, 217–18, 220
　visual attention and, 296–97
　yawning and, 62, 63t
prolactin, 111
threat and safety network and, 156–59
HPA axis, 148–49, 157f, 257, 313
humor, and letting go, 273
hunter-gatherers, 2–4, 109
hyperventilation, 239, 241, 313
hypochondriasis, see somatization
hypocortisolism, 257, 313
hypothalamus
　definition, 53, 313
　hormones of, 157, 158
　immune system function and, 159
　interoception and, 88f
　location of, 54f
　yawning and, 63t, 64
hysteria, see conversion disorder

IDS, see infant-directed speech (IDS)
imitation, 206, 223
immune system function, 117, 159–60
infant and child
　adolescents, 177, 254
　armoring in, 196–97
　attachment, 76–79, 173–77, 180–82
　body schema, 206–7, 213–14, 214f, 220
　brain development of, 177
　coregulation, 161–62, 173–74, 179
　crying, 112, 113t, 243–45, 244t
　embodied self-awareness and parent's role, 183, 213–14, 214f, 245–46
　emotions and, 20, 183, 204t–5t, 254–55
　humor development in, 274–75
　imitation in, 206, 223
　intersubjectivity in, 223–24
　language and internal state, 249–50, 249t
　memory and, 262, 263
　movement, in African culture, 213–14, 214f
　music preferences and, 246
　restorative influences and, 281–83
　rooting reflex, 89
　self-awareness, 12–13, 18–19, 20–21, 85–87, 89, 206–7

Index

threat effect and behavior, 177–79, 183
trauma and, 144, 264–65
vocalizations, 244–46
infant-directed speech (IDS), 245–46, 313
insecure anxious-resistant attachment, 175, 313
insecure avoidant-dismissive attachment, 175, 176, 313
inspiration, 242–44, 244t
insula
   definition, 314
   embodied self-awareness and, 88f, 96f
   interoception and, 55
   location of, 57f
   posttraumatic stress disorder (PTSD) and, 166
   rerepresentations and, 59, 317
   self-agency and, 92
   urge suppression and, 139, 140
intellectualization, 115, 116t, 314
interoception
   alexithymia, 114
   binge eating and, 123
   conjoined twins case study, 18–19
   definition, 10–11, 39, 314
   deliberate versus unconscious, 40
   emotions associated with touch, 217
   feelings versus emotions, 39–40, 312
   fetal self-awareness and, 11–12
   grieving process and, 40–41
   homeostasis and, 50–51
   infant self-awareness and
      conjoined twins example, 18–19
      limb movement, 89
      mirror neurons, 206–7
      nursing, 12–13
      twitching and, 85–87
      vocalizations, 244–46
   integration with body schema and emotions, 89–91
   memory and, 252–53, 260–67
   mirror neurons and, 207
   music preferences, in infants, 246
   nature and, 280–81
   neurophysiology of, 41–70, 60t, 88f, 96f, 152
   pain
      muscle tension, chronic, 192–94
      pain-threat cycle, 145f, 193–94
      perception of, 90–91, 95, 116, 117
   phantom limbs, 93–95
   in posttraumatic stress disorder (PTSD), 69–70
   posture and, 72–74
   psychiatric illnesses and, 82
   rerepresentations, 59–61, 63t, 65
   restoration principles, 23t, 39, 207–9
   self-awareness levels, 60t
   slowing down example, 47–49
   threat perception and, 144
   see also body schema; emotions; exteroception; limbic system; proprioception; receptors; suppression
intersubjectivity, 222–26, 314
interventions
   Aikido, 215
   Alexander Technique, 209
   awareness-based exercise therapy, 198, 285
   Biodynamic Massage, 209
   bioenergetic therapy, 197
   Body-Mind Centering, 209
   cognitive-emotional-behavior therapy (CEBT), 125
   craniosacral therapy, 136–37, 153
   dance movement psychotherapy, 76–79, 198, 309
   dance movement therapy, 284–85
   embodied self-awareness pain relief, 162–65
   Eye Movement Desensitization and Reprocessing (EMDR), 297
   Feldenkrais Method, 198, 215, 298–99
   functional integration, 209–12, 312
   Gestalt therapy, 209
   "good cry", 111
   Holotropic Breathwork, 241
   listening touch, 218, 224, 314
   massage, therapeutic, 34, 190, 198, 217, 220
   meditation, 33, 230–31, 240–41, 290–93, 291t
   mirror and video imaging, 125
   movement training, 285
   music, 33
   neuromuscular integrative action (NIA), 215, 315
   for phantom limbs, 93–95
   for posttraumatic stress disorder (PTSD), 69–70, 75
   progressive relaxation methods, 292, 316
   relaxation, 146, 198, 292
   Rosen Method Bodywork
      abdominal pain example, 133–35, 168–71, 199–202
      anger example, 34–37

Index

evocative language and, 33, 312
listening touch and, 218–19
self-regulation of practitioner during, 225–26
surgical trauma example, 265–67
twitching and, 86–87
Rosen Method of Movement, 285–89, 318
Slow Food movement, 120–22
somatic experiencing, 172, 319
somatic psychotherapy, 33, 125–27, 172, 198, 236–38, 319
tai chi, 33, 215, 240, 285, 290, 293
virtual reality therapy, 75
Watsu, 209, 321
yoga
  body schema and, 127
  evocative language and, 33, 312
  mindfulness and, 290, 314
  psychiatric illnesses and, 198, 215–16
  restorative, 74
intrafusal muscle fibers, 189
isometric contractions, 188
isotonic contractions, 188

James, W., 130
Johnson, D., 238

kangaroo care, 220

Lame Deer, 1, 279
language, evocative, 31–33, 247–51, 249t, 255
larynx, 242, 243f
lateral, defined, 51, 314
Leg to Stand On, A, 81
letting go, 24t, 270t, 272–73, 276
  see also muscle tension, chronic; restoration, principles for
leucine enkephalin, 111
Levine, P., 172
limbic system
  definition, 53, 314
  location of, 54f
  memory, autobiographical, 251–52
  safety-threat network, 155f
  structures of, 55–57
  see also amygdala; anterior cingulate cortex (ACC); emotions; hippocampus; hypothalamus; insula; thalamus
listening touch, 218–19, 224, 248, 314
lobes, cerebral, 51, 52f, 314

see also specific lobes
location terminology, related to brain, 52f
locus ceruleus, 158, 314
love, 278
Lowen, A., 197, 209

massage, therapeutic, 34, 190, 198, 217, 220, 320
medial, defined, 51, 314
medial prefrontal cortex (MPFC), *see* dorsomedial prefrontal cortex (DMPFC); ventromedial prefrontal cortex (VMPFC)
meditation, 33, 230–31, 240–41, 290–93, 291t
medulla oblongata, 153f
memory
  autobiographical, 251–54, 256, 257
  body schema impairments and, 92
  emotions and, 66
  experience dependent brain development, 61, 69, 312
  participatory, 198–202, 260–67, 295, 297
  procedural, 252–53, 256
  of threat and safety, 254–68
  working, 59
  see also posttraumatic stress disorder (PTSD)
mesencephalon, *see* locus ceruleus; periaqueductal grey (PAG)
Middendorf, I., 240
mindfulness, 290–91, 291t, 314
mirror and video imaging, 125, 208
mirror neurons, 206–7, 221, 224
misoplegia, 92, 314
modularity, 42–45, 314
motivation, 56, 67–68, 90–91, 186–87
motor cortex
  body schema and, 83
  embodied self-awareness and, 88f, 96f
  location of, 54f, 57f
  somatotopic organizaton, 84
  twitching and, 85
  see also cingulate motor area (CMA); premotor cortex (PMC); supplementary motor area (SMA)
motor unit, defiined, 314
movement, interpersonal, 207–9, 213–16, 214t
  see also multiple sclerosis case study; muscles
movement training, 285
MPFC, *see* medial prefrontal cortex (MPFC)
multiple sclerosis case study, 210–12
Murphy, R., 82

Index

muscles
  contraction types, 188
  extrafusal muscle fibers, 189
  extraocular, 298*f*
  intrafusal muscle fibers, 189
  respiration, 228–29, 229*f*
  skeletal, 187–94, 188*f*, 193*f*, 318
    see also armoring
  smooth, 194–95, 196, 200, 318
  spindles, 189, 189*f*, 314
  see also proprioception
muscle tension, chronic
  anxiety and, 193*f*
  armoring, 195–99, 209, 266, 307
  personal report, 301
  sources of, 190–94
  urge suppression and, 260
music, 33
myalgia, 117, 315
myelin, defined, 47, 315
myoclonic twitches, 85–87, 315
myopia, 302, 303

nature, as a restorative environment, 280–83
NE, *see* norepinephrine (NE)
neoplastic diseases, 117, 315
nerve cell fibers, 47
nerves, cranial, 299–300
neural integration
  body schema and, 83–84, 87
  definition, 185, 315
  interoception and, 58–61, 60*t*
  phantom limbs and, 93
  twitching and, 85
neural learning, 61
neural maps, *see* somatotopic organization
neural network, 315
neuraxis, 315
neuroception, 152, 315
neuroimaging, 43
neuromuscular integrative action (NIA), 215, 315
neurophysiology
  in addiction, 139–40
  during crying, 111
  embodied versus conceptual self-awareness, 95–101, 96*f*
  HPA axis, 148–49, 157*f*, 257
  neurogenesis, 257–58, 315

neurotransmitters
  dopamine, 139–40, 310
  locus ceruleus, 158, 314
  norepinephrine (NE), 158
  serotonin, 62, 63*t*
  urge suppression and, 139–40
  yawning and, 62
  receptors, 45, 45*f*, 140, 152, 189
  research methods, 43–45
  see also biobehavioral responses; body schema; homeostasis; hormones; limbic system; pain; suppression
NIA, *see* neuromuscular integrative action (NIA)
nociceptors, 152, 315
nonlinear transitions, 65, 98–99, 315
norepinephrine (NE), 158, 315
nursing, infant, 12–13

OBE, *see* out of body experiences (OBE)
OFC, *see* orbitofrontal cortex (OFC)
opiates, 155–56
orbitofrontal cortex (OFC)
  definition, 315
  embodied self-awareness and, 69, 88*f*, 96*f*
  hedonic value and, 57
  location of, 57*f*
  posttraumatic stress disorder (PTSD) and, 166
  urge suppression and, 139
out of body experiences (OBE), 93, 131, 315
oxytocin
  definition, 316
  threat and safety network, 158–59
  touch, interpersonal and, 217–18, 220
  visual attention and, 296–97
  yawning and, 62, 63*t*

PAG, *see* periaqueductal grey (PAG)
pain
  breathing and, 232, 240, 241
  crying in infants and, 244
  hypocortisolism and, 257
  leucine enkephalin, 111
  neurophysiology of, 152–60, 153*f*, 155*f*, 156*f*, 157*f*
  opiates, 155–56
  perception of, 90–91, 116, 117, 162
  relief through embodied self-awareness, 162–65, 221
  see also meditation

Index

as a warning, 143–44, 202
see also muscle tension, chronic
pain-threat cycle, 145f, 193–94
panic disorder, 166, 178, 239
paralysis, *see* body schema, impairments in
parasympathetic branch of ANS
  breathing and, 240
  crying and, 111
  definition, 316
  periaqueductal grey (PAG) and, 154, 316
  sympathetic branch of ANS versus, 62, 64, 148–50, 149t
  touch, interpersonal and, 217
parietal cortex, 83, 88f, 91–93, 96f
participatory memory, 198–202, 260–67, 295, 297
pathological dissociation, 128t, 130–33, 166, 167, 258, 316
periaqueductal grey (PAG), 153–56, 232, 316
Perls, F., 209
PET, *see* positron emission tomography (PET)
PFC, *see* prefrontal cortex (PFC)
phantom limbs, 93–95
phrenic nerve, 230, 233
physiatry, 284, 316
Piaget, J., 244, 258
Pickler, E., 240
plasticity, 84, 177, 185, 316
pons, 153f
positron emission tomography (PET), 43
posttraumatic stress disorder (PTSD)
  breathing and, 240–41
  in civilians, 183–84
  definition, 146–47, 316
  dissociation and, 167, 258
  embodied self-awareness and, 190–91
  Eye Movement Desensitization and Reprocessing (EMDR), 297
  handling intensity of, 69–70
  humor, and letting go, 273
  limbic system dysfunction in, 166
  memory, participatory and, 260–67
  statistics, 141–42
  symptoms, 146t, 259
  Veterans Affairs Medical Centers, 294–95
  virtual reality therapy and, 75
  see also interventions; threat
posture, 71–74, 89, 191, 194, 230, 316
  see also armoring

prefrontal cortex (PFC), *see* dorsolateral prefrontal cortex (DLPFC); dorsomedial prefrontal cortex (DMPFC)
prehistoric humans, 2–4, 109
premotor cortex (PMC), 56, 57f, 91, 92, 96f, 253
procedural memory, 252–53, 256, 316
progressive relaxation methods, 292, 316
proinflammatory cytokines, 133, 159, 317
projection, 115, 116t, 317
prolactin, 111
prolonged crying, 113t
proprioception
  balance, in elderly and, 285
  body schema and, 88f
  definition, 83, 317
  Golgi tendon organs, 189, 312
  interoception versus, 87–89
  muscle spindles, 189, 189f
  phantom limbs and, 93–95
  proprioceptors, defined, 317
  somatotopic organizaton and, 84
  twitching and, 85–87
Proskauer, M., 240
psychiatric illnesses, and interoception, 82
psychoperistalsis, 111–12, 317
psychosomatic disorder, *see* conversion disorder
psychotherapy, somatic, 33
PTSD, *see* posttraumatic stress disorder (PTSD)

qi, 239–40

Ramachandran, V., 93–94
receptors
  definition, 47
  dopaminergic receptors, 140
  ergoreceptors, defined, 45, 311
  exteroceptors, 46, 312
  Golgi tendon organs, 189
  muscle pain and, 193
  nociceptors, 152, 315
  proprioceptors, defined, 317
  skin receptors, 45, 45f
reengagement, *see* engagement
Reich, W., 197, 209
relationships
  armoring and, 197
  development of self-awareness through, 17–21
  with food, *see* eating disorders

infant-parent, 77–79, 180–82
romantic, 176, 184
suppression's effects upon, 118
threat to, in early childhood, 177–85
see also attachment; coregulation; self and others distinctions
relaxation, 146, 198, 292
relaxed breathing, 235, 317
repetitive motion injuries, 5, 7
representation, defined, 317
repression, 115, 116*t*, 317
rerepresentations, 59–61, 63*t*, 65, 68, 317
see also phantom limbs
resonance, 224, 246, 266–67, 317
resources, defined, 23*t*, 26, 317
see also restoration, principles for
respiration, *see* breathing
respiratory sinus arrhythmia (RSA), 233, 233*f*, 317
restoration
armoring and, 197–98
breathing and, 241
definition, 14, 317
embodied self-awareness characteristics and, 270*t*
environment for, 278–81
in infants, 173
neural learning and, 61, 207–8
oxytocin, 159
principles for, 21–28, 23*t*–24*t*
touch, interpersonal and, 221
twitching and, 86
see also biobehavioral responses
restorative environments, 280–83, 318
Restorative Yoga, 74
road rage, 110
Rogers, C., 272
Rolf, I., 209
rooting reflex, 89
Rosen, M., 197, 215, 240
Rosen Method Bodywork
abdominal pain example, 133–35, 168–71, 199–202
anger example, 34–37
definition, 318
evocative language and, 33
listening touch and, 218–19
self-regulation of practitioner during, 225–26
surgical trauma example, 265–67
twitching and, 86–87

Rosen Method of Movement, 215, 285–89, 318
rostral, defined, 51, 52*f*, 318
RSA, *see* respiratory sinus arrhythmia (RSA)
rumination, 129*t*, 137–38, 166, 205*t*, 318
Russell, R., 210–12

Sacks, O., 81
safety, *see* threat
Sander, L., 183
Schachtel, E., 277
schizophrenia, 56, 92, 178
secure attachment, defined, 318
self-agency, 211, 223, 318
self and others distinctions
balancing of closeness and distance, 271–72
body schema in infants, 206–8
humor development and, 274–75
mirror neurons, 207
movement, interpersonal, 207–9, 213–16, 214*t*
touch, interpersonal, 216–21
self-coherence, 211, 318
self-consciousness, loss of, *see* absorption, normal
self-regulation
cultural demands for, 115
definition, 26
expression, benefits of, 119
homeostasis and, 50–51, 55–56, 67–69
see also emotions
infants and, 162, 179
neurophysiology of, 41–70
restoration principles, 24*t*
suppression and, 104–8, 109–10, 117–18, 199
thought processes and, 100–101
see also biobehavioral responses; coregulation; posttraumatic stress disorder (PTSD); restoration
Selver, C., 240
Selye, H., 142
sensation, *see* interoception
sensorimotor integration, 19, 302–3, 318
sensory awareness, 240
sensory hypersensitivity, 302
serotonin, 62, 63*t*
shock trauma, 144, 318
shoshin, 249
skin receptors, 45*f*
sleep, and twitching, 86
Slow Food movement, 120–22
slowing down, defined, 26

395

Index

see also subjective emotional present
Smuts, B., 282
socio-sensual human organization, 2–4, 12–13
somatic awareness, 22
somatic experiencing, 172, 319
somatic psychotherapy, 33, 125–27, 172, 198, 236–38, 319
somatization, 104, 132–33, 258, 319
somatoform disorder, *see* somatization
somatoparaphrenia, 92, 319
somatosensory cortex (SS), 83, 84, 85, 88*f*, 96*f*, 222, 319
somatotopic organization, 84–85, 154, 319
spinal cord, 45, 47, 49–50, 50*f*, 54*f*, 82
spirituality, embodied, 293–96
SS, *see* somatosensory cortex (SS)
stage fright, 6
Stern, D., 18
stress
    breathing and, 231–39, 240–41, 311
    definition, 319
    homeostasis and, 142
    hypocortisolism, 257
    in infant-parent relationship, 180–82
    modern day afflictions, 141–42
    muscle tension, chronic and, 190–94, 193*f*, 301
    neurophysiology of, 148–49, 257–58
    pain, as a warning, and, 143–44, 202
    see also pain-threat cycle
    performance demands, 191–92
    as a precursor to trauma, 144
    respiratory sinus arrhythmia (RSA) and, 233–34, 233*f*, 234*f*
    Rosen Method Bodywork case study, 35–37
    see also abuse; eating disorders; meditation; threat
stretch reflex, 190
subjective emotional present
    avoidance of feelings, 102
    definition, 11, 269, 319
    engagement and, 14, 19–21, 24*t*, 26–27, 38, 80
    Eye Movement Desensitization and Reprocessing (EMDR), 297
    "good cry" and, 112, 112*t*
    impermanence of, 64–65
    language, evocative, 31–33, 247–51, 249*t*
    memory and, 256, 260–67

    mindfulness, 290–91, 291*t*
    neurophysiology of, 98
    restoration principles, 23*t*–24*t*
    suspension of time and, 60
    see also absorption; abuse; Rosen Method Bodywork; suppression; thought processes; trauma
sublimity, 247
supplementary motor area (SMA), 56, 57*f*, 106–7, 139, 319
suppression
    abuse and, 108
    anger and, 68–69
    armoring and, 195–99, 209
    conceptual self-awareness and, 33
    consequences of, 105, 106–8, 117–18
    crying, 110–13, 112*t*, 113*t*
    cultural demands for, 104, 108–10, 113
    defense mechanisms, 114–15, 116*t*, 309
    definition, 6, 319
    eating disorders and, 119–20, 122–27
    emotions and, 20, 21, 204*t*, 205*t*, 254–55
    experimentally induced, 104–6
    expression and, 104–6, 108–9, 113
    "false" smiles and, 113
    forms of, 116*t*
    immune system function and, 117
    interoception and, 40
    mediated by spirituality, 295
    muscle tension, chronic and, 145, 190–91
    neurophysiology of, 105–7, 116*t*, 117
    pain due to stress and, 143–44
    pain-threat cycle, 145*f*
    relationships and, 118
    resources to overcome, 23*t*, 37
    school and work environment and, 7
    threat, persistent and, 257
    urges and, 104, 106–8, 259–60
    visual acuity and, 302
    see also absorption, normal; breathing; Rosen Method Bodywork
surrender, 276
survival, *see* neuroception
sympathetic branch of ANS
    balance with parasympathetic branch of ANS, 148–50, 149*t*
    crying and, 111
    definition, 104–5, 320
    muscle pain and, 146

Index

parasympathetic branch of ANS versus, 62, 151
periaqueductal grey (PAG) and, 154
synapses, defined, 47

tai chi, 33, 215, 240, 285, 290, 293
TallMountain, 279
technology, 4–5, 15
temporal lobe, 55
thalamus, 55, 60t, 63t, 64, 83, 88f, 320
therapeutic dissociation, 136–37, 320
therapeutic massage, 34, 190, 198, 217, 220, 320
thoracic diaphragm, 228–29, 230, 320
Thoreau, H., 279
thought processes, 7, 96–97, 100–101, 195–96
  see also conceptual self-awareness; decision-making; embodied self-awareness; rumination
threat
  armoring and, 195–99, 209, 266
  cortisol, 148–49, 158, 309
  definition, 142, 320
  embodied self-awareness and, 161
  eye movements and, 297
  immobilization
    breathing and, 241
    definition, 313
    disorganized-disoriented attachment and, 175
    effects on body function, 148t, 150–51
    infant self-regulation and, 179
    periaqueductal grey (PAG) and, 154
  infant temperamental differences and, 183
  memory of, 254–68
  mobilization
    breathing and, 241
    definition, 314
    effects on body function, 148t, 150–51
    infant self-regulation and, 179
    insecure avoidant-dismissive attachment, 175
    periaqueductal grey (PAG) and, 154
  movement quality and, 186–87, 194
  muscle tension, chronic and, 190–94, 193f
  neurophysiology of, 178–79, 257–58
  pain-threat cycle, 145f, 194
  persistent, 256–57
  suppression of emotions and, 254–55

treatment principles, 194
  see also biobehavioral responses, to safety and threat; breathing; posttraumatic stress disorder (PTSD)
tics, 57
tool use, and body schema, 74–75
Tortora, S., 77–79
touch, interpersonal, 190, 209, 216–21
  see also multiple sclerosis case study
touch, listening, 218–19, 224, 314
Tourette's syndrome, 57
transitional objects, 162
trauma
  abdominal pain case study, 265–67, 268
  animals, as a restorative influence, 281–83
  definition, 142–43, 144, 320
  dissociation and, 258
  mediated by spirituality, 294–96
  memory and, 173, 251, 260–68
  nature, as a restorative environment, 281–83
  see also abuse; armoring; posttraumatic stress disorder (PTSD); threat
  treatment principles, see restoration, principles for
treatments, see interventions
True Self, 103–4, 250–51, 269, 320
Truitt, A., 304
twitching, 85–87

ultrasound, 11, 12f
unconsious, of emotions, 67
  see also embodied self-awareness
unease, 247
urges, 104, 106–8, 259–60

vagus nerve, 150, 232–33, 320
ventral, defined, 51, 52f, 320
ventral horns, 50
ventromedial prefrontal cortex (VMPFC)
  decision-making and, 98–100
  definition, 321
  embodied self-awareness and, 53, 96f
  location of, 54f
  posttraumatic stress disorder (PTSD) and, 166
verbalizations, defined, 23t, 26
  see also restoration, principles for
Veterans Affairs Medical Centers, 294–95
vigilance, 148t, 151, 175, 179, 297, 321
virtual reality therapy, 75

397

Index

vitality, 247
VMPFC, *see* ventromedial prefrontal cortex (VMPFC)
voice, 241–47, 243*f*, 244*t*, 250–51, 321
   see also breathing

Watsu, 209, 220–21, 321
Winnicott, D., 103, 162, 277
Wooten, S., 218, 219
working memory, 59

Xie He, 239

yawning, 61–64, 64*t*
yoga
   body schema and, 127
   evocative language and, 33
   mindfulness and, 290
   psychiatric illnesses and, 198, 215–16
   restorative, 74